Empathy and the Novel

Empathy and the Novel

Suzanne Keen

OXFORD
UNIVERSITY PRESS

2007

※ 70407721

OXFORD
UNIVERSITY PRESS

Oxford University Press, Inc., publishes works that further
Oxford University's objective of excellence
in research, scholarship, and education.

Oxford   New York
Auckland   Cape Town   Dar es Salaam   Hong Kong   Karachi
Kuala Lumpur   Madrid   Melbourne   Mexico City   Nairobi
New Delhi   Shanghai   Taipei   Toronto

With offices in
Argentina   Austria   Brazil   Chile   Czech Republic   France   Greece
Guatemala   Hungary   Italy   Japan   Poland   Portugal   Singapore
South Korea   Switzerland   Thailand   Turkey   Ukraine   Vietnam

Published by Oxford University Press, Inc.
198 Madison Avenue, New York, New York 10016

www.oup.com

Oxford is a registered trademark of Oxford University Press

Library of Congress Cataloging-in-Publication Data
Keen, Suzanne.
Empathy and the novel / Suzanne Keen.
p. cm.
Includes bibliographical references and index.
ISBN 978-0-19-517576-9
1. Fiction—Psychological aspects. 2. Empathy. 3. Empathy in literature.
I. Title.
PN3352.P7K44 2007
808.301'9—dc22   2006022453

9 8 7 6 5 4 3 2 1

Printed in the United States of America
on acid-free paper

for Fran,
soulmate

PREFACE

Empathy and the Novel presents a comprehensive account of the relationships among novel reading, empathy, and altruism, exploring the implications for literary studies of the widely promulgated "empathy-altruism" hypothesis.[1] Social and developmental psychologists, philosophers of virtue ethics, feminist advocates of an ethic of caring, and many defenders of the humanities believe that empathic emotion motivates altruistic action, resulting in less aggression, less fickle helping, less blaming of victims for their misfortunes, increased cooperation in conflict situations, and improved actions on behalf of needy individuals and members of stigmatized groups.[2] The celebration of novel reading as a stimulus to the role-taking imagination and emotional responsiveness of readers—in countless reading group guides and books on the virtues of reading, in character education curricula, and in public defenses of humanities funding—augments the empathy-altruism hypothesis, substituting experiences of narrative empathy for shared feelings with real others. Read Henry James and live well (*Love's Knowledge* 148); become a better world citizen through canonical novels, philosopher Martha Nussbaum advocates (*Cultivating Humanity* 90). Discover compassion through "The Lion and the Mouse" or "The Legend of the Dipper" writes William J. Bennett (*Children's Book of Virtues* 6–7). Shed your prejudices through novel reading, suggests novelist Sue Monk Kidd ("Common Heart" 9). Azar Nafisi affirms, "empathy is at the heart of the novel," and warns, if you don't read, you won't be able to empathize (*Reading Lolita* 111). Is the attractive and consoling case for fiction implied by these representative views defensible? Surveying the existing research on the consequences of reading, I find the case for altruism stemming from novel reading inconclusive at best and nearly always exaggerated in favor of the beneficial effects of novel reading.

There is no question, however, that readers feel empathy with (and sympathy for) fictional characters and other aspects of fictional worlds. As this book demonstrates, readers' and authors' empathy certainly contributes to the emotional resonance of fiction, its success in the marketplace, and its character-improving reputation. My discussion in chapter 1 of empathy as psychologists understand it and my historical survey in chapter 2 of the debates about the positive and negative results of feeling with fiction contextualize the current vogue for empathy, arising from two sources. We are living in a time when the activation of mirror neurons in the brains of onlookers can be recorded as they witness another's actions and emotional reactions.[3] Contemporary neuroscience has brought us much closer to an understanding of the neural basis for human mind reading and emotion sharing abilities. The activation of onlookers' mirror neurons by a coach's demonstration of technique or an internal visualization of proper form, and by representations in television, film, visual art, and pornography, has already been recorded.[4] Simply hearing a description of an absent other's actions lights up mirror neuron areas on fMRI imaging of the human brain.[5] The possibility that novel reading stimulates mirror neurons' activation can now, as never before, undergo neuroscientific investigation.

Neuroscientists have already declared that people scoring high on empathy tests have especially busy mirror neuron systems in their brains.[6] For the first time we might investigate whether human differences in mirror neuron activity can be altered by exposure to art, to teaching, to literature. This newly enabled capacity to study empathy at the cellular level encourages speculation about human empathy's positive consequences. These speculations are not new, as any student of eighteenth-century moral sentimentalism will affirm, but they dovetail with efforts on the part of present-day virtue ethicists, political philosophers, educators, theologians, librarians, and interested parties such as authors and publishers to connect the experience of empathy, including its literary form, with outcomes of changed attitudes, improved motives, and better care and justice. Thus a very specific, limited version of empathy located in the neural substrate meets in the contemporary moment a more broadly and loosely defined, fuzzier sense of empathy as the feeling precursor to and prerequisite for liberal aspirations to greater humanitarianism. The sense of crisis stirred up by reports of stark declines in reading goes into this mix, catalyzing fears that the evaporation of a reading public leaves behind a population incapable of feeling with others. Yet the apparently threatened set of links among novel reading, experiences of narrative empathy, and altruism has not yet been proven to exist. Empathy robustly enters into affective responses to fiction, but its role in shaping the behavior of emotional readers has been debated for three centuries. Chapter 2 surveys those debates, and chapter 6 revisits them by way of considering contemporary critiques of empathy by false empathy and failed empathy critics.

Unlike these critics, I regard human empathy as a precious quality of our social natures. Despite the disrepute of generalizations about universal human traits among postcolonial and feminist theorists, I observe that women writers and novelists from around the world endorse the notion of shared human emotions when they overtly call upon their readers' empathy. I sympathize with their ambition, while remaining skeptical about consequences beyond immediate feeling responses. However, I hold that narrative empathy need not definitively perform renovations of civic virtue nor of individual behavior to be recognized as a core component of emotional response to fiction, the loss of which (for large numbers of nonreaders) is indeed to be regretted. Understanding the aesthetic effects of narrative empathy illuminates the responses of feeling brains to the word-wrought spaces and inhabitants of fictional worlds. The most artful and complex evocation of shared feeling accomplished by the novelist's art deserves attention, not only because the insights of literary analysis may assist psychologists and neuroscientists in the framing of the next layer of questions about readers, empathy, and altruism. Discoveries about narrative empathy may also help explain aspects of literary response that have been neglected or disparaged by scholars even as they have been experienced by millions of readers.

This brings us to the problem of popular fiction, which has not often been praised for the beneficial effects attributed to great literature. If immersion in culturally valued fictional worlds—canonical literature and serious fiction—predisposes readers to good citizenship, then what happens to readers (most of those who are left in the dwindling tally) who choose mass-market fiction? Does exposure to attractively rendered vice make readers vicious? The deleterious effects of violent television and videogames documented in case law and social psychology do not extend, according to most accounts, to prose fiction.[7] The cultural tendency to value novels and denigrate cartoons or video games, however, contributes to assumptions about good and bad forms of narrative. In general, prose fiction benefits from the contrast with other popular cultural narrative forms. This book scrutinizes the notion, shared by many librarians, teachers, and millions of participants in book groups, that reading certain novels is good for people. From its boosters, key features of the reading experience receive positive emphasis. Limiting the effects of reading to those enjoyed by highly educated consumers of serious fiction shifts the emphasis to more rarified qualities of narrative such as defamiliarization. However, middlebrow readers tend to value novels offering opportunities for strong character identification. They report feeling both empathy with and sympathy for fictional characters. They believe that novel reading opens their minds to experiences, dilemmas, time periods, places, and situations that would otherwise be closed to them. They emphasize the universality of human emotional responses in their reports on reading, sometimes undervaluing real differences among people of diverse cultures. They unself-consciously judge the success of novels based on how well they could identify with characters' feelings. Though these claims have bearing on matters of narrative technique and form, readers tend not to adopt the analytical language of academic literary criticism when they defend the novel and novel reading. Empathy shapes their recommendations and judgments about fiction.

Empathetic reading does differ in some important ways from analytical reading, though I hope to show that the two modes are not incompatible. Indeed, they must not be, for if we hope to continue to recruit more people to the ranks of regular readers, then the ways in which they respond to texts ought to matter to literary professionals. Publishers, agents, and novelists themselves do not need to be convinced of this, but disdain for the preferences of feeling readers pervades academic literary criticism. Despite the now habitual questioning of the coherence of individual selves in literature, theory, and literary study, a vigorous notion of character identification entailing readers' responses to imagined persons persists in contemporary novels. According to Janice Radway, this quality may be the most common shared trait of fiction in English that reaches a wide audience. Novels that succeed in invoking strong character identification are likelier to reach large numbers of readers, such as the hundreds of thousands of women who participated in Oprah's Book Club. This study takes the experiences and opinions of these readers seriously. In addition to redressing an implicit gender bias in research on the effects of novel reading, enumerating the qualities of novels that elicit empathetic reactions from a broad range of novel readers points up some of the gaps in research into the effects of narrative techniques.

Narrative theorists, novel critics, and reading specialists have already singled out a small set of narrative techniques—such as the use of first person narration and the interior representation of characters' consciousness and emotional states—as devices supporting character identification, contributing to empathetic experiences, opening readers' minds to others, and even predisposing readers to altruism. Theorists and teachers often speculate that these techniques may change readers' attitudes. In the course of reviewing the available research on this subject, I point out the gaps in our knowledge of potentially empathetic narrative techniques. I also ask whether any set of narrative techniques overrides the resistance to empathizing often displayed by members of an in-group regarding the emotional states of others marked out as different by their age, race, gender, weight, disabilities, and so forth.[8] If empathetic reading experiences start a chain reaction leading to mature sympathy and altruistic behavior, as many believe, then discovering the narrative techniques involved matters, for it turns out in laboratory experiments that we humans, like other primates, tend to experience empathy most readily and accurately for those who seem like us, as David Hume and Adam Smith predicted.[9] We may find ourselves regarding the feelings of those who seem outside the tribe with a range of emotions, but without empathy.[10] If novels do extend readers' sense of shared humanity beyond the predictable limitations, then the narrative techniques involved in such an accomplishment should be especially prized.

In order to pursue these questions, this book sets forth a theory of narrative empathy, based on the reports of real readers. I also explore from a narrative theoretical perspective more fine-grained questions about empathetic responses to novels. For instance, consider the commonplace that first-person fiction more readily evokes feeling responsiveness than the whole variety of third-person narrative situations. Even a college sophomore with a few weeks' training in theoretical terms can tell you that within the category of first-person narratives, empathy may be enhanced or impeded by narrative consonance or dissonance, unreliability, discordance, an excess of narrative levels with multiple narrators, extremes of disorder, or an especially convoluted plot. Genre, setting, and time period may help or hinder readers' empathy. Feeling out of sorts with the implied readership, or fitting it exactly, may make the difference between a dutiful reading and an experience of emotional fusion.[11] Contrasting first person with third person puts the question too broadly, with too many other variables, to reach a valid conclusion. Careful use of narrative theory can improve the quality of research into discourse processing conducted by psychologists.

My approach to narrative empathy draws upon work in several areas beyond narrative theory. Developmental and social psychology, including the juncture of affect and social cognition, prove major resources. Philosophy offers provocative treatments of empathy and the intricate puzzle of our emotional responses to literature.[12] Within literary studies, reader-response criticism, reception theory,[13] and literary theories of affect[14] contribute insights and analytical methods. This book participates in the growing interdisciplinary field, cognitive approaches to literary study, but it emphasizes affect. For many decades, literary study has tacitly obeyed the strictures of W. K. Wimsatt and Monroe Beardsley in their 1954 essay, "The Affective Fallacy," which argued against treatment of readers' emotional responses as mere psychologizing. In my home field of narrative studies, the recent interest in the role of affect in cognition, stimulated by the popular works of Antonio Damasio and Joseph LeDoux, has brought emotion back into the critical conversation.[15]

The developing field of cognitive literary studies recognizes that "literary works—whether fictional or not—have an emotional and tangible effect on readers and on the real world in which we live with literature" (*Cognitive* 152). As Peter Stockwell writes, "Cognitive poetics aims to extend its coverage to encompass sensations such as feeling moved by a literary work, feeling immersed in the world of a text that seems almost as real as real life. The psychologizing of character that has been a prestigious feature of valued literature for the past two hundred years relies on readerly reconstructions of character that include identification and empathy, ethical agreement and sympathy, and other forms of emotional attachment that readers defend very strongly" (152). Though studying these effects empirically has proven a challenge, an energetic interdisciplinary group of scholars has begun producing fascinating, if preliminary, results. This book examines the findings of these studies and poses questions that should be of interest to those who study empathy and reading empirically. Throughout the following chapters,

Empathy and the Novel engages with contemporary psychological research on empathy, bringing affect to the center of cognitive literary studies' reexamination of narrative fiction. Along the way, I offer a series of hypotheses about narrative empathy that could be investigated by psychologists as well as by literature specialists.

A Theory of Narrative Empathy

Character identification often invites empathy, even when the fictional character and reader differ from each other in all sorts of practical and obvious ways, but empathy for fictional characters appears to require only minimal elements of identity, situation, and feeling, not necessarily complex or realistic characterization. Whether a reader's empathy or her identification with a character comes first is an open question: spontaneous empathy for a fictional character's feelings sometimes opens the way for character identification. Not all feeling states of characters evoke empathy; indeed, empathetic responses to fictional characters and situations occur more readily for negative emotions, whether or not a match in details of experience exists. Finally, readers' experiences differ from one another, and empathy with characters doesn't always occur as a result of reading an emotional evocative fiction.

Several observations help explain the differences in readers' responses. Most importantly, readers' empathic dispositions are not identical to one another. Some humans are more empathetic to real others and some feel little empathy at all. (Some research suggests that empathizers are better readers because their role-taking abilities allow them to more readily comprehend causal relations in stories.[16]) The timing and the context of the reading experience matters: the capacity of novels to invoke readers' empathy changes over time, and some novels may only activate the empathy of their first, immediate audience, while others must survive to reach a later generation of readers in order to garner an emotionally resonant reading. Readers' empathy for situations depicted in fiction may be enhanced by chance relevance to particular historical, economic, cultural, or social circumstances, either in the moment of first publication or in later times, fortuitously anticipated or prophetically foreseen by the novelist.

Novelists do not exert complete control over the responses to their fiction. Empathy for a fictional character does not invariably correspond with what the author appears to set up or invite. Situational empathy, which responds primarily to aspects of plot and circumstance, involves less self-extension in imaginative role taking and more recognition of prior (or current) experience. A novelist invoking situational empathy can only hope to reach readers with appropriately correlating experiences. The generic and formal choices made by authors in crafting fictional worlds play a role in inviting (or retarding) readers' empathic responses. This means that for some readers, the author's use of the formulaic conventions of a thriller or a romance novel would increase empathetic resonance, while for other readers (perhaps better educated and attuned to literary effects), unusual or striking representations promote foregrounding and open the way to empathetic reading.[17]

Psychologist Marjorie Taylor has demonstrated that a group of fiction writers score higher on empathy tests than the general population.[18] (Their high empathy may be innate, or the activity of fiction writing may cultivate novelists' role-taking skills and train them in habits of empathy.) If it were to be verified beyond the original study, Taylor's discovery has several implications for the study of narrative empathy. Most important, it suggests why authors themselves so often vouch for the centrality of empathy to novel reading and believe in the power of narrative empathy to change the minds and lives of readers. The belief mirrors their own experiences as ready empathizers. Yet even the most fervent employers of their empathetic imaginations realize that this key ingredient of fictional world-making does not always transmit to readers without interference. Authors' empathy can be devoted to socially undesirable ends that may be rejected by a disapproving reader. Indeed, empathic distress at feeling with a character whose actions are at odds with a reader's moral code may be a result of successfully exercised authorial empathy. Both authors' empathy and readers' empathy have rhetorical uses, which come more readily to notice when they conflict in instances of empathic inaccuracy (discordance arising from gaps between a author's intention and a reader's experience of narrative empathy). Experiences of empathic inaccuracy may contribute to a reader's outraged sense that the author's perspective is simply wrong, while strong concord in authors' empathy and readers' empathy can be a motivating force to move beyond literary response to prosocial action.

Some scholars of discourse processing believe that readers' empathy could produce verifiable results in the beliefs and actions of populations of actual readers. Psychologists such as Martin Hoffman, whose theory of empathy and altruism is treated in detail in chapter 1, believe that novel reading may participate in the socialization and moral internalization required for the transmutation of empathic guilt into prosocial action. In other words, reading experiences may indirectly lay the groundwork for real-world transmissions of empathy from fleeting feeling to willed steps taken on another's behalf. This would make the effects of reading difficult to measure because the altruistic actions might be taken at some distance from the reading experience, a point that emphasizes the need for longitudinal studies of readers' lives. My own research suggests that readers' perception of a text's fictionality plays a role in subsequent empathetic response, by releasing readers from the obligations of self-protection through skepticism and suspicion. Thus they may respond with greater empathy to an unreal situation and characters because of the protective fictionality, but (if Hoffman is right) still internalize the experience of empathy in a way that promises later real-world responsiveness to others' needs.

While a full-fledged political movement, an appropriately inspiring social context, or an emergent structure of feeling promoting change may be necessary for efficacious action to arise out of internalized experiences of narrative empathy, readers may respond in those circumstances as a result of earlier reading. The position of the reader with respect to the author's strategic empathizing in fictional world-making limits these potential results. I theorize that *bounded strategic empathy* operates with an in-group, stemming from experiences of mutuality and leading to feeling with familiar others. *Ambassadorial strategic empathy* addresses chosen others with the aim of cultivating their empathy for the in-group, often to a specific end. *Broadcast strategic empathy* calls upon every reader to feel with members of a group, by emphasizing common vulnerabilities and hopes through universalizing representations.

In the course of exploring this theory of narrative empathy, I also subject the existing theories of narrative empathy and its effects, including those offered by philosophers and psychologists, to critical scrutiny. Too often these theories have been marred by bias or by a tendency to confound the effects of teaching with those of reading. So, for instance, I suggest that if narrative empathy is to be better understood, then women's reading and popular fiction must be accorded the respect of experimental inquiry. It will not do to allow introspective accounts of reading (or teaching) canonical works of nineteenth-century fiction to substitute for broad inquiry into the effects of more popular, widely read fiction that succeeds with a female readership. This is not to say that trained readers' empathetic experiences with complex, experimental, difficult, and high literary texts hold no interest, rather that a theory of narrative empathy that cannot explain commonplace, frequent, and readily repeated experiences of feeling with fiction leaves a lot to be desired. While this criticism aims to expand the scope of inquiry into narrative empathy, another seeks to narrow it. Too often the discussion of effects of novel reading combines the social and pedagogical outcomes of group discussion and classroom experiences. If the value of discussion and the contributions of teachers in the intellectual and moral growth of readers are to be understood, then these elements must not be hidden within accounts that claim to study "effects of reading" but actually conflate reading, discussion, role-taking activities, writing tasks, and teaching. To conclude, as I do, that scant evidence exists for active connections among novel reading, experiences of narrative empathy, and altruistic action on behalf of real people only emphasizes the importance of discussion, directed introspection, and leadership through questioning and providing examples. Books can't make change by themselves—and not everyone feels certain that they ought to. If, however, a society judges that its peoples' novel reading ought to invoke empathy that yields in committed action for others, then it should be willing to invest in the teachers who will help readers make connections between their feeling responses to fiction and their subsequent behavior as citizens of the world. Rather than jumping to this conclusion, *Empathy and the Novel* asks its readers to consider that we have a great deal more to understand about narrative empathy before we place the novel in service to social goals, no matter how laudable they appear.

Feeling Good about Fiction

Bold claims have been made for the positive consequences of novel reading, and these contentions grow more urgent as the practice of literary reading in Anglo-American culture undergoes startling declines. This book questions the contemporary truism that novel reading cultivates empathy that produces good citizens for the world. I affirm the robustness of narrative empathy, as an affective transaction accomplished through the writing and reading of fiction, but I hesitate to tether readers' empathy to certain outcomes of altruistic action. Still, novel reading does a lot for readers. Few would doubt that a habit of consuming narrative fiction in prose improves the vocabulary and informs the reader about subjects, times, people, and places (real and imagined) in a way that extends knowledge beyond individual experience. Some studies of fantasy empathy suggest that people who readily imagine fictional others' perspectives also grasp the variety and individuality of real others, but this discovery about empathetic dispositions may simply explain why certain people gravitate toward novel reading (Stotland, *Empathy* 89). Do empathetic people make good readers, or do good readers become empathetic people? Both may be true without guaranteeing that novels routinely do more than entertain, inform, soothe, or excite their readers.

For immersed readers, entering fictional worlds allows a refreshing escape from ordinary, everyday pressures and preoccupations.[19] Encountering the routine enigmas that drive fictional plots may enhance a reader's fluency and comfort with print communication. Widely read popular novels give readers something to talk about and can contribute to the formation of those little ad hoc communities of fellow-feeling that arise when several who love a particular novel or novelist meet and share their enthusiasm. The contemporary phenomenon of book groups testifies to the social and personal benefits of novel reading, mainly enjoyed by women.[20]

Fictional characters can become mental companions to last a lifetime, and relationships across generations can be built around affection for a character or a fictional world. To this list of benefits we might add the potential for social advancement: the person who can casually chat about serious fiction may impress employers and those in circles with pretensions to culture. The unusual college student who reads fiction for pleasure enjoys not only the books themselves, but also the approbation of her academic elders. Many an English professor or librarian received encouragement to pursue a career path as a result of her enthusiasm for books. Because of their complexity and thematic links to history, politics, economics, and many other aspects of our embodied experience, novels make good objects of academic study, though one hopes this remains a secondary consequence of fiction's continued existence. Rarely, but vitally for the continuity of cultural forms, novel readers sometimes become novelists. What dedicated reader would question the importance of novel reading if it produces the vocations of writers themselves? That all of these desirable effects of novel reading fall into jeopardy when a nation stops reading certainly ought to give us pause.

In the summer of 2004, when I began writing this book, the National Endowment for the Arts released a sobering report, entitled *Reading at Risk*. It describes a nation sliding into a state of indifference to literature, of functional aliteracy. At the behest of the NEA, in 2002, the United States Census Bureau interviewed seventeen thousand adult Americans about their reading habits. They inquired whether these citizens had read a single work of poetry, drama, or fiction in the prior year. Keeping in mind that a reader who had turned the pages of a single volume of the *Left Behind* series would count as a literature reader by the survey's definition, the results may even be considered frightening. The NEA reports that over the past two decades, both book reading and literature reading have declined sharply. Only 46.7 percent of respondents had read at least a single work of literature, and the news about men, minorities, and younger people was especially disheartening: only 37.6 percent of males admitted to literary reading (balanced out by 55.1 percent of females); among Hispanics, only 26.5 percent were self-declared literary readers; and of 18–24 year-olds (a group that includes many of the nation's college students, who may be presumed to read at least a little under compulsion), only 42.8 percent admitted to recreational reading. As Dana Gioia, Chairman of the NEA, puts it, the report presents a "detailed but bleak assessment of the decline in reading's role in the nation's culture." He goes on to suggest that "anyone who loves literature or values the cultural, intellectual, and political importance of active and engaged literacy in American society will respond to this report with grave concern" (*Reading at Risk* vii).[21]

The reaction to the report highlights the benefits believed to accrue to individuals and the nation as a result of literary reading. Gioia worries about the increased passivity of Americans, whose short attention spans and desire for accelerated gratification lead them to video games, the Internet, television, and DVDs, rather than to books. According to Gioia, the active attention, engagement, and practice required by reading are in jeopardy, and the loss of contemplative engagement with complex works of literature impoverishes Americans. Cultural continuity, nuanced insights, informed debate, and independent judgment all suffer as reading declines (*Reading at Risk* vii). Though few of these assumptions have been subjected to systematic investigation, they strike a chord with cultural commentators who observe with trepidation the changes brought by new technologies of communication and entertainment. While some critics have reacted to the report as a jeremiad or as insufficiently attentive to the textual nature of our on-line activities, most authors, readers, editors, teachers, and librarians respond to the call to action with heartfelt anecdotes of the importance of reading in their lives (McLemee, "Literary Reading" A1, A16).

Personal testimony reveals the widespread perception that reading enriches the lives and stimulates the imaginations of dedicated readers, but as any bookworm knows, readers can also seem antisocial and indolent. Novel reading is not a team sport. It not only encourages but also requires a certain amount of couch time. An immersed reader possesses the irritating ability to shut out those around her, as my sisters can attest. Historically, novel reading has not always seemed virtuous. Thus a set of claims linking reading with other socially desirable activities deserves our attention. *Reading at Risk* announces that literary reading strongly correlates to other forms of active civic participation and reports that literary readers are more likely than nonliterary readers to perform volunteer and charity work, to visit art museums, and to attend and participate in performing arts and sports events. Thus, to put it in the negative, as the executive summary does, the decline in literary reading presages the erosion of cultural and civic participation (*Reading at Risk* xii). This logic suggests a causal connection among reading and volunteerism, charitable activity, and cultural participation (though other factors, such as education or social class, may better explain the correlations). The NEA seizes the opportunity to warn the nation about the consequences of a precipitous reduction in reading, for if literary readers decline further, then active participants in social and cultural events may also dwindle in number: "It is time to inspire a nationwide renaissance of literary reading and bring the transformative power of literature into the lives of all citizens" (xiii).

Paradoxically, the remedy for a populace inclining ever further toward the isolating behaviors deplored as "bowling alone" may lie in the cultivation of the mainly solitary activity of reading novels, for fiction comprises the bulk of the reading of literate Americans.[22] Dana Gioia's emphasis on employing arts funding to increase access to events and museums (rather than the traditional approach of funding individual artists or projects) capitalizes on the fear that we are becoming a people who fail to read: "We have a generation of Americans growing up who have never been to the theater, the symphony, opera, dance, who have never heard live jazz and who increasingly don't read. . . . In a country where we've lost 40 million potential readers in the last 20 years," Gioia questions "whether the problem is an insufficient number of new books" (Weber, "Poet Brokers" B1, B5). The gloomy prognosis and call to action have worked to garner conservative support and funding for the arts ("Poet Brokers" B1, B5). If Congress and the public take the report seriously, it is to be hoped that the nation's libraries will receive a similarly enriched infusion of support. The rhetorical groundwork has been laid by a variety of cultural commentators who weigh in on the importance of reading. Three voices from the fields of philosophy, psychology, and history represent here the common argument that novel reading results in civic good.

The influential philosopher Martha Nussbaum sees novel reading as one of the core strategies for building better world citizens capable of extending love and compassion to unknown others. Encountering Henry James or George Eliot (not coincidentally two canonical writers of Leavis's Great Tradition) helps the would-be world citizen become "a sensitive and empathic interpreter" of others.[23] Though Nussbaum's examples in *Cultivating Humanity* (1997) and *Poetic Justice* (1995) show a bias toward realism and canonical works (she stoops only so low as Dickens), she states her claims for the exercise of the narrative imagination broadly: "Habits of empathy and conjecture conduce to a certain type of citizenship and a certain form of community: one that cultivates a certain kind of responsiveness to another's needs, and understands the way circumstances shape those needs, while respecting separateness and privacy" (*Cultivating* 90). One builds these habits, starting in early childhood, through literary imagining, which "inspires intense concern with the fate of characters and defines those characters as containing a rich inner life, not all of which is open to view" (90). Nussbaum, following the lead of Lionel Trilling, believes that learning respect for the hidden inner life of fictional characters leads readers "to attribute importance to the material conditions of happiness while respecting human freedom" (90). This in turn leads to empathy, compassion, and social justice (91, 94). In the strongest terms, Nussbaum claims that reading must be consequential: "It is impossible to care about the characters [of Dickens and Eliot] and their well-being in the way the text invites, without having some very definite political and moral interests awakened in oneself" (104). Whether anyone, let alone large numbers of people, actually acts in traceable ways as a result of this conscientious prompting Nussbaum does not wonder: she assumes it must be so. Her strenuous efforts to promote reform in liberal education emphasize her faith in the efficacy of the right kind of novel reading.

For Steven Pinker, human beings need not be in school studying canonical writers to enjoy the benefits of what he names a "moral technology," storytelling. The evolutionary psychologist argues in a recent interview in *Seed* magazine that storytelling has made the human species "nicer" ("Seed Salon" 48); Pinker sees moral emotions as evolved traits that account for the statistical decline in the murder rate from the time of hunter-gatherer societies. In Pinker's rosy long view, "Much of the world has seen an end to slavery, to genocide for convenience, to torture as a routine form of criminal punishment for property crimes, to human sacrifice, to rape as the spoils of war, to the ownership of women. We seem to be turning into a nicer species" ("Seed Salon" 48). Most gratifyingly for those of us who spend our comfortable lives contemplating novels, Pinker attributes to storytelling the extension of the "moral circle" to include "other clans, other tribes, and other races" (48). He concedes that our near universal capacity for empathy does seem to be limited to a narrow compass of relations or villagers, but he holds that by allowing our projection "into the lives of people of different times and places and races, in a way that wouldn't spontaneously occur," fiction can change our perspectives on unlike persons "who might otherwise seem subhuman" (48). Thus fiction offers not only the "cognitive advantages of seeing how hypothetical scenarios play out," but also "the emotional pleasures of empathizing with a character" (97), and a payoff in understanding and better behavior.

The distinguished historian Lynn Hunt extrapolates from personal to political improvements. She argues that eighteenth-century novels played an important part in advancing the concept of human rights.[24] Indeed, if fiction can do what Nussbaum and Pinker believe, then why wouldn't history record some pretty dramatic effects of the rise of the novel? Hunt argues that the novel "disseminated a new psychology and a new social and political order" through its narrative form and "made the point that all selves are fundamentally similar because of their inner psychic processes" ("Paradoxical" 14). The eighteenth-century novel accomplished this by drawing readers in and making them feel "passionately" involved in the story. This new experience of empathy with characters gave new political concepts purchase: "Reading a novel (in the eighteenth century and not before) a reader identified with an ordinary person unknown to him or her personally but with whom the reader empathized thanks to the narrative form itself" (14). Hunt especially prizes the effect of novels on spreading the notion of women's subjectivity, but her conclusions take her beyond the renovation of opinion of mainly British and European middle-class readers about females and servants (who were not, she acknowledges, immediately granted full rights [15]). Novels trained readers to a broader conception of humanity, through "new forms of empathetic identification with individuals who are now imagined to be in some fundamental way like you" (13).

Well, it depends. Anyone who has read a fair number of eighteenth-century novels will be able to think of examples of stigmatized characters who are held up for ridicule and humiliation, to the delight of protagonists and implied readers alike. The elderly, the fat, and the gout-ridden all seem to be fair game. Eighteenth-century novelists often invite readers to laugh at rebarbative characters' misfortunes, often in support of general satiric aims, but sometimes just for fun. For instance, Frances Burney's *Evelina* (1778), a fiction inviting a sympathetic view of its eponymous heroine, also contains a sequence in which two aged women are recruited from local villages to run in a footrace, and one in which the heroine's vulgar old grandmother gets dumped in a ditch as the result of a carriage wreck. Hilarious? Do these scenes sustain a view of fiction as a fount of human sympathy? We don't in fact know how eighteenth-century readers responded to jokes that would be regarded as politically incorrect today, but it does seem a bit of a stretch to imagine that empathizing with Evelina counteracts all the moral consequences of howling with laughter at the humiliation of elderly females. *Schadenfreude* may be as robust an emotional response as compassion to the fates of eighteenth-century fictional characters.

Hunt concedes the difficulty of proving how eighteenth-century readers actually responded to the novels they had begun reading in large numbers. Other views have been offered about the widespread social impact of fictional representations on, for instance, the rise of nationalism.[25] Curiously, though Hunt situates her "imagined empathy" in parallel with Benedict Anderson's imagined communities (13), she does not address Edward Said's converse thesis about the impact of the novel on imperialism. Said argues that the novel was immensely important in the "formation of imperial attitudes, references, and experiences" (*Culture and Imperialism* xii), attitudes that were often at odds with the development of human rights. To put it baldly, how can we know that readers' passionate involvement with fictional others didn't inspire a desire to collect and control people they did not personally know? Or, perhaps, closer to the bone, might not novel reading enable individuals living on incomes from the investment funds that profited from the slave trade to feel moral indignation on the behalf of imaginary others brought near by fiction, while indirectly exploiting the suffering of real people far away?

Sometime during the Bosnian war, I was watching the news in my comfortable study. The camera showed refugees picking their way down a rough path, out of the mountains they had crossed to flee the conflict. I saw a professionally dressed woman in her thirties carrying a child about eighteen months old. I suddenly felt the weight of that toddler in my arms, the tension in my calves that governs slipping feet, and the spinal awareness that I might suddenly be thrown off balance. I felt not pity, but the apprehension the woman's face and movements showed. This was empathy—a spontaneous sharing of feelings, including physical sensations in the body, provoked by witnessing or hearing about another's condition. Human beings and other primates frequently experience fleeting empathetic sensations, which can be observed and measured by physical signs, including facial expressions, decreased heart rate, altered skin conductance, and palm sweat. These signs can be captured by observation and, in the lab, by electromyographic (EMG) recordings and even fMRI imagery of brain activity.[26] These common experiences may go by too quickly to register in our long-term memory, but most people, when asked, can recall times when they felt *with* another (as opposed to feeling *for* another, or sympathy).

Not so long after this episode, the bad news about the massacres in Rwanda began appearing in the paper. Just four days into the 1994 genocide, readers of *The New York Times* learned that thousands of Tutsis and moderate Hutus were being killed daily by machete, in systematic attacks by their Hutu neighbors. It wouldn't be quite accurate to say that I felt sympathy for the victims. I felt horror, shock, and, as time passed, disappointment at the tepid response to a faraway genocide. Then I felt a familiar American emotion—guilt. I wrote a couple of checks. What else could I do? I lapsed into a feeling of vague unease, as when an important task has been left unfinished. Among all the feelings that the real events in Rwanda provoked, empathy I do not recall. There was no moment when I shared the feelings of a Tutsi victim. I had not seen pictures: unlike the scenes of ethnic cleansing in the Balkans, the Rwandan genocide was not broadcast on television.[27] I wondered whether the large numbers of victims impeded my response—a strong possibility. Or perhaps the dearth of white, middle-class, English-speaking, professional women like me among the victims short-circuited my empathy. I couldn't identify with them; they were too unlike me; their circumstances and their suffering were unimaginable. This despite the fact that I had read dozens of novels set in African countries during times of crisis and had felt the strong, spontaneous kind of character identification that I call reader's empathy for fictional characters experiencing hunger, dispossession, rape, humiliation, and exile.

If my novel reading was to have cultivated my sympathetic imagination for the real people with whom I share existence, it had failed. If feeling bad and writing checks to relief organizations counted as being a good world citizen, then perhaps my lifelong novel reading did form something about my character. (Though now I know, sadly, that those checks probably did more to support the *genocidaires* fleeing from justice than to assist the victims.[28]) But there were so many other possible explanations for my minimal money-giving response to the genocide that novel reading scarcely seemed to rate. I began to wonder how one could ever tell what novel reading does to a person, for a person, if anything at all. For I have not been alone in my insufficient responses. Did a nation of book club readers rise up to protest the recent genocide in the Sudan?[29] We did not. Even Martha Nussbaum concedes, "sympathy inspired by literary imagining does not immediately effect political change" (*Cultivating* 97).

It would be comforting to believe that links between novel reading, empathy, and altruism or committed action in favor of human rights really exist. The fact that cultural authorities insist upon these connections just as reading becomes a minority pastime activates my skepticism as much as my concern, however. In the investigation that follows, I take a wide view of contemporary fiction and attend to the testimony of writers themselves. The purposeful invocation of empathy by many contemporary novelists attempts to alter readers' views about the extent of the empathetic circle. I respectfully observe writers' conviction that novels can make something happen, even though I question our certainty about the end results of reading. All over the globe, novelists exercise their empathic imaginations in acts of world creation, in the hope of reaching readers and changing hearts and minds. I respond in this book to their invitation to feel with fiction.

Organization of This Book

In chapter 1, "Contemporary Perspectives on Empathy," readers will find definitions of key terms, most importantly the related concepts of empathy and sympathy, and a broad account of the current popular understanding of empathy. Drawing primarily on the recent psychological literature on empathy and altruism, this introductory chapter explores some of the open questions about empathy, including its relationship to real-world "prosocial" helping behavior. I offer summaries of the most recent psychological and neuroscientific research in providing provisional answers to these basic questions: What is empathy? Who has it? How do psychologists study it? Does empathy involve emotion, cognition, or both? Finally, I turn to a first set of questions about readers' reactions to nonfictional and fictional appeals to their emotions. The chapter ends with a set of readings of three sample texts, showing that at least for a small sample of readers, the avowed fictionality of a text opens up the possibility for a feeling response by disarming suspicion.

Chapter 2, "The Literary Career of Empathy," traces the reputation of empathy and feeling responses to literature through three centuries. It demonstrates that significant components of what psychologists today call empathy appear under the label of sympathy in the works of eighteenth-century philosophers David Hume and Adam Smith. Moving in chronological order through literary periods to the twentieth century, I survey eighteenth-century sympathy and the literature of sensibility, Romantic and Victorian preoccupations with sensations and social problems, modern defamiliarization and estrangement, and the rise of the twentieth-century middlebrow reader. Each literary period contains voices advocating and contesting the value of a feeling response to literature. Thus, this chapter emphasizes doubts about empathy and records some of the gravest charges against empathy as well as some of the grandest claims for its social value. By the twentieth century, the end point of this chapter's brief survey, the reputation of empathetic response clearly depends upon contexts and genres. I illustrate my account of the ongoing debate with generous quotations from the original sources, so that the chapter serves as an anthology of empathy's controversial literary career.

In chapter 3, "Readers' Empathy," I present testimony collected from a variety of readers in addition to myself in order to move beyond introspection in discovering what readers say about the effects of their novel reading. I compare this anecdotal evidence with the few scholarly, empirical studies of reading, giving special attention to those that address empathy and changes of attitudes toward people regarded as fundamentally different Others. In a thorough examination of narrative techniques or aspects of the novel that have been identified as empathetic by narrative theorists or literary cognitivists, I identify the missing pieces of a comprehensive literary theory of readers' empathy, and I suggest areas where more careful research is required before conclusions can be made. Despite the provisional state of affairs in the area of study focusing on emotional responses to novels, in this chapter, I offer the first part of a preliminary theory of narrative empathy (the second part appears in chapter 5, "Authors' Empathy").

Chapter 4, "Empathy in the Marketplace," begins with a cautious assessment of the claim that reading novels extends the empathetic circle. Do empathetic novels sell better in the world fiction market because they appeal to female readers, or do women experience extension of their empathy because they read novels? Beginning with these questions, I discuss gender as a constitutive feature of the middlebrow reader, and I consider the central role of affect in the construction of the reading-group participant. Through a case study of the response to Rohinton Mistry's *A Fine Balance* (1995), the only postcolonial novel selected by Oprah Winfrey for her original book club, I examine the relationship between feeling readers and contemporary authors. I study how this audience (made up of Oprah's Book Club members) constructs ideal texts and characters with whom they can empathize and takes up the challenge of reading fiction about painful subjects by making it relevant to their own lives. The emphasis by readers, authors, and the novels themselves on a common emotional heritage and the universality of human feelings bridges social, cultural, economic, and geographical gaps that might otherwise impede empathy. However, the sharing of feeling may not translate into prosocial action on behalf of suffering others, as some authors hope. I speculate here that becoming a reader of an Oprah book, which is to say joining the vast audience of an instant bestseller, may activate the psychological response known as diffusion of responsibility: the assumption on the part of individuals, that because they are part of a crowd, they need not take responsibility for acting.

In chapter 5, "Authors' Empathy," I take up the topic of writers' intentions and their decisions about craft and content. Like my treatment of readers' empathy in chapter 3, this discussion ranges widely, deriving proposals about narrative empathy from the testimony and practice of a large number of contemporary novelists. Though many of the novelists discussed in this chapter are distinguished prizewinners, less well-known authors, including the writers of science fiction and novelizations from television series, contribute to the contemporary vogue for and interrogation of empathy. Some, such as Alice Walker, attempt to use their fiction and fame to effect change in the real world. Others, such as Keri Hulme, evoke empathy for characters that ordinary readers would usually find repellent. In this chapter I coin a term, *empathic inaccuracy*, meaning a strong conviction of empathy that incorrectly identifies the feeling of the subject. Authors sometimes succeed in evoking empathy unintentionally. When they explicitly invoke empathy, they do not present it as unambiguously beneficial. The contemporary thematizing of empathy as a character trait shows that novelists actively participate in the debate about the uses and perils of empathy. Indeed, novelists persist in what I call *strategic empathizing*, in which their own empathetic imagining goes out to meet particular audiences, not necessarily composed of educated Western readers. Authors' empathy flows in many directions, meeting the empathy of habitual readers wherever they are.

Chapter 6, "Contesting Empathy," addresses the most negative representations of empathy and explains why academic distrust of empathy has been so influential. Empathy earns distrust for its apparent directional quality—an empathetic performance may appear condescending to its object or to an observer. In addition, feminists, postcolonial theorists, and critical race scholars in legal studies resist the universalizing of human emotions inherent in much of the commentary on empathy. Some philosophers and experts in cultural studies regard the putative ethical consequences of empathy and reading emotionally evocative literature as impediments to justice. Many contemporary intellectuals point to the empathetic individual's erasure of suffering others in a self-regarding emotional response that affronts others' separate personhood. These criticisms place empathy in a negative light, and their authors certainly do not participate in the advocacy for empathy as an essential ingredient of good citizenship. Indeed, they regard it as a typical manifestation of Western arrogance, imagining common ground with the victims of global capitalism and fantasizing relationships of emotional recognition in place of the unseemly relation of consumers to the exploited. Empathy, in this light, becomes a delusion of the affluent West, which ought to be revealed for throwing up impediments to social change. Through discussion of fiction by Michael Ondaatje and Octavia Butler, I explore some of the most compelling stances against empathy. I distinguish *false empathy* from *failed empathy* critics and situate their views in relation to the critique of human universals that underlies some theorists' distrust of empathy.

Yet, despite this bracing critique, empathetic fiction (much of it written by women, racial and ethnic minorities, and postcolonial citizens) reaches a wide readership. In celebrated cases this fiction transcends barriers of difference represented by race, nation, gender, sexual orientation, and religion,

among others. Though the long-term political, social, and ethical consequences of empathetic reading experiences have yet to be demonstrated,
the ardency of readers and the perseverance of novelists give pause to the
skeptic who would argue that literature makes nothing happen. Simple
accounts of the utility of novel reading, I argue, should be replaced by more
nuanced study of the consequences of experiencing aesthetic emotions.[30]
The affective transaction across boundaries of time, culture, and location
may indeed be one of the intrinsic powers of fiction and the novel a remark-
ably effective device for reminding readers of their own and others' humanity. Narrative empathy is not an inconsiderable element of the creation and
reception of fiction, and it should be resituated to a central place in twenty-
first–century aesthetics.

This book pursues the question of what a habit of novel reading does
to the moral imagination of the immersed reader. Unlike the authorities
mentioned earlier, I do not assume from the outset that empathy for fictional characters necessarily translates into what Stephen Pinker calls "nicer"
human behavior. I ask whether the effort of imagining fictive lives, as George
Eliot believed, can train a reader's sympathetic imagining of real others in
her actual world, and I inquire how we might be able to tell if it happened.
I acknowledge that it would be gratifying to discover that reading Henry
James makes us better world citizens, but I wonder whether the expen-
diture of shared feeling on fictional characters might not waste what little
attention we have for others on nonexistent entities, or at best reveal that
addicted readers are simply endowed with empathetic dispositions. Like
most professors of literature, I would be delighted to affirm the salutary
effects of novel reading, but I am not prepared to take them on faith. How
might we verify when empathetic reading experiences have shaped our
behavior? We should begin by understanding what psychologists mean by
empathy, a term bedeviled by conflicting definitions.

Acknowledgments

A book about what happens to readers when they experience empathy for fictional characters (or other aspects of novelistic worlds) depends, first and foremost, on the generosity of readers. One can impose on one's students (and believe me, I did!), but the voluntary testimony of a variety of readers, including the pseudonymous posters at Amazon.com, made this project possible.

Exemplary among my informants were VICTORIA listserv correspondents. Without necessarily knowing me personally, they gamely responded to my query about empathetic reading experiences. I thank Diana Archibald, Alison Booth, Sarah Brown, Michel Faber, Richard Fulton, Sheldon Goldfarb, Kerryn Goldsworthy, Valerie Gorman, Jill Grey, Martha Stoddard Holmes, Susan Hoyle, Jack Kolb, Robert Lapides, David Latane, Mary Lenard, Anna Lepine, Margot K. Louis, Rohan Maitzen, Timothy Mason, Sara L. Maurer, Michael Hargreave Mawson, Pat Menon, Kathryn Miele, Ellen Moody, Deborah Denenholz Morse, Heather Morton, Lee O'Brien, Diana Ostrander, Meri-Jane Rochelson, Anne B. Rodrick, Heather Schell, June W. Siegel, Ann Shillinglaw, Suzanne Shumway, Kathleen O'Neill Sims, Beth Sutton-Ramspeck, Tamara S. Wagner, and Michael Woolf.

Many friends and colleagues supplied "true confessions" about what novels made them do, asked me those invaluable stumping questions, and provided ways into the daunting bibliographies of unfamiliar disciplines. For that and for responses to my work in progress, I thank Edward Adams, John Armstrong, Claudette Artwick, Theresa Braunschneider, Pam Burish, Gwyn Campbell, Marc Conner, Elizabeth Heckendorn Cook, Ed Craun, Kevin Crotty, Doug Cummings, Kelly Boyle Dailey, Scott Dransfield, Francoise Fregnac-Clave, Art Goldsmith, Jim Hentz, Sarah Kennedy, George Landow, Timothy Lubin, Nancy Margand, Richard Marks, Yolanda Merrill, David S. Miall, Brian Murchison, Nan Partlett, Domnica Radulescu, Brian Richardson, Elizabeth Samet, Lad Sessions, Kary Smout, Asali Solomon, Scott Sundby, Jim Warren, and Lesley Wheeler. I benefited from the public discussions and private conversations that went on at the Institute for English Studies conference, The Languages of Emotion, in London (October 2004), and at the Cognition in Literary Interpretation and Practice confer-

ence, in Helsinki, Finland (August 2004). Audiences at talks at Southern
Virginia University (Buena Vista, Virginia), University of Alaska Southeast
(Juneau, Alaska), University of Helsinki (Helsinki, Finland), University
of Washington (Seattle, Washington), and R. E. Lee Memorial Episcopal
Church (Lexington, Virginia) made comments and asked questions that
shaped my work.

In order to carry out this project, I had to find my way around several
fields that were new to me, specifically cognitive approaches to literary
study and the psychological study of empathy. Neuroscientist Tyler Lorig
and cognitive scientists David Elmes and Wythe Whiting were kind enough
to welcome me into their classrooms as an auditor. I received invaluable
suggestions and guidance from neuroscientist Len Jarrard, from social psychologists Martha McClintock and Julie Woodzicka, and from developmental psychologists Nancy Eisenberg and Nancy Margand. Tania Singer of the
Wellcome Institute at University of London was kind enough to respond to
the e-mail queries of a complete stranger. To Nancy Eisenberg I am especially indebted for expert guidance at the start and finish of this project.
In the field of cognitive approaches to literary study, I am grateful to Alan
Richardson, a generous and helpful reader, and to David Miall and Peter
Stockwell, both of whom offered encouragement and useful suggestions. I
am grateful to James Phelan for permission to publish in scattered chapters
here material that first appeared in an essay, "Narrative Empathy" in *Narrative* (Fall 2006).

Throughout my time at Washington and Lee University, I have benefited
from generous institutional support, and I owe specific thanks to Interim
Dean Jeanine Stewart, Acting Dean Lad Sessions, Provost Tom Williams,
and the members of the Advisory Committee. A Glenn Grant for summer
work in 2004 and a Class of 1962/Hewlett-Mellon grant augmenting sab-
batical salary in 2004–05 made the actual writing of this book feasible. The
Glenn Grant Publication fund provided timely subvention. Elizabeth Teaff
tirelessly processed my interlibrary loan requests, for which I thank her.
Sandy O'Connell pulled me through a year as Acting Chair and supported
me throughout the writing process.

Good book talk sustains real readers. I'm fortunate to enjoy frank conversations with my students, and I particularly thank my Washington and
Lee University undergraduates, especially those who participated in World
Fiction in English, Postcolonial Literature, Literary Approaches to Poverty,
and Children's Literature courses. For permission to quote their written
responses, I thank them. My graduate students at Bread Loaf in Juneau,
Alaska, deserve special mention. Their experiences as teachers in middle schools, high schools, and in K–12 schools in the Alaskan bush have
informed and inspired me. Even fleeting conversations with exceptional
readers can have a significant impact on the shape of a project. I am grateful

in this regard to Fakrul Alam, Carolyn Allen, Roy Blount Jr., Ian Duncan, Amy Elias, Michael Gorra, Jianjun Ma, Franco Moretti, Claude Rawson, and Robyn Warhol for their suggestions about novels and reading. Needless to say, the work that appears in these pages (and the inevitable errors) are my responsibility alone.

CONTENTS

Empathy and the Novel

1

CONTEMPORARY PERSPECTIVES ON EMPATHY

This chapter establishes a working definition of empathy, details the questions about empathy that psychologists and philosophers pursue, including the relation of empathy to altruistic behavior, and charts the representations of empathy in popular culture. In order to investigate what empathy invoked by novels might do to and for readers, I begin with the current psychological understanding of what direct experiences of empathy for actual humans appear to accomplish. While a well-regulated person may experience empathy that leads to sympathetic concern and altruism in real life, another individual may become distressed by exposure to another's condition. Research in psychology describes individual differences in empathy, addressing its heritability and its influence by the environment.[1] Twin studies show that genetic factors account for a great deal of the range in dispositional affective empathy.[2] Close and secure family relationships (a major component of environment) also contribute to individuals' feeling responsiveness to others.[3] While an emotional temperament is likely to contribute to empathy, little is known about the genetic sources or environmental antecedents of cognitive role taking,[4] an ability associated with empathy that may be involved in character identification. If novels can be considered a part of readers' environment, then fiction may elicit the expression of dispositional empathy, or it may cultivate the sympathetic imagination through the exercise of innate role-taking abilities. Could novel reading help an individual become better regulated and thus more likely to move from empathy to sympathy in real life? Or does the testimony about the role of fiction reflect the aesthetic preferences of readers already inclined to respond empathetically? As these questions show, much of the debate about empathy described in this chapter has relevance for the questions of narrative ethics raised in the preface, matters of narrative technique treated in chapter 3, and reader responses discussed throughout the book.

This chapter initiates that project by describing a collection of reactions to three brief texts that attempt to invoke emotional responses in readers. The discussion here leads to several baseline assertions about narrative empathy. Empathetic response to fiction is less consistent than it might at first seem. No one text evokes the same responses in all of its readers, and not all texts succeed in stimulating readers to feel and act as their authors apparently wish. I argue here that the very fictionality of novels predisposes readers to empathize with characters, since a fiction known to be "made up" does not activate suspicion and wariness as an apparently "real" appeal for assistance may do.[5] I posit that fictional worlds provide safe zones for readers' feeling empathy without experiencing a resultant demand on real-world action.[6] This freedom from obligation paradoxically opens up the channels for both empathy and related moral affects such as sympathy, outrage, pity, righteous indignation, and (not to be underestimated) shared joy and satisfaction. Before returning to my central topic of narrative empathy, however, the definitions of empathy and related responses demand attention.[7]

What Is Empathy?

Empathy, a vicarious, spontaneous sharing of affect, can be provoked by witnessing another's emotional state, by hearing about another's condition, or even by reading. It need not be a conscious response: the neonates who cry at the sound of other babies' cries are almost certainly unaware of their primitive empathy. Equipped with mirror neurons, the human brain appears to possess a system for automatically sharing feelings, what neuroscientists call a "shared manifold for intersubjectivity."[8] More complex cognitive responses to others' mental states layer atop this initial spontaneous sharing of feelings. Mirroring what a person might be expected to feel in that condition or context, empathy is thought to be precursor to its semantic close relative, *sympathy*.[9] Although the word *empathy* is a relatively young term, entering English in the early twentieth century as a coined translation of the German word *Einfühlung*, aspects of empathy have been described by philosophers since the days of Adam Smith and David Hume under the older term *sympathy*. Throughout this book I distinguish the spontaneous, responsive sharing of an appropriate feeling as *empathy*, and the more complex, differentiated feeling for another as *sympathy* (sometimes called *empathic concern* in psychological literature).

Personal distress, an aversive emotional response also characterized by apprehension of another's emotion, differs from empathy in that it focuses on the self and leads not to sympathy but to avoidance.[10] The distinction between empathy and personal distress matters because empathy is associated with the moral emotion *sympathy* (also called *empathic concern*) and thus with prosocial or altruistic action. Empathy that leads to sympathy is by definition other-directed, whereas an over-aroused empathic response that creates personal distress (self-oriented and aversive) causes a turning-away from the provocative condition of the other. I hazard that personal distress caused by novel reading leads people to stop reading, to put the book down, or to disengage full attention by skipping and skimming. None of the philosophers who put stock in the morally improving experience of narrative empathy include personal distress in their theories. Because novel reading can be so easily stopped or interrupted by an unpleasant emotional reaction to a book, however, personal distress has no place in a literary theory of empathy, though it certainly contributes to aesthetic emotions, such as those Sianne Ngai describes in her important book *Ugly Feelings* (2005).[11]

In this book I rely on an understanding of empathy derived from psychology, though not all psychologists agree on the components, processes, and outcomes of empathy. I do not attempt to resolve these disagreements through my use of terminology, but I do mention their differences when they are consequential.[12] In empathy, sometimes described as an emotion in its own right,[13] we feel what we believe to be the emotions of others.[14] This phenomenon is distinguished in both psychology and philosophy (though not in popular usage) from *sympathy*, in which feelings *for* another occur.

Empathy:
I feel what you feel.
I feel your pain.

Sympathy:
I feel a supportive emotion about your feelings.
I feel pity for your pain.

These examples emphasize negative emotions—pain and pity—but it should be noted from the outset that although psychological and philosophical studies of empathy have tended to gravitate toward the negative, empathy also occurs for positive feelings of happiness, satisfaction, elation, triumph, and sexual arousal.[15] All of these positive kinds of empathy play into readers' pleasure, a phenomenon French literary theorists have described with the felicitous term *jouissance*.[16]

Experts on *emotional contagion*, the communication of one's mood to others, have done a better job of studying the full range of emotional states that can be shared through our automatic mimicry of one another.[17] Indeed, primitive emotional contagion, or "the tendency to automatically mimic and synchronize facial expressions, vocalizations, postures, and movements with those of another person and consequently, to converge emotionally" (*Contagion* 81) offers a compelling explanation of a component of our empathy as arising from our physical and social awareness of one another, from birth. Inherited traits play an important role in our disposition to experience emotional contagion,[18] but our personal histories and cultural contexts affect the way we understand automatically shared feelings.[19]

So, for instance, emotional contagion comes into play in our reactions to narrative, for we are also story-sharing creatures. The same drive to affiliate with others for comfort and safety that expresses itself in empathy and sympathy may also play a role in our species' enthusiasm for narrative. The oral storyteller not only takes advantage of our tendency to share feelings socially by doing the voices and facial expressions of characters, but also tacitly trains young children and members of the wider social group to recognize and give priority to culturally valued emotional states.[20] This education does not create our feelings, but renders emotional states legible through their labels, and activates our expectations about what emotions mean. Narratives in prose and film infamously manipulate our feelings and call upon our built-in capacity to feel with others. We need not be present in the immediate audience to catch the feelings of others, as anyone who watched the events of 11 September 2001, on television will recall. (Remember also how many people said of that day, "It was like a movie," an evaluation that catches both the intensity of feeling and the sense of unreality that beset us then.) We humans can "feel with" fictional characters and faraway strangers when we are exposed to storytelling prose narrative and film fiction, or mass media broadcasts that call upon our emotions. It makes sense for all citizens to understand the circumstances and techniques that elicit our shared feelings, especially if an empathetic response does develop into more complex responses that contribute to (or impede) our moral development and civic engagement.

Who Has Empathy?

Humans feel empathy. We aren't the only animals to do so,[21] but empathy seems so basic a human trait that lacking it can be seen as a sign of inhumanity. *Blade Runner* (1982, 1992), Ridley Scott's film version of Philip K. Dick's *Do Androids Dream of Electric Sheep?* (1968), popularizes and troubles a notion of empathy as the one essential, recognizable trait of humanity. *Blade Runner*'s dystopic future world imagines society penetrated by nearly unidentifiable cyborgs engineered to believe in their wholly invented human lives, memories, and feelings, which have been supplied by their maker. These persecuted machines reveal themselves as cyborgs by failing an empathy test. Lacking empathy in this context means revealing oneself as a machine.

Popular culture represents empathy as a human and often also as a typically female trait, understandings to which science contributes. For instance, Cambridge scientist Simon Baron-Cohen's *The Essential Difference: The Truth about the Male and Female Brains* (2003) advances a theory about female empathy that confirms contemporary gender stereotypes and has received widespread coverage in the press due to its speculations about autism rates.[22] Baron-Cohen suggests that the capacity for empathy differs between men and women, specifically, that "the female brain is predominantly hard-wired for empathy" while "the male brain is predominantly hard-wired for understanding and building systems" (*Essential* 1). Baron-Cohen describes empathy by its behavioral consequences: for him it entails automatically feeling concern, wincing, and feeling "a desire to run across and help alleviate" the victim's pain (2).[23] He proposes that empathy "arises out of natural desire to care about others," and he argues that human females spontaneously empathize more than males (on average) (2).[24] This is not a new idea in sociobiology, philosophy, or politics.[25] For instance, it is axiomatic that women generally prefer reparative, humane solutions to social problems, while men prefer punishment and preventative measures.[26] Folk understanding of the gender gap in politics suggests that emotionality and empathy on the part of women incline them to caring solutions.

Real differences in the structures of female and male brains might seem to support this popular view with evidence from neuroscience.[27] Some aspects of emotional response are lateralized differently in men and women, and some brain areas involved in emotion differ in relative size between the sexes. Speculations about the evolutionary origin of human empathy often point toward the caregiver-infant relationship as a source for developing empathy.[28] It is important not to confound underlying structures with outcomes that may express cultural assumptions rather than biological fact, however. Some developmental psychologists and cognitive scientists reviewing the evidence question the assumption that empathy is a "female trait." Martin Hoffman believes that "mimicry is probably a hard-wired neurologically based empathy-arousing mechanism whose two steps, imitation and feedback, are directed by commands from the central nervous system" (*Empathy and Moral Development* 44). This means for all of us: human beings and other animals possess this fundamental "hard-wiring," evolved from primitive communication mechanisms that enhance cooperation with other organisms in the group.

Though some studies have shown gender differences (not all skewing toward females), in their second comprehensive review of the literature, Eisenberg and Lennon find that gender differences may arise from the methods of measurement rather than from genuine differences. Paper and pencil self-report studies produced large differences; picture/story indices yielded small differences; and physiological measures resulted in no differences. To Eisenberg and Lennon, this suggests that the subjects' assumptions about their own gender roles and appropriate emotional responses, especially when directly reported to a questioner, skewed results toward showing gender difference.[29] They conclude that fine-tuned definitions and methodology that guard against influence by cultural assumptions must be developed before any conclusions can be made about gender and empathy. Writing a decade later, social psychologists Tiffany Graham and William Ickes agree, although their use of empathy indicates cognitive perspective taking rather than affective empathy with others' feelings.[30] In their review of the evidence about "women's intuition," Graham and Ickes decide that "gender differences in empathic skills and dispositions appear to be small rather than large, and specific rather than general in their scope" ("Intuition"

139–40). Motivation rather than ability accounts for women's skills in judging others' thoughts and feelings.

Humanists and literary scholars are more familiar with feminist and post-colonial critiques of the essentializing universals that have often been used to narrow the definition of the human or to allocate traits rated low on a scale of values to subject races or to groups considered inferior. This perspective, too, brings into question any simple assignment of emotional traits to a gender or other group of humans. Certainly we should want to know what historical circumstances or social conditions influence the assignment of "caring" to women and "understanding" to men before we assume that a biological basis for a distinction exists. Despite critical reservations about claims such as Baron-Cohen's, however, the notion of gender difference in empathy persists in popular cultural representations of empathic individuals. Often such claims rely on a notion of the "natural" that does not always receive confirmation in the laboratory.

One clue that there may not be a biological basis for strong gender difference in empathy lies in the evidence of empathy among other primates. Though male and female monkeys may indeed have different sex roles in some areas, the account of empathy among bonobos published by Ellen J. Ingmanson about her observations at the San Diego Zoo features a young male bonobo's response to an older male's dejection. Ingmanson also reports cases in which male bonobos in the wild have taken over infant care of orphaned or neglected infants.[31] Male primates may not have gotten the social message that empathy is supposed to be a female trait! Recent work by Stephanie Preston and Frans B. M. de Waal reports many striking examples of empathy, including apparent cognitive perspective taking and sympathetic behavior, in both male and female animals. Chimpanzees console one another, responding to distress; macaques help handicapped group members; and as dog owners will anticipate, some animals respond to the distress of individuals from other species ("Communication" 283). Preston and de Waal regard empathy as "a general class of behavior that exists across species to different degrees of complexity" (285). Reviewing the experimental and behavioral data of empathy in rodents, monkeys, and apes, they conclude, "continuous contact and coordinated activities are characteristic of a bond that develops a physiologically adaptive response to stress, accurate communication of affect with others, and the capacity for empathic responding" (301). This bond may express itself in caregiver-child relations or in the coordinated activity of the hunt (though, to be sure, our capacity to disengage empathetic reaction may stem from the need to avoid feeling with the prey animal, where empathy would impede success). The uses to which we put our empathy may be subject to cultural influences, but the response itself, Preston and de Waal argue, occurs in humans and other animals. They argue that modern life inhibits the expression of empathy humans share with our primate and mammal cousins (301–2). Becoming more like apes would be a gain for disconnected and alienated human beings, regardless of gender.

Whether or not we feel comfortable with our empathy as an inheritance from our common primate ancestors depends on our attitudes toward evolution and the degree to which we regard humans as separate, special beings who are distinguished from the rest of living creatures. To those who regard empathy as primarily a matter of cognitive perspective taking (a view treated below), the homologous empathy of apes and humans may seem more difficult to accept. Apes cannot use language to confirm the motivations for their behavior. However, Preston and de Waal provide instances of animal behavior indicating perspective taking as well as affective empathy. A monkey that provides an appropriate tool to another after observing its struggles to solve a problem demonstrates perspective taking, and an ape that holds and strokes an unconscious human child who has fallen into her enclosure shows caring. That we share instinctive caring with our primate cousins need not diminish the uses to which humans put their empathetic responses. As Darwin's contemporary Herbert Spencer argued in 1855, our underlying sociality contributes to our group survival. Emotional response to others' condition has been seen as providing a basis for mature sympathy, morality, and social arrangements that seek the common good. Philosophers since David Hume and Adam Smith have argued this point, and recent evolutionary psychology has embraced the notion of the adaptive function of reciprocal altruism. A great deal more than shared sensations is attributed to human empathy.

Deficiencies in empathy impair human relationships and contribute to psychopathology. The difficulty may stem from a reduced ability to recognize others' sad, fearful, or distressed emotions.[32] Emotionally "tone-deaf" individuals who recognize neither their own nor others' feelings, may suffer from alexithymia, a dispositional deficit that shows in their inability to describe emotions verbally. Alexithymics' condition can interfere with relationships and their ability to use their imaginations. Lacking feeling rarely benefits the individual in popular representations (though the cold-blooded individualist gets credit for a successful strategy when he ignores others' feelings). Certainly, a complete freedom from empathy might be admired as a feature of ruthless competitiveness or hyperrationality, but in popular culture, characters exhibiting no empathy seem like monsters or machines. At best they seem odd to ordinary people. Mr. Spock of *Star Trek* and Data of *Star Trek: the Next Generation* represent two widely recognized pop culture versions of the emotionless being. Tellingly, the sophisticated robot Data wishes for nothing more than the acquisition of emotions, for he recognizes his lack of feelings as a cognitive disability that undermines his capacity to comprehend others' behavior. In popular culture, lacking empathy often correlates with sociopathic behavior, with the profiles of serial killers, and with developmental disorders such as autism.

To place an autistic child in the same list as a sociopath and a serial killer suggests one of the many disturbing consequences of emphasizing empathy as an intrinsic human trait. Certainly, suffering from autism does not predict a career of criminality (several recent novels have in fact emphasized the autistic child's gifts as a crime solver or a clever adversary of evil!).[33] No one disputes that autistic children are human beings. It helps to know that every psychologist studying empathy acknowledges the *range* of caring dispositions in people. Within every category, men, women, girls, and boys vary in their disposition to empathize.[34] The most serious impairments in empathic ability indicate disorders. For instance, Lorna Wing places lack of empathy at the beginning of her list of the main clinical features of Asperger's syndrome, and this problem appears to be at the root of some of its sufferers' other clinical indications, such as their poor nonverbal communication, difficulty in forming friendships, and inappropriate or one-sided interactions in conversation.[35] Having no empathy does not necessarily indicate low intelligence, however: Asperger's sufferers can be exceptionally bright.

Though understanding of Asperger's syndrome helps mitigate a prejudicial view of low-empathy individuals, the popular representation of the warped master criminal as simultaneously brainy and uncaring dominates in mass culture. Like many stereotypes, this one has its roots in reality. The fact that some criminals may be described as suffering from a syndrome known as antisocial personality disorder, which combines unlawful behavior with lack of remorse, or indifference to the pain, suffering, or material losses of their victims, reinforces the association of empathy with good citizens and the lack of it with problem cases. Worst of all are the well-publicized emotional failings of psychopaths such as serial killers. Psychopaths cannot construct mental and emotional facsimiles of other people effectively, so the feelings of others are of no concern to them.[36] This does not mean that they lack emotion, for these sadists may take joy from the suffering of their victims, but it underscore their lack of empathy.[37] All these understandings add up in the negative side of the tally. In the popular cultural view, lack of empathy spells social problems, danger to others, criminality, and inhumanity.

Being empathetic receives hearty endorsements from diverse voices in popular culture. The "empath" of popular science fiction represents the far extreme: unlike her unemotional opposite, she cannot help receiving and feeling the sensations of those around her. For fictional characters as well as many real people, empathy provides the basis for vocations in the helping professions. One can see figures such as Counselor Deanna Troi of *Star Trek: The Next Generation* as the direct descendent of real-world client-centered therapists whose therapeutic versions of empathy are widely diffused in popular culture.[38] As in the negative representations, a legitimate link to real-life practices exists. The successful psychotherapist needs to be able to harness empathy, using it to therapeutic ends without being overwhelmed by painful fellow feeling.[39] The field of narrative medicine emphasizes storytelling as an empathy-inducing methodology recommended to physicians who wish to practice medicine more efficaciously.[40] As Scott Sundby has argued, defense lawyers who effectively use narrative to call on jurors' empathy during the sentencing phase of capital convictions can win life sentences rather than the death penalty.[41] Perhaps the most compelling exhibit of empathy's rise in the contemporary roster of virtues appears in the huge success of Stephen Covey's best-selling self-help book, *The 7 Habits of Highly Effective People: Powerful Lessons in Personal Change* (1990), whose most recent cover boasts of over 10 million sales. Covey's treatment of principles of empathic communication (his fifth habit) urges the cultivation of role taking: "Seek first to understand, then to be understood."[42] CEOs and business leaders attest that Covey's renovation of character through empathy improves leadership ability. Covey's cognitive emphasis (seek to understand, he instructs, not seek to feel) may help make empathy acceptable to men in a culture that sees its expression as feminine. Yet the professionalizing of the empath's skills suggests the widespread cultural valuation of empathy, regardless of gender.

Even if one does not possess an empathic disposition, these professionalizing trends suggest, empathy ought to be cultivated in men and women to achieve best practices in medicine, business management, social services, and law enforcement, just to name a few of the targeted fields. The cultural consensus thus reveals both the importance of empathy and the anxiety that we may need to be better trained in order to empathize effectively. Humans empathize naturally, but perhaps we don't empathize with the right individuals automatically. Perhaps we feel, but fail to act—our empathy may not impel us toward offering appropriate help.[43] The possibility of changing social norms and teaching all citizens to care about one another and faraway human sisters and brothers (despite our apparent differences) motivates many educators, clergy, and human rights activists. All of these professionals, but teachers in particular, have employed narrative fiction to steer children toward greater empathy. This widespread practice raises the question of whether empathy can in fact be taught through reading.[44]

If empathy can be learned or developed, then novel reading might contribute to the cultivation of empathy. Encouraging thoughtful reading from an early age might overcome deficits in other areas contributing to empathetic behavior, thus compensating for failings in socialization or disposition. As chapter 3 will reveal, nearly all the studies on this topic work with young children, but educational ventures for adults also emphasize empathy. The field of narrative medicine, for example, requires expertise in narrative, as their program description establishes: "the Program attempts to train physicians and medical students in such narrative skills as close reading of literary and clinical texts, writing about patients in ordinary human language, and reflective autobiographical writing to reveal the self. . . . Narrative theory and knowledge provide fundamental conceptual frameworks for all of these dimensions of medicine while narrative skills and methods provide means of achieving narratively competent care" (narrativemedicine.org). Could training in these traditionally literary analytical skills and a course of novel reading actually instill empathic concern in a subject who lacks an empathic disposition? Perhaps it can only enhance empathy already present in a person. Despite the broad assumptions about the value of empathy embedded in educational programs such as narrative medicine, we still have limited knowledge about how well empathy can be taught through reading.[45] If empathy could be learned from fiction, then the technology of print culture might make up for some of human beings' alienation from their primate group behavior. The emotion-sharing dynamics that fostered empathy's contribution to group survival might be repaired by reading.

How Do Psychologists Study Empathy?

Though empathy matters to many academic disciplines (art history, education, philosophy, narrative medicine, and history, to name only the most obvious), developmental and social psychologists have studied it in the most detail. Since the 1980s, psychologists have employed a variety of tools to come to a better understanding of empathy in human beings. This section briefly describes the techniques used in empirical investigations of empathy. Recent trends in literary study, especially the focus on our embodied experience that has been brought to the fore by feminist theory, disability studies, cognitive approaches to literature, and ecocriticism, draw English professors closer to disciplines that accept the use of making measurements, doing tests and experiments, and interpreting empirical evidence.

Developing the conversation between literature and psychology ought to benefit both disciplines. Literary critics ask different kinds of questions than scientists about human behavior, some of which could be submitted to empirical testing with the collaboration of a colleague in psychology or neuroscience. Literary critics also have something to contribute to the empirical study of empathy by offering observations about the premises or tools used by psychologists. For instance, it may be of interest to narrative theorists to learn that psychologists often use small fiction as scenarios designed to elicit results about subjects' actual reactions or potential behavior. The use of short realistic fictions (narratives of hypothetical situations, etc.) and implicitly narrative storyboards is widespread in psychology. Narrative theory has had very little—if any—influence on the design of these small fictions. Results garnered from such studies are not framed as responses to fiction, *per se*, but perhaps they should be.[46] Experiments using fictions as tools of investigation may have something to say about how humans respond to these "true lies." As I will argue below, narrative fiction may in fact enhance the potential for subjects to respond feelingly to situations and characters, disarming them of their customary suspicions and learned caution. Literature professionals like myself may begin by respectfully comprehending psychology's methodologies.

Psychologists test and record empathy in a variety of ways. Physiological measures, sometimes combined with self-reports, can show the strength or weakness (or presence and absence) of empathic responses.[47] Psychologists measure changes in heart rate and skin conductance (palm sweat). They collect data on perceptible and imperceptible facial reactions, the latter captured by EMG (electromyographic) procedures.[48] They ask subjects how they feel or how they would act in certain situations, gathering responses through self-reports during or immediately after experiments and through surveys. Specialized surveys known as "empathy scales" are used to assess subjects' strength of empathic feeling.[49] As Nancy Eisenberg has repeatedly observed, cultural influences such as sex-role differentiation show up more in the kinds of tests that rely on surveys and interviews and much less (or not at all) in tests using physiological methods.[50] An unexamined bias originating from definition of terms or from methodology can skew results, and when those results happen to endorse a widely held view (such as the innate caring disposition of females), they can be hard to dislodge. As new tools come along that revolutionize knowledge by providing an entirely new way of collecting data, such as Functional Magnetic Resonance Imaging (fMRI), the need for careful analysis of methods and findings does not diminish.[51]

Understandably new fMRI studies of the brain excite speculation about empathy. Functional Magnetic Resonance Imaging allows dynamic records of oxygen use in whole brains to be made. The patterns in these records are associated with the cognitive tasks undertaken by the subjects. Tania Singer and her colleagues at the Wellcome Department of Neuroimaging at the University of London recently published a study in *Science* documenting empathetic responses to witnessing another's pain, supported by fMRI data. This study broke new ground in demonstrating why a person perceives that she feels another's pain, while not literally experiencing the identical sensation. Singer compared what happened in a subject's brain when she was actually shocked, when pain regions in the limbic system (the anterior cingulate cortex, the insula, the thalamus, and the somatosensory cortices) lit up on the fMRI, with what the brain looked like during observation of another's pain. When watching a loved one in the same room receiving a sharp shock, subjects showed active responses in the *affective* parts of the brain's pain matrix (in the anterior insula and anterior cingulate cortex, the lateral cerebellum, and the brainstem), but not in the somatosensory cortices of the brain. The affective brain areas responded to both real and imagined pain. A person not actually experiencing pain but observing a loved one being shocked showed brain activation of matching emotional areas, though not the sensory areas. Empathy alone did not light up the sensory areas for pain. Singer and her colleagues conclude that empathy is mediated by the part of the pain network associated with pain's affective qualities, but not its sensory qualities ("Empathy for Pain" 1157). They observed that subjects with higher scores on general empathy scales[52] "showed stronger activations in areas significantly activated when the subjects perceived their partner as being in pain" (1159). They also discovered that the same empathetic effects could be elicited without an emotional cue—in other words, subjects did not need to see their partners grimacing in pain in order to show empathic responses. An "arbitrary cue" signaling the feeling state of another was sufficient to elicit empathy (1158). This set of results affirms what philosophers since David Hume have been saying about empathy for centuries. For the first time, brain images supporting the long-standing introspective account of empathy have been recorded. Taking pictures of the brains of closely tied individuals as they experience or witness the beloved's pain is a good starting point, but it would be useful to compare such images with those made of brains of people regarding strangers' suffering. Then fMRI studies could contribute more to the understanding of what philosophers call POSE, or the Problem of the Other's Subjective Experience, a problem at the heart of novelists' imaginative representations of others' minds, motivations, and sensations.

The questions of how and why empathy works in the bodies and brains of human beings can still only be answered with theoretical speculations about the physiological substrate,[53] though the fMRI-based research described above and recent advances in the study of mirror neurons get researchers closer than they have been before. Stephanie Preston and Frans de Waal propose that witnessing or imagining another in an emotional state activates automatic representations of that same state in the onlooker, including responses in the nervous system and the body. They write, "empathy processes likely contain fast reflexive sub-cortical processes (directly from sensory cortices to thalamus to amygdala to response) and slower cortical processes (from thalamus to cortex to amygdala to response). These roughly map onto contagious and cognitive forms of empathy, respectively" ("Ultimate and Proximate" 12). Tania Singer's work bears out this hypothesis. The advantages of automatic responses lie in their speediness. Joseph LeDoux has written about how fear responses in the amygdala provide a quick and dirty, possibly life-saving response to environmental threats, which can then be evaluated as the slightly slower cognitive evaluation of threats kick in.[54] What is sometimes called "primitive empathy" may work in the same way, provided a first, fast, feeling response to seeing or learning about another's emotional state, before cognitive evaluation through deliberate role taking occurs.[55]

Primitive empathy, or the phenomenon of spontaneously matching feelings, suggests that human beings are basically similar to one another, with a limited range of variations. Martin Hoffman, for instance, believes that the structural similarities in people's physiological and cognitive response systems cause similar feelings to be evoked by similar events (*Empathy and Moral Development* 62). However, Hoffman would be the first to concede that similarity itself is not enough to guarantee an empathic response, and as I explain in the following section, he actually downplays the importance of an exact match in the emotion. Singer and her colleagues believe that our survival depends on effective functioning in social contexts, and that feeling what others feel, empathizing, contributes to that success. They suggest that "our ability to empathize has evolved from a system for representing our internal bodily states and subjective feeling states" to ourselves ("Empathy for Pain" 1161). In other words, empathy as Singer's group understands it participates in a theory of mind that links second-order re-representations of others to the system that allows us to predict the results of emotional stimuli for ourselves. Recent research suggests a mechanism at the neural level that would enable such representations of others' actions, including facial expressions and bodily postures that may convey emotional states.[56] Singer and her colleagues postulate a system for representation of others' feelings that participates in the task of enabling us to understand the motives, beliefs, and thoughts of others. This work on empathy thus supports the theories of evolutionary psychology that emphasize the adaptive function of our social relations.[57]

Just because we may be predisposed to care about others through our genetic inheritance, however, does not mean that we will choose to act on another's behalf when our feelings are aroused. We may employ our cognitive role-taking abilities to manipulate others. Empathy expert Mark Davis describes twin capacities in human beings, parallel affect and perspective taking, which may interact with each other: "the capacity for empathy-mediated altruism, to the degree that it indeed prompts behavior benefiting others, might serve to moderate the tendency to exploit others that accompanies Machiavellian intelligence. That is, instead of role taking abilities being given free rein to exploit one's social partners without limit, the tendency to experience negative affect in response to others' distress may serve as a countervailing force" (*Empathy* 36). When we do act altruistically, empathy and sympathy may not be the only or the most significant factors in instigating action. In one recent experiment, research conducted with 643 American college students of diverse backgrounds discovered that for spurring risky rescuing, "empathic concern made a significant but small contribution," while "the tendency for reciprocal altruism and kinship were the strongest predictors of rescue intentions" (Kruger, "Evolution and Altruism" 118).[58] D. J. Kruger argues that *expectancy of reciprocation*, or the belief that the beneficiary of helping would assist the helper if the situation were reversed, has eight times the impact on helping intentions than "the most powerful traditional predictor, empathic concern" ("Evolution and Altruism" 122). Though this one experiment affirms the "small but significant" role of empathy in a helping response, it does not address the inhibiting force of personal distress reactions. It may, however, indirectly clarify why the link between narrative empathy and altruism is so tenuous.

For a novel reader who experiences either empathy or personal distress, there can be no expectancy of reciprocation involved in the aesthetic response. The very nature of fictionality renders social contracts between people and personlike characters null and void. Unlike the children held hostage in Beslan who wished that Harry Potter would come to their rescue, adult readers know that fictional characters cannot offer us aid. Similarly, we accept that we cannot help them out, much as we may wish to intervene: Don't marry him, Dorothea! We may feel intense interest in characters, but incurring obligations toward them violates the terms of fictionality. Kruger's results may explain why the intense empathetic experiences of novel readers do not lead more often to prosocial behavior: the impossibility of reciprocation may interfere. That is, an empathetic response can be diverted from a prosocial outcome through interfering cognition.

Does Empathy Lead to Altruism?

Before we are ready to consider the potential effects of narrative empathy, several questions about human empathy should be examined. What role does empathy play in the morally desirable outcome of helping? Prosocial behavior, or voluntary actions benefiting another, can be motivated by concern for others, by internalized values, by desire for rewards, or by fear of punishment.[59] Typically only the first two motivations (concern for others and internalized values) contribute to altruistic behavior, and empathy often features as a first step in a process that expresses concern for others in voluntary action taken on their behalf. Psychologist Martin Hoffman has spent several decades studying the relationship between empathy and morality, especially as empathy contributes to the way we treat others. His definition of empathy emphasizes his focus on other-directedness: it is "an affective response that is more appropriate for another's situation than one's own" (*Empathy and Moral Development* 4). Far from assuming that empathy inevitably results in prosocial responses, he offers a usefully nuanced account of the possible paths from empathy to mature sympathy, including the byways that do not lead to constructive helping behavior.[60] Hoffman's interdisciplinary work connects social and developmental psychology with philosophers' conversations about moral development and emphasizes the emotional, cognitive, and motivational components of empathy as part of prosocial moral development.

In Hoffman's account, empathy may begin in five different ways, each occurring singly or in combination. Automatic, involuntary feelings of empathy may occur as a result of imitation, either in a simple reaction, as when a neonate cries at the sound of crying, or in the mimicry described above as emotional contagion. Hoffman also believes that automatic empathy can be stimulated as a result of conditioning and direct association: we can be taught (usually by parents) to respond automatically to another's feelings. He also describes two cognitive starting points for empathy, what he calls "language-mediated" association, or empathy for others one hears about or reads about, and the active, other-directed imagining, commonly known as "putting yourself in another's shoes."

These five starting points for empathy occur in different degrees in individuals depending on their age and developmental stage. Fusion of the self and other occurs in babies. The capacity to recognize the other as a physically separate being develops in early childhood. The recognition that others have independent feelings and the faculty of "perspective taking" that this recognition invites is cultivated in young children of preschool and grade-school age. Understanding that one's historically specific personal experience contrasts with others in different times, groups, or countries is generally understood as the most mature perspective, though it begins to occur in grade-school–aged children who are exposed to information about other cultures, peoples, and times.

When an empathetic reaction occurs in an individual at each of these stages, Hoffman believes, developmental levels of empathy can be observed. The crying neonate shows global empathy; the young toddler may focus more on the emotional effect on herself of another's feelings ("egocentric empathy"); the perspective taker should be able to experience empathy with another individual; and the mature perceiver may show empathy for an entire group of people, including those whose condition and prospects differ from hers. Hoffman argues that as soon as global empathy begins to move toward the more egocentric response, a sympathetic component can occur. By this logic, the empathy experienced by mature individuals ought to have a sympathetic element. Yet our position in relation to the victim also mitigates empathetic effects. We may be innocent bystanders, participants in the situation (transgressors), virtual transgressors (who feel responsible despite being uninvolved), and we may confront situations in which multiple claimants make contesting demands on us, or those in which caring seems to be at odds with justice (*Empathy and Moral Development* 3–4).

The transformation of empathy into other moral affects does not necessarily lead to a single kind of feeling. Noting in advance that Hoffman refers only to negative emotions experienced by "victims" explains why his follow-up emotions skew toward the negative options of guilt, anger, and distress. Hoffman describes five possibilities for the shaping of empathy into different moral affects, each related to the perceiver's evaluation of causes. If the victim has caused her own distress, she may no longer seem like a victim, and empathy may halt right there. If the victim has no control over the distress he experiences, he may invoke sympathetic distress in the perceiver, pity for his plight. If the perceiver actually has caused the victim's distress, the perceiver's empathy may morph into guilt; if the observer does nothing to relieve the suffering individual, she may feel guilt over inaction; and if the perceiver belongs to a group believed to be responsible for causing suffering, he may feel guilt by association.

These real transformations of empathy into a variety of guilty feelings may or may not impel a perceiver toward altruism or helping—guilty feeling may in fact incline a perceiver toward a feeling of helplessness in the face of others' suffering. Hoffman believes, however, that guilty feeling can be channeled into patterns of helping, but concedes that without teaching by parents or others, this outcome is less likely to develop (*Empathy and Moral Development* 9). He believes that empathy-based guilt is the key prosocial motive (113), but he describes a process that requires both socialization and moral internalization.

A question that I consider later in this book is whether novel reading might participate in the socialization and moral internalization required to transmute empathic guilt into prosocial action. One option would be to examine whether induction, as developmental psychologists understand it, plays a role. Readers might obtain socialization experience through characters' reactions to fictive situations, translating recognitions about characters back to their own lives. The parental strategy of induction, or taking victims' perspective and asking children to think about "how they would feel if they were in the victims' place" does bear a family resemblance to identification with fictional characters. Books often tacitly ask readers to step into a character's shoes. Induction differs from character identification, however, because induction occurs after a parent perceives a child's injury of another. Missing from the reading situation is the important sense—for induction and the writing of an internalized moral script—that the reader has somehow wronged the characters whose perspective he takes (cf. *Empathy and Moral Development* 151). Parental induction responds to wrongdoing by a child; reading involves voluntary imagining by an innocent reader (at least so far as the relationship to the text is concerned!). The unprompted application of lessons garnered through reading to the self would support the connection of induction and character identification, but the contempt in which many readers (including many children) hold overtly didactic fiction suggests that resistance also exists.

Hoffman sees two moral affects potentially arising from empathy that could lead to the outcomes posited by Martha Nussbaum. Empathic anger and an empathic sense of injustice can each lead to personal, social, and ideological responses based on understandings of unfairness or evocation of righteous indignation on behalf of victims. Yet even here, Hoffman promises no inevitable leap between the perception and action in the world. Many people feel others' distress but do nothing to alleviate it. Limits on empathy exist: for instance, people feel empathy for family members or for those who are close, but not to faraway others (*Empathy and Moral Development* 197). Even in circumstances in which helping others is affirmed as a core activity, as in churches, we can grow so used to appeals that the very familiarity of the suffering reduces an empathic response. Adults in the helping professions, whose lives are dedicated to making effective responses to others' needs, sometimes report developing compassion fatigue, a kind of empathy burnout (199–200). People experiencing empathic overarousal may react with aversion to the source of the negative feelings, as studies of personal distress indicate.[61]

Too much empathy can lead to an aversion to the victims or to the source of information. For instance, my seven-year-old expressed a desire not to go into the room if the radio was on, because the day before he had heard an NPR story about the many Russian schoolchildren killed in Beslan after being held hostage by Chechan militants. His empathetic distress of the day before had turned into what Hoffman calls empathic overarousal (*Empathy and Moral Development* 198). The novel reader discomforted by empathic overarousal might well simply stop reading and might avoid similar fiction in the future. If, however, a novel reader persisted in reading a text that initially caused overarousal and avoided the dead end of an aversive response, might that reader benefit from reduction of aversive distress in the future? This hypothesis, like many to be offered in subsequent chapters, could be subjected to empirical testing.

Experiments in social psychology have already taught us a great deal about limitations on empathy. Some of them have at their root biases, or in their strong form, prejudices. Whether it is construed as familiarity, similarity, or "in-group" bias, the reduction of response to those who seem strange, dissimilar, or outside the tribe has been attributed to human evolution (*Empathy and Moral Development* 206). This phenomenon can be read as prejudice or ethnocentrism or possibly as a practical response to a social world that makes too many demands on our feelings—we have to use some kind of sorting mechanism. We tend to choose to respond to the needs of those who are nearest us—flood victims in the Shenandoah Valley command my attention more readily than those rendered homeless by a typhoon in Bangladesh.

However, the "here and now" bias can be complicated by mass media broadcasting, as in the startling images of the 26 December 2004 tsunami, which can intermittently focus the nation's or world's attention on a particular group of needy people and create circumstances of "mass empathy." The net effect of television Hoffman questions in this way:

> With all of television's faults, has it, by depicting victims close-up, contributed to an enlarged awareness and empathic feeling toward victims around the world? Or, does exposure to victims repeatedly over time result in habituation and a lowering of people's empathic distress to the point of making them feel indifferent to another's suffering? Or . . . does depicting people in one's primary group as victims of another group foster ethnic hatred? Possibly all of the above apply and the net effect of television on "mass empathy" depends on the frequency and context of one's exposure. Only research will tell. (*Empathy and Moral Development* 214)

Versions of these troubling ideas have been in circulation since the eighteenth century. We should not assume that character identification mediated by video, film, or novels leads directly to empathy, altruism, and a commitment to human rights.

The two biases in empathy of "familiarity" (which impedes response to strangers) and "here-and-now" (which dilutes responsiveness to faraway or unseen claimants, sometimes interfering with justice) can be altered by education, according to Hoffman, but he and other scientists working on empathy believe that the response is a product of natural selection, and thus operates most powerfully in humans for those who share more of our genes (*Empathy and Moral Development* 4, 13).[62] He acknowledges that empathy may work best in homogeneous groups (216), and that in complex, multicultural, or (if I may extrapolate) global contexts, "*empathic morality alone may not be enough*" (original italics, 216). Hoffman believes, however, that empathy supports both caring and justice when it is embedded in moral principles adopted by a society.[63]

If novels do cultivate readers' empathy, and if empathy undergirds both caring and justice in society, then fiction apparently has a vital job to do today. However, the tethering of fiction (or novels, or narrative) to caring also shows a wish to raise the status of fiction and to boost a minority activity, reading. Linking novel reading to a widely shared moral principle—caring—without demanding that fiction be about caring allows broad claims about the medium to exist without evaluating content. This is a neat trick. Novels, by this logic, do not need to articulate the principle that people ought to care for one another. Didacticism is not required. Instead, the very action of reading fiction—any fiction—supposedly trains people to care for one another. (Martha Nussbaum offers a more canonical set of recommended readings; though classics, however, her favorite texts shy away from didacticism.) Then, the relationship among reading, empathy,

and caring justifies (by back formation) the cultural centrality, even necessity, of novels for a healthy society. These appealing connections may not
be justified, but they clearly have their attractions for defenders of the
humanities.

Fiction becomes even more implicated in socially beneficial processes
when Hoffman demonstrates the evident relationship between empathy
and caring. He writes, apparently of real people, "The link between empathy
and caring is reflected in the prosocial moral reasoning that accompanies
people's behavior when they encounter someone in distress" (*Empathy and
Moral Development* 225). This view has been substantiated by psychologists working on the relationship between empathetic responses and moral
reasoning, especially the judgments people make about moral dilemmas.[64]
However, Hoffman directs his reader's attention not to evidence from laboratory studies of prosocial moral judgment, but to exhibits from nineteenth-
century fiction. He recounts anecdotes of fictional characters' reasoning
about their helping behavior, drawn from Harriet Beecher Stowe's *Uncle
Tom's Cabin* (1852) and Mark Twain's *The Adventures of Huckleberry Finn*
(1884–85). Novels themselves thus provide Hoffman's evidence for affirmation of moral development as a result of empathizing, and he does not
acknowledge the fictionality of his examples. Hoffman slides right back to
the real world in his conclusion: "That is, empathizing with particular victims led to both affirming the caring principle and using the principle as a
premise for judging laws that violate it as morally wrong" (225). This will
not do. Fiction cannot document the effects of empathy as if the events
recorded happened to real people. The evidence Hoffman offers for the
function of empathy in cultivating caring and judgment tells us instead
what two nineteenth-century American novelists hoped for their readers.
True, both novels emphasize how unusual these helpers seem, and they
hold up their exceptional actions for praise and imitation. Regardless of
whether *Uncle Tom's Cabin* and *Huck Finn* changed the hearts and minds of
readers, however, the fictional characters' testimony simply cannot be considered evidence about empathy's real world efficacy. We cannot attribute
both causal effects and evidence of those effects to the same fictional texts,
especially when attempting to describe the grounds for moral development
in living human beings.

Hoffman could well have gone to Stowe's historical sources for legitimate accounts of real people's motivations to help fugitive slaves, but he
errs in making fictional characters stand for real people. Nonetheless, his
theory of moral development makes a strong case in favor of empathy's role
in justice and caring. His work openly acknowledges barriers to expressions
of empathy in prosocial action, barriers not always acknowledged by those
who cite him as an authority on the empathetic sources of altruism. In
addition to Hoffman's careful qualifications, alternative views weaken the

case for empathy as a fundamental cause of altruism. Not all psychologists agree with Hoffman's ambitious brief for empathy. Indeed, some believe that empathy may directly interfere with fairness and justice, leading to immoral actions.[65]

Empathy may precede and lead to sympathy, but as has been amply demonstrated, mature sympathy, pity, and compassion do not necessarily result from empathy, nor does empathy inevitably lead to helping. Each of these states, including a disposition to help, can be brought about by cognitive processes other than empathy. Further, psychologists Nancy Eisenberg and Janet Strayer, in studying prosocial development, find that "the relationship between empathy and prosocial behavior is neither direct nor inevitable" (*Empathy and Its Development* 11). J. A. Piliavin, J. F. Dovidio, and their colleagues, studying bystander intervention in emergencies, suggest that people upset about witnessing a crisis will sometimes intervene in order to stop their own distressed feelings. However, they may also calculate the "costs" of helping and decline to involve themselves.[66] This model deemphasizes the positive correlation between empathic feelings and helping.

Other psychologists believe that empathy does impel us to help others. Individuals predisposed to empathy (as measured by various empathy scales) show higher rates of what social psychologists call prosocial behavior, such as picking up a crying infant, comforting others, or offering help to a distressed person.[67] However, that response to caring may perpetuate or even create injustices. In a series of studies conducted over the past several decades, Daniel Batson and his collaborators have investigated the question of whether empathy can be considered a source for altruistic helping, and whether it may in fact interfere with just solutions that contribute to the common good.[68] While empathy has been demonstrated to contribute to moral reasoning and to altered attitudes about members of out-groups, it does not inevitably lead to just actions undertaken on behalf of others. For instance, in one study, Batson and his colleagues found that feeling empathy for another member of the group in a social dilemma created an altruistic desire to allocate resources to that person as an individual, thus reducing the collective good ("Collective Good" 619). Another study by Batson and his group showed that empathy-induced altruism can lead to actions that violate moral principles of justice. In contrast to Hoffman, Batson and his colleagues conclude that the two motives, empathy-induced altruism, and the wish to uphold moral principles of justice, "sometimes cooperate, but sometimes conflict" ("Immorality" 1042).

The cultural authorities who recommend novel reading as a practice cultivating empathy and leading to the formation of good world citizens (who volunteer and participate) do not worry that helping may violate principles of justice. Indeed, it may even seem perverse to point out that the altruistic acts prompted by empathy may conflict with justice. Practical ethicist Peter Singer offers a dramatic example of this kind of conflict. He contrasts the outpouring of support for victims of 9/11 with the lack of response to UNICEF's announcement that an estimated 30,000 children died of disease and malnutrition on 11 September 2001 (*One World* 151–52). Unjust, certainly, but understandable. In a world where so many people exhibit indifference to others and respond only to egoistic desires, an increase in altruism or even simple helping certainly seems like a good thing, even if multitudes of needy people still experience neglect. Some cast aspersions on voluntary helpers by suggesting that they donate time, treasure, and talent only to feel good about themselves, or worse, in an insulting exercise of *noblesse oblige* that degrades recipients of charity. (The squeamish may conveniently avoid these criticisms by not helping at all.) Truly selfless and unrewarded altruism, though rare, is harder to criticize without seeming churlish. The special case of holocaust rescuers offers a model of this true altruism, that is, helping that occurs in situations in which no benefit can accrue to the helpers, who may even risk their lives and those of their families to respond to another's need. Holocaust rescuers couldn't help every victim equally, but few would contest the value of their altruistic actions for survivors and their descendents.

Samuel and Pearl Oliner's studies of the altruism of holocaust rescuers offer a description of the personalities and motivations of these unusual individuals.[69] They were in a dramatic minority: less than half of one percent of the population of those Nazi-occupied European countries the Oliners studied participated in authenticated rescuing (*Embracing the Other* 6). Some others were active in the resistance, but the vast majority of people were bystanders or even collaborators. While we may agree that not everyone can live up to the example of these heroic rescuers and acknowledge that their more numerous nonresponding counterparts may have had practical reasons not to risk helping, rescuers surely exemplify the "good world citizen" imagined by Nussbaum and others. Did empathy motivate them? Did novel reading play a part in forming their characters?

The second question should be dealt with up front. The Oliners' interviewers inquired about education and religion of the rescuers and their parents, but not about reading habits. We may assume that education correlates with literacy, but no evidence emerges from the Oliners' study that would support a judgment about the importance or insignificance of novel reading in cultivating the sympathetic imaginations of people who helped Jews during the holocaust. Bystanders and active nonrescuers also offer no observations about the books that may have contributed to their life choices during the war years. They were not asked. This lack of information does not preclude influence through fiction reading, to be sure, but it does warrant caution when making claims about the formation of these particular good world citizens. To the Oliners and those who assisted in the research on the altruistic personality, other factors seemed more central. Prominent among these were education level, religious conviction, political affiliation, prior knowledge of Jews, and, most importantly, the example set by parents and other adults in the household of the future rescuer.[70]

The Oliners' work does verify the importance of empathy for some rescuers, but they did not find it a universal feature of the altruistic personality. Using an empathy scale to rate rescuers and nonrescuers, the Oliners found that the two groups did not differ in experiencing primitive emotional contagion when confronted with the feelings of others, but they differed markedly in terms of their sympathy. We may infer that widespread personal distress (and fear) account for the lack of altruistic responsiveness of most of the rescuers' contemporaries. Among the candidates for "rescuer status," people with substantiated anti-Nazi activities, the Oliners found striking differences. Those who reacted angrily to the Nazis were more likely to become active in resistance movements than in rescuing (*Altruistic* 148). Rescuers were more aroused by victims' pain (174). Rescuers did not show higher or lower levels of self-esteem than nonrescuers (178), but they were more affected by an internal compulsion to help when aroused to sympathy or compassion (169). Rescuers were more likely to perceive similarities with others, while nonrescuers reported perceptions of differences (176), and rescuers aroused by the pain of others also showed a general sense of responsibility and a tendency to make commitments (175).

More than 90 percent of rescuers assisted at least one person who was a total stranger (170). Nonetheless, the Oliners found that victims perceived as attractive and innocent were more likely to receive help than others (149). Religious affiliation did not distinguish rescuers from nonrescuers (156), but felt religious conviction correlated weakly to rescuing. A far more profound marker, the Oliners discovered, lay in egalitarianism and democratic political beliefs. Whether learned from parents or respected adults, at church, or from exposure to democratic ideas, the egalitarianism of rescuers marked them as different from nonrescuers. Eighty-seven percent of the rescuers interviewed by the Oliners' team described their motivations in terms of equity (fairness) or caring (163). Words expressing caring about others and terms characterizing victims as fundamentally similar dominate rescuers' descriptions of their wartime situations (168, 178).

The Oliners concluded that four different groups contributed rescuers. (1) Some were religious people with strong, cohesive family bonds. (2) Some found themselves in close contact with Jewish people through work or living situations. Others (3) had an abstract sense of connectedness or (4) believed in egalitarian principles (*Altruistic* 188). These different conditions contributed to the opportunity to help, but personal disposition also played a role. Some rescuers acted out of principle; that is, they responded to a situation that clearly violated a norm that they had internalized as individuals. Some responded to what they perceived as the breach of a social rule; these people believed that as members of a group, they had the obligation to react to violation of a norm. Some rescuers responded mainly because of their empathic orientation to others (188).[71] If we recall that emotional contagion shows up to a similar degree in rescuers and nonrescuers, this empathic orientation must combine with other factors to produce a stronger motive force. For the Oliners, the key trait that combines with prior shared feeling was egalitarianism.

Does novel reading inculcate egalitarian ideas? As I have already noted, the Oliners' team asked no questions about the reading habits of rescuers or nonrescuers. If they had, their focus might well have been on the sources of deeply held convictions, for they emphasize models and sources for beliefs in their questions about family, friends, religion, and politics. Novels can convey egalitarian ideas (though they may also contain strong representations of rank, hierarchy, or superiority over others). We should inquire, rather than assuming, whether novels make effective vehicles for messages of egalitarianism. This is a very different question from the point about novel reading and character identification made by Nussbaum, Lynn Hunt, and others. These theorists emphasize the moral renovation of the reader through the very experience of novel reading. They argue that the process of identifying with a fictional character leads to a revised view of other real human beings. Thus Lynn Hunt links the growth of human rights discourse to the rise of the novel.

This sort of argument avoids making judgments about the content of fiction. According to Steven Pinker, storytelling has made the human species nicer. Yet powerful stories about the racial supremacy of Aryans and the contaminating presence of Jews provided a rationale for genocide. The content of stories is not a neutral matter. If narrative fiction has the capacity to alter readers' characters for the good, it may also possess darker powers. If we were really to discover the whole impact of novel reading on Europeans of the Second World War period, we would need to know whether reading, like religious affiliation, cut across categories, or distinguished them from one another. Might novels have provided retreats from reality for bystanders? Elizabeth Bowen depicts such an escape into fantasy in her brilliant wartime short story, "The Happy Autumn Fields," in which the absorbing adventures of an imagined Victorian family overcome the reality, for the main character, of living under bombardment during the London Blitz.[72] Bowen's story offers an extreme case, but becoming absorbed in reading so far as to enter a trancelike state is not abnormal: Victor Nell describes it as "ludic reading," in a study offering a compelling account of the psychology of pleasure reading (*Lost in a Book* 73–83). Wartime may make that mental disappearing act all the more appealing.

Given that less than half of one percent of people living in Nazi-occupied Europe demonstrated their altruism by rescuing Jews, the impact of novel reading, even were it to be positively established, might well be statistically insignificant. Many more people read fiction sixty years ago than today. A vast majority of them must have been bystanders to the holocaust, and undoubtedly some participated in carrying out genocide. This might leave novel reading in a neutral position, neither distinguishing bystanders nor inspiring altruists. A more disturbing option must be confronted. Could fiction have participated in stirring up race hatred? Does anything guarantee that the technology of fictional world-making will always be used to good ends? As Geoffrey Hartman observes, "National Socialism used aesthetic pleasure"[73] to render its ambitions more glamorous, and as far as resisters' aesthetic experiences go, "there is no hard evidence that the altruistic personality is enhanced by exposure to higher education or 'culture'" ("Night Thoughts" 139). The literature on empathy and altruism, while filled with inspiring anecdotes of extraordinary individuals, does little to encourage reliance on empathy as inexorably leading to altruism. About the role of novel reading in setting individuals on the path to moral development, it has nothing to say.

We need not find ourselves at an impasse so early in the day, however. Many actions much milder than rescuing potential genocide victims constitute valued altruistic behaviors. Eighty-nine percent of Americans, according to the 2002 National Altruism Study, believe that people should be willing to help those who are less fortunate. A solid majority of Americans report empathic feelings as well as altruistic values. The rubber hits the road when feelings translate into actions, and the study reports that a majority of Americans did at least eight of these fifteen altruistic things in the past year: talked to a depressed person; helped with housework (!); allowed someone to cut in line; gave directions; gave money to charity; volunteered; helped the homeless; helped someone find a job; took care of things for an absent neighbor or coworker; gave up a seat; lent money; carried others' belongings; loaned possessions; returned extra change; and gave blood.[74] Though unpaid blood giving was also the least frequent activity, the prevalence of the other, easier activities among Americans gives reason to hope that our innate disposition to care may find ways of coming out. However, one may also regard this list of altruistic activities as the consequence of manners, principles such as duty, or even self-interested calculation. Within the moral philosophical and psychological discussions of empathy, the debate about motivations still goes on.[75] For some critics of empathy, a feeling response conflicts with rational aims. For others, a reasoned, principled act of altruism does not demonstrate the authenticity of the helper's empathy.[76] For defenders of empathy, identificatory emotions have a special role in spurring altruistic action.[77] This debate intersects with another hotly contested area, the relation of the emotions to cognition.

Does Empathy Involve Emotion, Cognition, or Both?

The idea that emotion and cognition (or thinking, or reason) oppose each other has a long history, not quite overlapping the venerable mind/body distinction, though sometimes confused with it.[78] The treatment of emotions and rationality as separate and dichotomous features of our experience has been challenged in recent decades. Thinking and feeling, for Antonio R. Damasio, are part of the same package.[79] In a series of academic articles and popular books, he has shown that clinical patients suffering from emotional disorders have cognitive difficulties. Ronald DeSousa has advocated recognition of the rationality of emotions and Joseph LeDoux's cognitive neuroscience focuses on *The Emotional Brain*.[80] Evolutionary psychologists Leda Cosmides and John Tooby[81] speak for a growing group of scientists who believe that "one cannot sensibly talk about emotion affecting cognition because 'cognition' refers to a language for describing all of the brain's operations, including emotions and reasoning (whether deliberative or non-conscious), and not to any particular subset of operations" ("Evolutionary Psychology" 98). Some neuroscientists informally refer to "cogmotions" to emphasize the fusion of the two concepts in their research.[82] Nonetheless, many experts in cognition carry out their work without regard to the emotions, and basic textbooks on cognition rarely refer to emotions.[83] The younger hybrid discipline of Social Cognition is more likely to reflect the understandings of affect and cognition as intertwined.[84] In the new field known as Cognitive Approaches to Literary Studies, in which the work of LeDoux and Damasio has virtually canonical status, matters of affect are generally considered to fall under the umbrella of the term *cognitive*. Few literary cognitivists acknowledge that a psychologist might not readily accede to the centrality of emotions to cognition. The subdisciplinary boundaries within the extremely diverse field of psychology result in different emphases and perspectives on the place of the emotions. Empathy studies have from the start challenged the division of emotion and cognition.

Human empathy clearly involves both feeling and thinking. Memory, experience, and the capacity to take another's perspective (all matters traditionally considered cognitive) have roles in empathy. Yet the experience of empathy in the feeling subject involves the emotions, including sensations in the body. Most experts consider empathy a phenomenon involving both emotion and cognition, but subtle differences in the phrasing of their definitions suggest their emphasis of one area over the other. For instance, philosophers Susan Feagin and E. M. Dadlez stress the role of the imagination in empathy: in Dadlez's words, "to empathize is to imagine having the thoughts and beliefs, the desires and impulses of another" (*What's Hecuba* 7). This view, like those of many philosophers', tilts in the direction of thinking or cognition, as the keyword *imagination* signals. Some psychologists also emphasize cognition: their key words include *role-taking imagination* and *empathic accuracy*. Psychologist William Ickes sees empathy as a feature of cognitive awareness and emphasizes empathic accuracy (or its biases and failures) in his edited collection, *Empathic Accuracy* (1997). Another group of developmental psychologists, most importantly Nancy Eisenberg and Martin Hoffman, acknowledge the role of cognition but regard emotion as an essential ingredient of empathy. Psychologists such as Martin Hoffman and Janet Strayer study the process of empathy, in a fashion that blends feelings and thoughts.[85] Throughout this book I rely most heavily on the multidimensional affective-cognitive understanding of empathy employed by both Janet Strayer and Nancy Eisenberg.[86] I frankly de-emphasize accounts of empathy that minimize the role of emotion, including emotional contagion and quick-match, involuntary sharing of feelings. This does not mean that I dismiss cognition and the role-taking imagination.

In any case, narrative empathy invoked by reading must involve cognition, for reading itself relies upon complex cognitive operations. Yet overall, emotional response to reading is the more neglected aspect of what literary cognitivists refer to under the umbrella term *cognition*. This does not need to be so. The discipline of aesthetics, which has historical ties both to philosophy and to psychology, as well as to literary studies, has been interested for over a century in empathy as a facet of creativity and an explanation of human response to artworks. In its strongest form, aesthetics' empathy describes a projective fusing with an object—which may be another person or an animal, but may also be a fictional character made of words, or even, in some accounts, inanimate things such as landscapes, artworks, or geological features.[87] The acts of imagination and projection involved in such empathy certainly deserve the label cognitive, but the sensations, however strange, deserve to be registered as feelings. Thus, for the purposes of this study, I do not quarantine narrative empathy in the zone of either affect or cognition: as a process, it involves both. When texts invite readers to feel, as I shortly show, they also stimulate readers' thinking.[88] Whether novel reading comprises a significant enough feature of the environment of literate people to play a critical role in their prosocial development remains to be seen. Even the leap between reading and empathizing can fall short, impeded by inattention, indifference, or personal distress. Readers' cognitive and affective responses do not inevitably lead to empathizing, but fiction does disarm readers of some of the protective layers of cautious reasoning that may inhibit empathy in the real world.

Moving Readers' Empathy

As Victor Nell observes, "we willingly enter the world of fiction because the skepticism to which our adult sophistication condemns us is wearying: we long for safe places—a love we can entirely trust, a truth we can entirely believe. Fiction meets that need precisely because we know it to be false" (*Lost in a Book* 56). An experiment I devised for my students collected their written responses to three sample texts designed to move readers' feelings. I wanted to test my idea that fiction deactivates readers' suspicions and opens the way to easier empathy. I had my students read two brief supplementary texts in one uninterrupted session. They had come to class prepared to discuss a third, fictional text, and I directed their attention to the pages I wished them to review.[89] The first text, an unsolicited e-mail I had received,[90] informs the recipient of a business opportunity involving a banking transaction. Like most people who have an e-mail account, I have gotten literally dozens of copies of this appeal, in slightly different versions, most often purporting to come from people in African countries. In both the United States and the U.K., official warnings have been issued about a type of fraud commonly known as "West African" or "419" advance fee fraud. According to the Metropolitan Police in the U.K., all these schemes entail requests to assist in moving large sums of money for a cash reward.[91] The e-mail appeals to the sympathies of its recipients by claiming to be from a helpless orphan in a corrupt country, but it also makes a bald attempt to play on the receiver's greed. With its first person narration and personal appeal, but evident fraudulence, I hypothesized that this text would elicit no empathy or sympathy from my students. The second text had arrived by post in a hand-addressed envelope. I displayed the original, which was written in neat blue ballpoint pen, with a photocopied grade report.[92] In it, an eighteen-year-old named "Noor N." appealed for financial assistance to continue her schooling at the St. Timothy Tailoring School in Uganda. Like the e-mail author, she represented herself as an orphan with sisters, mother, and grandmother to support after her father's death from AIDS. Noor writes, "With this letter I hereby appeal to you to come to my rescue and sponsor me so that I may complete my course." I anticipated that my students would respond favorably to this "stranded student" who had apparently taken the time to write me a real letter by hand.

The third text consisted of Motholeli's story from Alexander McCall Smith's novel, *Morality for Beautiful Girls* (2001). A little over the third of the way into this popular mystery, featuring the empathetic, helpful, and practical private detective Precious Ramotswe, the novel breaks from its dominant third-person voice to present a first-person narrative of the "three lives" of Motholeli, a wheelchair-bound orphan who has been taken in by Mma Ramotswe (82–86). The girl has rescued her baby brother from a burial pit and escaped from the bush to a situation of near enslavement. Bitten by a diseased dog, she loses the use of her legs. Now in a wheelchair, she is dismissed from her situation and ends up in an orphan farm. From there Mr. J. L. B. Matekoni and Mma Ramotswe rescue her and her younger brother. Cheerful, grateful, and optimistic, Motholeli dreams of becoming an auto mechanic. Because the narrative appears in first person and relates a harrowing life story, it formally resembles the two documents that appear above. Generically, it differs: it is not a letter, but a story within a story (an interpolated tale, embedded within a primary fictional world). Though fans of Alexander McCall Smith may well know that the orphanage that features in Motholeli's narrative has a real-world counterpart in Botswana, the appearance of this first-person account within a popular detective novel makes it easy to read as fictional. However, Motholeli's story ends with these words: "This story is true. I have not made any of it up. It is all true" (*Morality for Beautiful Girls* 86). I hypothesized that my students would respond feelingly to McCall Smith's skilful recreation of an African voice in his novel.

How did a cluster of real readers respond to the emotional appeals made by these three texts? To what degree did their fictionality or nonfictional status alter readers' ways of evaluating them? One is a lying, fraudulent appeal for assistance that, appealing to the recipients' greed, could lead to their fleecing. Another offers a possibly genuine but unverifiable appeal, written out by hand, for a fairly modest sum. It is a traditional begging letter. The third, contained inside a novel, claims in a first-person voice to be a true story and makes no demand on the reader's pocketbook. This contrast dramatizes fiction's freedom to evoke feeling and readers' option to feel without following through with action. In the discussion that follows, I quote the written reactions of my own college-age students, who read and then reported how they felt about the three texts. While virtually all the students rejected the scam e-mail's appeal, many felt confused by the ballpoint pen letter, and for most readers, the third text seemed most true and elicited the strongest feelings. Nonetheless, as I suggest below, empathetic response was uncommon.

My student Caitlin evaluated the texts as follows:[93]

> *The e-mail.* "Half of me believes that most of the scheme is true since I know little about the country but the letter seems to go along with the few stereotypes I am familiar with—that he is poor, his family is gone and he needs aid from a Western person. When he asked that whoever set up the account also be his guardian, that made the letter more believable. But the rational side of me is louder than the compassionate side—I would delete the e-mail."
>
> *The ballpoint pen letter.* "The handwriting of the letter and the talk of parents who died of AIDS rouses some compassion—this I could believe was true. But my guard is still up, especially with the transcript. I'd throw away the letter."
>
> *The excerpt from* Morality from Beautiful Girls. "Her story is so believable, immediately I feel compassion for the young girl. It makes me feel like no little girl should endure these things. I don't know

what I would do other than dwell on her story, when I would not dwell on the other 2 letters."

Caitlin's response captures well how the novel excerpt strikes readers as truthful, while the appeals from African correspondents puts them on guard. Martin Hoffman would identify Caitlin's response to the Motholeli's story as exhibiting her sense of empathic injustice. For now, let us note that Caitlin offers to "dwell on" Motholeli's story, while planning to discard or delete the other texts. Fiction demonstrates its capacity to command the reader's attention through feelings of compassion. Yet Caitlin's prospective actions as a result of reading are limited to ignoring or "dwelling on," a good phrase for the daydreaming thought that readers of fiction add to their comprehension of narratives.

Ian, one of very few male students in the group, posited more activist responses to the three texts:

> *The e-mail.* "It just constitutes another reason why my trust in humanity has fallen to an all time low. I only wish there was some authority that I could forward this letter to, so that the perpetrator of this scam could be prosecuted. Unfortunately that is not an option."
>
> *The ballpoint pen letter.* "This one seems even worse because it is so deceptive. A handwritten note, so seemingly trustworthy, and with such good intentions, could have such a scam behind the façade. There is little to do in this case other than ignore this shameless plea for funds."
>
> *The excerpt from* Morality from Beautiful Girls. "It is obviously a dramatized story, however it almost seemed more genuine than the other two letters. If it were a real scenario, I would possibly donate money to the orphanage that took the children in."

Ian reacts angrily to the e-mail, with irritation to the ballpoint pen letter, and with slightly more openness and trust to the novel excerpt. The conditional actions Ian imagines include ignoring, like Caitlin, but he also thinks about donating money (if Motholeli's story were real) and wishes that he could bring down the force of the law upon the email scammer. Interestingly, Ian rules out forwarding the e-mail to "some authority," perhaps not realizing that the Attorney Generals' Offices of most states in the United States operate fraud-alert hotlines and Web sites. Just possibly, if Ian learned the web address of the fraud prevention Web site or the name of the actual orphanage, the SOS Children's Village at Tlokweng, upon which Alexander McCall Smith bases Mma Potokwane's fictional orphan farm, then perhaps his disposition to act would result in responses in the real world.[94] His baseline assumption, however, holds that action is impossible—he rules it out.

Another student articulates the thinking that could lead to a real-world response to a scenario in a novel, but meets an impediment because of its fictionality. She feels sympathy for Motholeli, but notes that the character has already been saved in the story, which is, after all, only a story. Yet she makes the leap to observe that in real life lots of children are in Motholeli's situation, and that few of them will be saved. A student who identifies herself as West African (in her response to the e-mail appeal) writes of the novel, "This excerpt is very heartfelt. It is reminiscent of so many African Stories. I am not sure what I would do." (In another part of her response, this student points out that it is difficult to respond to begging letters when one is struggling oneself.) Megan, another student, explains why Motholeli's story is so touching—"because despite all the hardship the girl has experienced, she does not complain or feel bad for herself. Instead, she is thankful for all of the good fortune she has been met with. Since she isn't asking for help I suppose I wouldn't do anything—maybe I would consider donating to an orphanage that helped children with situations like hers." Megan also responds favorably and trustingly to the author of the ballpoint pen letter, commenting, "enlisting outside aid in order to finish one's education seems like a very mature and responsible things to do. I would try to help this person." Judgments about the appealing characters' motivations and behavior incline Megan toward imagining herself trying to help. For Meredith, the novel excerpt is the most touching of the three texts because it comes from an orphan and because it provides impressive detail that renders Motholeli's situation believable. Meredith ignores the text's fictionality and comments affirmatively, "I would definitely be more willing to help an individual in this situation through an orphanage."

Every student in my small sample responded skeptically to the e-mail appeal; indeed, some reported having received and deleted e-mails just like it from their own mailboxes. Most responded to the ballpoint pen letter cautiously, though just under half felt it could be genuine and the writer could be a deserving person. Many expressed their hesitancy to help a stranger who makes contact out of the blue. None responded to Motholeli as a stranger, and only some foregrounded the girl's fictionality in their responses. Character identification with a figure presented in a realistic (if formulaic) frame seemed to disarm suspicion of strangers and open the possibility for an emotional response to a scenario with a compelling relation to contemporary reality.

Courtney explains, "Since this excerpt is from a fictional novel, the story is 'real' to the readers (the characters are trustworthy)." Courtney's response to this "real" seeming "trustworthy" testimony is to revise her opinion of a continent and a country: "After reading the book, I have a new perspective on Africa/Botswana. The country seems more innately 'good' whereas before I only knew of the negative things about it." The student extrapolates from an evident fiction to alter her opinion about the real country, recognizing that her lack of information had prejudiced her against it in the past. If reading a single light detective novel can have such a result, then the real-world effects of novel reading may be considerable.

Two students responded to Motholeli's story with judgments of themselves.[95] While Courtney projected outward from the orphan girl to the continent of Africa, revising her view to emphasize its peoples' innate goodness, Amanda and Paige reflected on what the story revealed about themselves and their own inadequacies. Amanda writes, "This letter makes me angry and at the same time a little ashamed. Supposing this were a real letter, and I'm getting it for a good reason, I would be angry about her mistreatment and also ashamed that I am not able to handle the problems in my life with such humility and acceptance. The letter doesn't call for action, but I guess I would try to keep a better perspective." Of all the students I surveyed, only Amanda responded to the character's abuse by malefactors clearly described by Alexander McCall Smith. Amanda clearly engages in perspective taking when she applies a lesson from Motholeli's response to her own life. Similarly, Paige puts herself in Motholeli's shoeless footprints: "I don't know what the action would be here," Paige confesses,

> Yet, the letter makes me say: "wow"—for lack of a better word. Here is this girl, removed from situations of "comfort" 3 times to live what she calls "3 lives." If anything happened to me as it happened to her, I would be so devastated that I probably would be completely helpless. The fact that such a small girl was able to overcome such hardship and take care of not only herself, but also her brother at such a young age really speaks to my heart—and she is not cynical and upset, as I or many privileged Westerners would be, but she is grateful.

Having just demonstrated her capacity to engage in sophisticated moral analysis through perspective taking, Paige comments, unconscious of the irony, "This situation is one I could never put myself in."

Garnering an empathetic response was harder for the three authors of the sample texts than might have been predicted. The fact that all three texts employed first-person narrative situations calls into question many of the common notions about the special values of "I" narration. Though apparently some hapless individuals have fallen victim to the e-mail scam, surrendering their bank account numbers and losing their savings, my students recognized this "I" as the front of an untrustworthy spammer. The ballpoint pen used by the stranded student, "Noor N.," disarmed some of my students, since they recognized the letter had to be written out, stamped, and mailed by an individual person. Their skeptical interpretation of the accompanying materials (what narrative theorist Gerard Genette calls paratexts) made them suspicious. The poor quality of the photocopied transcript, which looked as if its dates had been crudely altered, undermined

Noor N.'s authenticity. Though nearly half still felt Noor was worth help-ing, none of my students responded to the explicitly religious content of Noor's appeal. The effort made in the letter to connect writer and recipient through faith made little impact, but the deaths from AIDS and the writer's status as a student (albeit a student of tailoring) resonated with these col-lege students. Chapter 3, "Readers' Empathy," discusses in detail the narra-tive techniques that contribute to empathetic responses from readers. An important one appears here, in Noor's construction of her autobiographical persona as a student whose family members have died. She makes of her-self what I call a bridge character, with whom faraway readers can feel they have something in common. Nonetheless, Noor's appeal received cautiously compassionate responses, at best, and some students rejected the ballpoint pen letter as obviously fraudulent.

Fiction, as we know, depends upon its persuasive lies for its world-mak-ing powers. But fictional world-making is only ever as effective as the partic-ipatory reader makes it, through active cocreation. The capacity of human beings to engage intellectually and emotionally with imaginary worlds and their denizens places narrative empathy at the intersection of aesthetics, psychology, and philosophy. As the cognitive literary theorist Lisa Zun-shine speculates, "The enjoyment of fiction may be predicated—at least in part—upon *awareness* of our 'trying on,' so to speak, mental states (of the characters) *potentially available* to us but at a given moment *differing* from our own" ("Richardson's" 132). For Zunshine, Theory of Mind theory sug-gests that "the very process of making sense of what we read appears to be grounded in our ability to invest the flimsy verbal constructions that we generously call 'characters' with a potential for a variety of thoughts, feel-ings, and desires" (132). Vitally for this conception, fictional characters play a different role for readers than the regard of real others encountered in the world. While the fact of human others' perspectives and motivations activates our caution, the fictiveness of characters' mental states invites our participation and playful engagement. This view was borne out by my stu-dents' responses. The very fictionality of the excerpt from Alexander McCall Smith's *Morality for Beautiful Girls* overcame the guarded reading habits of my students and permitted emotional responses to emerge. As we have seen, the language of sympathy and compassion appeared in several of their responses. Did Motholeli's story invoke empathy, however? The novel suc-ceeded in getting two students to engage in perspective taking. One leapt to a perception of injustice. One taught herself to regard Africa and Botswana as good. None of the students wrote anything in the empathetic register of "I feel what Motholeli feels." The closest to come to that was the West Afri-can respondent, who wrote of a sense of recognition: "It is reminiscent of so many African Stories."

Does exposure to just a few of the many African stories cultivate the empathy of readers who might otherwise regard Africans (in all their diversity) as a single mass of impoverished, disease-stricken, starving, or violence-prone strangers? As this preliminary survey of the scholarship in empathy studies has shown, empathy may be innate, it may be felt by most human beings, and it may be a small factor in our altruistic behavior, but it has not yet been demonstrated to be as robust a feature of our moral and social lives as has been posited. Empathy is easy to feel, but like all fleeting emotions, it passes, and relatively few altruistic actions (or even simple helping) can be securely linked in a causal chain to our empathic feelings. This has not impeded authorities such as Martha Nussbaum, Martin Hoffman, and Lynn Hunt from making large claims for empathy. That the novel should be singled out as a technology most adept at invoking empathy and shaping moral behavior challenges what psychologists have been able to discover about empathy, but it endorses what many people believe about the transformative power of reading and of reading fiction in particular.[96] Perhaps repeated entrances into fictional worlds must occur to benefit the developing mind. Possibly the effects on younger readers are stronger than those on mature consumers of fiction. Personal dispositions toward fantasy empathy—such as the capacity to project internal visualizations of scenes and imagined persons—may make some readers more susceptible to influence by fiction than others.[97] These are open questions, for although fantasy empathy has been identified as a facet of the empathetic disposition,[98] little is known about the process that would transpose experiences of feeling with fictional beings to actions taken on behalf of real others. The subsequent chapters of this book strive to bring psychology, philosophy, and narrative theory to bear upon the matter of how, if at all, human beings can learn empathy from novels.

THE LITERARY CAREER OF EMPATHY

The fact that novel reading receives credit from policy makers and bureaucrats for renovating potential marks a noteworthy development in the history of a form that has not always been celebrated for its positive influence on civic life.[1] In 1749, the *London Magazine* suggested that the vogue for novel reading resulted in the loss of human spirit in the pursuit of a nonentity, exchanging reasonable delight for "negligence and folly" (*Novel and Romance* 127). Many reviewers worried that readers' appetite for frivolity would drive out useful and serious (nonfictional) works and that "obscene" works pouring in from France would corrupt the young (209). In 1791, the Reverend Edward Barry warned that novel reading ranked among the incentives to seduction. Fiction could prime an explosion of the reader's inner bulwarks of virtue and reputation by agitating unrelieved sensations (375). The official disrepute of the popular form registers in the somewhat defensive claims made by the now-canonical heavyweights of the eighteenth-century novel. In his Preface to *Robinson Crusoe* (1719), Daniel Defoe insists: "The Story is Told with Modesty, with Seriousness, and with a religious Application of Events to the Uses to which wise Men always apply them (*viz*) to the Instruction of others by this Example, and to justify and honour the Wisdom of Providence in all the Variety of our Circumstances" (56). Testimonial advertisements for Samuel Richardson's *Pamela* (1740) affirm, "As to *Instruction* and *Morality*, the Piece is full of both. It shews Virtue in the strongest light and renders the Practice of it amiable and lovely" (96). The influence of the romantic experiences of fictional females on unmarried women readers was an especially sensitive point, as cultural watchdogs fretted that novel reading would lead not to the imitation of Pamela's virtue, but to unrealistic expectations about marriage. The perverted imagination would devolve to wasted lives and bitter disappointments. Novels threatened to make readers do too much, stirring up passions that could find satisfaction only in illicit sexual activity, and too little, inducing indolence and indifference to real life.

These eighteenth-century criticisms of novel reading persisted well into the Victorian period, receiving a boost from the evangelical distrust of fiction and the religious convictions of librarians such as Mr. Mudie. *De facto* censorship of the more licentious aspects of fiction set in as circulating libraries such as Mudie's bought most of the print runs of Victorian novels and enforced a representational code that ostensibly prevented a blush from rising to the cheek of the young person. Editors of family magazines colluded in the cultural project of cleaning up a form that had the reputation of tending toward inappropriate, even scandalous, representation. Eighteenth-century novels fell into disrepute as reading for respectable women. Even a bestseller such as *Jane Eyre* (1847) received reviews cautioning readers that it was appropriate fare only for grown men and married women. Sensation fiction of the 1860s freshened the sense that novel reading could be dangerous and corrupting.

The reinvention of the novel as a form that might do something positive in the world by swaying readers' minds rather than activating their passions we may also date to the Victorian period, particularly to the mid-century when social-problem novelists used fiction to diagnose the condition of England. Charles Dickens's *Oliver Twist* (1837–38) permanently tarnished the image of the New Poor Law and its workhouse system. Benjamin Disraeli's now largely unread *Coningsby* (1844) and *Sybil* (1845) outlined a political program and described the division of Britain into two nations. Elizabeth Gaskell's *Mary Barton* (1848) urged well-off Christian readers to bridge the growing gulf between the rich and the poor in a homiletic fiction that invoked the fear of revolution as well as the threat of perdition. Gaskell, a Unitarian minister's wife, had the credentials to offer her sermon, but the most eloquent advocate for the moral usefulness of fiction was the unbelieving and officially immoral George Eliot (Mary Ann Evans lived in sin with a married man, George Henry Lewes). Eliot's novels, most especially *Adam Bede* (1859) and *Middlemarch* (1871–72), articulated a project for the cultivation of the reader's sympathetic imagination. Novel readers might learn, by extending themselves into the experiences, motives, and emotions of fictional characters, to sympathize with real others in their everyday lives. Thomas Hardy notoriously pushed the envelope in the last generation of Victorian fiction by presenting for sympathetic imagining characters such as Tess, a fallen woman, and Jude, a member of the disenfranchised working class. We owe to these Victorian novelists the notion that novel reading can be a personally improving activity and one that may even, as in the famous case of Harriet Beecher Stowe's bestseller *Uncle Tom's Cabin* (1852), inspire allegiance to a political cause, in that case the eradication of slavery.[2]

The appearance in the twentieth century of difficult and relatively inaccessible high literary modernist fiction such as James Joyce's *Ulysses* (1922) raised the status of a form whose more ordinary instances still commanded little respect. By this time, serious fiction had achieved critical sanction as literature, while the numerous descendents of romance devolved into the popular subliterary genres that commanded an increasing share of the fiction market after the 1880s. The modes of criticism that followed the identification of a Great Tradition in English fiction (by F. R. Leavis in 1948) enforced the process of separating the novel from its origins as a consumer product sustained by buyers (or paying borrowers) in a commercial marketplace. The novel's reputation and generic status had risen higher by mid-century, in part as a result of the academic study of English literature. Yet popular fiction—and writing lives sustained by its sale—persisted. Despite the remaining distinctions of (higher, more culturally valued) literary fiction and (lower, mass market) genre fiction and the serious challenge posed by film and television, the novel has made it to the twenty-first century, during which it has become a global commodity, thanks in part to the European empires that spread both languages and cultural forms worldwide. Even though the number of readers continues its lamented decline, the novel as a form currently enjoys the best press of its three-century career. Novels get credit for the character-building renovation of readers into open-minded, generous citizens.

The key term in the transformation of novel reading from a morally suspect waste of time to an activity cultivating the role-taking imagination, *empathy*, appeared in English as a translation of *Einfühlung* in the early twentieth century.[3] Since then, its verb form, "to empathize," and its interchangeable adjectival spin-offs "empathic" and "empathetic," have passed into common parlance. In the twenty-first century, real human empathy enjoys good press as a concept and a desirable character trait (given the improved cultural status of emotional intelligence [Goleman, *Emotional Intelligence* 96–110]). Its application in representational empathy, through the invocation of shared feelings through words, sounds, and images, leaps forward with the newer entertainment technologies. Film effectively exploits empathy— it is at least a happy coincidence that the invention of motion pictures and the modern term *empathy* occurred in the same decades.[4] Imax theatres are wonderful places to observe people engaged in motor mimicry, especially while they watch 3-D films. Empathy's lexical spread in the realms of high-tech gear, gaming, and fantasy and science fiction reaches its apotheosis in virtual reality machinery. In popular fictions of virtual reality, and even in the real world, commercially available goggle and glove sets make it possible for consumers to replace their own experiences and sensations with sensory inputs that construct entirely computer-generated worlds. This extreme case of voluntary exchange of one's own reality for the sensations of another takes to its furthest logical extension the fusing with another object that aesthetics' *Einfühlung* set out to describe in the 1890s. It also raises worrying questions about the purposes of fictive representation: does virtual reality's evident usefulness in training jet pilots or producing green screen animation make up for the unseemly pornographic possibilities foreseen by science fiction? The reputation of narrative empathy is tainted by association with popular technologies for sharing feelings. This goes a ways toward explaining why advocates of the ethical benefits of novel reading nearly always insist that great literature—Greek tragedies, Shakespeare's plays, canonical novels, and serious literary fiction—best stimulates literary empathy.

Sharing Good and Bad Sensations

Virtual reality and pornography render empathy legible as a commercially exploitable quality of consumers. To discover which representational devices most commonly invoke strong sensations of "feeling with" another, the student of empathy might well turn to the market's most successful vehicle for rendering feelings in a stimulating way: porn. Pornography depends upon reliably conjuring physical sensations in the bodies of its consumers and appears to activate mirror neurons in the brains of its consumers (Blakeslee, "Cells That Read Minds" F4). It need not be realistic. Porn can be a cartoon; it can feature protagonists with fantastical proportions and superhuman abilities. It revels in stereotypical characterization and unabashedly ludicrous plotting. All that is required for porn's success is an effective transfer of the arousal and gratification of the protagonist to the bodies of its viewers. Vicious representations play on our human proneness to emotional contagion and motor mimicry just as readily as innocent or even socially beneficial world-making.

If fictions can move our feelings, then they can push us in degrading and dangerous directions. As Cristina Nehring rightly observes in the *New York Times Book Review*, "you can learn anything from a book—or nothing. You can learn to be a suicide bomber, a religious fanatic. . . . You can acquire unrealistic expectations of love . . . you can float forever like driftwood on the current of text; you can be as passive as a person in an all-day movie theater, as antisocial as a kid holed up with a video game . . ." ("Books Make You a Boring Person" 23). Fiction might be bad for readers. This view coexists comfortably with the positive view of reading advanced by ethical theorists, justifying as it does the work of cultural guardians who sort worthy novels from mass-market trash. Arguments in favor of censorship (or regulation by labeling) of television and film depend upon public fears of corruption and a widely shared belief that vicious narratives have baleful influences on those who so avidly seek to consume them. (Indeed, the prohibition against harmful fictions and their makers goes back at least as far as Plato.) Too rarely do the celebrators of reading concede that, as Mark Edmundson writes, "the force of reading, the power of words, is not always a force for good" ("Risk of Reading" 11). Deleterious emotional responses to vicious narratives also activate the neural shared manifold for intersubjectivity.

Like novels, empathy itself also receives disproportionate credit for encouraging positive and commendable emotions, especially fellow feeling with suffering others. Popular versions of empathy de-emphasize its potential to spread sensations such as sexual arousal. The dominant concern with the effects of negative emotions in empathy studies reflects researchers' beliefs that empathy with pain moves us more surely toward sympathy and altruism than shared joy does. Over two hundred and fifty years ago, Adam Smith noted that although fellow feeling applies to the whole range of human feelings, our sympathy is more fully engaged by the negative emotions: "the agreeable passions of love and joy can satisfy and support the heart without any auxiliary pleasure. The bitter and painful emotions of grief and resentment more strongly require the healing consolation of sympathy" (*Moral Sentiments* 15). To be sure, Smith also imagined a social role for positive sympathy, in that our private benevolent affections render us more capable of being good citizens (*Moral Sentiments* 227–29). Focusing on empathy with ecstatic, joyful, or sexually aroused emotional states of others can swerve in the direction of hedonism, and any concessions involving novels' titillating or corrupting influences can raise the specter of censorship. It is therefore not surprising that from Adam Smith onward, the power of negative feelings has received the main emphasis: "Our sympathy," Smith writes "with deep distress is very strong and very sincere . . . we weep even at the feigned representation of a tragedy" (43). Though questions have persisted about the disturbing element of pleasure onlookers take in the representations of another's suffering,[5] empathy with negative emotional states has dignity and a pedigree that goes back to Aristotle.[6]

If we were to trace the terms that appear in empathy's family tree, its relations would include fellow feeling, pity, compassion, and benevolence. Aspects of empathy can be discerned in theories of the sublime.[7] Love and affection contribute traits, but by far the most influential source for the English tradition lies in the concept of sympathy, as elaborated by eighteenth-century thinkers. As the following narrative of the literary career of empathy suggests, each period that has seen a positive role for spontaneous sharing of emotional states has also witnessed the expression of reservations about its efficacy and its contribution to morality. The consequences of reading or viewing works that engage the emotions have also been contested in each literary period celebrating the cultivation of feeling readers. Attitudes about the social class, gender, maturity, and generic preferences of readers in turn contribute to the reputation of literature that invokes shared emotional responses.

While poetry rides high as an appropriate vehicle for conveying feelings to the sympathetic and refined reader, the novel often arouses suspicion in the eighteenth and nineteenth centuries, so effectively does it provoke emotional responses in women, servants, and the poor. By the twentieth century, the end point of this chapter's survey, the reputation of empathetic response depends upon contexts and genres. While the rise of the middlebrow (often female) readership for the novel makes empathetic character identification a central feature of most fiction reaching a large number of readers, some varieties of *avante garde* literary practice eschew empathy in favor of shock and defamiliarization. Thus, I argue here, an underlying disagreement about the moral consequences of reading, persisting from the eighteenth century to the present day, reappears whenever critics except popular fiction and women's writing from their optimistic visions of the benefits of the role-taking imagination. The account that follows illustrates the ongoing debate with copious extracts from the critical sources in which aspects of empathy appear, even under the historically precedent term *sympathy*.

Eighteenth-Century Sympathy and Sensibility

In eighteenth-century usage, the reaction modern psychology calls empathizing was covered by the verb form of *sympathy*. Samuel Johnson's *Dictionary of the English Language* (1755) defines "to sympathize" as "to feel with another; to feel in consequence of what another feels; to feel mutually." A contributor to moral sentiments, the basis of benevolent affection, sympathy is a valued quality of human nature for both David Hume in *A Treatise of Human Nature* (1739) and Adam Smith in his *Theory of Moral Sentiments* (1759). Their accounts of sympathy include clearly recognizable aspects of empathy, though neither philosopher uses that term. Hume's sympathy includes an empathic first stage of what contemporary psychologists would call emotional contagion: "the minds of men are mirrors to one another," he writes, "not only because they reflect each other's emotion, but also because those rays of passions, sentiments, and opinions may often be reverberated" (*Human Nature* 365). "No quality of human nature is more remarkable," Hume writes (316), though he observes sympathy "thro' the whole animal creation" (353), especially among social animals.[8] Similarity facilitates the desire for the company of one another (318), so the resemblance of men to one another underlies sympathy, especially in men of the same nation (317, 359). Hume notices the biases toward familiar and "here and now" claimants: "The sentiments of others have little influence, when far remov'd from us, and require the relation of contiguity, to make them communicate themselves entirely" (318). When people are close enough together, however, their feelings strike upon one another's souls. Hume employs physical metaphors and analogies drawn from music to explain motor mimicry and emotional contagion: "As in strings equally wound up, the motion of one communicates itself to the rest; so all the affections readily pass from one person to another, and beget correspondent movements in every human creature" (576).

However, Hume also speculates about the cognitive elements that contribute to these transmissions of emotion:

When I see the *effects* of passion in the voice and gesture of any person, my mind immediately passes from these effects to their causes, and forms such a lively idea of the passion, as is presently converted into the passion itself. In like manner, when I perceive the *causes* of any emotion, my mind is convey'd to the effects, and is actuated with a like emotion. Were I present at any of the more terrible operations of surgery, 'tis certain, that even before it began, the preparation of the instruments, the laying of the bandages in order, the heating of the irons, with all the signs of anxiety and concern in the patient and assistants, wou'd have a great effect upon my mind, and excite the strongest sentiments of pity and terror. No passion of another discovers itself immediately to the mind. We are only sensible of its causes or effects. From *these* we infer the passion: And consequently *these* give rise to our sympathy. (*Human Nature* 576, italics in original)

Rejecting clairvoyance, Hume emphasizes the actions of the imagination that lead to the excitation of feeling in a beholder. As Adela Pinch notes, Hume characterizes feelings not as individual possessions, but as "transpersonal," as "autonomous entities that . . . wander extravagantly from one person to another" (*Strange Fits of Passion* 3).[9] The feelings people catch from one another may seem as if they undermine our individual autonomy, but for Hume, this human capacity vouches for our fundamentally social nature.

Adam Smith's 1759 *Theory of Moral Sentiments* offers a complementary account of imaginative transport under the term sympathy.[10] Since the eighteenth century, the responsive and imitative phenomena that Smith described have been differentiated and given separate labels, whereas in Smith's treatise, we find a good description of empathy under the label "fellow feeling." Smith writes, "whatever is the passion which arises from any object in the person principally concerned, an analogous emotion springs up, at the thought of his situation, in the breast of every attentive spectator" (*Moral Sentiments* 10). Smith also notices the human propensity to motor mimicry that leads to an empathetic response: "When we see a stroke aimed, and just ready to fall upon the leg or arm of another person, we naturally shrink and draw back our own leg or our own arm; and when it does fall, we feel it in some measure, and are hurt by it as well as the sufferer" (10). Emotional contagion in crowds does not escape Smith's notice: "The mob, when they are gazing at a dancer on the slack rope, naturally writhe and twist and balance their own bodies as they see him do, and as they feel that they themselves must do in his situation" (10). Smith posits that perspective taking enables humans to feel copies of others' sense impressions: "by the imagination we place ourselves in his situation, we conceive ourselves enduring all the same torments, we enter as it were into his body, and become in some measure the same person with him, and thence form some idea of his sensations, and even feel something which, though weaker in degree, is not altogether unlike them" (9). Smith even anticipates the problem of projection, writing, "we sometimes feel for another, a passion of which he himself seems to be altogether incapable; because, when we put ourselves in his case, that passion arises in our breast from the imagination, though it does not in his from the reality" (12).

Both Smith and Hume link sympathy to the organizational principles of society. Smith believed our sympathy made us good citizens, and Hume insisted that our sympathy tempered our self-interest: "*Thus self-interest is the original motive to the* establishment *of justice*: but a sympathy *with public interest is the source of the* moral approbation, *which attends that virtue*" (*Human Nature* 499–500, emphasis in original). The sympathy and social feeling for fellow creatures described by Hume and Smith constitute core elements of subsequent English utilitarian philosophy, and they are linked through that tradition with aims of social reform. The nearly automatic association of spontaneously shared feelings with socially beneficial action in the world owes a great deal to this transmission from the eighteenth century to the Victorians, who were to develop the romantic idea of the sympathetic imagination into a device for personal and social renovation. As we will see, some Victorians especially prized the novel as a popular narrative form well suited to cultivate the feelings of readers and instruct them in political and social issues. Though their fiction—and indeed the late twentieth-century fiction fiction that is the subject of this book—employs very different representational strategies than the eighteenth-century novel, the novel of sensibility contributes an important positive vision of the moral force of reading.

Sensibility refers to responsiveness both to others' emotions and to inanimate features, such as sublime landscapes. The novel of sensibility was regarded by its appreciators as sowing the seeds of virtue in the hearts of responsive readers.[11] Between the time of Hume and Smith's two philosophical treatises, the English novel had made a good start in gaining its first wide audience, including many women readers. Sympathy features prominently in the themes and effects of the literature of sensibility. Novels that invoked strong feelings enjoyed widespread popularity,[12] in part because such fellow feeling was esteemed as the source of social bonds: sensibility was believed to lead to compassion and active benevolence. Sensibility in a reader showed in her feeling responses; in a fictional work, sensibility suggested its capacity to invoke feeling reactions.

Fiction was especially esteemed for its capacity to extend a reader's imaginative capacity beyond a narrow circle of acquaintance, as in Henry Home, Lord Kames's observations about the emotions caused by fiction from his *Elements of Criticism* (1762).[13] Henry Lord Kames appreciates the power of language to call up ideal representations that lead to readers' virtuous actions:

That extensive influence which language hath over the heart; an influence, which, more than any other means, strengthens the bond of society, and attracts individuals from their private system to perform acts
of generosity and benevolence. Matters of fact, it is true, and truth in
general, may be inculcated without taking advantage of ideal presence;
but without it, the finest speaker or writer would in vain attempt to
move any passion: our sympathy would be confined to objects that
are really present; and language would lose entirely its signal power
of making us sympathize with the beings removed at the greatest distance of time as well as of place. Nor is the influence of language, by
means of ideal presence confined to the heart; it reacheth also the
understanding and contributes to belief. ("Emotions Caused by Fiction" v. 1. 74)

Kames regards language as enabling the creation of ideal presences, that
is, the persons and situations of fiction. From these representations both
the feelings and the intellect receive instructions that would otherwise be
impossible, given our limited experiences. Kames celebrates the power of
fiction to move sympathy, and he believes that both social bonds and benevolent actions occur as a result of sympathetic feelings.[14]

Yet not all contemporaries believed that reading *Pamela* (1741) or other
novels of sensibility would lead to benevolent behavior. Delusional hopes,
corrupted desires, and a damaging unawareness of the real world were negative consequences of reading fiction according to novels' detractors. By the
late eighteenth century, cultural watchdogs had begun to worry about the
kinds of fictional representations that excited readers' sensations. Romances
had been condemned in similar terms in an earlier period, but far fewer
people read them. By the late eighteenth century, circulating libraries had
become widespread in London and provincial towns, and most of what they
offered for rent was novels. This change made fiction affordable for working
people, a phenomenon that did not meet with universal approbation. John
Tinnon Taylor quotes an anonymous commentator of 1795, who complains
in the pages of *The Sylph* that "I have actually seen mothers, in miserable
garrets, crying for the imaginary distress of an heroine, while their children
were crying for bread" (quoted in Taylor, *Early Opposition* 53). Clearly the
baseline social class for sympathy and sensibility ordinarily cut off far above
these impoverished mothers; the affront Taylor records in this comment
derives from a neglectful poor person revealing herself as both a sympathizer
and a novel reader. For this representative late eighteenth-century voice, to
be an appropriate person of sensibility, one must be at least a respectable
consumer, not a likely recipient of charity.

Sensibility operated in a market for fictions and feelings in which poor
people's place was to be felt for rather than to feel. Raymond Williams
notes that sensibility comes close to sentimentality in this period, for both

entailed "a conscious openness to feelings, and also a conscious consumption of feelings" (*Keywords* 281). Sentimental literature exploited its consumers' appetites for feeling, taking on a pedagogical role and training its readers in emotional responses through exemplary responses of characters. As Janet Todd explains, sentimental literature assumes that "life and literature are directly linked, not through any notion of a mimetic depiction of reality, but through the belief that the literary experience can intimately affect the living one" (*Sensibility* 4). Even for the respectable middle classes and their social superiors, however, enthusiasm and sentimentality were not universally esteemed. Sentimentality was condemned by eighteenth-century critics who regarded readers' appetite for feelings morally suspect, especially if immersion in the literature of sensibility failed to alter the conduct of its consumers. The novelist Henry Mackenzie (author of *The Man of Feeling* [1771]) had his doubts about the underlying premises of the literature of sensibility.[15] He writes damningly in a *Lounger* essay of 1785 of

> refined sentimentalists, who are contented with talking of virtues which they never practise, who pay in words what they owe in actions; or perhaps, what is fully as dangerous, who open their minds to impressions which never have any effect upon their conduct, but are considered as something foreign to and distinct from it. This separation of conscience from feeling is a depravity of the most pernicious sort; it eludes the strongest obligation to rectitude, it blunts the strongest incitement to virtue; when the ties of the first bind the sentiment and not the will, and the rewards of the latter crown not the heart but the imagination. (*Works* 183–84)

Mackenzie sees even well-regarded high-quality novels (not just circulating library trash) as potentially debilitating, especially for young people. With novelists themselves doubting the results of the literature of sensibility, apologists for the promulgation of benevolence through reading had their work cut out for them.

In 1773, Anna Laetitia Aiken (later Mrs. Barbauld, the abolitionist poet) was not convinced that feelings invoked by distressing reading material would in fact lead to social change. She writes:

> Much has been said in favour of [such representations], and they are generally thought to improve the tender and humane feelings; but this, I own, appears to me very dubious. That they exercise sensibility is true, but sensibility does not increase with exercise. By the constitution of our frame our habits increase, our emotions decrease, by repeated acts; and thus a wise provision is made, that as our compassion grows weaker, its place should be supplied by habitual benevolence. But in these writings our sensibility is strongly called forth

without any possibility of exerting itself in virtuous action, and those emotions, which we shall never feel again with equal force, are wasted without advantage. Nothing is more dangerous than to let virtuous impressions of any kind pass through the mind without producing their proper effect. The awakenings of remorse, virtuous shame and indignation, the glow of moral approbation, if they do not lead to action, grow less and less vivid every time they occur, till at length the mind grows absolutely callous. The being affected with a pathetic story is undoubtedly a sign of an amiable disposition, but perhaps no means of increasing it. On the contrary, young people, by a course of this kind of reading, often acquire something of that apathy and indifference which the experience of real life would have given them, without its advantages. (*An Enquiry* 289)

Aiken's critique echoes down through the centuries to the present day, when it has become a critical commonplace in some schools of thought to see the novel as dulling readers' sense of responsibility to real people, either by habituating them to the idea of faraway others' suffering, or by providing representative fictional characters who replace real others, and (being fictional) make no demands on readers.[16] Other eighteenth-century detractors of sympathy saw different risks because they felt, in contrast to Aiken, that sympathy was all too effective: it spread alarmingly from person to person. For the influential William Godwin of *An Enquiry Concerning Political Justice* (1798 edition), the social nature of sympathy conflicts with individuality. The enthusiasm generated by crowds spontaneously sharing feelings evokes the spectre of the out-of-control mob or the contagious disease.[17] Though Godwin felt that the fleeting moods of sensibility that resulted in momentary tearful reactions had no staying power, he still wrote propagandistic fiction that attempted to channel human sympathy of readers into useful courses of action.

Twentieth- and twenty-first–century readers tend to notice additional bothersome features of sympathy and the literature of sensibility. While sympathy in Hume and Smith emphasizes mutuality of feeling, for later readers, the fiction of sensibility presents excessive scenes of compassion and pity that can seem condescending to the suffering recipient. Sympathy becomes tainted with a sense of social as well as moral superiority, and the suspicion that it exists only to shore up middle-class identity taints its exercise.[18] Empathic scenes of shared feeling can seem vampiric, as if the person of sensibility feeds on the pain of others. It gets worse. A recent historical rereading of the late eighteenth-century literature of abolition sees the representations of suffering slaves as pornographic, appealing to the sadomasochistic appetites of persons of sensibility. In a direct confutation of the claim that empathy for fictional characters started human rights discourse, Marcus Wood writes that "the dirtiest thing the Western imagination ever did, and it does it compulsively still, is to believe in the aesthetically healing powers of empathetic fiction" (*Slavery* 36).

These views from the turn of the millennium bring us to the far extreme of the case against sympathy. Though under suspicious interrogation today, the eighteenth-century idea of sympathetic role taking as the highest moral and aesthetic exertion of the imagination[19] has a robust legacy in nine-teenth-century literature (especially in Romantic poetry and Victorian fiction). The effects of novelistic invitations to sympathy were still questioned in the nineteenth century, but the explosion of both social fiction and sensation fiction in the Victorian period attests to the novelists' sustained belief in their ability to move the feelings, and even the convictions, of their readers.[20]

Nineteenth-Century Sensations and Social Problems

The Romantic poets not only believed in the powers of sympathy, but they also attempted to bring their readers into contact with others, animate and inanimate, in order to guarantee the conversion of feeling into benevolent action. Though some Romantic writers felt qualms about the conversion of others' suffering into aesthetic pleasures for readers, they emphasized the beneficial opportunity to engage in imaginative transport beyond the bounds of the self.[21] Despite their oppositional stance toward the earlier generation of poets, the Romantics belonged still to a philosophical tradition that linked self-love to love of community and regarded the human race as an extended family:

> Self-love but serves the virtuous mind to wake,
> As the small pebble stirs the peaceful lake;
> The centre moved, a circle straight succeeds,
> Another still, and still another spreads,
> Friend, parent, neighbour, first it will embrace,
> His country next; and next the human race,
> Wide and more wide, the o'erflowings of the mind
> Take ev'ry creature in, of ev'ry kind;
>   (*Essay on Man*, 4, lines 363–70)

Though the closed couplets of Alexander Pope would be eschewed after 1798, most early nineteenth-century writers agreed in general with his argument that self-love yields social benefits.

William Hazlitt, for instance, argues in his 1805 *Essay on the Principles of Human Action* that the human mind "is naturally interested in the welfare of others" ("Human Action" 3), that the imagination carries the person out of himself into the feelings of others, and that self-love entirely depends upon the experience of loving others (4–5). Hazlitt sees sympathetic imagining as the more persuasive account of self-knowledge (over self-interest), writing

> a sentiment of general benevolence can only arise from an habitual cultivation of the natural disposition of the mind to sympathize with the feelings of others by constantly taking an interest in those which we know, and imagining others that we do not know, as the other feeling of abstract self-interest . . . must be caused by a long narrowing of the mind to our own particular feelings and interests, and a voluntary insensibility to everything which does not immediately concern ourselves. (14–15)

For Hazlitt, insensibility requires practice and willful disregard of others' feelings, against the natural tendency of humans to sympathize, particularly with others' pain. However, in Hazlitt's essay, one may also find a rare acknowledgment of the role of pleasurable sympathy in human sexuality, for "the gratification of the same passion in another is the means of gratifying our own, that our physical sensibility stimulates our sympathy with the desires of the other sex, and on the other hand this feeling of mutual sympathy increases the physical desires of both" (41). Hazlitt regards this physical sensibility as the "chief foundation of the sexual passion" (41), in a positive account that sharply contrasts with later Victorian fears about the perils of stirring up passionate sensations. Hazlitt anticipates recent psychology's understanding of physical and emotional attunement in lovemaking (Daniel Stern, *Interpersonal World* 30).

Hazlitt's younger contemporary and acquaintance Percy Shelley regards the effects of disinterested benevolence as less automatic, but for Shelley this only heightens the imperative nature of sympathy. While Hazlitt regards sympathy as a basic human trait, Shelley requires its cultivation in order to be good. In his *Defence of Poetry* (1821), Shelley writes that a good man "must imagine intensely and comprehensively; he must put himself in the place of another and of many others; the pains and pleasures of his species must become his own" (*Defence* 487–88). In this cultivation of role-taking imaginative engagement with the pleasures and suffering of others, poetry assists.

The passage from private affections to broader social bonds that Hume and Smith assume receives special emphasis from Romantic writers who attempt to ensure that personal feelings develop in the proper direction. In 1795, Coleridge writes, "Jesus knew our Nature—and that expands like the circles of a Lake—the Love of our Friends, parents and neighbours lead[s] us to the love of our Country to the love of all Mankind. The intensity of private attachments encourages, not prevents, universal philanthropy" ("Lecture 3" 163). Coleridge defined active benevolence in 1796 as "Natural Sympathy made permanent by an acquired Conviction, that the Interests of each and all are one and the same" (*Watchman 4* 132), though he also worried, in concert with Anna Laetitia Aiken, that novels of sensibility could impede the development of benevolence. Imagining a sweet tea–drinker who reads a novel unconscious that her sugar consumption supports slavery, Coleridge deplores the fine lady who "sips a beverage sweetened with human blood, even while she is weeping over the refined sorrows of Werter or Clementina." Sensibility, or susceptibility to feelings, "by making us tremblingly alive to trifling misfortunes" often prevents benevolence and "induces effeminate and cowardly selfishness" (*Watchman 4* 139). Still, emotional responsiveness was not therefore to be eschewed: according to Coleridge, he and Wordsworth agreed in their collaboration on the *Lyrical Ballads* (1798) that the first of two cardinal principals of poetry was "the power of exciting the sympathy of the reader by a faithful adherence to the truth of nature" (*Biographia Literaria* 5). Shelley concurred about the civilizing effects of reading poetry, though he expressed himself more chauvinistically and emphasized the egoistic gratification of sympathy:

> Every one has experience of the fact, that to sympathize with the sufferings of another, is to enjoy a transitory oblivion of his own. . . . The inhabitant of a highly civilized community will more acutely sympathize with the sufferings and enjoyments of others, than the inhabitant of a society of a less degree of civilization. He who shall have cultivated his intellectual powers by familiarity with the highest specimens of poetry and philosophy, will usually sympathize more than one engaged in the less refined functions of manual labour. . . . The only distinction between the selfish man and the virtuous man is that the imagination of the former is confined within a narrow limit, while that of the latter embraces a comprehensive circumference. ("Treatise on Morals" 188–89)

For Wordsworth, Coleridge, and Shelley, poetry did the best job of the varieties of available literature in extending the sympathetic circle and cultivating the capacity to feel with others, in what is now described as empathetic connection. Though my account of early nineteenth-century ideas has observed the convention of using the contemporary terminology, elements of empathy embedded within nineteenth-century sympathy (as in the eighteenth-century sources) should be clear: the spontaneous overflow of powerful feeling, prompted by memory, landscape, or personal encounters, involves what contemporary psychologists call emotional contagion. The questionable accuracy of the empathetic projections of Wordsworth, in poetic conversation with his sister, laborers, or vagrants, should not obscure the centrality of spontaneous emotional sharing to the Romantics' thought.[22] For Wordsworth, exercising this faculty aided moral growth and repaired the wounded soul.

For the Romantics, the emotionally involved reader and the sympathetically imagining writer joined in a mutually reinforcing process of cultivating feeling selves.[23] Indeed, because of the powerful invocation of sympathetic responses to people and scenes in Romantic poetry, literary texts (particularly poetry) become the preeminent place of sympathy in the early nineteenth century. This is not to say that real individuals living in the 1800s ceased to experience the psychological phenomena of spontaneous shared emotion, fellow feeling, sympathy, or pity for real people—quite the contrary—but that literary representations of sympathetic encounters became so influential in the culture at large that the evidence of textual and real-world sympathy become difficult to disentangle. A lyric poem offering an account of sympathy on the part of the speaker that also records the poet's sympathy (and elicits it from readers) offers a complex of sympathies, some of which continue to operate outside of their original historical moment. This fusion and ongoing transmission of sympathies complicates our view of nineteenth-century sympathy in many ways, not only because we rely on textual sources as records of real (but no longer living) people's feelings. Texts articulating theories of emotional connections between self and other become erstwhile records of moments of sympathy in history. Yet the status of a poem as a record of a lived feeling depends in part on a theory of poetry, still vigorous today, that emerges in the Romantic period through intertwined poetic and emotional practices.

The circulation of sympathy through author, reader, real world, and text still underwrites most of the boldest claims for the consequences of reading and writing. This legacy of romanticism passes directly to theories of Victorian fiction. By the Romantics' logic, writers invite readers to fuse with themselves and with the objects of their representation. Readers feel with writers and with characters or representations, and readers in the real world regard the objects of their gaze as if they were representations. Writers in the real world do the same thing with their subjects, recognizing and representing them as material for sympathetic identification—the loop goes on. In testifying to the effects of fiction, readers' responses to characters in novels often elide the difference between fictive constructions and actual experience: the training in sensibility offered by fiction often becomes evidence of its own efficacy. Whether one judges the net effect of this aesthetic practice as the stimulus for the changes of heart that accompanied or brought about the social changes of the nineteenth century, or as a phenomenon ultimately isolating, selfish, and dehumanizing to others, depends on temperament and opinion, not established fact.

There is no doubt that Victorians had high hopes for the moral consequences of novel reading, though editors, publishers, and proprietors of libraries also presided over an informal censorship that kept fiction safe for young people. Raised in status by the productive career of the popular poet Walter Scott, novels in the Victorian period dominated the collections of circulating libraries and were widely disseminated through weekly and monthly periodical publications. Serialized fiction appeared in the company of nonfictional essays in many of the magazines of the day, and editors exploited the connections between fictional representations and the topics or issues they raised. Sympathy for fictional characters (including animals) could be turned to persuasive advantage by editors advancing causes of the day, or so they believed.[24]

By the end of the Victorian period and the first 150 years of the novel, slavery had been abolished, child labor had been curtailed, free public education had been established, factories had been made safer for workers, the franchise had been extended, and a host of other reforms had occurred. Literary representations calling upon the sympathetic imaginations of readers had been marshaled to these and other causes in an outpouring of didactic and sensational fictions. Both the social-problem novels of the earlier part of the Victorian period (up until the 1848 climax of the Chartist movement) and the sensation fiction of the 1860s–70s depended upon moving readers' feelings about topical problems. The earlier industrial or social-problem fiction gravitated toward the plight of workers or the rift between the two nations of the rich and the poor, while sensation fiction drew its lurid topics of bigamy, false imprisonment, madness, and divorce from scandals of the day.

Whether the fiction on these topics appealed because it connected to concerns of the present or recent past, confirming readers' previously formed opinions, or because it offered new ways of thinking that challenged complacency, it is difficult to know. Literary critics and novelists of the day often deplored open didacticism (a legacy of the use of fiction in tracts and pamphlets produced by various reform-minded societies), but successful forms of didacticism included those that exemplified political or religious arguments through convincing characters.[25] Thus, Harriet Beecher Stowe's *Uncle Tom's Cabin*, condemning slavery, and Elizabeth Gaskell's *Ruth* (1853), about a fallen woman, both received approving reviews even from periodicals otherwise hostile to fiction of overt didactic purpose (Stang *Theory* 70). The contemporary reviews offer at least a record of paid opinion. Whether novels-with-a-purpose actually swayed readers, changed minds, and resulted in different behavior is difficult to ascertain at a far remove. On the one hand, strong claims of efficacy include the critical commonplace that Charles Dickens's condemnation of the New Poor Law's workhouse system in *Oliver Twist* (1837–38) prevented the full implementation of the law, so prejudiced against the system were his readers. Further, the depiction of a Yorkshire orphanage, Dotheboys Hall, and its sadistic headmaster, Wackford Squeers, in Dicken's *Nicholas Nickleby*

(1839) provoked threats of libel suits from Yorkshire schoolmasters. Dickens had indeed exaggerated, but within a few years many of the allegedly abusive establishments had closed down.[26] Dickens had a lively sense of the power of his celebrity and large circulation and believed that he could influence public opinion. On the other hand, countless sensation fictions evoked strong but ephemeral reactions that cannot be causally linked to legislation or shifts in popular opinion.[27] Out of the tens of thousands of Victorian novels avidly consumed by circulating library patrons, only a few can be causally linked to documented consequences, and serve better as records of Victorian assumptions and anxieties than as proofs of the successes of purposeful representation.[28]

It may then seem too portentous a question to put to Victorian fiction: what effects did it have, and does it continue to have, on its readers? That sympathy, specifically sympathy evoked by the situations of fictional characters, was at the center of novelistic practice few contemporaries would have disputed. The term "sympathy" appears with predictable frequency in reviews of Victorian fiction (as well as in the novels themselves), and novelists' success or failure in rendering characters that could invoke sympathetic reactions played a significant role in reviewers' responses. Occasionally a writer earns a rebuke for inviting sympathy for a character judged unworthy by a reviewer, but in most cases, for Victorian reviewers, fictional characters either garner sympathy or they fail. The capacity to create sympathetic characters, justly rewarded, becomes a basic test of a novelist's competence. Novelists were expected to affirm readers' emotional reactions to their characters with appropriate plots of poetic justice, so the development of psychological realism only tells part of the story.

For one of the greatest of the Victorians, the cultivation of the reader's sympathetic imagination lay at the center of her art. To be sure, George Eliot had a notion of character-construction as calling forth "tolerant judgment, pity, and sympathy" in her readers (Eliot to John Blackwood, 18 February 1857; *Letters* 2, 299). Yet she also hoped that the activity of reading would renovate the reader, in Wordsworthian fashion. She writes in an 1855 review of Charles Kingsley's *Westward Ho!* that a successful author may teach "by giving us his higher sensibility as a medium, a delicate acoustic or optical instrument, bringing home to our coarser senses what would otherwise be unperceived by us" (*Essays* 126). She warns that open didacticism, preachiness, and the riding of hobbyhorses all mar the effectiveness of sympathetic composition. Extending readers' sympathies is hard to achieve, and authors fail when they make false assumptions about the psychology of the objects of their representations. Eliot relies on her own empathy for her creations in rendering what she "*feel*[s] to be *true*" in mixed characters (Eliot to John Blackwood, 18 February 1857; *Letters* 2, 299).

Eliot's famous 1856 essay, "The Natural History of German Life," written at a time when Eliot was readying herself as a fiction writer, articulates the role of art and letters in actively shaping the reader's imaginative capacity. The views of Wordsworth about the renovating virtue of extended sympathies receive in Eliot's version a reworking that applies to narrative fiction, as this extract makes plain:

> The greatest benefit we owe to the artist, whether painter, poet, or novelist, is the extension of our sympathies. Appeals founded on generalizations and statistics require a sympathy ready-made, a moral sentiment already in activity; but a picture of human life such as a great artist can give, surprises even the trivial and the selfish into that attention to what is apart from themselves, which may be called the raw material of moral sentiment. When Scott takes us into Luckie Muckle-backit's cottage, or tells the story of "The Two Drovers,"—when Wordsworth sings to us the reverie of "Poor Susan,"—when Kingsley shows us Alton Locke gazing yearningly over the gate which leads from the highway into the first wood he ever saw,—when Hornung paints a group of chimney-sweepers,—more is done towards linking the higher classes with the lower, towards obliterating the vulgarity of exclusiveness, than by hundreds of sermons and philosophical dissertations. Art is the nearest thing to life; it is a mode of amplifying experience and extending our contact with our fellow-men beyond the bounds of our personal lot. ("Natural History" 270–71)

The moral consequences of response to works of art thus animate Eliot's career. Her sense of her own contribution to her readers' moral development comes through in one of her letters to Charles Bray, in which she writes that "the only effect I ardently long to produce by my writings, is that those who read them should be better able to *imagine* and to *feel* the pains and joys of those who differ from themselves in everything but the broad fact of being struggling erring human creatures" (Eliot to Charles Bray, 5 July 1859; *Letters* 3, 111). Importantly, Eliot's stated goals lay in the extension of readers' feelings, not necessarily in any particular real-world action to follow.

The assumption that feelings so cultivated by exposure to great fiction will lead to active good citizenship underlies Martha Nussbaum's strenuous recommendation of a diet of canonical novels (Dickens, James, Stowe, and Eliot herself). The great English Marxist critic Raymond Williams takes the opposite view of the long-term effects of sympathetic fiction. Williams suggests in his influential account of the Victorian industrial novels that readers feeling sympathy for a character in a book (for instance, an impoverished worker) experience a general structure of feeling that leads not to good citizenship, but to apathy and inaction in the real world: "Recognition of evil was balanced by fear of becoming involved. Sympathy was transformed, not into action, but into withdrawal" (*Culture and Society* 109). This conviction has permeated subsequent novel criticism, casting doubt on the effects of the sympathetic imagination that major realist writers so assiduously sought to cultivate. Not that they were entirely naïve about sympathy—they knew it could be abused, especially by charlatans who preyed on charitable individuals.[29] Because they deliberately invoked it in support of favorite causes, they were also aware of its manipulation.[30] That missionaries and colonizers deliberately employed sympathy to political ends in what we now call their discourses of power would not have surprised Victorians. Fictive representations of sympathy-inducing subjects competed for the attention of the public, so perhaps indifference to the plight of Williams's industrial workers actually reflected the fickleness of sympathy, which could be swayed by a new and fresh appeal on behalf of another group, such as Hindu widows or animal victims of vivisection. Distraction, rather than withdrawal, might be a fairer explanation of the disconnection of art and action.

The notion that great art ought to do anything at all through sympathetic connection with readers, or by exerting moral influence on them through their emotions, was about to receive a serious and lasting challenge. At the end of the Victorian period, just as the modern concepts of *Einfühlung* and empathy began to emerge in German aesthetics and psychology, several influential writers changed the terms of the debate by eschewing sensibility and empathetic connection.[31] At least from an academic perspective, the emotional bases of moral sentimentalism would never recover from the blow.

Modern Defamiliarization and Estrangement

In the beginning of the twentieth century, the English novelist Vernon Lee brought *Einfühlung* and empathy to a broader literary audience. In a public lecture followed by a magazine piece in a popular journal,[32] she advanced a theory of aesthetic perception of form involving empathy, though not (at first) so named. Originally Lee's aesthetics focused on bodily sensations and muscular adjustments made by beholders of works of art and architecture and downplayed emotional responsiveness. By the time she revised and expanded her ideas for presentation in book form as *The Beautiful* (1913), Lee had adapted Lipps's understanding of empathy, a parallel development from common sources in German aesthetics. Defining the purpose of art as, in part, "the awakening, intensifying, or maintaining of definite emotional states" (*Beautiful* 99–100), Lee makes empathy a central feature of our collaborative responsiveness (128). In an account that combines motor mimicry, memory, and psychological responsiveness to inanimate objects, Lee argues that empathy enters into "imagination, sympathy, and also into that inference from our own inner experience which has shaped all our conceptions of an outer world, and given to the intermittent and heterogeneous sensations received from without the framework of our constant and highly unified inner experience, that is to say, of our own activities and aims" (68). An explanation for our figurative language (62), empathy for Lee is ubiquitous, a matter of cognition. She remarks, "If Empathy is so recent a discovery, this may be due to its being part and parcel of our thinking; so that we are surprised to learn of its existence, as Molière's good man was to hear that he talked in prose" (69). No sooner had the term been announced and situated so centrally in aesthetic theory for an English-language audience, however, than it received brisk challenge from high modernist quarters.

Literary modernism took on sympathy, empathy, and sensibility not by questioning the claims of social and personal benefit that earlier writers ascribed to these psychological experiences of emotion. Instead, it sought to break with the aims that Philip Sidney framed in the Renaissance, Henry Lord Kames recast in the eighteenth century, and the Romantic poets and Victorian novelists such as Dickens, Gaskell, and Eliot sought to implement in the nineteenth century. Modernists revised the purposes of art, broadly conceived. Appeals to sentiment and feeling fell out of favor as merely conventional. Poets eschewed empty phrasing. Experimental techniques disrupted the surface of discourse so that it could not be read by getting "lost in a book," with the reader submerged in an unchallenging, absorbing, reading trance. Inducing readers to work as strenuously thinking collaborators meant depriving them of the emotional effects they had come to rely upon getting from literature.[33] To see how the critical evaluation of empathy changes just as the term itself begins to gain an audience in the fields of aesthetics and psychology, we turn to the areas of poetry and drama, where highbrow cultural arbiters expressed disdain for the empathetic effects of character identification and crude appeals to emotion.

Perhaps the best known assault on empathy as an aspect of artistic reception in the modern period comes from Bertolt Brecht's so-called alienation effect, a translation of the *Verfremsdungseffekt* (V-effekt), which can be better rendered as an estrangement effect.[34] Brecht offered his theory in essays and interviews, but critics have also singled out aspects of his theatrical practice that reach for the defamiliarization or making strange that would promote a rational response and deflect viewers' emotional reactions. In particular, Brecht sought to discourage his audience from identifying with characters. He took an interest in plays from non-Aristotelian traditions that were "not dependent on empathy" ("Chinese Acting" 91). Brecht wanted playgoers to experience detachment, rather than absorbed suspension of disbelief. His techniques included the rejection of both the illusion of the fourth wall and Stanislavskian acting. By reversing the conventions in both these areas of dramaturgy, Brecht attempted to interfere with "the automatic transfer of the emotions to the spectator," a phenomenon Brecht deplored as "emotional infection" (94). He wished instead for the presentation of dramatic figures "quite coldly, classically and objectively. For they are not matter for empathy; they are there to be understood" ("Conversation" 15). Brecht's own examples of the V-effekt emphasize the disruption of ordinary affective ties and attitudes ("Short Description" 144) and his technique, rendering character and action alien, remote, and strange to viewers, attempts to make the audience see things afresh, separated from their ordinary, expected appearances. The effort to block a viewer's role-taking fusion with dramatic characters makes the anti-empathetic thrust of the V-effekt clear.[35] Brecht regarded the universalizing tendencies of viewers experiencing empathy as an affront to the historical specificity of experience. Emotions, he felt, "have a quite definite class basis; the form they take at any time is historical, restricted and limited in specific ways" and were "in no sense universally human and timeless" ("New Technique" 145). Furthermore, a recent example of the uses of the emotions discredited them in Brecht's eyes. He recalled with disgust "Fascism's grotesque emphasizing of the emotions" (145). Far better, he felt, to invite estrangement and defamiliarization:

> The old A-effects quite remove the object represented from the spectator's grasp, turning it into something that cannot be altered; the new are not odd in themselves, though the unscientific eye stamps anything strange as odd. The new alienations are only designed to free socially-conditioned phenomena from that stamp of familiarity which protects them against our grasp today. ("Short Organum," section 43, 192)

The legacy of Brecht's anti-empathetic aesthetics can be plainly seen in Marxist-descended postcolonial theory and criticism, in which the implausibility of universal emotions makes empathy a suspect end of representation.

If Brecht's drama rejects empathy outright, modernist poetic theory laments the layers of convention and failures of perception that interfere with a direct and fresh poetry.[36] Admiration for poets who look "into a great deal more than the heart" underlies a second influential modernist evaluation of literary empathy. T. S. Eliot's famous phrase, "the dissociation of sensibility," comes from his 1921 essay "The Metaphysical Poets," which describes a lamentable loss of "the direct sensuous apprehension of thought, or a recreation of thought into feeling" ("Metaphysical Poets" 246). T. S. Eliot admired those early seventeenth-century poets whose emulation would require that one "look into the cerebral cortex, the nervous system, and the digestive tracts" (250). Eliot especially prized the empathetic connection between poet and reader that he discovered in the Metaphysical poets, and he regarded the crude appeals to emotion and the consciously elevated language of later poets as a falling off from the achievements of the seventeenth century. Eliot's criticism played an important role in the denigration of the Romantic poets, whose emphasis on empathetic connections with readers and subjects comprised a central part of their poetic theory and practice. This change in taste (celebrating seventeenth-century poets and downgrading more emotionally expressive writers such as Percy Shelley) had an enormous impact on the teaching of literature, through practical criticism and the New Criticism.[37] W. K. Wimsatt and Monroe Beardsley's condemnation of the mere psychologizing they associated with "the affective fallacy" owes a great deal to Eliot's rewriting of the hierarchy of literary values (*Verbal Icon* 21–39).

However, the fate of empathy as a representational goal in the early twentieth century looks quite a bit different when one approaches it from the perspective of the novel. Suzanne Clark has persuasively argued that the change in fashion took the form of a gender division: "from the point of view of literary modernism, sentimentality was both a past to be outgrown and a present tendency to be despised. The gendered character of this condemnation seemed natural: women writers were entangled in sensibility, were romantic and sentimental by nature, and so even the best might not altogether escape this romantic indulgence in emotion and sublimity" (*Sentimental Modernism* 2). It also depended upon the separation of the more difficult, high literary modernist novel from the mainstream of literary fiction, which continued to rely upon evocation of character identification and other techniques that seek empathetically responding readers. As I argue below, the rise of the middlebrow (often female) reader sustains empathy as a goal of literary representation even while fragmentation, difficulty, deliberate obscurity, and exploitation of alienation effects enjoyed their vogue. This does not mean, however, that modernist experimental fiction eschewed empathy, rather that it recast the representation of consciousness and feelings as one of the primary tasks of novels rejecting conventional representation.

The thrust of experimentation in modernist fiction (with some notable exceptions[38]) emphasized techniques that would render character and consciousness more vividly. E. M. Forster proclaimed in his 1927 lectures, published as *Aspects of the Novel*, that "it is the function of the novelist to reveal the hidden life at its source" (*Aspects* 45). Though humorously critical of novelists for neglecting the main facts of human life (birth, death, food, sleep, sex), Forster celebrates the capacity of fiction to allow readers to "know people perfectly" (63), for fictional characters are "people whose secret lives are visible" (64). Henry James's "centers of consciousness" eschewed the old-fashioned authorial narrator for a figural narration rooted in the lovingly rendered perceptions of a central observer.[39] Virginia Woolf, criticizing the conventionality and materialism of her contemporaries H. G. Wells, Arnold Bennett, and John Galsworthy in her 1919 essay "Modern Fiction," called for a different kind of psychological realism, one that she would perfect in her own novels. Woolf regarded James Joyce as one of the few "spiritual" writers, "concerned at all costs to reveal the flickerings of that innermost flame that flashes its messages through the brain, and in order to preserve it he disregards with complete courage whatever seems to him adventitious, whether it be probability, or coherence, or any other of these signposts which for generations have served to support the imagination of a reader when called upon to imagine what he can neither touch nor see" ("Modern Fiction" 214). Woolf saw Joyce's rendering of Bloom in the Hades episode as "undoubtedly" coming close "to the quick of the mind" (214), and many subsequent critics would agree that Joyce's wandering Jew of Dublin represents a triumph of the novelistic sympathetic imagination. Joyce's rendering of internal, bodily, and psychological states of mind and feeling challenged the conventional boundaries of representation (as did D. H. Lawrence's frank representations of sexuality) by developing forms of inwardness that opened characters up in a new way.

For Woolf, the matter and manner both required renovation. A spiritual fiction, in Woolf's terms, redresses the failures of earlier materialist fiction, about which she asks, "Is it due to the method that we feel neither jovial nor magnanimous, but centred in a self which, in spite of its tremor of susceptibility, never embraces or creates what is outside itself and beyond?" ("Modern Fiction" 215). In other words, a writer's empathetic exertions must extend to both "the dark places of psychology" and the broad field of other peoples' experiences, for no material is barred (215). "Everything is the proper stuff of fiction, every feeling, every thought," writes Woolf, "every quality of brain and spirit is drawn upon; no perception comes amiss" (218). The challenge for the common reader she addresses is to adjust both to the new techniques (a guiding, authorial comment on characters' states of minds was less likely to be provided) and to welcome representation of unfamiliar, disconcerting, and even frightening thoughts and feelings. From this combination comes the common belief, noticed by Wayne Booth, that literature can and ought to "challenge" readers. (The same critics who would vehemently resist the legitimacy of an openly didactic or polemical work of literature will often implicitly endorse the capacity of difficult writing to improve the reader who struggles with it.) Woolf's classic statement of the novelist's task demands empathetic work on the part of both author and reader, transmitted through the rendering of the ordinary mind of a character:

> Examine for a moment an ordinary mind on an ordinary day. The mind receives a myriad impressions—trivial, fantastic, evanescent, or engraved with the sharpness of steel. From all sides they come, an incessant shower of innumerable atoms; and as they fall, as they shape themselves into the life on Monday or Tuesday, the accent falls differently from of old; the moment of importance came not here but there; so that if a writer were a free man and not a slave, if he could write what he chose and not what he must, he could base his work upon his own feeling and not upon convention, there would be no plot, no

comedy, no tragedy, no love interest or catastrophe in the accepted style, and perhaps not a single button sewn on as the Bond Street tailors would have it. Life is not a series of gig lamps symmetrically arranged; but a luminous halo, a semi-transparent envelope surrounding us from the beginning of consciousness to the end. Is it not the task of the novelist to convey this varying, this unknown and uncircumscribed spirit? (212–13)

Arguably, Woolf makes the rendering of a mind, empathetically conceived by the novelist and recognized by the reader, a priority over all the usual aims of narrative fiction, including telling a story (E. M. Forster sighed, "oh dear, yes— the novel tells a story . . ." [*Aspects*, 26]).

As we will see in the last section of this chapter, character identification, which may be enhanced by representations such as the one Woolf imagines, remains the single most important facet of response to fiction articulated by middlebrow readers. Even authors now considered difficult often strove to reach that broad readership with representations generated out of sympathetic imagining that George Eliot would have recognized. Joseph Conrad's 1912 credo "A Familiar Preface" sounds the hopeful note: "I would fain claim for myself the faculty of so much insight as can be expressed in a voice of sympathy and compassion" (*Personal Record* xvii). Modernist reaction against it never eliminated empathy from the novel as a part of composition or a goal of representation: modern novelists considered it part of their craft and an ingredient in their relationships to both their inventions and their readers.

The Rise of the Middlebrow Reader

In the twentieth century, a large group of educated general readers sometimes known as common readers (Woolf) or as middlebrow readers developed influence in the market for English-language fiction. Neither the lowbrow consumers of mass-market fiction (who have now gone over completely to television, film, and video), nor the expensively educated trained highbrows who embraced the hard work of interpreting complex, experimental modernist fiction, middlebrow readers tended to be educated people who wished to read the right thing, and were happy to be told which books would suit them by book reviewers. Many of them were women.[40] Empowered by education and informed by Oprah, book reviews, word-of-mouth, and Readers' Guides, the descendents of these middlebrow readers populate the informal book clubs that make up such an important feature of the reading landscape in the twenty-first century, while publishers depend upon them to buy books as fewer and fewer people read literature at all.[41] A number of factors influenced the growth in middlebrow readership from the late 1920s onward. First, the demanding nature of high modernist literary fiction meant that novel reading (and novel writing) became a more dignified activity. This change in the status of fiction accompanied the growth of a new category, literary fiction, which split off from the mass of publications in areas now labeled as subliterary "genres."[42] A person such as Virginia Woolf could be a celebrity, with her picture in *Vogue*, even if her novels were read by relatively few. Eager to read for pleasure and edification, but insufficiently invested in the strenuous interpretative work to make a steady diet of high literary modernism, middlebrow readers patronized bookshops and circulating libraries in large numbers. They read excellent short fiction in popular magazines, especially in the United States. They read the advice of book reviewers writing for the weeklies and dailies. Despite the disdain of cultural arbiters, best-seller lists became powerful devices for the recommendation of reading material, fictional and nonfictional, to numerous middlebrows attentive to fashion.

Several publishing houses, such as the Modern Library and Penguin Books, were founded to reach this readership. Book clubs such as the National Book League, the Literary Guild, and the Book of the Month Club capitalized on middlebrow readers' willingness to have their reading chosen for them, particularly as books became part of the appropriate furnishings of the middle-class home. Advertisers emphasized novels as consumer products. In the meantime, literary criticism split off from book reviewing as a newly professionalized class of interpreters trained university students (including growing numbers of women and working-class students) in the technical analysis and judgment of literature. Women had always made up a large part of the audience for novels, but now more college-educated and professional women brought their disposable income to the bookshop or to the automatic billing subscription service. For these middlebrow readers, aims of escapist pleasure reading needed not conflict with the desire to stretch a little intellectually, so long as the work was not so demanding as to interfere with immersion reading habits. Aims of self-improvement and social awareness were not absent from the middlebrows' vision of what reading might do for them.[43] Fiction was valued for introducing readers to new worlds and experiences. Indeed, the use of literature in the secondary schools as a vehicle for teaching values, history, heritage, and civics laid the groundwork for a later generation's use of fiction to promulgate values of tolerance and cultural understanding (Pinsent, *Children's Literature* 5).

Reading fiction was esteemed throughout the century, especially as it was regarded as a personally improving activity. Writing in 1926, just around the time when Virginia Woolf's first volume of *Common Reader* essays brought her work for the periodicals and her vision for a spiritual modernism to a wider audience, the American professor Frank Luther Mott articulated the value of novels for ordinary readers in his *Rewards of Reading*. Thoughtful men, according to Mott, benefited in practical fashion from the empathetic experience of immersion reading. Novels offered insight into human motives, as well the friendship of characters such as David Copperfield. Wholeheartedly recommending both canonical fiction, historical fiction, and selections of the popular writers of the day (such as Booth Tarkington), Mott praises the egalitarian zone created for the fiction reader: "all classes, and more than that, all races, meet us in fiction's pages" (*Rewards* 23). Fiction overcomes the challenges of cultural, national, and racial difference by offering opportunities for empathetic identification: "We dramatize the events of the novels in our own persons. . . . we are there; we are caught up into the whirl of things; the whole aggregate mass of emotions, social conditions, characters, influences, environment, takes hold of us and becomes personal to us; and we emerge from it, when we close the book, bigger, stronger, richer in personality, because we have experienced these phases of life, however vicariously" (28). Even for this enthusiastic popularizer of reading, however, the old worry about the moral peril of vicarious emotion (as in the novel of sensibility) remains; tellingly, Mott's victim of fiction is the idle female: "A housewife who sits down in her rocker after breakfast, morning-cap over uncombed hair, leaving dishes standing in the sink and beds unmade, to read the latest novel about impossible loves of impossible people till she gets into a glow of false emotion, is a pitiable figure" (20). The danger of the self-improving motive for reading devolving into such masturbatory scenes haunts apologies for fiction. Who is to guarantee that the feelings-for-sharing offered by novels will result in the robust forms of self-help imagined by Mott, or the expansion of the perceptive capacities implied by Woolf?

Late in the century, as novel reading no longer seems such a certain part of the cultural, intellectual, and pleasure-seeking practices of literate people (even middlebrows), its valued social consequences have become ever more overdetermined. Empathy offers an almost magical guarantee of fiction's worthiness. Martha Nussbaum assesses the situation in terms of the challenge we face in realizing and respecting others' consciousness and experience, in a passage with clear links to Virginia Woolf: "We see personlike shapes all around us: but how do we relate to them? All too often, we see them as just shapes, or physical objects in motion. What storytelling in childhood teaches us to do is to ask questions about the life behind the mask, the inner world concealed by the shape. It gets us into the habit of understanding that that inner world is differently shaped by different social circumstances."[44] For Nussbaum, the reading practices of the middlebrow are more likely to result in good ethical effects, while highbrow (analytical) professional readers are least likely to benefit, a sad message for English professors: "Reading can only have the good effects we claim for it if one reads with immersion, not just as a painful duty. Professors of literature are often jaded and detached; they don't read with the freshness and responsiveness of ordinary readers" ("Exactly" 353). For the distinguished theorist and literary critic Robert Scholes, the task at hand is to persuade his readers (mainly those benighted, jaded professors) to teach literature in such a way that readers make connections with their real lives and actions: "reading, though it may be a kind of action, is not the whole action but a part of it, remaining incomplete unless and until it is absorbed and transformed in the thoughts and deeds of readers" (*Protocols* x). Scholes believes that "reading can and should answer to social and ethical concerns" (x). Wayne Booth puts faith in what he calls the *coduction* enacted by readers discussing their appraisals of literary works. The comparative, communal evaluation of the work, "a thoroughgoing particular engagement with this narrative, considered neither as based on nor leading to general rules but as an ever-growing awareness of what is humanly possible" could make novel reading and even literary criticism ethical activities (*Company* 76). Booth also believes that novel reading can have moral consequences. He collects dozens of examples of witnesses who testify to the power of fiction to change lives, from the Austen reader who learned to stand up for herself by reading *Mansfield Park* (1814), to the repentant racist brought to guilty consciousness by Toni Morrison's *Song of Solomon* (1977), to those who treated Jews, or female academics, or Africans, or Southerners, differently because they'd taken to heart a novel (*Company* 278–79). Booth candidly points out the inherent untrustworthiness of such reports (though they are legion), and he does not censor the regrettable effects of fiction—those Ayn Rand readers, swearing off charitable giving!—but he believes, at least, that the reports of real readers about the effects of novels on their lives deserve critical reflection.

As each literary period treated in this brief survey of the effects of empathetic reading experiences has had its skeptics, let not the recent past be represented only by those who see, or wish for, a defense of fiction in terms of its virtuous actions. Writing in the 1980s, novelist Elizabeth Hardwick observed that the emphasis on resonance with readers' experiences might in fact narrow the reach of literature: "the personalization of fiction, the reduction of it to the boundaries of the reading self, often one who has lived for only a few decades in the twentieth century, is an intensive democratization not quite so felicitous for the spread of literature as one might have predicted" ("Reading" 15). This is not simply a version of the antiegalitarian sentiments that often undermine the arguments of defenders of literature, as in this extract from the late Victorian Andrew Lang: "People who deserved to be able to read, did read, and now that every one can read, few people deserve to do so, for few go beyond a newspaper. It is but a small minority who even aspire to study a novel. What is the result? The result is that authors endeavour to reach that vast public which, in no age and in no country, has cared for the pleasures of literature. We hear it said of a book that it does not appeal to a man on an omnibus, or to a man lunching in a public-house. That condemns a book, therefore authors debase their wares, to captivate indolent women, and the man on the omnibus" ("Introduction" 9–10). Lang participates in the long tradition of hand-wringing about the power of reader-consumers to debase the novel through their purchasing power. This kind of criticism is alive and kicking in the late twentieth and early twenty-first century, as the churlish response to Oprah Winfrey's power to move books through her television book club more than demonstrates.[45]

Hardwick, in contrast to Lang and his fretting about novelists selling out to readers, worries more about the way we (teachers, authorities) recommend reading. By advertising novels as so relevant, personally beneficial, and immediately useful to self and society, do we not render unpalatable the very product we wish to place in the hands of the young? Even if empathy for fictional characters were to be demonstrated a short cut to altruism and compassion, should novel reading be asked to bear that heavy freight? Hardwick wonders, "so, perhaps we should not solicit, insist, badger, embarrass, on behalf of this almost free pleasure" ("Reading" 18). Perhaps the guerilla promoters of literacy who offer a shag to anyone spotted reading a novel are on the right track. Novels, surely, can still be sexy, time wasting, and subversive—or do they have to be vitamin-enriched bowls conveying good-for-you moral fiber? It is helpful to recall that the very centuries in which novels were frequently condemned as corrupting influences on the young enjoyed burgeoning growth in the numbers of novels and novel readers. Bring on the prohibitions; print the warning labels. Novels can be dangerous. They convey disturbing ideas. They awake strange desires. They invite identification with criminals and prostitutes and assassins. They give people, not just children, nightmares that they can't forget. Years ago my parents put the hardcover first editions inside the bookcases with leaded glass doors. These were banned books, the Updike with the three-way sex, the signed Isaac Singers, the valuable collection of Horatio Algers. You bet I read them.

3

READERS' EMPATHY

The distinguished novel critic Wayne Booth troubled to ask a variety of readers of different ages and backgrounds about the novels that had led them to do something specific: to make a change in their behavior or beliefs (*Company* 278–79). In this chapter, I follow Booth's lead, giving priority to several different kinds of evidence about reactions to reading fiction. First and most important, I describe and liberally quote what other readers have told me about their experiences of narrative empathy. Though this procedure does not render my research empirical, it significantly broadens the scope of my inquiry, certainly beyond my own personal responses to fiction. From these reports by other readers I distill a set of working hypotheses about the qualities of novels that evoke empathy in readers, hypotheses that in turn contribute to a working theory of narrative empathy. Subsequently, I examine the empirical studies on the effects of reading, and I collect the ideas about readers' empathy that feature in that scholarly literature. This prepares the way for consideration, in chapter 4, of potential impact in the marketplace of reading materials deemed likely to evoke empathy. Though this project has formalist qualities, in that it seeks to identify narrative techniques that tend to evoke empathetic responses, its inevitable emphasis on what readers feel about novels departs from the purely textual focus of New Criticism and much of narratology. Professional readers will recognize the influence not only of Booth, but also of Louise Rosenblatt's *Literature as Exploration* (1938), in which she explores readers' transactions of texts into fully realized literary works. Chicago School rhetorical criticism is also a major influence. My interest in readers' feelings participates in the project of assuring that the umbrella of cognitive literary studies arches over the affective dimensions of literary response, but it departs from much of that literature in one way: I do not assume that social good necessarily comes of empathetic reading.[1] Novels' intellectual and emotional influences may certainly lead to socially consequential results, but good effects of novel reading ought to be analyzed in context with neutral and negative effects. Empathetic reading experiences that confirm the empathy-altruism theory, I argue, are exceptional, not routine.

Wayne Booth inquired of his interlocutors, "Name fictions that changed your character—or made you want to change your conduct," an imperative instruction that implies fictions *ought* to do both things. When I took the early versions of this book around as talks to a variety of different venues (including church groups, friends of the local library, book clubs, as well as university audiences), I found that a majority of my interlocutors agreed with Booth's premise—reading fiction *ought* to change your character or make you want to alter your conduct. When asked my more neutral version of the question, however, they often confessed, "I just read to relax," or "Novels are just for fun, to get away from things for a while." Adult women readers in particular resisted the sense that novels were supposed to be doing anything more than interesting or entertaining them. They often commented quite appropriately and analytically about particular novels that had made a strong impression on them, but demurred when asked if the strong character identification or immersion in a fictional world that they reported had any specific results in their real lives. My question didn't imply that novels ought to do anything—I just inquired, "Can you think of any time where a novel made you do something specific in the world, something you might not have done or thought of if you hadn't read the novel?" This way of asking the question gave many readers the permission to answer no.

Nonetheless, some readers confided (privately, or by e-mail) instances of their influence by a novel. One member of my Bread Loaf audience in Juneau, Alaska, told me that reading a number of novels by the popular South Asian writers made her less shy around subcontinental Indian people: she struck up a conversation with a woman in a sari who had sat down next to her on the bus. A colleague reported, only partly facetiously, that he had started making Spanish rice because Perry Smith, the murderer in Truman Capote's *In Cold Blood* (1965), especially liked the dish. A beautifully turned out octogenarian Episcopalian lady won the attention of her peers when she spoke out in response to my question, "Has a novel ever made you do anything differently?" "Ye-es," she announced in a genteel drawl, "*Lady Chatterley's Lover*," and she let our imaginations take it from there.

The example of D. H. Lawrence, so positive for my informant, brings us once again to the topic of the possible negative consequences of novel reading. A. S. Byatt blames Lawrence for misleading an entire generation of women readers into false expectations about sex and poor choices of sex partners.[2] If these topics raise the spectre of fiction's often condemned tendency to misinform, titillate, or even corrupt readers, other testimony appears to confirm the novel's relationship to consumerism. Writers and publishers have an obvious financial interest in getting readers to purchase another novel in the series, or one in the same genre, or by the same author. For better or for worse, the novel is a commodity, whose relationship to other products in the marketplace matters when the effects of reading are under investigation. Acquiring particular accessories, garments, and other purchasable tokens of a desired identity can be the direct result of novel reading. The toy industry capitalizes on this phenomenon when it offers action figures, costumes, party decorations, and updated versions of old games as thematic tie-ins to movies, cartoons, and even books. Adults are not immune to being influenced as consumers by their exposure to fictional worlds and their denizens. Some late Victorian relative of mine collected a set of Dickens plates, decorated with well-known characters from the fiction: the heroes and villains appear in the dining room, emerging from under the dessert. Using these plates acknowledges the tackiness of celebrity knick-knackery, but also inevitably announces a degree of erudition—everyone knows Little Nell and Bill Sikes, but Captain Cuttle? (He's in *Dombey and Son* [1848].) As the displays in the Dickens House suggest, Dickens was a celebrity, a figure more like Madonna than Stephen King, and his fictional universe compares to George Lucas's *Star Wars* in its cultural iconicity. Thus, perhaps buying Dickens plates indicates enthusiasm for a fashion rather than direct influence by a novel.

Contemporary evidence suggests, however, that books can indeed make us buy things. The jewelry company Bulgari believes so: it recently commissioned a novel from Fay Weldon, complete with embedded references to its products. *The Bulgari Connection* (2001) was at first privately printed by the company before being reissued by a commercial publisher. A friend reports purchasing a three-piece Italian wool tweed Polo suit under the influence of Patricia Highsmith's *The Talented Mr. Ripley* (1955). (In his own defense, he observes that the suit was on sale, 40 percent off.) Before I swore off D. H. Lawrence, I sought out colorful tights, inspired by Gudrun's stockings. In the same period (my teenaged years), a friend of mine more influenced by Victorian fiction wore form-fitting grey dresses in emulation of Jane Eyre. If it were not so embarrassing to admit, we might have more evidence of the effects of reading if we were to scrutinize records of our purchases. Typically, a reader called upon to reflect upon the ethical effects of her reading will suppress the knowledge that her scarlet winter cape pays homage to the descriptive power of scenes of consumer desire in Elizabeth Gaskell's *Sylvia's Lovers* (1863). It is one thing to concur that the novel (historically speaking) participates in the formation of the bourgeois subject, and quite another to notice proof of that thesis in one's own behavior in the marketplace.

Before going on to examine the commonly held assumptions about the effects of reading, I tackle in the immediately following section my primary subject—the phenomenon of readers' experiencing empathy with fictional characters and with other aspects of novels.[3] Nine proposals about readers' empathy emerge from this discussion. In the second full section of this chapter, six more proposals emerge as I examine the scholarship on the effects of reading. I show there that this research reflects an intention to reveal positive effects of reading in the world, as well as bias in favor of culturally sanctioned *literary* texts (including poetry). The researchers in this area have been more curious about the good that reading quality fiction may do, and less assiduous in tracing possibly disreputable consequences of reading or in evaluating the ethical effects of reading popular fiction (the books most novel readers choose). While I certainly do not think that novels have a primarily negative influence on readers, I observe that their impact is considerably more unruly than advocates of narrative ethics would lead us to believe.

Readers on Empathy for Fiction

When large numbers of readers are consulted about their empathetic reading experiences, a strong pattern emerges supporting the notion that character identification lies at the heart of readers' empathy. These characters need not be human:

> The first novel that came to my mind was *Black Beauty*. Some might see it as problematic to claim that one can feel empathy with an animal (real or fictional), but I think it is very possible to do so.[4]

> As a child, my favourite book was *Black Beauty*, which I read six times. I fear this means I identified with a horse, albeit a highly anthropomorphized horse who greatly resembled a powerless child.[5]

Novels and stories featuring animals, miniaturized figures such as Tolkien's hobbits, and toys come to life provoke empathetic reactions of readers who report ready identification with nonhuman figures. This suggests that character identification and empathy felt for fictional characters requires certain traits (such as a name, a recognizable situation, and at least implicit feelings) but dispenses with other requirements associated with realistic representation. Readers' tendency to anthropomorphize nonhuman characters even in texts strongly resistant to normalizing character, such as the early stories in Italo Calvino's *Cosmicomics* (1965, trans. 1968), persists well beyond their attainment of the developmental sophistication that enables humans to distinguish between people and unconscious or inanimate others. The literature and orature of most cultures feature talking animals, and anthropomorphism, sometimes disapproved of by educators, has proven difficult to stamp out. Tricksters alone present a compelling body of material from widely dispersed cultures: Anansi, Raven, Reynard the Fox, Coyote, Brer Rabbit, and their adversaries need not be human in order to invite character identification.[6]

If character identification routinely overcomes the significant barrier of species difference, as it appears to do, then readers' empathy may be swiftly activated by a simple sign of an active agent. Merely naming a character may

set readers' empathy in motion; indeed information leading to precise place-
ment of a character in terms of species, race, age, gender, and other aspects
of status often appears after an emotional hook has connected reader and
character. Thus I propose that *empathy for fictional characters may require
only minimal elements of identity, situation, and feeling, not necessarily complex
or realistic characterization.* This first hypothesis, which has been observed
in experiments with real readers as they begin reading a story,[7] runs counter
to common assumptions about complexity and realism as prized elements
of canonical fiction. Two possibilities that undergird this hypothesis deserve
special emphasis. First, if the very start of a narrative can evoke empathy at
the mere gesture of naming and quick situating, then readers may be primed
by the story-receiving circumstance to get ready to empathize. The mirror-
neuron manifold for shared intersubjectivity may be activated by simple
cues announcing the existence of another being. Second, something about
the signal alerting readers or listeners to a text or performance's fictionality
apparently permits identification to occur regardless of factuality or verisimilitude, though the first reaction may later be revised. Whether mature,
experienced readers show a similar degree of swift emotional responsiveness to just-introduced characters as children (not yet habituated to the
conventions of psychological realism) would make an interesting research
question. At stake is the basic question of whether our fiction habit plays
upon our human empathic disposition, develops it, or possibly even trains
us in delaying or disengaging it. Human empathy may arise from a set of
responses so swift and automatic that cognition, including lessons learned
from stories, functions to limit it.

Childhood reading, recalled across the decades, provides examples of
many readers' most memorable (or admissible) empathetic reactions to fiction. It may be that early, striking reading experiences occurring before a
reader has been socialized into the kinds of responses that win praise at
school stand out, even in academic readers' memories. A question remains
as to whether mature readers feel differently about fictional characters as
they grow up, or whether they learn to assess and present their responses
differently. (As we will shortly see, the notion that a badly written book or
stereotyped character can invoke empathetic response particularly bothers trained readers, for whom quality matters.) Whatever authorizes their
disclosures, many readers report that novels in which child characters are
subjected to cruel or unfair treatment evoke empathy, as these exemplary
reports suggest:

> I also deeply identified with Jane Eyre, especially during her child-
> hood. I also identified with the young David Copperfield, when my
> mother read that book aloud to me when I was about twelve. In both
> cases my strongest empathetic responses were aroused by the scenes
> of abuse by cruel relatives and abusive school teachers, even though

I was a happy lovingly-nurtured child who adored my teachers and school. Perhaps there's something about the fundamental powerlessness of childhood that explains the continuing appeal of suffering characters, from the March girls to Jane and David, to all those other orphans and fairy tale victims.[8]

Certainly when I first read *Jane Eyre* at 14 I felt in complete empathy with Jane through her early experiences—the narrative voice, the intensity of the passion, the experience of isolation and injustice and lability and rage she evokes.[9]

Jane Eyre is a magnet for reader empathy—encouraging anyone who has ever felt victimized as a child by more powerful adults to identify with her (a small subset being girls who attended boarding schools up to and including the nineteen fifties as I can personally attest). The choice of first person narration also contributes to increase the reader's empathetic reaction in this novel and in others.[10]

I doubt whether anyone who has read *Tom Brown's Schooldays*, and who has himself attended an English Public School as a boarder, has failed to empathise with at least one of the characters—probably Tom. I boarded in the late 1970s and early 1980s, and, as unbelievable as it may sound, there were many parallels in both emotions and experiences.[11]

All four readers emphasize the cruelty, injustice, and victimization of the children in their reports, though only one directly identifies with the fictional character's experiences. These mature readers remember strong fellow feeling even as they acknowledge differences from characters' situations. They testify that a reader does not have to be an orphan, a maltreated victim, or a beaten animal to experience a strong empathetic response through character identification. My second hypothesis can be drawn from these readers' observation: *character identification often invites empathy, even when the character and reader differ from each other in all sorts of practical and obvious ways.* Indeed, the opportunity to share feelings underwrites character identification that transcends difference: *I am not an orphan, but I feel with Jane Eyre.* This nearly ubiquitous readerly experience suggests that the opposite hypothesis also deserves exploration: *spontaneous empathy for a fictional character's feelings opens the way for character identification* (even in the face of strong differences, e.g.: *the protagonist is a rabbit*). This chicken-and-egg pair of proposals has important implications for the way teachers and narrative ethicists understand the consequences of reading fiction. If, on the one hand, empathy precedes (and invites) character identification, then empathy may be better understood as a faculty that readers bring to their imaginative engagement with texts—a human default setting—rather than as a quality gained from or cultivated by encounters with fiction. (The absence of interest Apsberger's syndrome sufferers and high-functioning autistics show in fictional worlds, made up stories, and characters may connect to their lack of normal human empathy.) If, on the other hand, character identification opens the opportunity for empathy (this is the more common and more widely disseminated assumption), then representation of characters with strong differences might be used didactically, to develop a reader's moral sense. Of course, readers of different dispositions may experience character identification and empathy in varying orders, and their experiences of both phenomena may change depending on the novel, the author, or their age and condition while reading.[12]

Looking at college students' reports about empathetic characters verifies the sense that a character's negative affective states, such as those provoked by undergoing persecution, suffering, grieving, and experiencing painful obstacles, make a reader's empathizing more likely.[13] College students and precocious young readers' experiences also confirm the observation that a sense of empathetic connection with a character or situation can be felt without an exact match in identity. Texts eliciting readers' deeply held fears seem especially successful in provoking empathy:

> Although I have never been in a situation in which I was charged with murder, I have experienced empathy for Vernon, the 15–16 year old boy in *Vernon God Little*. In my reading I have been overcome with stress and frustration for him as he has been ignored by the "grown-ups," wrongly accused, and tricked.[14]

> I experienced empathy with Jimmy/Snowman in *Oryx and Crake*. Although I do not share his dystopic environment, his sense of loss, confusion, and inability to retain some pieces of knowledge are consistent with everyday life: it is bewildering and nobody shares our exact history to remind us what we've lost.[15]

> *Age of Innocence, Little Women*, any novel where the father or younger brother dies—I cry in all of these books because, although my dad or mom or little brother are still obviously with me, I am so protective of them that these events always make me extremely upset.[16]

> I think I felt empathy for Jimmy in *Oryx and Crake*. He felt bad about being an "art person" as opposed to Crake the "science person." My boyfriend is a science person—sometimes I feel that my major is less important.[17]

> I think if anything at all I felt empathy with Edwidge Danticat's *Krik? Krak!* Coming from a war-torn country myself, I could honestly feel what the characters were feeling. The story that sticks out to me the most is the one where the woman finds an abandoned child which we discover is dead.[18]

In this sequence of comments from articulate teenaged readers, the effort to connect a response to personal experience or familiar feelings ranges from the assertion that reader and character have nothing in common, all the way to a close match in personal history. The match contributes to a sense of certainty ("I could *honestly* feel . . .") but does not constitute a requirement for empathetic reactions. Instead, a continuum of degrees of emotional recognition can be observed in these and other readers' reports. Many assert shared feelings despite different experiences. Many report strong identification with the character. Some discover aspects of their own identity through imaginative fusion with a character. Each of these background states can be accompanied by an empathetic reaction, in these cases, to characters experiencing negative feelings. The students were at liberty to mention any text that came to mind, but they did not choose upbeat novels and short stories with joyful or comical characters. A fourth hypothesis may thus be added to the tally: *empathetic responses to fictional characters and situations occur more readily for negative feeling states, whether or not a match in details of experience exists*. The emphasis on shared *negative* feelings is a striking feature of the voluntary responses I have collected—readers could certainly have reported sharing feelings of joy or pleasure, but they tend not to, or not to recognize those readerly sensations as empathy.[19]   Perhaps the circumstances of fictionality enable exploration of negative feeling states that might otherwise be avoided or repressed for personal or social reasons.

My fifth hypothesis, based on readers' testimony, points out that narrative empathy cannot be expected invariably to work, for *empathy with characters doesn't always occur as a result of reading an emotional evocative fiction.* What causes this variation in response to a fixed text may be readers' individual dispositions, aspects of their identity, their age and experiences, their location in a remote culture or historical period, their knowledge, their fluency in genres and conventions, or even the quality of the attention they give to reading. Negative factors such as prejudice, bias, impatience with a particular literary style, or feeling rushed or pressured might also account for unresponsive reading. Indeed, there are so many possible reasons for interference with intended emotional effects that great care must be taken not to confound causes: if lack of familiarity with generic conventions corresponds roughly to gender in a group of readers, which factor would account for the lack of an empathetic response? An alternative way of phrasing this proposal would state the obvious truism that no one novel evokes empathy in all its readers, but that formulation would downplay the fact that some readers seem less disposed to empathize with fiction than others. Readers' dispositions matter: as Michael Steig observes in *Stories of Reading: Subjectivity and Literary Understanding* (1989), "Because of personality and experience, some readers are capable of more original and deeper understanding of emotionally puzzling aspects of particular literary works than are others; and such understandings can be conceptualized by such a reader through a reflection upon the emotions experienced and upon personal associations with those emotions" (xiv).

A few readers assert that they *never* empathize with fiction (though a subset of these volunteer that autobiography moves them). Real readers also confess to occasions when something about a text blocks empathy or invites a different response from the one the central character apparently feels. For instance, one of my students observes that she experienced "different feelings with the mother's view of the daughter's marriage to a non-Haitian man" in Edwidge Danticat's *Krik? Krak!* (1995): "I was angry whereas the daughter simply let her mother's protests roll off her back."[20] Arguably, this response belongs to the range of appropriate emotions invited by Danticat's close-to-the-bone representation of intergenerational conflict. Much of what we feel while reading depends upon responding to differences between a character's reaction and what we believe to be the narrator's or implied author's point about a situation. A reader who especially appreciates ironic effects may be less likely to experience spontaneous emotional sharing with a character. This sort of resistance to empathy is cultivated by academic modes of analysis that privilege critical distance and observations about style. Paradoxically, professionals often disguise their own, passionate reading habits from their students. These young avid readers are often rewarded most generously for their argumentative brio and technical analysis (regardless of how they feel about the texts), while they learn to suppress discussion of certain emotional responses—outrage and indignation can still be mentioned, while "gushy" feelings cannot.

While readers who dissent from an authorized reaction to a text sometimes suppress this fact, some readers invited to meet and match an authority's endorsement of particular feelings evoked by fiction outspokenly rebel. Any ardent recommender of novels well knows that the recommending formula, "you'll love this book," encodes a wish rather than a prediction. Despite the popularity of some particular texts among cohorts of readers, my correspondents honestly reflected on the fact that an empathetic response of one's own might well not be shared by other readers, even (especially) one's children:

> And then there's the salutary (bracing) experience of trying to share your empathetic experience with a child, say a daughter. When my daughters . . . reached an age where they could read *Little Women*, *Jane Eyre*, *Heidi* (a little earlier), I presented these books to them in the full expectation they would like them. They didn't. *Heidi* was a bore. *The Secret Garden* was barely tolerated; both preferred *The Little Princess*. When we got to *Jane Eyre* (the process took several years—I never presented more than one book at a time), the older one turned round and said to me, Mom, what is it that you liked [about] these punished goody characters? . . . I've wondered if the difference my two

daughters (very different in character) both displayed is a generational change. Why read about abused children? I almost take this as a good sign, as showing my pair were somehow healthier than me at their age, didn't expect to be punished and would not buy into the ideas implicit in these scenes.[21]

We witness generational changes of taste in character types and situations as well as in genre, and these large shifts can have an impact on a classic text's empathetic potential. Vernon Lee's theory of aesthetic empathy stresses the sensitiveness of people living in particular times and periods to shapes to which they have been habituated: "Nothing is so routinist as imagination and emotion," she writes, " and empathy, which partakes of both, is therefore more dependent on familiarity than is the perception by which it is started" (*The Beautiful* 134–35). The hypothesis that comes out of this observation confutes the notion of a timeless classic: *The capacity of a particular novel to invoke readers' empathy may change over time (and some texts may only activate the empathy of their first, immediate audience)*. Evidence of an earlier empathetic reaction to novels that no longer reach readers emotionally may be useful to both literary and cultural historians, as well as to teachers hoping to bring classics to life for a new generation of readers.

Another kind of dissent from mainstream empathy occurs when a reader connects emotionally with the "wrong" character. Readers such as this listserv discussant embrace the emotional stretching—to include the perspectives of unsavory characters— that this kind of empathizing seems to demand:

> Isn't the whole point of empathy to find it in ourselves to feel for others we wouldn't ordinarily identify with? . . . Isn't it our empathy for fools, villains and other unattractive types that deepens our understanding, in that, against our inclinations, we identify certain aspects of their humanity with our own?[22]

This interpretation recuperates empathy for nasty characters to the broad project of character education for tolerance, by emphasizing the humanity of the vicious or the risible. A more complicated circumstance occurs for readers who respond against the grain and know (as this reader does) that their feelings are anomalous. In private correspondence, readers confessed not only to disliking certain popular characters, but to empathizing with or identifying with despised characters apparently held up for scorn by authors:

> I also identified with and thus empathized with many unattractive characters whose mistakes isolated them, like Dombey and Mr. Dorrit. . . . I have felt empathetic to Fagin, the hook-nosed caricature, especially in his last scene, alone in the condemned cell. Though I was still a boy in the late 1940s, when I first read *Oliver Twist*, I had

already begun to think that being an outlaw was a reasonable response to persecution.[23]

Secretly, I also empathize with Rosamond in *Middlemarch*, Gwendolyn . . . all the nasty, frivolous self absorbed types! I think they tap into one's self-critical streak . . .

This is a little embarrassing, but I had a strong empathetic reaction to the character of Casaubon in *Middlemarch*. I read the novel for the first time in graduate school, when I was struggling to regain a sense of purpose for my life. . . . I was also convinced—and this conviction still occasionally torments me—that I was just on the verge of pulling together all my ideas into some grand cultural unified field theory, which would not only unite the very disparate chapters of my dissertation but also explain the world in some transformative way. And there's Casaubon, patient, pathetic pedant, working on his Key to All Mythologies. As a reader, I could recognize that his goal was a phantasm, that his life was barren, that he was doomed to ruin his only chance at happiness, and that his whole career would be, to an outsider, an object of ridicule. At the same time, I thought, "Yes, he's right! That's exactly it—the Key to All Mythologies!" The sense of recognition was visceral. I had faith in the same ridiculous thing, and I could resist neither the idea nor the scholar. I picture Casaubon, rejecting Eliot's portrayal, as an attractive, enticing figure, tragically misplaced in his community. At the same time, my disgust is just as real. I love Casaubon (so exclusively that all the novel's other characters made almost no imprint in my memory) and I loathe him.

The keywords of this third reader's response to Casaubon—the visceral recognition of a pictured character, his goals, and his situation; the love and loathing; the attraction and disgust—speak eloquently to the complex of feelings that can be activated by an empathetic connection with a character, even a risible one. One of the many contributions that the study of narrative empathy can make to the study of human empathy lies in the complicated combinations of different affects, as in this report, that comprise an empathetic response.

These candid accounts also point up the fact that *empathy for a fictional character need not correspond with what the author appears to set up or invite* (a seventh hypothesis). Self-reported readers' empathy appears to be unpredictable and sporadic. Readers accustomed to discussing their reactions to books with others will recognize the phenomenon of being surprised by the ways other readers feel about, or judge, negatively portrayed figures. Though earlier I use the word "wrong" to label these empathetic surprises, instances of anomalous readerly identification are only wayward in so far as readers feel uncomfortable disclosing them. The phenomenon of empathy for unattractive characters actually strengthens the case for the idea of minimal requirements for identification: a name (or a pronoun), a situation, and an implicit feeling might be all that is required to spark empathy. The character need not be admirable. The characterization may indeed be quite sketchy. The author need not like the character nor lavish representational attention on the character's state of mind to invoke a reader's empathy.

By no means do authors completely control the range of available reactions to their fictional people, nor should readers feel limited to identifying with a central character (either a center of consciousness in a third-person fiction or a self-narrator in first person). A participant in the VICTORIA-L online discussion correctly observes:

> It's interesting to me to take note of identifications with the sisters in *Little Women*—not everyone goes for Jo. My mother came around to Jo but told me she started out with Beth; one of my sisters liked Meg best, though she traveled further than any of us from the domestic sphere; I always liked Amy, possibly because Jo got on my nerves as the clear center of the story and the one I was "supposed" to travel with. And Amy, though spoiled when we meet her, grows: and she stood up to Jo more than the others, as well as being the other overtly creative sister.[24]

Even when the narrative technique employed by the author says, "I'm Pip—travel with me," real readers may waywardly feel with Estella, or Miss Havisham, or (as Peter Carey demonstrates) Magwitch. Indeed, a vigorous subgenre of contemporary fiction takes a misunderstood, disreputable, or demonized character from an earlier writer's novel and recenters a revisionist fiction upon the marginalized other.[25] This imaginative procedure is honored as a creative practice, but for a regular reader, identifying or feeling with the "wrong" character may produce discomfort, shame, or self-censorship. In the twenty-first century, our book talk often takes place in classrooms, libraries, auditoriums, and online chatrooms: spaces of the public sphere that invite performance of our most admirable guises.

Under these circumstances, self-consciousness about being judged for having a naïve, sentimental, or socially unacceptable reaction to a novel can alter readers' self reports about reading. One member of the VICTORIA-L listserv discussion noticed this phenomenon:

> I'm also interested that there were a few people on the list who felt the need to "apologize" for having been moved by characters like Beth in *Little Women*. Why apologize? Why cling to the remnants of the New Critical hostility to sentimentality? Surely it's that hostility— I. A. Richards went so far as to compare sympathetic emotional reactions to a disease—that has resulted in the degradation of so much of

Victorian women's literature. . . .[and] the anti-sentimentality reaction obviously affected Dickens' critical reputation as well. When are we going to stop apologizing for liking books that "Jones at the Club" (see Thackeray's *Vanity Fair*) sneers at down his oh-so-intellectual noses? Down with Jones!!![26]

This strong comment draws attention to the social aspect of novel talk: we say who we are, and we reveal our training and taste, when we confess our feelings about characters. David Bleich, an early advocate of reader-response criticism, believes that "when tastes are publicly presented on the basis of response statements, it is possible to distinguish between tastes based on motives for compliance or for self-satisfaction" (*Subjective Criticism* 166). Mary Lenard's challenge to the listserv discussion members suggests that our different kinds of taste and the social aspirations that shape them do show and that we share them fully conscious that we will be judged by others. Bleich offers what I regard as a utopian account of what will happen when real readers disclose their true likes and dislikes. He believes that if motives of self-pleasing are "taken seriously in public, the principles of public taste-formation are altered, since the element of compliance is significantly reduced" (166). Lenard's comment suggests that thirty years of reader-oriented criticism has not brought about this change, at least not yet. Bleich's subjective paradigm puts a great deal of weight on "collective similarity of response" to a symbolic object, which, he acknowledges, depends upon "each individual's announcement of his response and subsequent communally motivated negotiative comparison" (98). Bleich concludes that the "investigation of the nature of popularity in this way is likely to change what is considered popular," and this may turn out to be true, over time (166). In the short term, public disclosure about our feelings for fictions still places us into categories, generic, gendered, and marked by education and social class. This phenomenon becomes all the more personal and revealing when we admit sharing feelings with fictional characters.

Certain fictional characters even possess the power to resist professional technical analysis, so strongly do readers identify with them. One teacher reflects:

For sheer intensity of the readerly relationships she inspires, Jane Eyre stands by herself, among my students. They are expert at explaining her motivations, defending her faults, applauding her decisions, and analyzing her romances. There's something generously empathetic in the work they do to protect Jane from the professor who wants to talk about her as just an effect of a literary work. None of my students, by the way, are British orphans facing a world in which educated women have precious few channels for making money or acting independently.[27]

Individual readers do dissent from the critical consensus, and in this class-room they clearly feel empowered to articulate their own positions. Often discussion situations move toward a shared interpretation; sussing out the implied author's intentions is a common strategy for arriving at a reading acceptable to a group. Those presented with a received interpretation may resist professional literary analytical explanations for their feelings about a character or an author. These readers may be encouraged to speak up, but they may also fall silent in the face of an authoritative interpretation offered by a teacher, a critic, or an articulate participant in a discussion. A caution to researchers pursuing information about readers' responses through their self reports (the methodology of this chapter) would be: *discussion of fiction that takes place in public settings, while extremely valuable in itself, may not be the most reliable source of evidence for emotional responses to fiction.* The effects of conscious or unconscious desires to please can even occur when anonymity and privacy are guaranteed. As Nancy Eisenberg and her collab-orators observe about research on gender difference in empathy, question-naire and interview methods that allow subjects conscious control of their performance appear to skew results toward cultural norms (see 7–8 above). A challenge for future scholars of emotional response to literature will be to develop, in collaboration with colleagues in psychology, methodologies that can overcome the effects of social expectations on reports about read-ing experiences. As reader's empathy is valorized by our culture at large and connected (whether justifiably or not) with social goods such as tolerance, volunteerism, and altruism, the pressure to respond acceptably to a fictional character may increase. In a worst-case scenario modeled by *Blade Runner*, identifying and empathizing with a featured character could become a test, in which readers who gravitate toward other textual features (or simply dislike the novel!) reveal their moral failings or inhumanity. This sort of adjudication of right empathy and wrong empathy should be avoided, if we hope to learn how empathy for characters and other textual features works in real readers.

Professionally trained readers are more likely than regular readers to recount experiences of empathy with other aspects of fictional worlds: the projected "implied author," particular situations, settings, atmosphere, and (much more rarely) the language or style of a novel. Authors (the real people or the imaginary figures that readers construct out of the effects of their works) command empathy as if they were characters, even when colossal differences between text and creator exist. Ellen Moody describes this well:

> Readers "empathize" with c19th novels . . . through their imagined
> identification with what they think is true of the author's mental life
> . . . how we feel about the author as a presence in his or her work as a

projected personality and as revealed in the text's apparent belief-system is central to our experience of empathy with the characters. I have loved Fanny Price and Elinor Dashwood because Austen-in-the-novel makes me feel she loves them too—even if she can treat them with irony and distance at moments.[28]

This macro view of empathy with an author's mind is counterbalanced by a reader's testimony of empathy with brief moments in the depiction of particular characters, in which a situation becomes so compelling that empathy overcomes distance or dislike. Despite finding the character Anna Karenina "mostly annoying," Kerryn Goldsworthy experiences "moments of feeling with" her . . . the unreasonable, unjustified jealousy and fear that eventually destroy both her and Vronsky."[29] Empathy with a situation responds to plot as much as to character, though it often finds its focus in a character's feelings. Narrative theorists know how difficult it is to disentangle plot from character, for without events, the agents of fiction are inert. Reading for plot certainly involves attention to character, but it engages with action-sequences, development of complex circumstances, and the hoped-for resolution of suspenseful enigmas. As psychologist Richard J. Gerrig observes, "to a large extent, a theory of suspense must include within it a theory of empathy," since the motivation for caring about the consequences of actions is bound up in "active thought" about characters' fates (*Experiencing* 80). Yet liking or approving of the characters may not be a requirement for the situational empathy that occurs for some readers.

Empathy with situations tends to zero in on episodes, circumstances, or states of relationship at points of irresolution. That is, empathy with plot situation gravitates toward *middles* of plots, when problems and enigmas have not yet been solved or brought to closure. Thus, a twenty-first century student who is separated from her illegal alien husband can react with tearful recognition to Catherine Earnshaw's doom, loving the screwed up Heathcliff, unable to escape by making a better choice.[30] The ongoingness of a fictional situation (never really over because never really occurring) lends itself to empathetic engagement. Empathy with situations resembles (and may feed into) empathy with characters with whom close identification can be made, but huge character-reader differences do not interfere with situational empathy. Thus a middle-class divorced American woman may tremble in recognition of the fear, invoked by Amy Tan in *The Kitchen God's Wife* (1991), that a despised first husband might turn up to wreck her happiness. This kind of reader's empathy may appear more egocentric than empathy for characters, since it requires much less effort in role taking and imaginative extension. It is also extremely idiosyncratic: if you haven't been divorced, or diagnosed with a fatal disease, or shamed as an unwanted child, you may simply not feel it when those circumstances turn up in a story. A summary hypothesis suggests that *situational empathy, which responds primarily to aspects of plot and circumstance, involves less self-extension in imaginative role taking and more recognition of prior (or current) experience.*

This kind of empathy is particularly vulnerable to criticism as a form of easy egotism, such as these listserv discussants describe:

> Where does empathy stray into narcissism? When does the mirror cease to be a magic portal into another life, another dimension, another view, and become merely a self-serving portrait of our own desires and aspirations?[31]

> It is possible for readers—even relatively discerning readers—to feel empathy with characters in poorly written books. All that's necessary is that the characters go through experiences resembling (or symbolically encapsulating) the reader's own. . . . The literary characters with whom we feel empathetic thus reveal more about our own psychology and our own personal histories than they do about the author's conceptions or skills.[32]

One theorist of character identification who studies the reading autobiographies of "motivated" readers like the listserv discussants actually distinguishes "wish identification" and "similarity identification" from empathy in her rubric of relationships between readers and the realms of fiction.[33] This neatly solves the problem of potentially discreditable, selfish-seeming experiences of empathy by calling them by another name. However, situational empathy can have a social dimension that may redeem it from charges of narcissism. So, for instance, the Thackeray scholar Sheldon Goldfarb sees a moment of situational empathy in *Vanity Fair* (1847–48), "where Thackeray conjures up the fearful side of high society and I think inspires fear in us, or at least reminds us of our fears."[34] This connection closes the gap between Becky Sharp's world and the actual world of twenty-first–century readers, as empathy transcends historical and contextual differences.

While experiencing empathy for a character placed against a remote or unfamiliar backdrop may be partly responsible for the sense that reading fiction extends the imagination over barriers of unfamiliarity, sometimes a chance resemblance of circumstances does the trick. Some of the empathy-inspiring situations readers recall point to particular historical moments that render fictional characters' dilemmas especially affecting. For instance, the children in *Heidi* (1885) and *The Secret Garden* (1911) who learned to walk again moved a reader who encountered these characters before the development of the polio vaccine:

> I suppose I identified with headstrong little girls who hoped nevertheless to help people somehow—and what could be more dramatic in the age of polio than the miracle of wasted limbs becoming strong again?[35]

A moment of relevance may heighten the empathetic opportunities presented by a novel, only to diminish as the cure for polio (in 2007 nearly eradicated worldwide) reduces the chances of spontaneous recognition.

This phenomenon suggests that the study of narrative empathy ought to be attuned to historical and social contexts in the period of reception. Rigorous historicizing of the nature of human feelings in different periods should counter the psychologists' tendency to generalize from results garnered from the study of the present generations to all humans in all times.[36] Even if basic human emotions remain the same, the situations that provoke empathetic recognition of complex blends of feeling are quite likely to differ in tone, mixture, and intensity in different contexts. Thus, a hypothesis emerges: *Readers' empathy for situations depicted in fiction may be enhanced by chance relevance to particular historical, economic, cultural, or social circumstances.* Both successes and failures of empathy may arise as much from the specific context and conditions of the reader as from the representation itself. Preliminary confirmation comes from the comparative experiment of János László, in which responses of Danish and Hungarian readers, elicited by an emotionally-charged story about Nazis (by contemporary Hungarian writer Ferenc Sánta), showed a more passionate engagement on the part of more culturally knowledgeable Hungarian readers. László's experiment showed that Danish readers felt empathy, apparently on the basis of "universal emotions," while Hungarians resonated more strongly with the protagonist's dilemmas, especially the "unpleasant and aggressive aspects" of it, "because it related to a number of personal experiences" ("Cognition" 140).[37] It remains unclear whether a reader's deliberate attempt to live up to a novel's demands (thus joining what Peter J. Rabinowitz calls the authorial audience) can alter the likelihood of situational empathy occurring.[38]

Where, the professional literary critic may wonder, does this leave the teachers and scholars who have spent their lives practicing the elucidation of texts and contexts, theories and interpretations? Does attending to readers' empathy mean valuing the reports of what Virginia Woolf called common readers over the reactions of trained novel critics?[39] I believe that an emphasis on readers' empathy allows an important role for literary criticism, if psychologists are willing to engage themselves with the complex structures of feeling embedded in texts and embodied in the attuned reader. An excerpt from an e-mail to the VICTORIA-L discussion group provides an exhibit of what elucidation of empathy might look like as an element of interpretation:

> Now one Dickens scene has been teasing me ever since I read the question: the wonderfully rich and terrible scene in *Little Dorrit* in which Mr. Dorrit, at the height of his fortune and social success, cracks and goes into a delusion, before all his guests, that he's back in the

Marshalsea [a prison]. Reading that I feel an agonized, tormentingly embarrassed empathy with *someone*, but whom? Not him—he's not sane enough to be aware of how ill he is; not Little Dorrit, who's far too concerned about him to feel the social embarrassment; not the guests, who don't really understand . . . can it be Dickens? The whole scene seems to shimmer and writhe with complex feelings that none of the characters on the spot seems big enough to hold—so who else could it be? Dickens, then, or the narrator: whoever's floating over the scene feeling that wonderfully controlled mixture of love, raw social anguish, visceral horror at the sudden inbreak of madness, angry yet clear-eyed and compassionate condemnation of Mr. Dorrit's terrible emotional mistakes, angry contempt for the class represented by the guests, and along with it all an intense aesthetic satisfaction as the novel reaches its perfect symbolic crisis—the feelings are there, I feel them, yet I feel reasonably sure I wasn't big enough to conceive them in the first place! So it must be empathy. . . .[40]

Though composed in a casual mode as a contribution to a listserv discussion in the informal medium of e-mail, this analysis of empathetic feeling with a complex of emotional currents evoked by Dickens's great novel *Little Dorrit* (1857) strikes me as an exemplary use of professional analytical skill. The questions of where cues to empathy reside in a text, and with whom (or with what) a reader might be empathizing can provide sufficient starting points for guided discussion and critical analysis. While it is difficult at the moment to envision the discourse analysis experiment that would get at the complex of feelings with which this reader resonated, the challenge should at least be posed as a goal of narrative empathy studies.

Nonetheless, it must be acknowledged that discussion of readers' empathy levels the playing field in a way that some professional critics may find unnerving or simply unacceptable. If the reactions of *any* feeling reader count as evidence of a novel's effectiveness, then suddenly all sorts of popular fiction, including formulaic romance novels, demand attention. If the exercise of professional judgment means weeding out the worthwhile fiction from ephemera (as it does for book critics and teachers of contemporary fiction, who work without the armature of a teaching canon), then readers' empathy may be a positive feature assisting critical judgment, or it may be an annoying reminder of the power of popularity. For instance, millions of readers resonated empathetically with the protagonist of Robert James Waller's *The Bridges of Madison County* (1992), but the MLA Bibliography reports only a single peer-reviewed journal article on the novel.[41] The book stayed on *The New York Times'* Bestseller list for nearly three years, and its publisher TimeWarner characterizes *Bridges* as the best-selling novel of all time. As far as I can tell, the novel is not taught in colleges or university literature courses, though it has a presence in communications, composition, and print-to-film courses. Though the critical consensus appears to be that the film improved on the novel, ordinary readers' enthusiasm for Francesca's love story propelled the success of this novel. Copies of the authentic first edition of the novel now go for hundreds of dollars to collectors, and over a decade later, readers still endorse the novel on the pages of Amazon.com and Barnes and Noble.com, where it is available as a downloadable e-book and an audiobook, as well as in hardcover and paper. At a basic level, novels that enjoy such phenomenal popularity are self-discrediting to most professionals in literary studies (agents, would-be-authors of bestsellers, and editors obviously feel differently). The success of novels such as *The Bridges of Madison County* demands attention if readers' empathy is to be understood, and certainly should compel respect if the empathy of readers could actually be turned to socially desirable ends. An empathy-inducing blockbuster would be a powerful tool, if feeling readers acted upon their sensations as Martha Nussbaum believes readers of Henry James, Charles Dickens, and George Eliot do. However, literary studies and philosophy (including novel criticism and narrative ethics) have a largely unexamined vexed—often openly contemptuous—relationship with popular fiction.

I take up this subject at greater length in the following chapter ("Empathy in the Marketplace"), but I mention it here because many educated readers believe that the quality of a novel somehow inheres in the empathy it evokes. This widespread conviction represents a continuation of the Victorian critical standard, expressed in countless book reviews, that successful fictional characters command readers' sympathies. Though the twenty-first–century style replaces Victorian sympathetic feeling *for* with contemporary empathetic feeling *with*, teaching at the primary and secondary level inculcates the view that readers vicariously experience novels by identifying with characters. In the prevailing circular logic, good novels invite empathy and empathetic responses verify the quality of the novel. A typical comment of this sort uses empathy as a test of literary greatness: "I wonder if most, if not all, great works inspire empathy, otherwise readers wouldn't take an interest in them?"[42] Another reader emphasizes how great writing can evoke empathy for a wide range of fictional characters, regardless of gender or position of the character in the story.[43] Greatness, embodied in the author, the technique, or the works themselves, registers as both a cause and consequence of empathy.

Unfortunately, in order to diminish the power of the evidence suggesting that lowbrow fiction evokes empathy more reliably than treasured classics, some critics end up denigrating the readers who respond to popular, mass-market texts. This seems to me a counterproductive strategy in an era of diminishing reading. Better to admit, as this reader notices, that personal bias may be the foundation for much of our estimations of greatness:

> I suppose everyone wants to believe that the books they love most passionately are great works of literature. As adults, we don't like to think that we have been "taken in" by shoddy, perfunctory fictions for no better reason than that we could relate to the characters/situations. However, it may be helpful to remember that all literature "takes us in." Every author seeks to manipulate us with artificial inventions. It's not as though bad authors seek to deceive us into empathy while good authors channel real life for us, unmediated and pure. Fiction is a crafty business and most writers, whether they're good or bad, will use "every trick in the book."[44]

The question of quality, or of the relationship of empathy to literariness, may well prove a stumbling block to the understanding of empathy and the novel as a phenomenon. The traditional critical task of distinguishing great works from worthless trash is a useful practice—no one has time to read everything and critics help readers choose. However, carrying over the critical habit of elimination of unworthy texts may obscure more than it reveals about human empathy and our appetite for narrative. Thus I conclude this section with a caution, that *readers' empathy may have little to do with the quality of fiction as acclaimed by professionals.* Understanding readers' empathy almost certainly requires attending to the novels that real readers choose for themselves and may demand a discomforting de-emphasis of prized qualities of literariness.

Scholarship on the Effects of Reading

Empathy figures prominently in the investigations of recent empirical research on the effects of reading, conducted primarily by psychologists, discourse processing experts, and education specialists. Despite weak results for the causal relationships among reading, empathy, and prosocial action, empathy continues to loom large as an element of reading theories under empirical investigation.[45] The forms of inquiry employed by scholars of reading vary from surveys or questionnaires administered to large or small numbers of readers, to controlled reading-speed experiments in which short stories are broken up into bits to be read in sequence on a computer screen.[46] Some researchers, including many reader-response critics, ask readers to write out personal responses after completing reading,[47] while others record the comments made aloud as reading takes place. Both methods in effect study verbal responses rather than reading itself. Arguably, reading changes when it is interrupted to provide intermittent commentary aloud, while surveys or written responses elicited after reading emphasize the completed experience over the dynamic process. Statistical methods, such as the U.S. Census Bureau's survey of 17,000 adult Americans, *Reading at*

Risk, produce the broadest kind of study of reading habits, but these questionnaires are necessarily retrospective and tell us nothing directly about either the experience or effects of reading. Studying reading "online," especially with long texts like novels, has proven a challenge. A small number of experiments conducted in the 1970s measured skin conductance (readers' sweating) as works about racial others were perused.[48] Computers have enabled eye movements to be measured and reading speeds quantified. Victor Nell observed subjects in a laboratory setting as they immersed themselves in self-selected pleasure reading and combined his observations with interviews of subjects. Though new brain imaging techniques (fMRI and diffusion tensor imaging) hold out the promise of understanding the reading brain better, such a research program has not been a priority among neuroscientists.[49] What little is known about the neural networks involved in symbolic text processing has yet to be correlated with questions about emotions evoked by reading.[50] In particular, the question of whether readers' empathy resembles fMRI images of the empathetic brain (activated in the anterior insula and anterior cingulate cortex, the lateral cerebellum, and the brainstem) remains to be investigated. Because this body of work rarely receives attention from post-secondary literature specialists, I review it in some detail here.

To represent empirical approaches to literary reading, which typically blend basic concepts from literary study with social-psychological methods (including questionnaires and self-reports, delivered aloud or composed in writing), I draw here on the work of several of its most respected practitioners. These include David S. Miall and Don Kuiken of the University of Alberta (in literature and psychology, respectively) and the Utrecht University scholar Jèmeljan Hakemulder, whose research into the effects of reading treats both social perceptions and morality. I augment this group with a report on the work of Tammy Bourg, a psychologist at California State University at Sacramento, for Bourg focuses tightly on empathy. Miall, Kuiken, and Hakemulder pursue broader research programs, each of which addresses the role empathy plays in literary reading.[51] In this section I review their insights about empathy and point out some of the assumptions that underlie each researcher's questions and methodology.

A primary assumption, with implications for the study of fiction, holds that reading literature differs from reading generally. I argue above that readers' empathy may have little to do with the *quality* of fiction as affirmed by professionals, that is, on the distinction of serious from popular fiction (including the often-dismissed categories of "junk reading," "trash," "airport books," and genre fiction such as romances). This does not eliminate *kinds* of fiction from consideration, for testimony of readers suggests that *generic differences are likely to play a role in inviting (or retarding) empathic response.* Certain fictional genres should not be equated with higher literary status if empathy is to be a factor in value. The scholars who study literary reading often assume and sometimes describe this kind of distinction in level or quality.[52] To some extent their assumption mirrors commonsense understandings of literature as qualitatively different from texts in general. Few would contest the observation that a modernist lyric poem makes special demands on a reader, compared, say, to the ads on the back of a cereal box. There are lots of different kinds of reading other than perusing literary texts. Reading, for the fluent literate person, ranges from automatic comprehension of instructions and signs, to scanning for specific information, to speedy consumption of narrative, to slower, more meditative engagement with texts.

Two kinds of reading seem especially desirable to specialists: slow, careful reading represents one ideal (once the halting pace of the beginner is no longer necessary); and the trancelike absorption of the immersed reader (when not being disparaged as an advanced form of idleness) often results in a faster page-turning pace. These practices make possible literary reading. However, as Leah Price has described beautifully in *The Anthology and the Rise of the Novel* (2000), even literary reading involves a great deal of skipping and skimming. In contrast, reading literature analytically, with an aim of sharing or comparing insights with others or producing interpretations, is a highly specialized activity that (for most people) requires training. This education disrupts students' habitual reading patterns with new demands— attention to privileged details and patterns, to symbolic objects, to loose ends, to contextually relevant information—depending on the approach. The rarified form, academic reading, moves beyond appreciation to analysis in its now quite various modes. Nonetheless, this last kind of reading, "reading" as analytical interpreting, is what most literature specialists mean when they use the word.

The scholars whose work I describe here focus on reading defined more broadly than literary interpreting, but their location in universities, their reliance on college students as research subjects, and to some extent their research agendas conspire to preserve literary reading's position in the hierarchy of types of reading. The role of interpretation and the importance of training students to interpret literature more acutely receive challenges in a body of work that focuses more directly on reading, but the values of literary reading are very much embedded in this scholarship.[53] Whether it stands out from ordinary reading because it defies convention, employs defamiliarizing techniques, slows the reader's pace, or flirts with open-endedness or indeterminacy, "literature" seems to these researchers a legitimate category of its own.[54] If we were able to agree where the boundary between trash and literary fiction lies (a line ignored by the National Endowment for the Arts' *Reading at Risk*), it might well be worthwhile to investigate readers' emotional responses to see if the assumptions about the values of quality literature indeed hold up under empirical scrutiny.

David S. Miall and Don Kuiken have an interest in discerning the effects of literary reading through empirical studies, and to that end Miall in particular has sought to define the qualities of literariness.[55] Indeed, most researchers in the field distinguish the effects of particular kinds of texts from others (literary from nonliterary texts; narratives from descriptive prose) in an effort to establish the consequences of reading culturally valued literature, or to understand how that reading differs from reading in general. Since my concern is empathy in particular, not literariness, I focus here on the role of empathy as Miall and Kuiken's work invokes it: a central feature of their experiments and a key trait of literary experience in their accounts. Miall writes that the two principal features responsible for the reader's engagement (through imagery and emotion) with a literary text "appear to be the dehabituating power of literary forms, and empathic projection into the lives of others through narrative" ("Necessity" 50). This pairing, which makes of empathy a companion to defamiliarization (Miall's "dehabituating power"), brings formal traits into conversation with readers' behavior. Supported by experiments done in collaboration with Don Kuiken, Miall sees foregrounding as a means for slowing the reader's pace, gaining his or her attention, and allowing for empathy as well as other insights into texts to transpire. In essence, following Miall, *unusual or striking representations in the literary text promote foregrounding and open the way to empathetic reading.*

This thesis might imply that the more difficult and discontinuous texts promote empathy more effectively than their simpler relatives. Miall and Kuiken take care to avoid this assertion, and indeed investigation of the range of responses evoked by works arranged on a scale of difficulty (particularly longer works) remains to be done. Virtually all of the empirical research on actual readers' responses uses literary short stories, very brief excerpts from novels, or lyric poetry. The application of findings from this research to the experience of immersion novel reading makes a leap that may not be substantiated by research in the future. Nonetheless, some findings may suggest relevant questions to pose about novel reading. For instance, on the question of difficulty's relation to empathy, one might ask whether it ever acts as a barrier to empathy? Is there a point at which alienation effects impede empathetic response, as Brecht believed. Some research reveals that a reader's ability to understand cause and effect precedes role taking and empathizing with characters.[56] This suggests that relatively basic aspects of narrative (coherent plot units and/or the relation between characterization and characters' actions) must be met for empathy to occur.

Psychologist Tammy Bourg proposes that comprehension of causal relations in literary stories assists cognitive empathy and that empathy with fictional characters leads to greater comprehension. Her experimental results from work with both adults and children confirm what others have also observed in studies of children, that empathizers make better readers in the first place than nonempathetic people. Not only does empathic ability at eight to nine years predict reading achievement at ten to eleven years,[57] but also sixth graders instructed in role-taking strategies better comprehend literary short stories. This research suggests that readers' innate or cultivated capacity for empathy helps their reading succeed and that obstacles to comprehension may be overcome by employing empathetic strategies. Further, individual dispositional differences among readers will affect which ones achieve narrative empathy during particular reading experiences and which ones do not. Some texts may be too strange to invite empathy in many readers. Defamiliarization may, as Brecht intuited, throw up obstacles to empathizing if it blocks or delays comprehension. The habitual role taker, or successful empathic reader, may possess the means to overcome these obstacles, but the techniques may not work: hence the reaction, "I just couldn't get into this story." Thus empathy in this research looks less like a phenomenon arising from readers' response to texts and more like a disposition that may be employed as a reading strategy. Tammy Bourg's research supports David S. Miall's contention in "Beyond the Schema Given" that emotional responsiveness enables understanding, but it also suggests that overall, texts may do more to get in the way of most readers' innate empathic tendencies than the other way around.

Human empathy, with its roots in primate behavior, developed long before we began mediating emotions through inscribed symbols. Indeed, as Paul Ekman observes, "Although there is no doubt that we can become emotional by reading about a stranger, it is amazing that something that came so late in the history of our species—written language—can generate emotions."[58] Ekman hypothesizes that written language changes into sensations, pictures, sounds, smells, and even tastes in our brains, subsequently to be "treated like any other event by the automatic-appraisal mechanisms to arouse emotions" (*Emotions Revealed* 35).[59] This is only one view of many on the highly contentious subject of the literary emotions.[60] It is important to keep in mind as we review the research on readers' emotional responses to literature that the underlying brain processes accounting for both empathic disposition and emotional responsiveness to fiction are still little understood.

Writing is a fairly recent development in human history, but our propensity for narrative and fiction may run nearly as deep as our use of language. As I argue earlier, *readers' perception of a text's fictionality plays a role in subsequent empathetic response, by releasing readers from the obligations of self-protection through skepticism and suspicion.* David Miall has noticed a similar effect. The fiction reader who suspends disbelief, Miall argues, encounters devices that vouch for a novel's fictionality and that are "capable of eliciting the decentering response of empathic projection" ("Necessity" 54). As a consequence of this fusion of fictional technique and reader response, novels and short stories have a special role in theories about readers' empathy. Miall and Kuiken have developed the Literary Response Questionnaire (LRQ) to discover the role of empathy, among seven features, in readers' orientation toward narrative fictional texts.[61] The questions rating empathy of the reader all focus on character identification and indicate the reader's strength of projective identification:

> Sometimes I feel like I've almost "become" a character I've read about in fiction.
> I sometimes have imaginary dialogues with people in fiction.
> When I read fiction I often think about myself as one of the people in the story.
> I sometimes wonder whether I have really experienced something or whether I have read about it in a book.
> I actively try to project myself into the role of fictional characters, almost as if I were preparing to act in a play.
> Sometimes characters in novels almost become like real people in my life.
> After reading a novel or story that I enjoyed, I continue to wonder about the characters almost as though they were real people. (LRQ 56)

These survey questions allow a researcher to discover dispositional differences among individual readers (with the caveat that self-reports may be biased by the subjects' perceptions of desirable answers). They place aspects of empathy (role taking) in a continuum with fantasy projection and behaviors that in other circumstances might be regarded as signs of mental illness. These questions might be used to ascertain the degree of a subject's empathic disposition and compared to reading comprehension. In the context of Miall and Kuiken's orientation toward the evaluation of textual features and their interaction with readers' feelings, an empathic response to fictional character contributes to a positive evaluation of the function of literary fiction. Miall approvingly cites studies of the influence of working-class writers on working-class readers[62] as well as present-day programs employed by localities to reduce criminal recidivism by encouraging literary and philosophical reading ("Necessity" 48–49). He concedes that the empirical evidence for good effects on novel readers is "too little known" and "so far lacks paradigmatic status" but believes that further empirical research will bear out the positive links between reading, experiencing empathy, and garnering socially beneficial results from literature's "innate power" ("Necessity" 55). Miall implies that *readers' empathy could produce verifiable results in the beliefs and actions of populations of actual readers.*

The Dutch scholar Jèmeljan Hakemulder has gone the furthest in reviewing the available experimental evidence and conducting his own studies on effects of literary reading, both of which he reports in his book, *The Moral*

Laboratory (2000).[63] Hakemulder's work is valuable not only because he reports some success in improving readers' role-taking skills with respect to culturally marginalized others, but also because he dispassionately reports the results of many studies. He avoids cherry-picking for positive ethical outcomes and frankly admits that the evidence for links between readers' empathy and even rudimentary forms of altruistic behavior is mixed at best. This does not prevent him from taking an upbeat position on the significance of positive results, even those garnered from studies of preschool children. Because Hakemulder breaks each contention down to a manageable dimension and examines the evidence for each, I present his judgments in selective sequence, emphasizing those that pertain to readers' empathy.

Observing Richard Rorty and other philosophers' arguments that reading narrative fiction "enhances the ability to make psychological inferences about the emotions, thoughts, and motives others have in certain situations" (*Moral Laboratory* 13), Hakemulder finds some supporting evidence and conducts experiments with students confirming that "enhancement of insight into human thoughts and emotions may bridge individual as well as cultural differences" (13). Like others working in this field, Hakemulder shares the bias against popular genres, especially women's romances. He feels that the role-taking effort required of romance readers "does not demand much reflection or imagination" (15). Thus only a certain kind of reading, complex enough to require imaginative effort on the readers' part, yields the valued difference-bridging insight. Indeed, following the lead of Allan Bloom's *The Closing of the American Mind* (1987), Hakemulder entertains the notion that "a diet of texts that offer oversimplified and shallow prototypes of emotional life may hamper the development of readers' imagination about or their view of other peoples' emotions" and "may even impair the development of their own emotions" (15). However, he reports that empirical work confirming the special power of complex literary characters over simple stereotypes in increasing readers' sophistication about others' emotions does not exist (15, 52). When it comes to literary texts that represent ethical problems "related to contemporary developments in society," Hakemulder finds some evidence of alterations in readers' norms and values (22, 53), but for the use of defamiliarization or foregrounding to enhance open-minded ethical reflection, or for readers' acquaintance with a wider range of moral perspectives on issues, Hakemulder finds no evidence yet (23, 53).[64]

Reviewing four studies[65] on the effects of reading narrative on aspects of empathy (including subsequent prosocial behavior), Hakemulder concludes that "reading narratives may enhance awareness of others' emotions and motives, but that it does not seem to stimulate self-denying behavior" (*Moral Laboratory* 32–33, 36). Specifically, two empathy studies showed character identification enhancing comprehension of others' feelings (57). However, the one study looking into effects on altruism found no changes as a result of encountering narratives (57). All of the empathy studies judged reliable by Hakemulder present by his own account "confounded" results because the experiments included activities other than reading, as for instance, role-taking games (38). More recent work by C. Daniel Batson and his collaborators affirms Hakemulder's belief that reading narratives can induce empathy for members of stigmatized groups, even when the individual is fictional.[66] Batson argues, "the belief that inducing empathy for a fictional character can be used to improve attitudes and stimulate concern for a stigmatized group may well be valid" ("Empathy, Attitudes, and Action" 1666). His observations come from an experimental situation in which research subjects exposed to an empathy-inducing interview with a drug addict were asked immediately afterward to allocate funds from a charitable student group (not real money from their own pockets) to organizations including an addiction counseling service. Like the confounded results in the research Hakemulder examines, the experimental design at least implies that there *ought* to a correlation between reading and giving, a condition that does not pertain to normal fiction reading circumstances.

This point raises a question seldom addressed by advocates of literature as a method for developing empathy. Reading alone (without accompanying discussion, writing, or teacherly direction) may not produce the same results as the enhanced reading that involves the subsequent discussion (what Wayne Booth calls *coduction*). As Hakemulder has it, "it remains to be seen whether empathic effects, moral development, and the enhancement of critical thinking can be achieved by reading, or whether these effects are due to a combination of reading and post-reading tasks" (49). Despite these mixed or inconclusive results, for Hakemulder, "readers' empathy forms the centerpiece of the Moral Laboratory, because . . . it is essential to the effects of reading narratives" (68). Hakemulder speculates that "readers may empathize with morally good characters and inhibit their empathy for morally bad characters"—a model in which readers' self-concept guides empathic response—and he also opines that "an engaged, empathic response to characters may cause changes in a [reader's] self-concept" (72, 84).[67] He acknowledges, however, that direct evidence of such changes is missing and that "effects of stories are probably marginal compared to other social influences" (84). A point he de-emphasizes is that most of the existing research features the empathetic responses of very young children, some of them not yet readers.

Hakemulder's own research focuses on adults, who may be assumed to be somewhat less malleable than young children engaged in role-taking exercises. Hakemulder finds good evidence that "reading stories with positive portrayals of outgroups leads to a reduction of social distance" (*Moral Laboratory* 98) and that a "narrative presentation causes stronger effects on our beliefs about the emotions and thoughts of others" than nonnarrative presentation of the same content (56, 107). Even though he concedes that reading stories may also introduce biases into social perceptions (54, 143, 162), invite cruel (unjust) responses to those perceived as harming victims (54), or teach incorrect beliefs about others (162), Hakemulder maintains that readers' empathy stimulates moral reflection and the adoption of a "habitual empathic attitude towards fellow humans" (154). Hakemulder keeps readers' empathy at the center of his Moral Laboratory by exaggerating the conclusiveness of the link between human empathy and altruistic behavior (93, 167). Even psychologist Martin Hoffman and others who investigate the empathy-altruism thesis describe a variety of responses to others' feeling states that often fail to lead to prosocial action. Hoffman does suggest in *Empathy and Its Development* that a particular subvariety of empathy, empathic guilt, may be excited by readers' exposure to fiction, making actual responsiveness to real people in need more likely. Hoffman thus argues that *novel reading may participate in the socialization and moral internalization required for transmutation of empathic guilt into prosocial action.* Hakemulder takes his inspiration not only from psychology, but also from philosopher Martha Nussbaum's endorsement of literary reading (167). Hakemulder's empirical approach checks his enthusiasm for Nussbaum's project, however, and he quite rightly calls for an effort to falsify theories of literature that promise positive outcomes (167). Scrutiny of the available research on the specific narrative techniques associated by theorists and actual readers with empathetic responses carries the project of cautious evaluation of the causes and consequences of readers' empathy a step further.

Empathetic Narrative Techniques

A variety of narrative techniques has been associated with empathy by narrative theorists and by discourse processing experts carrying out empirical research into literary reading. This section enumerates specific techniques or aspects of narrative fiction that receive emphasis in discussions of narrative empathy by scholars. The formal devices themselves are regarded as empathic in nature by some theorists and researchers, while for others the disposition of the reader toward the text can be measured by inquiring about particular consequences of literary reading. The observations made by this latter group often lead to speculations about narrative technique. Gathering the formal qualities and techniques of narrative fiction emphasized in the existing literature permits comparison with the strategies employed by authors attempting, by their own account, to evoke empathy in readers or to address the idea of empathy in their fiction. Mapping ostensibly empathetic narrative techniques also draws attention to the many aspects of narrative form that have not yet been associated with readers' empathy, but which ought not to be ruled out without careful consideration.

The most commonly nominated feature of narrative fiction to be associated with empathy is *character identification*. Specific aspects of characterization, such as naming, description, indirect implication of traits, reliance on types, relative flatness or roundness, depicted actions, roles in plot trajectories, quality of attributed speech, and mode of representation of consciousness, may be assumed to contribute to the potential for character identification and thus for empathy.[68] The link between readers' reports of character identification and their experiences of narrative empathy has not yet been explained. Furthermore, the nature of emotions invoked by fiction is hotly contested by philosophers (I hold a Deweyan view).[69] A close second for formal quality most often associated with empathy would be what narratologists call *narrative situation* (including point of view and perspective): the nature of the mediation between author and reader, including the person of the narration, the implicit location of the narrator, the relation of the narrator to the characters, and the internal or external perspective on characters, including in some cases the style of representation of characters' consciousness.[70] Many other elements of fiction have been supposed to contribute to readers' empathy, including the repetitions of works in series,[71] the length of novels,[72] genre expectations,[73] vivid use of settings,[74] metanarrative commentary,[75] and aspects of the discourse that slow readers' pace (foregrounding, uses of disorder, etc.).[76] The confirmation of many of the hypotheses about specific narrative techniques and empathy has yet to be undertaken in most cases, but the work that has been done as often fails fully to support the commonplaces of narratology as it authenticates them.[77] Whether this has to do with faulty experimental design, insufficient grasp of the nuances of narrative theory, or verifiable confutations of theory has yet to be discovered. The following paragraphs fill out a catalog of commonplaces with formal possibilities less often believed to elicit empathetic responses.

Character Identification

To begin with the necessary clarification, character identification is not a narrative technique (it occurs in the reader, not in the text), but a consequence of reading that may be precipitated by the use of particular techniques of characterization, as listed above.[78] These qualities have not been investigated in a comprehensive fashion. Marisa Bortolussi and Peter Dixon emphasize aesthetic qualities of narrative that open the way to personal involvement.[79] In contrast, Jèmeljan Hakemulder suggests that readers experiencing strong admiration of an author's writing style may engage less readily with the fictional world and its inhabitants (*Moral Laboratory* 73–74). Readers' personal involvement with a fictional character may (or may not) be contingent upon the use of a particular technique or the presence of certain representational elements that meet with their approval.[80] Keith Oatley believes that readers' personal experiences of patterns of emotional response provoke sympathy for characters, especially as readers identify with characters' goals and plans.[81] David S. Miall and Don Kuiken argue that emotional experiences of literature depend upon the engagement of the literary text with the reader's experiences,[82] but they emphasize foregrounding effects at the level of literary style that shake up conventions, slow the pace, and invite more active reading that opens the way for empathy.[83] Don Kuiken's research shows that readers who linked themselves to story characters through personal experiences were more likely to report changes in self-perception, if not actual empathy.[84] Max Louwerse and Kuiken suggest that empathy may work as a gap-filling mechanism, by which a reader supplements given character traits with a fuller psychologically resonant portrait.[85] Readers' judgments about the realism of the characters are supposed to have an impact on identification,[86] and the similarity of the reader to the character is widely believed to promote identification.[87] None of these phenomena, however, inhere in particular narrative techniques contributing to character identification.

A few techniques of characterization have actually been tested for their relation to readers' emotional responsiveness or empathy. Characters' involvement in a suspenseful situation provokes physiological responses of arousal in readers even when they disdain the quality of the narrative.[88] Plot-laden action stories have been shown to promote faster reading than narratives focusing on characters' inner lives,[89] which (if the assumptions about slower pace and greater empathy are accepted) may suggest greater reflectiveness on the part of character-focused readers, as Hakemulder supposes (*Moral Laboratory* 74). However, this does not account for the quick, apparently involuntary responses to particular plot situations inspired by trashy novels. Speedy reading may be a token of involvement in a character's fate, identification, and even empathy. With the exception of appraisal of causality, virtually nothing about the role of plot structure has been associated with readers' empathetic responses or tested in controlled settings.[90] Aspects of plot structure and narration that might have a role in invoking readers' empathy include the control of timing (pace), order (anachronies), the use of nested levels of narrative (stories within stories),[91] serial narrative, strong or weak closure, the use of subsidiary (supplementary, satellite) plot events, repetition, and gaps. Since each one of these structural categories contains an array of possibilities for characterization, their neglect leaves us with an incomplete picture of the devices whose use makes character identification possible.

Many aspects of characterization have not yet been tested in controlled experiments, despite their nomination by theorists. The naming of characters (including the withholding of a name, the use of an abbreviation or a role title in place of a full name, or allegorical or symbolic naming, etc.) may play a role in the potential for character identification. The descriptive language through which readers encounter characters is assumed to make a difference (content matters!), but what about grammar and syntax? Does the use of present tense (over the usual past tense) really create effects of immediacy and direct connection, as many contemporary authors believe? The old "show, don't tell" shibboleth of creative writing class remains to be verified: direct description of a character's emotional state or circumstances by a third-person narrator may produce empathy in readers just as effectively as indirect implication of emotional states through actions and context.[92] David S. Miall has suggested that characters' motives, rather than their traits, account for the affective engagement and self-projection of readers into characters,[93] though it remains unclear when, and at which cues, readers' emotional self-involvement jump-starts the process of interpretation. Bortolussi and Dixon believe that "transparency," or the judgment of characters' behavior as sensible and practical, contributes to identification (*Psychonarratology* 240). This may be too simple: even traditional novels are complex, polyvocal, and various, and Wayne Booth offers this sensible caution: "What we call 'involvement' or 'sympathy' or 'identification,' is usually made up of *many reactions* to author, narrators, observers, and other characters" (*Rhetoric* 158, my emphasis). Some way of accounting for the multiplicity of reactions making up a normal novel-reading experience needs to be devised in order to study the transition from distributed characterization in narrative fiction and readers' everyday synthesis of their reactions into an experience of character identification.[94]

This may require setting aside some common value judgments about techniques. For instance, E. M. Forster's famous distinction between flat and round characters operates within virtually every fictional world populated by more than one character. The typical critical preference for psychological depth expressed by roundness, in those characters 'capable of surprising in a convincing way' (*Aspects* 78), does not preclude empathetic response to flat characters, minor characters, or (as we have seen in the earlier discussion) stereotyped villains and antagonists. Drawing on the literature of cognitive social psychology, Richard J. Gerrig has suggested that readers are likely to make category-based judgments about fictional characters and to emphasize attributed dispositions of characters over their actual behavior in situations.[95] This theory suggests, as Forster intuited, that flat characters—easily comprehended and recalled—may play a greater role in readers' engagement in novels than is usually understood. Fast and easy character identification suffers in theorists' accounts of the reading process, which often privilege more arduous self-extension and analogical reasoning.

Patrick Colm Hogan, for instance, regards categorical empathy (with characters matching a reader's group identity) as the more prevalent form, while situational empathy, the more ethically desirable role taking, depends upon a reader's having a memory of a comparable experience, which is never guaranteed.[96] If situational empathy alone, as Hogan argues, leads to the ethics of compassion, then quick-match categorical empathy looks weaker and more vulnerable to bias through ethnocentrism or exclusionary thinking. We do not know, however, that categorical empathy does *not* lead to compassion, no more than we know the ethical results of situational empathy for fictional characters. Neither hypothesis has yet been tested. While literary critics and professionals value novels that unsettle convictions and contest norms, readers' reactions to familiar situations and formulaic plot trajectories may underlie their genuinely empathetic reactions to predictable plot events and to the stereotyped figures that enact them.[97] The fullness and fashion by which speech, thoughts, and feelings of characters reach the reader are very often supposed by narrative theorists to enhance character identification, as I discuss below, but relatively externalized and brief statements about a character's experiences and mental state may be sufficient to invoke empathy in a reader. Novelists do not need to be reminded of the rhetorical power of understatement, or indeed of the peril of revealing too much. Indeed, sometimes the potential for character identification and readers' empathy *decreases* with sustained exposure to a particular figure's thoughts or voice.[98]

Narrative Situation

A commonplace of narrative theory suggests that an internal perspective best promotes character identification and readers' empathy. Achieved through first-person self-narration, figural narration (in which the third-person narrator stays covert and reports only on a single, focal center of consciousness located in a main character), or authorial narration that moves omnisciently inside many characters' minds, an inside view should increase the chance of character identification. Wayne Booth, for instance, writes, "*If an author wants intense sympathy for characters who do not have strong virtues to recommend them, then* the psychic vividness of prolonged inside views will help him (*Rhetoric* 377–78, emphasis in original). Of course, the technique also works for characters in which readers have a natural rooting interest, and Booth's detailed account of how Jane Austen uses the inside view to promote sympathy for the flawed Emma is a classic of narrative theory (245–56). Booth asserts, "By showing most of the story through Emma's eyes, the author insures that we will travel with Emma rather than stand against her" (245). It is not an accident that Austen is one of the early masters of the technique of representation of characters' consciousness, *narrated monologue*, to allow smooth transitions between the narrator's generalizations about characters' mental states and transcriptions of their inner thoughts.[99] Also called free indirect discourse, narrated monologue presents the character's mental discourse in the grammatical tense and person of the narrator's discourse.

Subsequent theorists have agreed that narrated monologue has a strong effect on readers' responses to characters. David Miall specifically mentions free indirect discourse as a means of providing "privileged information about a character's mind" likely to cue literariness and invite empathic decentering ("Necessity" 54). Sylvia Adamson arrives independently at a similar point, arguing that narrated monologue should be understood as "empathetic narrative."[100] In Adamson's language, the representational technique and its ostensible effects fuse. *Quoted monologue* (also called interior monologue, the direct presentation of characters' thoughts in the person and tense of their speech) also has its champions, who regard the move into first person as invariably more authentic and direct than the more mediated or double-voiced narrated monologue. *Psycho-narration*, or the narrator's generalizations about the mental states or thoughts of a character, has fewer advocates perhaps because it is associated with traditional narratives such as epics. However, both Wayne Booth and Dorrit Cohn suggest that psycho-narration can powerfully invoke character identification, and Cohn points out that both poetic analogies and metaphors for feeling states (as Virginia Woolf often employs) require the use of psycho-narration.[101] Despite the frequent mention of narrated monologue as the most likely to produce empathy,[102] quoted monologue and psycho-narration also give a reader access to the inner life of characters. Most theorists agree that purely externalized narration tends not to invite readers' empathy.[103]

In addition to these speculations about modes of representing inner life, the person of the narration often seems likely to effect readers' responses to narrative fiction and its inhabitants. In particular, first-person fiction, in which the narrator self-narrates his or her own experiences and perceptions, is thought to invite an especially close relationship between reader and narrative voice. For instance, Franz Stanzel (a major theorist of narrative situation) believes that the choice of internal representation of the thoughts and feelings of a character in third-person fiction and the use of first-person self-narration have a particularly strong effect on readers.[104] Novelist and literary theorist David Lodge speculates that historical and philosophical contexts may explain the preference for first-person or figural third-person narrative voice: "In a world where nothing is certain, in which transcendental belief has been undermined by scientific materialism, and even the objectivity of science is qualified by relativity and uncertainty, the single human voice, telling its own story, can seem the only authentic way of rendering consciousness" (*Consciousness* 87).

However, the existing experimental results for such an association of technique and reaction are not robust. In several studies of Dutch teenagers, W. van Peer and H. Pander Maat tested the notion that first-person narration creates a "greater illusion of closeness . . . allowing the reader a greater and better fusion with the world of the character."[105] It did not. They conclude "it remains unclear why point of view has no more powerful and no more overall effect on readers, given the effort devoted by authors in order to create these devices that produce a point of view" ("Perspectivation" 152). While noting that readers certainly express preferences about point of view and prefer consistency over inconsistency, they found that enhancement of sympathy for protagonists through positive internal focalization actually weakened as teenagers matured (152–54). David Lodge concedes that the first-person voice "is just as artful, or artificial, a method as writing about a character in the third person," but he insists that it "creates an illusion of reality, it commands the willing suspension of the reader's disbelief, by modeling itself on the discourses of personal witness: the confession, the diary, autobiography, the memoir, the deposition" (*Consciousness* 87–88). I have been pursuing the opposite argument, that paratexts cuing readers to understand a work as fictional unleash their emotional responsiveness, in spite of fiction's historical mimicry of nonfictional, testimonial forms. For Lodge, the fact that first-person narration provides writers with the greatest opportunity for the creation of unreliable or discordant narrators plays on the practically automatic trust readers are assumed to bring to their part of the fiction-reading project,[106] but the effect of narrative unreliability can be added to the long list of techniques not yet tested for effects on readers' emotional responses.

To that list a further set of questions about narrative situation accrues. What effect (if any) does consonance (relative closeness to the related events) and dissonance (greater distance between the happening and the telling) have on readers of first-person, self-narrated fictions? Does a plural, communal narrative voice, a "we" narration, bring the reader into a perceptive circle in which empathetic reactions are more readily available? Does the use of second-person "you" narration, enhance the intimacy of the reading experience by drawing the reader and narrator close, or does it emphasize dissonance as it becomes clear that "you" can't include the reader?[107] In third-person fiction, does the use of a figural reflector, rather than an authorial (omniscient) narrator, make any difference in readers' emotional responsiveness to situations and character?[108] Does the location of the narrator inside (or outside) the story world affect readers' reactions to the content of the narration? Does a covert narrator, who scarcely does more than provide cues about characters' movements and speech, disinvite empathy for those characters, or invite readers to see the action with a greater sense of immediacy, as if it were a play, as Bortolussi and Dixon suggest (*Psychonarratology* 202)? In the most fully polyphonic novels, in which a single narrative perspective is simply not available to the reader, does readers' empathy increase, dwindle, or vary according to the page they are on? Finally, to bring the questions back to what happens in actual readers, if a narrative situation devised to evoke empathy fails to do so, does the fault lie in the reader or in the overestimation of the efficacy of the technique? While I am inclined to agree with Wayne Booth that no one ethical effect inheres in a single narrative device, the commentary on narrative form often asserts (or assumes) that a specific technique inevitably results in particular effects—political, ethical, emotional—in readers. These views, in my opinion, should be sub-jected to careful empirical testing before any aspect of narrative technique earns the label of "empathetic."

Real readers believe that they have legitimate empathetic experiences as a result of their encounters with fictional characters and the imagined worlds they move in. Indeed, when questioned, readers report a wide range of emotional responses to novels, not only the culturally sanctioned feel-ings of catharsis and compassion. Scholars studying the effects of reading using controlled experiments seek to verify their beliefs that fiction reading evokes empathy, which in turn results in improved attitudes toward oth-ers and prosocial action in the real world. Though the evidence for these effects is still scanty, the faith in the relationship between reading narrative and moral or social benefits is so strong and pervasive that it remains a bed-rock assumption of many scholars, philosophers, critics, and cultural com-mentators. Real readers are more hesitant about the results that reading has worked in them, however. Most readers value empathy as one of the desired experiences brought about by reading, and to that end they seek out novels that will allow imaginative identification with characters and immersion in vividly rendered fictional worlds so that they can feel with fiction. The mass appeal of empathetic fiction may not translate directly into altruism, but its very success in the marketplace demands attention.

4

Empathy in the Marketplace

Generations of novel readers have believed that books open up to them the perspectives of others who are markedly different, to their enrichment, and this belief has been woven into the literary history of the novel.[1] In a typical recent example, Mark Edmundson writes, "The rise of the novel coincides with a realization expressed, or perhaps created, by the development of democracy. That realization is of the great span of individuals to be found in the world, of the sheer proliferation of divergent beings" (*Why Read?* 69). The fiction reader, who in Edmundson's formulation is likely to be a citizen of a democratic state, develops virtuous understandings of otherness and diversity. Certainly, a reader uninterested in people will be unlikely to develop a habit of novel reading. Through fictional characters, we can imaginatively inhabit the circumstances, dilemmas, and desires of person-like figures, some of whom represent socially or temporally remote people. We often respond to characters as if they were human beings like us, and we have to learn the professional convention of treating them as "word masses" rather than as people.[2] Some, of course, like the characters of fantasy, don't even resemble humans, but that seems to prove no obstacle to our imagining and feeling for them.

The range of fictional characters (synthetic, thematic, and mimetic, according to James Phelan) affords readers many different kinds of opportunity to stretch imaginatively.[3] I argue in the preceding chapter that characters need not be realistic, particularly lifelike, or even fully rounded to invite engagement on the part of readers. Whether we feel with characters in the emotional accord of empathy, identify with them through deliberate role taking, or experience spontaneous character identification, we come away from engrossed reading with the sense of knowing more about others, and sometimes also about the alien cultures and times called up by fictional worlds. I recall feeling that way in different decades of my reading career about Arthur Golden's *The Memoirs of a Geisha* (1997), Nevil Shute's *The Pied Piper* (1942), and Henry Treece's *Horned Helmet* (1963), so I associate the sensation with historical fiction, a hybrid of realism and romance. For my mother, an avid reader, nineteenth-century Russian novels in translation created a lifelong sense of connection to a country and people remote from her experience. Readers' testimony documents the power of fiction to persuade us, contrary to fact, that we really understand individuals and worlds of which we have no direct knowledge.

Needless to say, the insights and convictions that we garner from reading fiction may be dead wrong. We may learn prejudices from fiction as we share others' biased perspectives. Philosophers interested in narrative ethics have tended to emphasize the positive effects of imaginative extension, and they have also repeatedly endorsed the worthiness of canonical realistic fiction. As chapter 2 documents, however, worries about the consequences of character identification and the vicarious emotional experiences offered by fiction trouble the literary history of the novel from the eighteenth century to contemporary condemnations of women's light romances. A common way of attempting to regulate readers' unruly responses to fiction has been to distinguish "good" or "serious" literature from popular fiction, especially genre fiction.[4] However, no empirical research yet demonstrates that the effects of reading "highbrow" serious literary fiction differ from the results of immersion in "middlebrow" or even "lowbrow" mass-market fiction.[5] In fact, it would be difficult to say for certain which fictional works exemplify these categories of taste, though that hasn't stopped the disparagement of certain genres and their readers.

What drives the desire to limit the positive consequences of reading to literary fiction? Do we wish to promote or sequester valued books because we believe in the good they do? Or do we wish to curtail the deleterious effects of reading popular fiction? Could our arguments about merit reflect our reading preferences, dressed up to represent "tradition" or "innovation"? How do we account for the many texts (such as the work of Dickens) that have migrated from popular fiction to canonical literature? Trends in the academy play a role, but how much influence on regular readers' behavior can really be attributed to the opinions and teaching of literature professors like myself, or an earlier generation of professors whose taste differed? These and other questions trouble the effort to verify the merits of novel reading through prophylactic categorization.

Rather than assuming that some genres promote desirable changes in readers while others debase them, we should ask whether a relationship between kind and effect could be confirmed. Genre may enhance *or* play down the effect of connecting with characters that seem like alien others. Certain genres of fiction may depend upon readers' strong recognitions of sameness or contemporary relevance. What do we crave more, realism or romance? We may find in fiction confirmation of our sense of self and social experiences in novels that invite comfortable recognition perturbed only by plot, or we may escape from reality into a richly furnished alternative world whose characters' strivings strike heroic notes. These are not the only alternatives, but the descendents of romance (fantasy, science fiction, thrillers, horror, westerns, many mysteries and historical novels, and of course women's romances) vie with varieties of realism, and with hybrid forms in which elements of romance and realism mix, for the attention of readers.[6]

It is not beyond us to know that success in the marketplace more often correlates with lowbrow status, that respectful reviews and small sales to educated readers suggest highbrow status, and that widespread adoption by book groups labels a novel as middlebrow. Even in a commercial context in which a significant percentage of books bought are works of fiction, a very tiny percentage of all the books published receive the official approbation of a review in a magazine, journal, or paper.[7] Gender inflects estimations of cultural status, with male majorities among both book reviewers and authors of books reviewed in the major weeklies and dailies.[8] Sales figures and library circulation data provide us with a rough sense of adult fiction readers' preferences: in Great Britain, general fiction is the most popular category overall, with mystery and detective stories and light romances following, and historical fiction coming in a more distant fourth.[9] These categories of borrowing accounted for about 93 percent of the total of fiction checked out in the U.K. (according to statistics compiled in 1999). In order of their significantly lesser popularity, war stories, science fiction, westerns, horror fiction, humor, and short stories made up the remaining 7 percent (*Bestsellers* 247). These statistics do not separate ambitious literary fiction and canonical novels from "general fiction," but very few books of these kinds become bestsellers.

The exceptions to this general rule deserve attention. Film adaptations can propel literary fiction, including classics, onto best-seller lists. For instance, Michael Cunningham's novel *The Hours*, which had won several prestigious awards and had been enthusiastically reviewed when it came out in 1998, sold 636,000 copies in 2003. A year earlier, the celebrated 2002 film version of *The Hours*, starring Meryl Streep and Nicole Kidman, had collected half a dozen Oscar nominations (Kidman won for best actress). Perhaps even more impressively, the film version of Virginia Woolf's life contained within *The Hours* sent 425,000 buyers back to Woolf's 1925 novel *Mrs. Dalloway* (McEvoy and Maryles, "Paperback Bestsellers" 584). I speculate that many book groups and college students read the two novels back-to-back in 2003, but Amazon.com's automated recommendation system, which pairs books and offers a discount on joint purchases, may well have played a role in boosting Woolf's sales. The annual Booker Prize winner normally sells very well, but not always well enough to reach the top 10 in the paperback bestseller list.[10] Other prizes, early notices in mass-market outlets such as *Good Morning America*, and adoption by Book of the Month Club can give a novel a chance to catch on: Alice Sebold's *The Lovely Bones* (2002) and Sue Monk

Kidd's *The Secret Life of Bees* (2002) went from modest first print runs to million sellers in just a year.[11] Exceptionally, Oprah Winfrey's selection of a novel for her Book Club can propel even a quite difficult literary novel (such as Toni Morrison's *Beloved* [1987] and *Song of Solomon* [1977]) right to the top the best-seller lists. Winfrey's imprimatur grants middlebrow status to works that would otherwise seem either too difficult or beneath notice.[12] However, as Jonathan Franzen notoriously emphasized when he wished to keep Oprah's signature sticker off the cover of his novel *The Corrections* (2001), becoming an Oprah book also brands a work as especially suitable for female readers. For a DeLillo *manqué*, increased readership does not necessarily compensate for the association with the topicality and emotional invitation that Oprah books promise their empathetic readership.

No individual has more influenced the book purchasing and reading of adult Americans in recent years than Oprah Winfrey.[13] At a conservative estimate, she was responsible for the purchase and reading of twenty-one million copies of works of adult fiction in the United States, between 1996 and 2002. The figure soars when one adds library patrons and international buyers to the tally. Now that Oprah's Book Club has returned after a brief hiatus, in a new form featuring backlisted books by dead authors, the evidence of Winfrey's power to shape Americans' reading has become clearer than ever. When she selected John Steinbeck's 1952 novel *East of Eden*, it immediately shot to the #1 spot on the best-seller list and sold 1.6 million copies in 2003 (McEvoy and Maryles, "Paperback Bestsellers" 584). A less dramatic but still impressive result occurred when Winfrey chose Alan Paton's *Cry, the Beloved Country* (1948), a novel that had sold a respectable 80,000 copies in 2002, no doubt as a result of its presence on school and university syllabi. With Winfrey's attention, Paton's novel sold 617,000 copies in 2003 (584). Sales figures and television ratings combine to suggest that around half a million adults, mostly women, read each of her selections. An astonishing thirteen million viewers tuned in to her book club segments, and anecdotal evidence suggests that Winfrey influenced some of these viewers to resume reading or to become novel readers for the first time (Rooney, *Reading with Oprah* 126).

Given the dramatic drop in the number of novel readers, especially among men, rational inquiry into the effects of reading ought not to be limited to the putative effects of serious literary fiction, a thin slice of the action by any measure. Attention to the interests of the middlebrow reader, who populates the book clubs and buys most of the fiction sold in the United States and Great Britain, suggests that she seeks empathetic reading experiences.[14] I propose that novels inviting empathy do better in the marketplace (perhaps because they get better word-of-mouth recommendations) and that empathetic reading habits make up a core element of middlebrow readers' self-image. This self-reinforcing pair of observations (empathy sells books; empathetic readers seek books that will allow them to feel with characters) complicates the attempt to discover what novel reading does to and for readers. Narrative empathy may be less influential as an effect of reading and more important as a sought-after experience—tantamount to a precondition for success with a large segment of the book-buying and novel-reading public. The opportunity to read empathetically certainly seems to matter to tastemaker Oprah Winfrey.

Before turning to a case study of one of the last of the original Oprah Book Club selections, Rohinton Mistry's novel *A Fine Balance* (1995, selected in 2002), this chapter examines a belief about fiction that is normally presented as a baseline assumption: Does novel reading really extend the empathetic circle? The emphasis by readers, authors, and the novels themselves on a common emotional heritage and the universality of human feelings promises that novel reading can bridge social, cultural, economic, and geographical gaps that might otherwise impede empathy. Though the sharing of feeling with fictional characters may not translate into verifiable prosocial action on behalf of suffering others, as some authors and psychologists hope,[15] people validate their reading by honoring novels' renovating virtue, which is understood to operate through imaginative extension. The potential of fiction to open readers' hearts and minds to markedly different others invites an understanding of storytelling as a moral technology. Does it work?

Does Novel Reading Extend the Empathetic Circle?

When we read novels, we often experience empathic reactions to characters and their situations. The analogy with the way real people invoke our emotional responses inspires the idea that we may learn how to respond to those who are different from us through the safe trial runs of fiction reading.[16] Jèmeljan Hakemulder reports that some studies show reading enhances the ability to make inferences about others' thoughts, feelings, and motives, which confirms both commonsense assumptions and evolutionary biological arguments about the uses of fiction (Hakemulder, *Moral Laboratory* 13, 50–52). Making accurate inferences about others' thoughts, feelings, and motives does not at all guarantee that a reader shares, supports, or regards them as anything but tools to be employed in gaining the upper hand over others, however. Empathy may be used as Robert MacNamara presents it in Errol Morris's 2004 documentary *The Fog of War*: "empathize with your enemy." MacNamara states in the film, "We must try to put ourselves inside their skin and look at us through their eyes, just to understand the thoughts that lie behind their decisions and their actions." Though MacNamara claims that successful empathizing led to a peaceful resolution to the Cuban Missile Crisis, this kind of empathy exercised for strategic purposes differs from the socially beneficial imaginative extension as a source of altered attitudes, upon which Hakemulder focuses in *The Moral Laboratory*. Hakemulder's own experiments suggest that reading stories featuring positive depictions of members of "outgroups" leads to a reduction of social distance. Like the empathy studies he discusses, however, his own work complicates literary response by engaging subjects in role-taking tasks, which may in fact *cause* the reductions in social distance he records (*Moral Laboratory* 98–100). Hakemulder's study of the empathetic effects of story reading, in which he employs standardized empathy tests and omits role-taking exercises, produced no evidence of a correlation, though it did suggest that stories can introduce biases into social perceptions (143). Empathy with persecuted victims can increase hatred of their tormenters, which may then be extended wholesale to a whole group, including to innocent members.

A positive way of putting Hakemulder's findings emphasizes the boost that the incorporation of role-taking exercises into the teaching of fiction gives ("Foregrounding" 195). Reading alone, or reading brief extracts or short stories, may well be insufficient to extend the empathetic circle to include members of outgroups. Hakemulder found that reading short (translated) excerpts from Salman Rushdie's novel *The Satanic Verses* (1988) (and paraphrases that deleted Rushdie's baroque language) failed to influence a group of sociology students' opinions about immigrants ("Foregrounding" 204). Literature students showed different responses to the literary version (as opposed to the manipulated summary), but their scores on scales measuring perceptions of immigrants' adaptation problems, experiences of intolerance and low acceptance, and motivation by necessity were not altered by reading Rushdie (206). An earlier study conducted by Canadian education specialists John Kehoe and Charles Ungerleider found neither reduction in dogmatism nor increase in empathy as a result of reading passages from John Marlyn's novel *Under the Ribs of Death* (1957), a book about the experiences of Hungarian immigrants in Winnipeg ("Effects of Role Exchange" 48–52). Changing students' empathic perceptiveness to include ethnically diverse others, and reducing their discriminatory attitudes and intolerance seem to require more than simple novel reading. These preliminary studies do not disprove the widely held belief that novel reading extends readers' sense of the humanity of members of outgroups, but they fail to lend empirical support to the popular theory.

Other kinds of evidence may be brought to bear on the question, however. I have suggested above that the very fictionality of novels licenses our feeling responsiveness because it frees us from responsibility to protect ourselves through skepticism and suspicion. Fiction may evoke empathy in part because it *cannot* make direct demands for action. We readers find ourselves in a position even less implicated than real-world bystanders. We may ask, with the philosophers, how strong and authentic are our reactions under these special, fictional circumstances? Can we say that fleeting shared feeling matters if it does not result in changed attitudes or deliberate actions? To begin to answer this question, I turn to the testimony of readers, gathered from my own students.

While a majority of my students believe that "if everyone still actually read, there would be a lot more awareness of people's feelings and needs,"[17] and some report reinforcement of beliefs through reading, very few are able to report actual effects of reading on their behavior. The effects, when discernable, rarely impel the reader far beyond their comfort zones. For instance, one student writes, "After reading [Bharati Mukherjee's] *Desirable Daughters* I was reminded that no matter our backgrounds or appearances we all have similar emotions and concerns. It really made me want even more to be sure that I looked everyone in the eye as I walked by and said hello."[18] On a small rural campus that prides itself on its friendly Speaking Tradition, this resolution could be carried out easily, and I hope that the student acted on her impulse. Another student reports, "Whenever I read works that emphasize family (like [Edwidge Danticat's] *Krik? Krak!* or [Mukherjee's] *Desirable Daughters*) I always make sure to call my parents immediately. Especially since I now live so far from home, our family time is limited and easily pushed down the list."[19] Like the first comment, this one reports a good side effect of reading, but not one that directly alters behavior to those outside the community or family circle. Both cases record the opposite directionality from empathetic extension, in fact. Reading texts about characters from distinctively different cultures brings to the surface these readers' desires to make human contact with people in their immediate community or kinship network.

While older adults often mention being inspired to travel to a faraway place by a novel, the second most common view among my college-aged students emphasizes internal changes, as opposed to outward actions: "Novels often make me think very hard for days on a certain subject. I often change my views according to novels and adopt views from novels into the mix of my own but I can't say that any particular novel has moved me to any direct or specific course of action. Yet I have been moved to adopt stances on issues/feelings that have indirectly changed my outlooks/behaviors."[20] The most common opinion among college-aged readers affirms that while an empathetic reading experience *might* make a reader do something, it hasn't done so as far they can recall. This anecdotal gathering of opinions confirms a surprising result in a recent empathy study conducted by psychologists Krystina A. Finlay and Walter G. Stephan.[21] While discovering that reading about commonplace discrimination or receiving empathy instructions improved attitudes toward both in-group and out-group members, they unexpectedly discovered that neither manipulation affected the *reactive* empathy "usually associated with an increased willingness to help others or with more positive attitudes toward others" ("Improving" 1731). As my review of Hakemulder's work has already suggested, reading by itself may be insufficient to extend the empathetic circle beyond its predictable reach of family, community, and tribe.

The explanation for this underperformance of fiction may lie in the very textuality of novels. Psychologist Martin Hoffman believes that verbally mediated empathic arousal should be expected to evoke a weaker response than when we witness another's emotions in person. He attributes this weakness to three differences. First, the act of reading (actually processing, comprehending, and picturing the text's contents) takes a longer time than seeing someone in distress. Second, reading requires more mental effort; and third, the technology of prose puts psychological distance between sender and receiver (*Empathy and Moral Development* 50). However, Hoffman also speculates that exposure to films and novels such as *The Grapes of Wrath* (1939) or *Les Miserables* (1862) could add an "empathy-charged, need-based component to one's distributive justice principles" (259). In other words, a reader might find a moving novel altering her values about how rewards and punishments should be allocated.[22] Hoffman points out that film and novelistic narrative have the advantage of offering a reader the opportunity to empathize with another's "entire life (hard work, expectations, disappointment) and respond, where appropriate, with empathic feelings of injustice" (259). This comment suggests that fiction in the *Bildungsroman* tradition (novels of development relating a whole life story), naturalist fiction (emphasizing the inexorable determination of experience by environment), and realistic social fiction (focusing on identifiable social problems) may have a special role to play in cultivating empathy. Not all genres of narrative emphasize the plot trajectory implied by Hoffman's telegraphic "hard work, expectations, disappointment," however. Would novels in other genres offer readers comparable opportunities? Did Rushdie's novel fail to alter Dutch students' opinions of immigrants because of its phantasmagoria, its ornate prose style, its irony, or its unrealistic conventions?[23] Studies comparing the effects on the opinions of readers could be designed to discover if particular genres garner stronger empathetic effects (or alteration of readers' opinions) than others. So far, these studies do not exist.[24] The testimony of readers and their behavior in real and virtual bookstores (and libraries), however, suggest some avenues for future investigation.

One direction would be to examine the disproportionate gendering of novel reading as a female activity as aliteracy rates accelerate. I have already commented on the gender gap in fiction reading: women outnumber men among novel readers in western countries (not just in the United States: in the European community, an average of 45 percent of citizens described themselves as *book* readers, not necessarily fiction readers; but 65 percent of the book buyers are women, and they do prefer fiction).[25] Reading has declined in Europe and North America in terms of both numbers of readers and in numbers of hours spent reading, but the decline has been sharper among men, making women a greater majority of the remaining readers. One result of this phenomenon may be summarized this way: in the early twenty-first century, female gender has become a constitutive feature of the middlebrow reader.[26]

Since publishers and book professionals, equipped with market research data, claim that women do 70 percent or more of the book purchasing, the shift in demographics may be assumed to have an influence on which novels get published, promoted, and widely distributed.[27] Choosing a future bestseller or even solid mid-list performer is not an exact science, however, so the desires of reading public cannot be regarded as dictating the qualities of published fiction. The way an audience represents its taste in books or its reading habits may nonetheless influence the market over time. One notable development that indicates publishers' responsiveness to middlebrow readers can be spotted in the availability of reading-group guides (online and in special edition paperbacks aimed at reading group members) for a wide range of fiction from popular bestsellers to canonical classics.

At Oprah.com, a curious reader can find queries, suggestions, and expert answers to frequently asked questions about her featured novel. While some of these materials inevitably carry a whiff of academic instruction, they also reveal the contours of Oprah Winfrey's interests and the preferences of her readers. Typical Oprah reading-group questions ask for evaluations of characters, delve into their qualities and feelings, and pose role-taking scenarios. Asking readers to compare or contrast their real-world experiences with the novel's representation augments the role-taking exercises with elaboration of human connections despite different circumstances. Finally, the questions often invite readers to apportion blame for the social ills or unfortunate events of the story. Winfrey's readers are invited to make moral evaluations of the real-world issues embedded in novels, not just the actions of characters within fictional worlds. Though other questions focus on images and symbols, Winfrey's discussion cleaves quite closely to stages of empathetic response and often dramatizes for viewers the effects of reading, represented by readers who have written in and have been selected to appear on the show or have dinner with the author. This emphasis endorses Winfrey's evident belief that reading fiction promotes positive changes in her viewers' lives. Looking closely at the appreciation and analysis of a single book chosen by Winfrey can only reveal a part of the complex profile of the new middlebrow readership, but their emphases confirm the perception that empathy matters to many novel readers. In the section that follows, I consider the central role of empathetic response for Oprah's reading-group participants.

A Fine Balance and Oprah's Book Club:
Breaking Us Out of Our Comfort Zones

> Oprah: Has anybody read a book like this before? I've never encoun-
> tered pages that took me so far, and removed me from my own way
> of life and way of thinking the way *A Fine Balance* did.[28]

Rohinton Mistry's novel, *A Fine Balance*, may at first glance appear an
unlikely choice for Oprah's Book Club, which most often featured women
writers' books.[29] Though Winfrey does not shy away from tough subjects
or difficult prose, by her own account, she responded to the book as an
unusual reading experience. By 2002, many readers were already enjoying
the craze for works by South Asian writers ("Indo-chic"), which received a
boost from the celebration of fifty years of Indian independence in 1997.
Arundhati Roy's *The God of Small Things* (1997), Vikram Seth's *A Suitable
Boy* (1993), and Jhumpa Lahiri's *Interpreter of Maladies* (1999) were just
the most widely read of a rich field of fiction including the works of Salman
Rushdie, Anita Desai, R. K. Narayan, and many others. Few of these novels or collections of short stories presented such a stark representation of
poverty and exploitation as Rohinton Mistry's *A Fine Balance*. A critically
acclaimed, very long novel, *A Fine Balance* had already won the Giller Prize,
the Commonwealth Writers Prize, and the Los Angeles Times Book Prize
for Fiction, and had been shortlisted for the Booker Prize, the International
IMPAC Dublin Literary Award, and the Irish Times International Fiction
Prize by the time Winfrey announced its selection on November 30, 2001.
In short, it had been marked as a highbrow's novel, a modern-day Hardy or
Zola, before Winfrey resituated it and brought it to a broader middlebrow
audience.

A Fine Balance holds the distinction of being the only postcolonial novel
from outside the Americas that Winfrey selected for her readers.[30] Contrary
to the impression that reading the likes of Salman Rushdie is a highbrow
pursuit, many novels by writers from all around the globe fit the bill for
middlebrow pleasure reading.[31] Postcolonial novels differ from the usual
reading group fare only in the degree to which they invite readers to faraway worlds and unfamiliar cultures. As Nico Israel has observed, many
postcolonial writers "shun the low affect irony associated with postmod-
ernism" ("Globalization" 4). Wide readers of world fiction will be able to
think of many contemporary postcolonial novels that seem suitable for discussion by Winfrey: Keri Hulme's *the bone people* (1983), Sunetra Gupta's
Memories of Rain (1992), Bharati Mukherjee's *Jasmine* (1989), Anita Desai's
Fire on the Mountain (1977), and Tsitsi Dangarembga's *Nervous Conditions*
(1988) immediately spring to mind. She appears to prefer American fiction,
but by her own account, Winfrey made the selection of *A Fine Balance* at
what seemed like an unusually appropriate time for reflection about a wider

world: "After September 11, I started taking more time for myself. I read [*A Fine Balance*] and thought 'This will do, in some ways, what September 11 has done. Take us out of our own little shell. Expose us to a whole other world out there going on beyond our backyards.' And it did exactly that" ("Discussion").

A Fine Balance provides an unremittingly grim depiction of life in an unnamed Indian seaside city (recognizably Bombay) during the 1975–1977 State of Emergency. This disruption of democratic governance occurred when Indira Gandhi, having been convicted of election fraud, ruled by dictatorship, suspended civil liberties, and dealt with overpopulation by sterilizing eleven million people, many of them by force. Most Americans do not recall this traumatic period for India. As Winfrey comments on the show, "That's the year I graduated from college . . . we were all in our own little worlds in 1975 . . ." ("Discussion"). *A Fine Balance*'s confronting of contemporary events that transpired during many of her viewers' lifetimes, but failed to make a lasting impression, assists in Winfrey's goal of "breaking us out of our comfort zones." Winfrey's treatment of the novel emphasizes role taking with its sympathetic characters and the difficult search for an adequate moral judgment about social evils affecting those characters. Her show also elucidates the realities lying behind Mistry's representation of poverty, violence, and caste prejudice.

Mistry's narrator provides an overarching perspective on the period of the Emergency through focus on four major characters, the widow Dina, the student Maneck, and the tailors Ishvar and Om. Within individual sections, the third-person narrative reflects a tighter focus on the perspective of a particular character or pair, so the novel provides a variety of opportunities for character identification. Dina, who struggles against cultural expectations for widows, and Maneck, who strives to justify his parents' sacrifice in sending him to school, make fairly accessible bridges for American readers. However, the two untouchable tailors and their acquaintances on the street push these readers to extend the empathetic circle to suffering others who would normally seem remote and incomprehensible. Mistry insists on linking the four lives he narrates, and he uses the emblem of a quilt to make their connection vivid. Dina creates this frugal artwork out of scraps, recording the friends' good times and bad, and defying the barriers of caste that would normally separate them. She intends it to give it as a wedding present to Om. Unfortunately, when Ishvar and Om get rounded up in a sweep of the slums, Om is not given a simple vasectomy in the sterilization camp. Instead, he suffers castration. Ishvar, who has only been sterilized, gets infected and loses his legs. Mistry's last mention of the hopeful emblem of the quilt occurs when it can be glimpsed cushioning the legless beggar on his wheeled cart.

In *A Fine Balance*, Mistry's claustrophobic determinism leaves its lovingly depicted central characters Ishvar and Om no escape routes. Mistry relates their attempt to improve their lot from leatherworking, the task of the untouchable caste to which they are born. Ishvar and Om succeed for a while, but true to the naturalist logic that governs Mistry's story, they get pounded down into degraded conditions and end the novel as maimed beggars. We read on, horrified, as Mistry loads yet another tragedy, gleaned from newspaper accounts of atrocities, abuses, corruption, and crime, onto Ishvar and Om's frail shoulders. This runs a risk of compromising the novel's realism, as a contributer to a SASIALIST listserv discussion complains: "The novel telescopes dozens of experiences suffered by many from the disadvantaged groups into the lives of two people, and by making it all happen to the two, it transforms the tale into melodrama. It made the suffering appear so commonplace as to be dismal."[32] Another contributor to the SASIALIST discussion laments that the powerful representation of suffering emphasizes how little has changed in over two decades: "What bothers me is that these things happened, and unfortunately still happen. . . . Nothing has changed, no lesson has been learnt due to the 'emergency.' That is what I find to be extremely disturbing, because it nullifies any hope I would have otherwise had."[33] These readers, knowledgeable about India and familiar with its modern history, respond to the novel's ambitious representation of injustice with ambivalence. Both complaints, that hope suffers nullification and that melodrama mutes the response to suffering, assume that successful representation *might* do something positive with readers' emotional responses, but deny that *A Fine Balance* achieves that goal.

For *Oprah* viewers, the show anticipates a different kind of response: simple disbelief. In film sequences of the slums of Bombay and in discussions of the condition of India's poorest citizens, the show insists upon the verisimilitude of Mistry's novel. Discussions with participants chosen for their first-hand knowledge of India pass on to Winfrey's viewers some of the nitty-gritty details about caste prejudice, for instance, and forcible sterilization during the internal Emergency. The task that remains is to forge a meaningful response to this unwelcome knowledge. The characters may have no escape routes, but Winfrey emphasizes the moral value of struggling to feel kinship with despised others. In a discussion with Mistry, Winfrey exclaims, "It's different, though, when you have to open your home, your porch, your veranda, to someone who you didn't even think was in your touching zone. That's a whole bigger thing." Rohinton Mistry responds with a gloss of his intentions, "It's a big stretch, what you just mentioned. It's a big stretch. And many big stretches will reduce the amount of injustice in the world. There's no other way than making the big stretch" (Oprah and Rohinton, "Discussion"). Winfrey's presentation of *A Fine Balance* thus enables the viewer to connect the dots between an emotional response through character identification and the goal of reducing injustice in the real world. Her representative readers, featured on the show in conversation with Winfrey and the author, strive to make that connection, with varied results.

Among Winfrey's featured readers, "Madhavi" has the closest ties to India and struggles with the difficulty of assigning blame or finding solutions to the problems Mistry describes: "This book was really hard for me. I felt like everyone who struggled and tried in this book failed. And I had a hard time understanding, because I can't get through my day thinking that no matter what you do, it isn't going to help in the end. . . . And the fact that no one is responsible. There's no clear villain!" (Madhavi, "Discussion"). Madhavi's original letter to Winfrey emphasizes the difficulty of pinning down right and wrong. The letter shows a strong sense of shared humanity but honestly comments on the impulse to distance oneself from others' suffering: "Every page was emotionally exhausting. . . . This book opened my eyes to how difficult it is to define wrong and right on an individual level. It showed me the remarkable interconnectedness of everyone and everything and the complex, multifaceted nature of human beings, particularly where there is rampant poverty, with religious and social norms that allow human suffering to be reasoned away. But maybe that's what one needs to be able to [do to] survive" (Madhavi, "Discussion"). Perhaps because Madhavi feels closer to the country and culture being described, the pressure to understand root causes and address real suffering results in an impasse. The empathetic response of this reader reaches the mature phase that Martin Hoffman describes as an empathic sense of injustice, but it does not result in a clear program for action. Ironically, the compelling representation of injustice frustrates this reader's wish to blame a villain.

For "Mohammed," a second participant in Oprah's show on *A Fine Balance*, the novel's scene was familiar as a result of four periods of service in the slums of Bombay. Having actually met and worked with real people like the characters in the novel, Mohammed asserts confidently, "I know them intimately. They are real. They are still there" (Mohammed, "Discussion"). Mohammed also shies away from a prosocial response to the novel, perhaps because he has already given of himself in earlier years, as his original letter suggests. Mohammed's particular experience of the realism of Mistry's representation leads him to insist, in that letter, on the universality of the emotions experienced by the characters: "The book is deeply entrenched in Indian themes, peppered with Indian slang and set in contemporary and local political events indigenous to the Indian sub-continent. Yet the appeal of the book is universal. Look at its worldwide sales. . . . Human emotions, regardless of nationalities, are universal. Grief, joy, hope and despair know no cultural boundaries. Herein lies Mistry's skill. Though the events may be foreign and some linguistic references incomprehensible, the reader rarely stumbles, because the emotions that the characters elicit are intuitively recognizable, thus making the characters archetypal" (Mohammed, "Discussion"). For Mohammed, the novel succeeds because it presents recognizable, verisimilar characters in situations that not only resonate with his experience, but also reach out to a wider audience through feelings that any reader would know. The representation of the characters' emotions achieves universality though the book itself is "entrenched" in an India Mohammed knows firsthand.

In the context of Oprah's Book Club, the possibility of universal feelings, shared by humankind, is a baseline assumption. This popular belief echoes the attitude of many psychologists toward human emotion, but it differs markedly from the view of emotion as culturally constructed that holds sway in many academic disciplines. (I take up this debate at greater length in chapter 6, "Contesting Empathy.") In support of the sort of universality of feeling that Mohammed notes, we may consider what psychologist Dylan Evans writes about our reading: "When we read poems and novels written by authors from different cultures, we recognize the emotions they describe. If emotions were cultural inventions, changing as swiftly as language, these texts would seem alien and impenetrable" (*Emotion* 8). The logic of this statement may be reversed in order to illuminate Mohammed's insistence on the archetypal emotions evoked by *A Fine Balance*: were we not to find recognizable feelings, then whole cultures and peoples, not just texts, might seem alien and impenetrable. Certainly many people *do* find other cultures, countries, and individuals alien, strange, and threatening. This fact only increases the importance of recognizing universal feelings, as a second excerpt from Dylan Evans suggests: "Our common emotional heritage binds humanity together, then, in a way that transcends cultural difference. In all places, and at all times, human beings have shared the same basic emotional repertoire. Different cultures have elaborated on this repertoire, exalting different emotions, downgrading others, and embellishing the common feelings with cultural nuances, but these differences are more like those between two interpretations of the same musical work, rather than those between different compositions" (*Emotions* 8). We find a not very subtle recipe for achieving universal harmony embedded in Evans's metaphors. Whether or not human emotions are universal, the expression of *belief in universality* carries with it an optimistic program for transcending cultural differences.

For readers with no direct connection to India, the emotional demands made by the novel did not, however, lead to an effort to overcome difference. Their responses pointed back to their own situations and contexts.[34] Participant "Carlyn" seeks books that "enrich the spirit" and reveal "emotions that the reader didn't know were possible." Stretching to comprehend the pain of Mistry's characters, and questioning how well she would endure this pain, led Carlyn to a cathartic process regarding the trauma of the terrorist attacks of September 11, 2001. Caryln writes, "For the first time, I began really feeling for the effects and implications of the September 11 attacks on America. I watched from a screen, imagining the terror and loss. And in this sense, the circle has become complete for me through the reading of

Mistry's book. *A Fine Balance* serves as a gateway for me to walk through with these feelings" (Carlyn, "Discussion"). Carlyn comes to the realization that the human family is interconnected, and she takes as a challenge the message that "we have to open our hearts to one another, or all of us will perish in the face of poverty, terrorism or violence toward each other" (Carlyn, "Discussion"). We do not learn what steps Carlyn takes in order to achieve this goal, but her conviction resonates with Winfrey's intentions of getting beyond our comfort zones. For "Patty," a fourth featured reader, the forging of bonds of friendship in the face of misery also inspires reflection on the indomitable human spirit. The result of reading for Patty is more practical, but also in keeping with Winfrey's emphases on self-actualization. Patty writes, "I came away with a powerful reminder of some valuable life lessons, that you, Oprah, have stated many times over. 'Strive to live your best life, stand within your truth and keep your own counsel.' Since finishing the book, I was inspired to launch my own management consultancy and continue my career development" (Patty, "Discussion"). From a novel about the bravery of the suffering poor, Patty takes the impetus to risk a career change. As Kathleen Rooney has recently observed, Oprah's show imposes its own narratives of self-improvement on the novels, explicitly inviting readers to garner "life lessons" from reading. Patty's response, though far from traditional literary criticism, fits Winfrey's formula neatly (*Oprah* 142–46), and indeed she comes the closest to representing the typical Oprah reader, even when responding to this atypical novel.[35] In this case, Winfrey's featured readers all struggle with their heartfelt reactions to Mistry's novel. Each one expresses empathetic feelings, but each one ends up in a different place as a result of the reading experience. This readerly phenomenon echoes in the writer's comments about his intentions. Though Mistry invokes the spread of justice as his writerly intention, in an interview he confesses that, like Camus, he believes that "one can redeem oneself by writing." He comments, "I think that is why I began to write. I wasn't sure how redemption would come through writing but I'm still writing" ("Rohinton Mistry with Robert Mclay" 206). The motivation to write fiction may involve a reaching out to readers as brothers and sisters for the benefit of the writer, and empathetic effects may then play a different role in the emotional transaction between author and readers than inspiring prosocial action.

It is not at all surprising to find empathy and its potential effects foregrounded in an Oprah book discussion. Empathy is an Oprah touchstone. As an admirable trait it links the show and Web site's presentation of Barack Obama, the Dalai Lama, Pearl S. Buck, and Mary-Louise Parker, all of whom apparently possess it and recommend it to Winfrey's viewers. Empathy plays a central role in the show's recommendations about love, "marriage repair," child rearing, grieving, and "lifestyle makeover." As a quality of a book, the Web site attributes empathy to Andre Dubus's *House of Sand and*

Fog (1999), Sol T. Plaatje's *Mhudi* (1930), Tolstoi's *Anna Karenina* (1878), and Lalita Tademy's *Cane River* (2001). Winfrey encourages her audience to employ empathy in their life-improving efforts, including in their reading.[36] In turn, the Oprah audience constructs an ideal author with whom they can empathize and seeks a way of understanding the challenge of reading painful fiction by empathizing with characters. That they do not inevitably reach the desirable end point of prosocial action, engaging in altruistic helping or working to end injustice, does not diminish the centrality of empathetic feeling as an aspect of a fulfilling emotional life. Feeling with others, including fictional others, can be an end in itself. It draws some of its power from the analogous experience of compassion, experienced in a religious context, for Oprah's show owes a great deal to the forms and function of testimonial religion.

Oprah Winfrey's very influential guidance on how to read a novel contributes to the contemporary scene's unprecedented cultural valuation of empathy, which in turn participates in an optimistic understanding of the process of social formation. This emphasis has become widespread in the cultural commentary on books. The choices that readers make for themselves, and perhaps even more importantly, for children, are felt to contribute to social renovations that stem from empathy. We find this emphasis even in the religious press, in which compassion, forgiveness, and loving one's neighbor might be considered the more traditional goals (Donnelly, "Studies Abroad" 22–24). One may ask whether this social formation through reading reaches everyone. If novel reading does open readers up to the perspectives of markedly different others, as many teachers believe, then women and girls may disproportionately benefit from this exercise of their sympathetic imaginations. Though Oprah Winfrey does not exclude men from the beneficial effects of empathetic reading, her audience is mainly female. This matches up to the well-documented observation that women do most of the novel reading today.

Does women's novel reading then exaggerate the culturally sanctioned gender roles of "feeling women" and "thinking men"? If so, then the efforts of individuals such as Oprah Winfrey exercise considerable cultural influence by bringing particular texts to the attention of a broad potential readership and reminding that readership how to use the novel-reading experience. Winfrey acts as a teacher in her Book Club segments, encouraging role taking, judgment making, and application of life lessons from novels to the real lives of her viewers. Whether novels on their own can actually extend readers' empathetic imagination and make prosocial action more likely remains uncertain, but Winfrey's advocacy for the force of fiction creates the circumstances that have been shown to increase empathetic understanding of others. By dignifying empathetic response to fiction, Winfrey may increase the role-taking efforts of her considerable readership, and that may change attitudes, if not actions.

Bestsellers and the Diffusion of Responsibility

When a reader commits herself to an Oprah book, she joins a vast audience. If she heeds Winfrey's recommendations on how to read, she may feel that the novel presses her to respond in the real world. In the case of Rohinton Mistry's *A Fine Balance*, the emotions invoked may impel a reader to feelings of helplessness in the face of insuperable injustices, as we have seen above. More positively, it may provoke self-evaluation that leads to action in a purely personal realm. It may provide an opportunity for cathartic healing and expanded understanding. However, social psychology suggests another possibility. Becoming a reader of a bestseller means joining a crowd, though not the kind of throng that surrounds a person physically. The best recent example of this phenomenon occurs when J. K. Rowling issues one of her Harry Potter books: readers all over the world simultaneously obtain and then read the novel together, conscious that millions of others are doing the same thing. Harry Potter books, engrossing and excellent as they are, make few direct demands on readers' behavior.[37] When Winfrey chooses a novel that centrally addresses questions of injustice, she opens the way for socially committed responses. However, joining the crowd of readers of *A Fine Balance* may also activate the psychological response known as *diffusion of responsibility*: the assumption on the part of individuals, that because they are part of a crowd, that they need not take responsibility for acting. By this logic, if everyone else—hundreds of thousands of other readers, and millions of other viewers—becomes aware of caste prejudice, oppression of the poor, and the cruel treatment of widows in India, then surely someone else must already be doing something.

Researchers on altruism in the real world have already demonstrated the rarity of a truly risk-taking altruistic response to others' needs (see 22–23 above). Latane and Darley's classic research on "diffusion of responsibility," or bystander apathy, suggests that in some circumstances, being part of a crowd reduces the speed of response to another in need, and in some cases thwarts responding at all.[38] A bestseller that galvanized a large group into taking action would confute this observation. To the degree that literary history ever notices bestsellers, it honors a scant few novels with having made a significant impact on public opinion and subsequent legislation. The *locus classicus* for a bestseller "changing the world" would be the outcry against food impurity in the wake of Upton Sinclair's novel *The Jungle* (1906). Though Sinclair hoped to sway his readers' political views, his graphic descriptions of the meatpacking industry had the unintended effect of spurring lawmakers to regulate the purity of food. His readers, after all, were also eaters. Nowadays, investigative journalists and documentary filmmakers aspire to reach a wide public in order to effect change, but very few novelists attempt to use their medium to sway the opinions of a mass readership. (I treat Alice Walker, a provocative exception to this generalization, in the following chapter.) After all, very few fiction bestsellers can live up to the oft-cited exemplars, *The Jungle, Uncle Tom's Cabin*, and *Oliver Twist*. The number of bestsellers that have distinguished themselves simply by selling extremely well suggests that most readers do not look to their fiction reading to suggest programs for action in the real world.

When a novel does make explicit demands on its readers, as I believe Rohinton Mistry's *A Fine Balance* does, the responses of those readers do not necessarily oblige the author by channeling into the fight against injustice. At the end of January 2005, 411 readers had spontaneously shared their responses to *A Fine Balance* through Amazon.com's Web site. Accompanied by a rating in numbers of stars, readers wrote in their reasons for recommending (or much more rarely, not recommending) the novel to other readers. All of the responses are in English (like the novel), but the readers write from all over the world. A significant proportion comes from American readers. Approximately one third of the responses provide a simple recommendation. The remaining two thirds are more expansive, elaborating on their reactions to the novel. Forty-six percent of all respondents emphasize the emotional experience of reading the novel, frequently describing empathetic responses and even tears. Twenty-eight write about their improved comprehension of the historical circumstances of Mistry's characters; in other words, they testify to an intellectual expansion of sympathetic understanding. Ten percent come to moralized conclusions about the message of the novel (as when one reader condemns moral relativism and urges Christian faith on other Amazon users).[39] Two reviewers, both writing after 11 September 2001, feel inspired by Mistry's depiction of the suspension of civil rights during the Emergency to comment on the fragility of the rights that American citizens enjoy. Many come to the conclusion that privileged readers ought to "count their blessings," the most common of the moralizing responses. Not a single soul reports doing something specific in the real world as a result of reading the book, other than recommending the novel to others, reading more about India, or seeking out other works by Rohinton Mistry.

Just because more than four hundred readers omit mention of the specific prosocial actions they have taken as a result of reading an extremely moving, absorbing, and eye-opening novel does not prove that *A Fine Balance* fails to inspire altruism. Modesty may be a factor. Readers of Mistry's novel may be more likely to give money to tsunami victims. They may be more likely to extend a hand to someone outside their "touching zone," as Winfrey puts it. They may react with compassion rather than indifference to the next indigent person who asks them for spare change on the street. They may indeed already be the kind of people who routinely do all these things, in which case their affinities may predispose them to the novel's invitation to feel and even act. We must confront the possibility, however, that an experience with a book leads most readily to other bookish activities, as study of the impact of Oprah's Book Club reveals (*Oprah* 126–33). No less prominent an authority than Harold Bloom argues that "the pleasures of reading indeed are selfish rather than social. You cannot directly improve anyone else's life by reading better or more deeply" (*How to Read and Why* 22). Bloom expresses skepticism about "the traditional social hope that care for others may be stimulated by the growth of individual imagination" and wariness about arguments that "connect the pleasures of solitary reading to the public good" (22). Bloom's readers may search for another work that absorbs them so completely and makes them feel so intensely. Oprah Winfrey's readers may seek out others who have emerged from a novel desperate to talk about it. These readers, who may even be the same readers, demonstrate their appetite for narrative empathy in the marketplace, when they purchase and read more novels that allow them to feel with fiction. The next chapter turns to the authors who produce empathetic fiction, in hopes of reaching this significant proportion of the novel-buying public. For like Oprah and her readers, many contemporary novelists believe that fiction can make something happen through empathetic representation.

5

Authors' Empathy

We laymen have always been intensely curious to know . . . from what sources that strange being, the creative writer, draws his material, and how he manages to make such an impression on us with it and to arouse in us emotions of which, perhaps, we had not even thought ourselves capable.
—Sigmund Freud, "Creative Writers and Day-Dreaming" (1907)

The relationship of empathy to novelists' craft of fiction presents puzzles just as intriguing as the conundrums of readers' empathy discussed in the previous two chapters. Contemporary novelists frequently connect fiction with empathy in their comments on creativity and the effects of novel reading.[1] Writers themselves may in fact be the primary source of this widespread belief, so often do they repeat it. Despite the apparent popular consensus that fiction develops readers' empathy, however, contemporary novelists approach empathy from a variety of angles. Representations of empathy in contemporary fiction run the gamut from moral approval to subversive deconstruction. (The following chapter, "Contesting Empathy," discusses several contemporary novelists who represent empathy most negatively.) While this chapter can only selectively mention some of the copious examples of textually rendered empathy, it does so with an aim of mapping the variety of techniques and attitudes embodied in contemporary fiction's versions of empathy. A lively debate about the uses and value of empathy emerges, as well as an additional set of proposals about narrative empathy.

Many novelists call up empathy as a representational goal by mirroring it within their texts: they present empathetic connections between characters or thematize empathy explicitly in fiction meditating on the vagaries of social relations. This ubiquitous form of empathy depends heavily on character identification and on reading habits that emphasize the feeling connection of readers to imagined beings in novels. Despite the disdain of some literary theory for such a traditional notion of character, this kind of felt connection should be acknowledged as the normative version of narrative empathy, one that persists even when novels engage in surface-level postmodern play that undermines certainties.

For instance, Margaret Atwood's feminist dystopia, *The Handmaid's Tale* (1985), purports to be transcriptions of a series of tapes, recovered and reassembled in the distant future, by a remote civilization looking back with dispassionate academic curiosity on an earlier North American society (subsequent to our own) that savagely represses women and dissenters through an alliance of fundamentalist religion and radical feminism. A careful reader attuned to postmodern technique recognizes that, by the end, Atwood has destabilized the foundations of her fictional world. Nonetheless, the alternating first- and third-person segments that comprise the novel, despite their gaps and uncertainties and the implausibility of Atwood's extreme scenario, evoke strong feeling responses of empathy with Offred, as well as outrage, pity, shock, and horror. Readers of *The Handmaid's Tale* readily make connections between Atwood's fictional world and parts of the real world in which women are similarly exploited. This kind of novel doesn't need to mention empathy directly in order to provoke vicarious emotional response in readers, some of whom go so far as to report physical symptoms such as pounding hearts and breathlessness.[2] In spite of Atwood's deliberate emphasis on the constructedness of her characters, readers persist in feeling with the titular handmaid and hating her oppressors.

When empathy receives direct reference by a contemporary novelist, it most often appears as a character trait or as a feature of relationships. This does not mean that empathy is always figured as purely positive or beneficial. Indeed, it sometimes marks a character as especially vulnerable or a relationship as unhealthy. For instance, in Sarah Schulman's novel *Empathy* (1992), a lesbian character who has undergone a dissociative personality split into male therapist and female client diagnoses the state of mind that cripples her female side: "You're suffering from empathy" (31). Understanding that one's own happiness may not be the central fact in a situation sometimes leads empaths to self-sacrifice. A character in a young adult novelization by Ellen Steiber spontaneously bleeds in the blood type of a kidnap victim who shares her experience of abduction. Empathetic fusion results in death for the empath. In *Parable of the Sower* (1993), Octavia Butler's hyperempath Lauren Olamina suffers debilitating pain when she witnesses others' suffering, a trait that makes her and other "sharers" especially vulnerable to enslavement. In Lois Lowry's dystopian children's book, *The Giver* (1993), a society that mutes its citizens' human feelings with mandatory drugs chooses one person to do the feeling for all of them. The official empath receives the memories of an entire culture, including all of its experiences of pain. Not surprisingly, he flees for his life, demonstrating the possibility of empathy swerving in the direction of personal distress.

Some figurations of empathy work more positively, even miraculously. In contemporary romances of the archive,[3] empathy becomes a magical device for solving mysteries of the past, as when a character dons virtual reality gear and steps back in time, entering the body, consciousness, and memory of a long-dead historical figure. In Bharati Mukherjee's version of technologically assisted historical empathy in *The Holder of the World* (1993), the full surrender of the quester's personality results in the finding of a long-lost treasure (Keen, *Romances of the Archive* 227–29). Other romances of the archive, such as Stevie Davies's *Impassioned Clay* (1999), celebrate the connections of personal identity that transcend huge differences in historical context to permit understanding. Historical fiction as a genre is particularly reliant on empathetic imagining, not only in women's historical romances, which often thematize empathy explicitly. While science fiction valorizes empathy as a form of advanced knowing, and depicts empaths as canny strategists (as, for instance, in Orson Scott Card's *Ender's Game* [1985]), it also advances the depiction of cold, monstrously rational, or cyborg characters that lack empathy. Paradoxically, some recent fiction sets about to evoke sympathy for characters who themselves lack empathetic skills, as in Mark Haddon's *The Curious Incident of the Dog in the Night-time* (2003).

A more didactic version of textual empathy explicitly recommends empathy by way of a character's expressed personal philosophy. Alexander McCall Smith has his Botswanan detective, Mma Ramotswe, comment directly on the social value of empathy in *Morality for Beautiful Girls* (2001): "If you knew how a person was feeling, if you could imagine yourself in her position, then surely it would be impossible to inflict further pain" (77). The naiveté of this view brings Mma Ramotswe to no grief in the sunny detective series, that testifies to the fundamental humanity of African people. As the more traditionally realistic determinism of Rohinton Mistry's *A Fine Balance* suggests, however, some cruel individuals feel sadistic pleasure in imagining others' pain. A few novelists, such as Rohinton Mistry and Alice Walker, attempt to employ empathy to spur prosocial action on behalf of suffering others.

In sum, while the popular genres of science fiction, gothic horror, and detective fiction all frequently involve plots of empathetic connection and empaths as characters, contemporary fiction considered more broadly proves a site of contestation, where the meaning and value of empathy receive a thorough going-over. Representations explicitly valuing empathy cannot be guaranteed to appear in all or even most works of recent fiction, but few manage to avoid alluding to it or eliciting it from readers. When authors dedicate their empathetic imaginations to the creation of characters and fictional worlds, it is perhaps not surprising that they so frequently embed representations of empathy and empathizing within their works. Like the scenes of reading that have been so assiduously sought out and interpreted in the past several decades of literary criticism, scenes of empathy can also be read metatextually, as slightly disguised commentary on the art of fictional world-making as understood by its makers.

The Empathy of Authors

A wealth of anecdotal testimony suggests that novelists themselves most frequently celebrate the value of narrative empathy. Women writers very often promote the positive consequences of empathic reading experiences, not only for women readers. Sue Monk Kidd, author of the best-selling *The Secret Life of Bees* (2002), writes, "While, as a writer, I want to affect the reader's mind—to educate and enlighten—what I wish for even more is to jolt the reader's heart. I want my words to open a portal through which the reader may leave the self, migrate to some other human sky and return 'disposed' to otherness" ("Common Heart" 9). For Kidd, the Emersonian quest for the common heart motivates fiction that "creates empathy" in even the most resistant (male) readers (9). She cites with pride an encounter in a bookstore with a well-dressed forty-nine-year-old business executive. A reluctant reader of *The Secret Life of Bees*, he told Kidd that he now feels "disposed to the South, to black women and to white girls who need their mothers" (9). For Kidd, this encounter epitomizes the value of "seeing the world through someone else's eyes, feeling it with someone else's heart" (9). For novelist Jane Smiley, the loss of male readers by the sidelining of the novel to "the seraglio" threatens to brutalize and coarsen our society (*13 Ways* 177). She writes, "When we talk about the death of the novel, what we are really talking about is the possibility that empathy, however minimal, would no longer be attainable by those for whom the novel has died" (176). Men in particular lose access to the "inner lives of their friends and family members" if the novel dies for them (176–77). For Smiley, the loss of empathetic reading experiences threatens apocalypse: "In a world where weapons of mass destruction are permanent features of the landscape, I cannot help believing that a lively sense of the reality of other consciousnesses on the part of those whose fingers are on the trigger is essential to human survival" (176).[4]

Male novelists also participate in the celebration of narrative empathy. David Lodge, a prolific novelist as well as a respected literary theorist, writes, "One might suggest that the ability novelists have to create characters, characters often very different from themselves, and to give a plausible account of their consciousnesses, is a special application of Theory of Mind. It is one that helps us develop powers of sympathy and empathy in real life" (*Consciousness* 42). Like many novelists, Lodge equates the value of advanced role-taking imagining on the part of writers with the end result garnered by readers: authors' use of their imagination to create fictional beings with persuasive inner lives somehow helps "us"—readers operating in "real life"—develop sympathy and empathy. By now it should be clear that the empirical evidence for causal links between fiction reading and the development of empathy in readers does not yet exist, though ingenious studies are underway to shore up the case that novel reading assists in moral development by training readers in empathy. Lodge's statement can be chalked up alongside Smiley's jeremiad and Kidd's hopes for the common heart as evidence of a still unsubstantiated but prevalent *belief* in a link between fiction reading and the cultivation of the empathetic imagination.

Another interpretation of Lodge's words leads us to a more defensible assertion. Lodge supposes that "the ability novelists have to create characters . . . helps us develop powers of sympathy and empathy in real life" (*Consciousness* 42). If his observation about effects on "us" can be interpreted as referring to processes internal to novelists, those special people who spend their lives imagining unreal persons and events for the entertainment and edification of others, then, indeed it may be true. Novelists may emphasize aspects of empathy as part of the creative process and as a goal of their fiction writing in part because they are more empathetic themselves than the average person, as we will see.[5] Their empathy may spur imaginative invention that finds valued expression in a writing career. Qualities of empathetic responsiveness and imaginative role taking may be cultivated most assiduously by novelists as a matter of craft, and they may indeed experience "real-life" improvements in their abilities to feel with others as a result of their long practice with imagined beings. This scenario has recently received support from an unexpected quarter: developmental psychology, in which the study of young children's imaginary friends transpires.

Nearly a century ago, Sigmund Freud suggested that there might be a link between the creativity of adult fiction writers and the imaginary play of children ("Creative Writers" 141–54). Developmental psychologist Marjorie Taylor of the University of Oregon, in *Imaginary Companions and the Children Who Create Them* (1999), has helped rehabilitate children's practice of talking and playing with invisible friends, previously seen as a sign of psychological or social problems. Taylor recasts imaginary companions as a healthy part of children's emotional and cognitive development. Taylor and her collaborators have recently extended research into the "illusion of independent agency" frequently reported by children about their imaginary companions, into the area of adult creativity. Accounts of this illusion, in which fictional characters seem to their creators to have minds and wills of their own, can be discovered in the interviews, memoirs, and casual commentary of many writers. Taylor specifically mentions Alice Walker, J. K. Rowling, Sara Paretsky, Philip Pullman, John Fowles, and E. M. Forster's comments reporting the illusion of characters' independent agency, but this sampling should not be taken as an unusual group.

Perhaps the most famous literary rendering of this very common creative experience occurs in playwright Luigi Pirandello's *Six Characters in Search of an Author* (1922), a play that dramatizes the notion of the independent existence of characters from their creator. Pirandello writes in his preface, "I can only say that, without having made any effort to seek them out, I found before me, alive—you could touch them and even hear them breathe—the six characters now seen on the stage. And they stayed there in my presence, each with his secret torment and all bound together by the one common origin and mutual entanglement of their affairs, while I had them enter the world of art, constructing from their persons, their passions, and their adventures a novel, a drama, or at least a story" (preface). Though his status as an innovative dramatist whose work anticipates aspects of theater of the absurd may impede such a reading, Taylor's research emboldens us to take Pirandello's report at face value. He may indeed have been reporting an imaginative experience as much as a frame-breaking invention.

Literary history records many such remarks of authors regarding the origins and fates of their fictional characters. Long before her Alzheimer's disease set in, Iris Murdoch was well known for referring to the continued post-novel existences of her creations and would sometimes inform her visitors or correspondents about what the characters had been up to recently. Because Pirandello and Murdoch are reputable writers, their self-reports of what might otherwise seem to be delusions or hallucinations are taken as perfectly normal. Indeed, the experience of "having a character in your head who won't go away" is widely regarded as a common reason for writing fiction in the first place.[6] Not only famous writers feel this way, although success as a fiction writer may be in part dependent on experiencing inspiration by way of characters who appear in the mind's eye, demanding attention. That they "go on existing" after the author finishes the books helps explain the drive to write sequels, as well as Murdoch's counterfactual assertions.

In a remarkable study of fifty fiction writers, Taylor and her collaborators discovered not only that 92 percent of the authors reported some experience of the illusion of independent agency, but also that the more successful writers (those who had published their fiction) had more frequent and more intense experiences of it. Taylor and her group hypothesize that the illusion of independent agency could be related to writers' expertise in fantasy production ("Illusion" 361, 376–77), suggesting that it occurs more easily and spontaneously with practice, or that writers naturally endowed with creative gifts may experience it more readily. Writers report looking at and eavesdropping on their characters, engaging in conversations with them, struggling with them over their actions, bargaining with them, and feeling for them. Taylor writes, "The essence of this conceptual illusion is the sense that the characters are independent agents not directly under the author's control" (366). Though clearly novelists still do exercise their authority by choosing the words that end up on the page, they may experience the creative process as akin to involuntarily empathizing with a person out there, separate from themselves. Several tests administered by Taylor to her subjects support this connection.

Taylor found that the writers as a group scored higher than the norm (in the general population) in empathy ("Illusion" 361). Using Davis's Interpersonal Reactivity Index (IRI), a frequently used empathy scale, Taylor and her colleagues measured her subjects' tendency to fantasize, to feel empathic concern for others, to experience personal distress in the face of others' suffering, and to engage in perspective taking (369–70). Both men and women in her sample of fiction writers scored significantly higher than Davis's reported norms for the general population, with females scoring higher in all four areas than males. Writers of both genders stood out on all four subscales of Davis's IRI, but they were "particularly off the charts" for fantasy and perspective taking. Taylor speculates that "these two subscales tap the components of empathy that seem most conceptually related to IIA [the Illusion of Independent Agency] and might be seen as 'grown-up' versions of variables associated with children who have imaginary companions (pretend play and theory of mind skills)" (377). The work of Taylor and her group leads to the first hypothesis about narrative empathy from the authors' side: *novelists as a group may be more empathetic than the general population.* A second hypothesis must follow immediately, acknowledging the difficulty of pinning down the difference between innate dispositions and results of practice and habitual use in groups of people: *the activity of fiction writing may cultivate novelists' role-taking skills and make them more habitually empathetic.*

These proposals do not imply that the actual behavior of novelists is any better than the population at large. Even the most ardent advocates of narrative ethics hesitate to argue that being a novelist correlates with being a better person. Literary biographies provide too many counterexamples to risk going down that path. Novelists known to be nice people may exercise their empathy on behalf of nonexistent beings and indeed on behalf of nasty characters. Furthermore, nasty people may become novelists! Nothing prevents a novelist with appalling personal convictions from employing his creative empathy to render, for instance, the plight of white supremacists in a fashion designed to stir the feelings of those who fear having their guns taken away. This is precisely what William Pierce, founder of the white supremacist organization The National Alliance, did when he published a novel under the pseudonym Andrew MacDonald. *The Turner Diaries* (1978) is credited by the FBI and the Anti-Defamation League for having stirred up race hatred and anti-Semitic activities in the United States.[7] Most notably, Timothy McVeigh, the bomber of the Federal Building in Oklahoma City (in 1995), had apparently made a careful study of *The Turner Diaries* and emulated its protagonist by building a fertilizer bomb to explode a government building. The novel provides a careful account of how such a bomb might be made and deployed in a small truck.

Pierce's hateful representations of blacks, Jews, homosexuals, and so-called mud people, all of whom face extermination in his paranoid near-future world, have all but obscured his representational success in creating a long-suffering white revolutionary character, to whom a certain kind of reader (in all likelihood much more passive than McVeigh) clearly responds.[8] These readers report being thrilled by the novel, even when they disagree with some of the attitudes it expresses. As F. R. Conway, an Amazon reviewer observes, "The target audience for this book is a person, usually young, who's already on the edge. . . . Take a kid that's already angry at the world, at the government, show him this book with these things that already tick him off, highly exaggerated and he'll feel a connection with it. Then the story is an engaging and empowering one with a frightening message."[9] Though William Pierce (who died in 2002) was not a violent criminal like Timothy McVeigh, he indulged his genocidal revenge fantasies in a future-world thriller that clearly has the capacity to stir the feelings of some readers. The notion that empathy *could not* be involved in such an act of creation should be treated with skepticism, for empathy and ethnocentrism have often been fellow travelers. This unpleasant example prompts the observation that *authors' empathy can be devoted to socially undesirable ends.* Even then, it takes a McVeigh to transform a novel into an action plan for terrorism. Most readers recognize the novel, whether or not it appeals to them, as fiction and therefore see it as exempt from attributions of cause-and-effect agency. It may be especially an author's fantasy to believe that readers will be prone to implement the programs embedded within fiction.

Intriguingly, in the same research project described above, Taylor and her collaborators also discovered that fiction writers as a group showed higher scores of dissociation than the norms for the general population. Dissociation, in psychological terms, means an abnormal separation of mental processes from conscious awareness and can be involved in an array of disorders, including amnesia, memory loss, and schizophrenia. In its least pathological forms, dissociation takes place during intense daydreaming, especially the kind during which the absorbed subject loses track of time and bodily awareness. Taylor and her team used a standard questionnaire,[10] as in the empathy component of her study, and discovered that the fiction writers scored significantly higher than the average, due especially to high scores on daydreaming and absorption. Taylor comments that the writers' scores are closer to the average Dissociative Experiences Scale (DES) score for a sample of schizophrenics ("Illusion" 373–74) but hastens to reassure readers that scoring in this range does not constitute a diagnosis of a dissociative disorder. Indeed, she and her colleagues conclude that "the profile of our writers . . . is that of a group of people who readily adopt other people's perspectives, and who revel in the imaginative worlds of fictional characters, fantasy, and daydreams" (377). Fantasies and daydreams, delightful though they may be, however, do not inevitably contribute to the social good, and they may sometimes allow a person to indulge in imagined actions that would be judged criminal, immoral, or dangerous if carried out. This is part of the attraction of fiction for many readers, even sophisticated ones, and should not be dismissed from a broader consideration of narrative ethics.

The comments of authors about their craft of character creation affirm the connections discovered by Taylor and in the process highlight more problems with authors' empathy. First among these problems is the necessity of empathizing with unlikable characters, the readerly counterpart of which I have discussed earlier (see 74–75 above). Native American novelist and poet Leslie Marmon Silko puts it this way: "My second novel has some pretty outrageous villainous characters, and I have to admit, I was right inside them. I have to own up to saying that everything that they imagined and felt, I imagined and felt. I think that if a writer can't put herself inside the skin of all of her characters, if she's not sympathetic with them or doesn't like them enough, it will show, and the readers will feel a distance. And so I just imagine that I'm standing right there. I'm there doing it."[11] In this case, Silko describes her conviction that the creation will suffer if she fails to exercise her own empathetic imagining on their part. Like Silko, other novelists regard role taking as a fundamental part of the craft of fiction. This aspect of writers' practice crosses significant boundaries of difference, not just the borders between good and evil characters. The ability on the part of a male author to create a convincing female character is often remarked as if it were an unusual attainment, but authors who have accomplished it, such as Arthur Golden, author of *Memoirs of a Geisha* (1997), treat role-taking imagining more matter-of-factly, as a basic requirement of the craft. Golden comments, "There are differences between the genders. But I think that a fiction writer's job is to put himself into the mind of someone different from him or her."[12] This chapter considers the effort of a female writer, Keri Hulme, to portray a male child abuser in a fashion that evokes empathy as well as horror, employing the representation of interiority to cross barriers of otherness more extreme than race and gender. Like Silko and Golden, Hulme uses her empathetic skills to craft a character whose reprehensible behavior becomes shockingly understandable.

One of the reasons that authorial intentions can be so tricky to discover lies in the automaticity of expert writing. Novelists frequently claim "not to know" how or why their representations turned out the way they did, and they are not always being coy or hiding their sources. In keeping with Taylor's findings, novelists in the flow of creation may engage in empathetic role taking with an imagined projection without realizing how much of the writer's self has been projected into that fictive being. Sometimes a novelist will admit to discovering after the fact that an inadvertent act of empathetic sharing has occurred in the course of writing. J. K. Rowling, who has also described discovering her character Harry Potter as an image complete with his lightning-bolt–shaped scar in a clear example of the illusion of independent agency, also admits to discovering unintended empathetic projection in her writing. Rowling comments,

> There's a part of Book One where Harry sees his stepparents in an enchanted mirror. I was quite taken aback when I re-read that chapter to see how much I had directly given Harry my own feelings because I wasn't aware of that as I was writing. As I was writing, I mean, I'm try-

ing to do the thing properly that needed to happen for plot reasons. If people have read the book, they will know Harry had to find out how that mirror worked. But when I re-read the chapter, it became very clear to me that I had given Harry almost entirely my own feelings about my mother's death.[13]

In the context of authors' empathy, the discovery that writers unconsciously lend characters their feelings highlights what has often proved a worrisome aspect of imaginative role taking for those who theorize empathy. What if our empathy with others is only egoism, recognition of the self, painted over the other's true experience? The contemporary disparagement of empathy (a minority view, to be sure) often focuses on this possibility.

If empathy demonstrates only egoism and fantasy projection, then accurate apprehension of another's feelings will be difficult to achieve. Most theories of narrative empathy, though sketchy, assume that empathy can be transacted accurately from author to reader by way of a literary text. Thus, in J. K. Rowling's example, she gives her character her own feelings, allowing a reader to share grief with Harry and herself in a triangulated empathic bond. Though in the case of a fictional character such as Harry Potter no one is being deprived of his true feelings by his creator's empathy, real people—for instance, objects of pity presented by charitable organizations—might find their position in that empathic triangle discomforting. The transaction of feeling might result in sensations of misunderstanding or even erasure. The following chapter takes up the political critique of empathy that inheres in this notion. For now, the issue of empathic accuracy (and the struggle against what I term "empathic inaccuracy") belongs to a discussion of authors' empathy, in this hypothetical form: *Though a key ingredient of successful fictional world-making, authors' empathy does not always transmit to readers without interference.* As this chapter goes on to discuss in a section on Flora Nwapa's novel *Efuru* (1966), authors sometimes represent a practice or experience that evokes empathy in readers, against authors' apparent or proclaimed representational goals.

The opposite situation, in which authors set about deliberately to manipulate readers' emotional responses in hopes of provoking altruistic action in the real world, raises questions of whether success should be measured either by readers' feelings or by their subsequent actions. Arts of persuasion are commonly evaluated by their success in motivating people; we judge whether a political candidate has won or lost a debate, or whether a leader has swayed public opinion. As Aristotle observed, the evocation of a feeling response serves as a rhetorical tool. Most novelists who employ narrative empathy rhetorically do not make a mark. Despite the difficulty of influencing readers' behavior, many authors, including authors from postcolonial nations, report world-changing intentions. For politically engaged writers, the worry that experiencing narrative empathy short-circuits the impulse to act compassionately or to respond with political engagement does not discourage their effort to evoke it in readers. Though an author's didactic use of empathy may invite critics' suspicion, for offering "a kind of cannibalistic pleasure in consuming the suffering of others" (Rooney, *Reading with Oprah* 137–38), many novelists persist in purposeful empathetic representation. The fearful view of authors' empathy as corrupting readers by offering them others' feelings for callous consumption leads in some quarters to the depiction of empathy itself as a quality that weakens humans and makes them vulnerable to others' cruelest manipulations.

Feeling with Villains

In the earlier chapter "Readers' Empathy," I cited several cases in which readers confessed to feeling with negatively portrayed characters. This sort of readers' empathy may have its roots in the empathetic process of character creation as described above by Leslie Marmon Silko. If an author has felt with all her creations as she imagines them, not just reserving emotional investment for favored protagonists, then the opportunity for readers to bond temporarily with monsters, madmen, and villains can be regarded not as anomalous, but as a standard feature of fiction. Indeed, this kind of risk-mitigating opportunity to think and feel with those from whom we might ordinarily recoil in horror provides one of the much-touted advantages of fictional world-making. Novels can provide safe spaces within which to see through the eyes of the psychopath, to occupy the subject position of the oppressive racist, to share the brutalizing past of the condemned outcast. Don DeLillo's *Libra* (1988), Nadine Gordimer's *The Conservationist* (1974), and Peter Carey's *Jack Maggs* (1997) all offer versions of this fictive extension of role-taking imagination. Such serious literary experimentation with inhabiting the perspective of stigmatized or repulsive others may play on readers' appetites for vicious imagery or play with taboos, but it has not been generally understood as a corrupting aspect of narrative.

Feeling with villains has been recuperated as an aspect of ethical reading practices through its opportunity to warn, caution, instruct, and safely defuse social tensions through carnivalesque inversions of norms. Considerably more social anxiety accrues to texts judged crude and simple enough to appeal to young people. In the past, William Ainsworth's racy, melodramatic novel *Jack Sheppard* (1839) was regarded as a dangerous text that glamorized criminality. In more recent times, the Anti-Defamation League warns its readers about National Vanguard Books' *New World Order Comix*, featuring "White Will" and aimed at white high school students ("Q and A"). The lower the cultural estimation of the form under consideration, the more likely it is to receive condemnation for inciting consumers to imitative violence or expression of anger and hatred. Thus, the gory narratives of video games, which require advanced gaming skill even fully to preview, are assumed to have a corrupting influence on the young people who play them, but few literary fictions, no matter how transgressive, achieve the spotlight of public reprobation.

Keri Hulme's Booker Prize–wining novel *the bone people* (1983)[14] makes a useful case study of a work that violates taboos in its empathetic presentation of a child abuser. The novel's violence has attracted quite a lot of comment, not all of it disapproving,[15] for out of the breakdown of her three central characters, Hulme forges a new beginning and way of living, which she labels *commensalism* (*bone people* 434). Hulme goes so far as to suggest that the victim of child abuse, a mute European child (Simon), invites his beatings from his adoptive alcoholic Maori father (Joe). Her representation goes far beyond contemporary understandings of codependency, implying that the child victim incites violence against himself in order to bring peace, healing, and reconciliation to the wounded adults who harm and love him. Her brief glimpses into Simon's consciousness show him intentionally provoking fights, and her depiction of his behavior (he is a sneak thief and disobedient to the point of self-endangerment) suggests how he drives his caregiver to distraction, then to assault. Hulme naturally also plays up Simon as a sympathetic character, gradually revealing the layers in his history of abuse, from the funny marks he has on him already, as a half-drowned toddler, when his foster parents take him in, to his near obliteration at Joe's hands late in the novel. Abandoned by his natural parents, drugged-out aristocratic Eurotrash, Simon serves as a self-sacrificial catalyst of Maori healing through reconstitution of (nonbiological) family.

As one might expect from this bald summary, the novel has received some negative criticism, though it won both the Pegasus Prize (1984) and the Booker Prize (1985). Responding to the fact that Keri Hulme is one eighth Maori, C. K. Stead took her to task for speaking inauthentically about Maori legends and practices and for receiving an award designated for Maori writers.[16] This ham-handed appraisal of the novelist's identity and authority has all but obscured the rest of Stead's critique. In the same article, Stead identifies the novel's "bitter aftertaste, something black and negative deeply ingrained in its imaginative fabric" ("Pegasus" 107) with *the bone people*'s representation of "extreme violence against a child" (108). The failure of the novelist adequately to punish the child abuser (he does serve a brief prison term after nearly killing Simon) provokes some readers: Stephen Fox of Gallaudet University reports that "in classes or discussion groups the usual reaction is horror and anger at the situation, the hope that Simon (the victim) will be allowed to escape his tormentor, and the expectation that Joe will eventually be punished. When no such outcome occurs, readers can become quite upset, as I know from having used this book in college literature classes" ("Beneficial" 46). Amazingly, very few professional critics after Stead have explored the extent to which Hulme's representation of violence invites the reader to inhabit the position of the abusive adults.[17] An exceptional view comes from Mark Williams, who notices that "we are made to identify emotionally with the victim of an evil" ("Negative" 86), but also to understand Simon's abuser Joe sympathetically. Williams argues, "At this point the novel's relation to the social evil it dramatises comes dangerously close to complicity" (108). I acknowledge that the scarcity of critics who agree with Stead and Williams suggests that empathizing with Joe may well not be a common response, but the author's evident empathy for Joe certainly plays a role in scripting one of the most disturbing novel-reading experiences that I can recall encountering in my adult life. I didn't like it, but I felt with Joe.

At the time of Simon's most vicious beating at the hands of Joe, the child has just broken all the plate glass shop windows in town. Just prior to this act of destruction, Kerewin has hit him, after he attacks her. He has stolen a precious knife from Kerewin and damaged her guitar. Arguably, being hit by Kerewin sets off his window-breaking spree. In any case, she is still angry when the authorities hand Simon over to Joe. Over the phone, Kerewin communicates her disgust to Simon:

> She has finished having anything to do with him.
> She hates him.
> She loathes every particle of his being.
> Did he know what that guitar meant to her?
> Did he know what that knife meant to her?
> Did he know what he had wrecked?
> She hopes his father knocks him sillier than he is now.
> She has every sympathy for his father.
> She didn't realize what a vicious little reptile he had to endure.
>
> (*bone people* 307–8)

In effect, Kerewin gives Joe permission to beat Simon, as she later realizes (325).

In this excruciating brief scenes that follow, Hulme conveys in terse, lyrical lines the consciousness of Simon as he receives a nearly fatal beating, which he brings to an end by stabbing his assailant Joe with a shard of glass. Among the most difficult pages of the entire novel, these passages convey the anger and pain of a triple-bound situation. Hulme not only invites empathy for the victim, Simon, but also brings her readers close to the infuriated adults in the triangle. While the character Kerewin ostensibly "has every sympathy" for the long-suffering Joe, the author Hulme asks not just for sympathy but for a more painful sharing in the emotions that drive Joe to violence. She charts the escalation from exasperation to shame to money anxiety ("you have ruined me") to unleashed rage. As other critics have observed, she describes Joe's racial and socioeconomic position in such a way virtually to determine his violent response.[18] Hulme explains this at a public reading, when she remarked, "I think he's an astoundingly nice person, in his own way, given his warped background" ("Reconsidering" 139).

In case any doubt remains about where the novelist hopes to bring her readers, her central character Kerewin makes this speech to Joe just before he is convicted and imprisoned for the assault:

> I've been fascinated by you two these past few months. You've got, you had genuine love between you. You've given him a solid base of love to grow from, for all the hardship you've put him through. You've been mother and father and home to him. And probably tomorrow they'll read you a smug little homily, castigating you for ill-treatment and neglect. And they'll congratulate themselves quite publicly for rescuing the poor urchin from this callous ogre, this nightmare of a parent. . . . (*bone people* 325)

Though it may seem impossible to fathom from this abbreviated account of the novel's content, Hulme succeeds in bringing readers into temporary congruence with this perspective, in which social welfare officers and the justice system actively impede the spiritual healing of the novel's quest by jailing Joe. While no reader I have met will agree with the argument the author makes here, they will admit to the sickening feeling of being made to see a child abuser in a sympathetic light and the even more upsetting sensation of temporarily feeling with him (always still feeling with his victim at the same time). The word many readers use to describe the book's evocation of this complex of feelings is "manipulative." This term of disapproval embeds within it the sense that an author has somehow employed craft to get her readers to feel things that they don't at all wish to feel. I hazard that Hulme's depiction of the rich interiority of intersecting characters involves narrative empathy in the making and invites readers' empathic distress. The hypothesis I draw from this example registers that *empathic distress at feeling with a character whose actions are at odds with a reader's moral code may be a result of successfully exercised authorial empathy.*

In the case of Keri Hulme's *the bone people*, internal references within the novel strongly suggest that a reader intent on following the writer's cues will arrive at an experience of empathic distress as I have described above. This reaction strongly correlates to Hulme's own experience of the illusion of independent agency (as described by Taylor), a view that receives extra-textual support from remarks made in some of the reclusive author's infrequent interviews. To the charge of manipulating readers she would accede, acknowledging that she communicates by "trapping your mind, eyes, and inner ear" (*Spiritcarvers* 57). Hulme explicitly connects her style of trapping or netting readers with her experience of the illusion of independent agency. Just as readers must listen to her, she must listen to her characters: "Sometimes they tell me things I didn't actually want to hear. . . . Not infrequently, I see my characters as much as I hear them; but I don't hear words—the trick for me is putting it into words" (59). Hulme recognizes the alarming congruence of this writerly experience and mental illness in her description of her worries about the illusion as a "private nightmare":

> What would you say if one of your characters came to the door? Would you say "piss off, I killed you ages ago"?—because some of my characters seem to come from nowhere, and they are very real. I'm delighted to hear that other writers think this too; you wonder if you're making it up or not. You get to live with them—once they inhabit you for a long while, they become as real as anybody else. I once got jumped on quite heavily by a person who belonged to a Schizophrenia Fellowship, by saying that Schizophrenia is a writers' disease. But actually, quite seriously, it is. I have met writers who no longer maintain the borders and are no longer sure of what's real and what's not. (65)

The unsettling feeling of invasion by unwelcome characters who won't obey or go away is then passed on to the reader. Communicating a private nightmare through fiction to a group of unwitting readers may seem more like the compulsive storytelling of Coleridge's Ancient Mariner than the exercise of constructive imagining. Hulme comments, "you actually can, if you like, induce that reading trance" ("Reconsidering" 145). For all the fantasy woven through *the bone people*, however, Hulme's comments on the novel suggest that she sees it as an intervention in the real world. In addition to the novel's recommendation of an uncompetitive commensalism as a model for relations among contemporary New Zealanders (Maori and Pakeha), *the bone people* also attempts to alert a society to the plight of abused children. To that end, Hulme told an interviewer, "I made it as real as I could' ("Reconsidering" 153).

What readers swept up in empathic distress for both Simon and his abuser Joe are to do with their reactions remains unclear: the confusion of fictional world-making with social criticism in *ex post facto* interviews does not settle the question of why Hulme makes violence so real to her readers. If they feel sick as they share Simon's feelings during the beating, then perhaps they are okay. But what about readers who shudder with recognition at Joe's wrath? C. K. Stead records his uneasiness with the representation of abuse in *the bone people*, which "demands sympathy and understanding for the man who commits it. In principle such charity is admirable. In fact, the line between charity and imaginative complicity is very fine indeed" ("Pegasus" 108). Readers finding themselves responding charitably (or not) with their embroiling in Joe's situation may be victims of emotional contagion communicated through a text. Narrative empathy may in fact involve a darker aspect of emotional contagion, by which an author inflicts feeling on readers in order to exorcise her involuntary empathic experiences of feeling with and being inhabited by fictional characters.

"Empathic Inaccuracy" and Authorial Intentions

My discussion of readers' empathy in chapter 3 includes the following observations about the variability of response to potentially empathetic fiction. (1) Empathy with characters doesn't always occur as a result of reading an emotionally evocative fiction. (2) The capacity of novels to invoke readers' empathy may change over time (and some novels may only activate the empathy of their first, immediate audience). (3) Empathy for a fictional character need not correspond with what the author appears to set up or invite. All three premises become involved when the question of empathic accuracy is brought to bear on the novel-reading experience. Empathic accuracy matters to those who study it because its obverse, false empathy can be a result of bias or egocentrism. From the failures of empathetic individuals to question whether their assessments of the other's feelings could be off base comes a great deal of the negative reputation of empathy as a particularly invasive form of selfishness. (I impose my feelings on you and call them your feelings. Your feelings, whatever they were, undergo erasure.) Contrary to this fearful scenario, the psychological research on empathic accuracy records the remarkable degree of rightness in human empathy, though to be sure more cross-cultural verification of these findings would be welcome.[19] Whether from expert reading of facial cues, body language, tone of voice, context, or effective role taking on the part of the empathizer, ordinary subjects tend to do pretty well in laboratory tests of empathic accuracy. Verification can be achieved readily enough through interviews cross-checked with physical measurements and observations.

When we respond empathetically to a novel, we do not have the luxury of questioning the character: we cannot ask, Is that how you really felt? The text, however, may verify our reactions even as it elicits them. Some narrators employ psycho-narration, or generalizations about the characters' inner states, including thoughts and feelings, with the result that the text itself announces how the character feels. First-person narration (self-narration) may also allow for direct confirmation of a shared feeling, as may the inclusion of quoted monologue (interior monologue), like Keri Hulme's representation of Simon's feelings during his beating, quoted above. Narrated monologue (free indirect discourse) may combine with psycho-narration to suggest the character's thought stream in the narrator's language. For characters represented externally, dialogue and action may provide clues, but no one of these techniques assures us that our empathetic reaction precisely catches the feelings embedded in the fictional characters. For this reason, extratextual sources, such as interviews with authors, become important tools in assessing literary empathic accuracy. "Empathic inaccuracy," a term I coin here, describes a potential effect of narrative empathy: a strong conviction of empathy that incorrectly identifies the feeling of a literary persona. Empathic inaccuracy occurs when a reader responds empathetically to a fictional character at cross-purposes with an author's intentions. Authors sometimes evoke empathy unintentionally. This accident contributes to empathic inaccuracy. Unlike in real-world, face-to-face circumstances, the novel-reading situation allows empathic inaccuracy to persist because neither author nor fictional character directly confutes it. Indeed, literary study privileges against-the-grain interpretations of fiction that may be founded on deliberate acts of role taking that subvert the authors' apparent intentions.

Authors are not helpless in the face of empathic inaccuracy. Their commentary can guide readers' responses. When my students and I discuss Opal Palmer Adisa's novel, *It Begins with Tears* (1997), for instance, I can be fairly sure that the female students nervously crossing their legs are responding empathetically to the scene in which a group of women punish Monica, a prostitute and "man-stealer," by tying her to a bed and stuffing fiery chopped red pepper into her nose and vagina (*Tears* 131–32). The novel firmly disavows Monica's assailants' perspective by keeping them anonymous during the attack and by quoting her rescuer, Miss Cotton: "No one deserve dat, no one" (132). Adisa further verifies the empathetic horror of readers in direct phrasing— "she lay tied to her pain" (132), "the lips of her vagina were swollen and blistered" (133), and "When they managed to force the spout of their improvised douche into her vagina, Monica's scream cut through the night" (136). Finally, Adisa cues readers to the appropriate response by marking the rescuers with the symptoms of emotional contagion: "They all ached. The crime was too violent for words. The lips of their vaginas throbbed in sympathy, their wombs ached, and their salty tears left stain marks on their faces" (136).

How male readers respond to this sequence in the novel, beyond being disturbed at having to talk about it in mixed company, I have not been able to discover. It may be that, as Beryl explains when she summons the group of women who will tend Monica, "is oman business dis" (133); even sympathetic men are disinvited. By opening the world of the novel to any reader, however, Adisa shares the healing art of her fiction with a broader array of people, and she uses the scene of healing and reconciliation at the river to build community (212–19). Pain, if survived, offers the opportunity for healing and creativity, as Adisa emphasizes in an early statement of *ars poetica*, "She Scrape She Knee." Adisa describes her writing as a curative process, "I am the work, and the work is womanish. . . . female, spirited, sponging Winnie Mandela's feet, rubbing the shoulders of the basket women in Kenya, raising the backs of Indian women; my writing is an introduction into the world of womanism" ("Scrape" 150). Adisa sets up the wounding of her character Monica at the hands of jealous wives in order to stage a communal healing ritual of reintegration near the end of the novel. This healing extends beyond the circle of women (a point to which some feminist critics have objected, arguing that Adisa lets complicitous males off too easily).[20] Adisa comments in an interview:

> My first objective in this novel was to look at healing and try to understand why there is so much pain among black people apart from the issue of slavery. What I realized is that we have not healed from slavery because we have not done any rituals. . . . In all cultures, not just African cultures, whenever there is some kind of trauma there is a ritual performed to bring back balance to the community.[21]

The aftermath for the perpetrators (expulsion, pain, and death) and the positive turns in community life leave no room for doubt that Adisa aligns herself with traumatized black people generally (and their healers). This novel leaves no room for empathic inaccuracy.

My reading of empathic cues in Adisa's fiction may appear to essentialize female readers as especially capable of accurate response; this is a function of my gender and the relative comfort of my female students in discussing the novel. I assume that most male readers would also follow Adisa's directions in reading the novel, though they might feel offended by or implicated in the novel's attack on patriarchal values. One must take care not to reinscribe gender distinctions with respect to the capacities of imaginative extension, just because the social circumstances of book discussion favor the contributions of one gender over the other. Female and male readers sometimes differ in their tastes, and this may have an impact on publicly confessed empathetic responses. No work yet verifies, however, that adult female readers are better readers than their male counterparts, though in the United States, Europe, and the United Kingdom, women apparently like reading fiction more than men do. Liking to read emotionally evocative fiction does not guarantee that an individual reader responds accurately to a novel's invitation to feel. Female readers, myself included, can still be terribly mistaken in their empathy.

Empathic inaccuracy can be an effect of cultural background as well as gender. Flora Nwapa's *Efuru* provides an example of a novel almost certain to create confusion through the empathic inaccuracy of Western readers. Nwapa's text presents the experience of genital cutting in preparation for childbearing in a positive light.[22] This "bath," as Nwapa refers to the Female Genital Cutting of her central character, does carry the risk of excessive bleeding (*Efuru* 13), but the female elders emphasize the graver risks of childlessness or child mortality associated with the failure to undergo the ritual surgery. Nwapa does not deny the pain involved in the straight razor operation (on the clitoris and sometimes the labia).[23] The description of the event invites the reader to join with Efuru to share the agony: "Efuru screamed and screamed" and "Efuru's husband was in his room. He felt all the pain. It seemed as if he was the one being circumcised" (14). Thus far any readers who recognize what the surgery involves may flinch in tandem with the feelings of the fictional characters. However, the novel rapidly moves to convey the benefits of undergoing "circumcision." Efuru grows plump and beautiful with the feasting and grooming that follows the painful genital cutting. She enjoys the admiration of those in her society. Efuru goes out with the other circumcised women, dressed in the honorable outfit of the mature females: "They were objects of attraction; men, women and children stopped to watch and to admire them" (17). At this point in the narrative, readers who have joined with the suffering Efuru several pages earlier are not always ready to make the rapid transition to follow her into the states of happiness and pride so clearly signaled by the text. Indeed, they sometimes react with outrage at what they regard as an unjustifiable or implausible turn of events in the emotion cues offered by the novel. Some readers resort to ironic explanations, as indeed Efuru later enters the despised state of childlessness against which the ritual is supposed to guard a woman.

Nwapa herself does not make the point ironically, choosing instead to celebrate Efuru's dedication of herself to the childless goddess of the lake.[24] Nwapa's message in this novel and others concerns the value of economic independence for all adult women (Nwapa and Umeh, "Poetics" 22–30). She does not directly contest practices (such as female circumcision and polygamy) that many Western readers would regard as interfering with women's rights in traditional societies. Understandably, students in the United States find themselves empathizing inaccurately, for their own cultural context condemns female genital cutting (FGC). Indeed, the United States has legislated against the practice of FGC as child abuse or torture. It is illegal to perform FGC on an American girl under the age of eighteen.[25] The historian Sandra E. Greene, who teaches Nwapa's *Efuru*, confirms my sense of the difficulties emerging from students' responses. Greene writes, "How are we to understand a novel that so resolutely challenges a culture yet also takes for granted certain practices—female circumcision, bridewealth, and polygyny—that most of my students understand as degrading to women and therefore anti-female?" ("Flora Nwapa's" 220). Greene struggles to bring her students to the point at which they may "contend with the fact that there is no one legitimate perspective on these issues" (223).[26] Experiences of narrative empathy, accurate or inaccurate, may make such a relativist insight more difficult to achieve, if it is indeed the goal of instruction. Empathy often underwrites readers' convictions about the universality of human nature, as the case study of Oprah's readers shows. A reader persuaded that she has felt with a fictional character may defy the stated or implicit intentions of an author, as we have seen in an earlier chapter. When the author's intention matches the reader's feelings and the agreement resonates with empathic accord, then the introduction of alternative perspectives on the matter at hand may meet with disbelief or outrage. *Empathic inaccuracy*, to craft a hypothesis out of this circumstance, *may then contribute to a strong sense that the author's perspective is simply wrong.*

Rather than attempting to eliminate empathic inaccuracy by arguing with readers' feeling responses, recognizing the conflict between author's empathy and reader's empathy opens the way to an understanding of narrative empathy as rhetorical: *both authors' empathy and readers' empathy have rhetorical uses, which may be more noticeable when they conflict in instances of empathic inaccuracy.* By using their powers of empathetic projection, authors may attempt to persuade readers to feel with them on politically charged subjects. Readers, in turn, may experience narrative empathy in ways not anticipated or intended by authors, as we have seen earlier. When those readers articulate their differences with a text's and author's apparent claims, they may call upon their empathetic response as a sort of witness to an alternative perspective. Arguments over empathic differences between authors and readers, or among readers with different emotional reactions to a shared text, give feeling responsiveness to fiction a status it has not often been granted in academic analysis of literature. Feeling responsiveness can impede or assist arguments about an issue that transpire in the public sphere. The existence of an empathetic novel-reading experience, whether accurate or not, can enter into debates without even being identified as a response to fiction. These untraceable influences upon readers' passions cannot be documented, but every so often, a novel leaves a mark.

Occasionally, a text so resonates with its readers and their knowledge of the author's intentions that it has the power to draw the world's attention to an issue or problem. Throughout this book I have emphasized the relative rarity of such occurrences. The impressive social and political impact of Stowe's *Uncle Tom's Cabin* and Dickens's *Oliver Twist*, for instance, should be set against the sixty thousand or more works of fiction published in Britain alone in the Victorian period. Few would nominate the nineteenth-century novel *en masse* for the honors heaped on the unusual representatives by Stowe and Dickens. Documented examples of successful interventions in the public sphere by novelists are cherished but scarce. In the few cases that literary history documents, the novelist appears to succeed by evoking empathy for suffering characters while delivering salient information to the reading public. Personal celebrity on the part of the author may also be an essential ingredient. This was certainly the case when Alice Walker turned her attention to the practice of Female Genital Mutilation (FGM, the term Walker uses for FGC).

By the time that Alice Walker published *Possessing the Secret of Joy* (1992), she was already the world famous author of *The Color Purple* (1982). Linked to that earlier text by a character in common (Tashi), Walker's *Possessing the Secret of Joy* makes a direct plea to readers, in an afterword, on behalf of the millions of women and girls who have been subjected to genital mutilation. Walker assists readers in informing themselves by providing bibliography and announces that a portion of the profits of the novel will be "used to educate women and girls, men and boys, about the hazardous effects of genital mutilation, not simple on the health and happiness of individuals, but on the whole society in which it is practiced, and the world" (*Possessing* 283). Within a few years of publication, Walker's stated intention of publicizing FGM had been realized, though the practice of genital cutting still persists. Walker used her novel to raise the Western world's awareness. Since the publication of *Possessing the Secret of Joy*, Amnesty International has emphasized FGM as torture, the World Health Organization and UNICEF have taken steps to eradicate FGM, and both state and federal laws in the United States have been enacted banning the practice. Walker's novel has also been vigorously criticized for its very success when African activists were ignored[27] and for the elitist representation of an imaginary Africa,[28] apparently in need of an external messiah,[29] but its impact remains indisputable.

Preston N. Williams, a legal scholar, recalls how the novel raised his consciousness of the issue: "A reading of Alice Walker's *Possessing the Secret of Joy* shortly after its publication persuaded me that the custom of female circumcision should no longer be considered the possession of any one people or continent. Travel, migration, immigration, and a host of other interactions among peoples, cultures, and traditions have made female circumcision a matter of international concern" ("Personal" 491). Even her critics concede that Walker has brought the world's attention to the issue: "By virtue of Alice Walker's accomplishments as a powerful, well known feminist writer—taken seriously by most people who read her writings across the globe—her views on female 'genital mutilation' have come to constitute the last word of the subject of female circumcision" ("Elitist" 464). Walker's sensational novel may persuade Western readers to take her version of genital cutting as authoritative, and criticism of its inaccuracies and exaggerations may never reach as broad an audience. This situation can be a frustrating one for activists, who want the world's attention and recognize that Walker has brought them that but hope to inform the world without interference from a fictional character. This case shows that *concord in authors' empathy and readers' empathy can be a motivating force to push beyond literary response to prosocial action* (if the potential for change exists). It also draws attention to the irritation caused by empathic inaccuracy on the one hand (no, that's not how we feel about it at all!) and the imposition of Western values on other cultures in the name of a universalizing feeling response on the other.

Strategic Empathizing

Empathy intersects with identities in problematic ways. Do we respond because we belong to an in-group, or can narrative empathy call to us across boundaries of difference? Even this formulation could be read as participating in a hierarchical model of empathy. The habit of making the reactions of white, Western, educated readers "home base" for consideration of reader response has not yet been corrected by transnational studies of readers, though narrative theorists such as Peter J. Rabinowitz offer subtle ways of understanding the various audiences narrative fiction may simultaneously address. When the subject positions of empathizer and object of empathetic identification are removed from the suspect arrangement that privileges white Western responses to subaltern suffering, the apparent condescension of empathy can be transformed by its strategic use. Strategic empathy is a variety of authors' empathy, by which authors attempt to direct an emotional transaction through a fictional work aimed at a particular audience, not necessarily including every reader who happens upon the text. Three varieties of strategic empathizing may be observed at work in contemporary fiction, though I feel sure they also pertain to the hopes of authors in earlier periods as well. First, *bounded strategic empathy occurs within an in-group, stemming from experiences of mutuality, and leading to feeling with familiar others.* This kind of empathy can be called upon by the bards of the in-group, and it may indeed prevent outsiders from joining the empathetic circle. Certainly some experiences of empathic inaccuracy can be accounted for by recognizing that a reader does not belong to the group invited to share bounded strategic empathy. Second, *ambassadorial strategic empathy addresses chosen others with the aim of cultivating their empathy for the in-group, often to a specific end.* Appeals for justice, recognition, and assistance often take this form. Mulk Raj Anand's *Untouchable* (1935) provides a good example of ambassadorial strategic empathy in a novel. Third, *broadcast strategic empathy calls upon every reader to feel with members of a group, by emphasizing our common vulnerabilities and hopes.* The Kenyan novelist Ngugi wa Thiongo has deliberately employed broadcast strategic empathy in his fiction, provocatively embracing the universality so often rejected by contemporary champions of difference.

In the next and last chapter, I take up critiques of empathy from feminist, postcolonial, and critical race legal perspectives. They run counter to the case for empathy and sympathy as sources of social bonds and altruism. To those who contest its value, empathy occludes the others' true feelings by imposing Western ideas about what ought to be felt. For these critics, empathy erases the subjectivity of the other, disables effective political responses, and demonstrates the egotistical (and even perverse) motivations of privileged Westerners as they regard suffering others. As I establish in an earlier chapter, every period that celebrates empathy as a starting point for personal morality, the basis for healthy civic relations, or as a source of altruism, also records dissenting voices. Our own period proves no exception to this pattern of contestation.

6

CONTESTING EMPATHY

Up until this point, I have been making the case that the evidence for a relationship between narrative empathy and the prosocial motivation of actual readers does not support the grand claims often made on behalf of empathy. Far from denying the centrality of empathy to an accurate description of emotional responsiveness to fiction, however, I have described in detail the factors that appear to evoke readers' empathy. These may be dispositional, contextual, keyed to knowledge or experience, or they may hinge on matters of literary taste. I have placed my exploration of potentially empathetic narrative techniques in the contemporary context, in which narrative empathy is typically highly valued; but women's reading and subgenres associated with female readerships are often devalued. I have suggested that if narrative empathy is to be understood, all genres of fiction and all kinds of readers should be taken into consideration. A theory of the prosocial value of empathetic response to *A Portrait of a Lady* (1881) that cannot also account for the consequences of far more numerous empathetic readings of *The Bridges of Madison County* (1992) should be regarded with wariness.

It will not suffice, I have argued, to rely on the assertions of authors, on introspection, or on personal conviction to prove that reading certain canonical works of fiction inevitably yields the cultural and civic good of altruism and engaged world citizenship. Indeed, I note that even advocates of the empathy-altruism hypothesis, who see less fickle helping, less aggression, more cooperation, and improved attitudes toward outgroups as benefits of empathy-induced altruism, also document its liabilities, such as harming the target of help, addressing some needs better than others, and inducing empathy-avoidance. Most seriously of all, empathy-induced altruism can lead to actions showing partiality rather than care for the common good and can result in injustice and immorality (Batson, "Empathy-Induced Altruism" 380). These studies concern real-world empathy; the evidence for effects of literary empathy, I have argued, appears even weaker. By drawing on empirical studies conducted by psychologists and experts in discourse analysis, I have sought to mitigate the effects of exaggerating the prosocial value of narrative empathy. Unlike most of the critics discussed in the ensuing pages, however, I do not quarrel with the intrinsic value of human empathy, nor do I regard narrative empathy as a cheat or a fake. Readers' empathy clearly exists and quite likely contributes to the success of emotionally evocative fiction in the marketplace. Through strategic empathizing, authors' empathy may join with readers' empathy to raise awareness of issues through resonant feeling responses. Especially when literary texts explicitly recommend empathetic procedures, as the character Atticus Finch does in Harper Lee's *To Kill a Mockingbird* (1960), some readers respond to the importance of being urged to climb inside another's skin and walk around a bit. Most empathetic fiction calls less didactically for emotional engagement, and many novels stir the emotions of readers without having an explicit message. These novels, too, result in feeling responses that by no means always or even often lead to prosocial actions in the real world. When a novel becomes a popular bestseller, I have suggested, the psychological effect of diffusion of responsibility may deter readers from acting upon their empathetic reading. The link between feeling with fictional characters and acting on behalf of real people, I have argued, is extremely tenuous and has yet to be substantiated either through empirical research into the effects of reading or through analysis of demonstrable causal relationships between novel reading as a cultural phenomenon and historical changes in societies in which novel reading flourishes.

Though novel reading certainly involves role-taking imagination, for novels to change attitudes about others and inspire prosocial action requires more than just reading. Larry P. Nucci's research, summarized in *Education in the Moral Domain* (2001), reveals that the development of social and moral understanding requires *discussion* (173). This conclusion echoes the narrative ethics of Wayne Booth, who regards the active *coduction* that follows reading as a valuable step in connecting novel reading with the formation of readers' characters. The affirmation and challenge to convictions that can occur when readers discuss fiction, especially with the guidance of a teacher who connects the dots between reactions to fiction and options for action in the real world, can be considerable. The belief in the power of a teacher to influence at least those of her students who arrive in a state of readiness to the task of reading animates both the moralists who hope to teach through literature[1] and the cultural conservatives who fear that politically correct indoctrination occurs in the literature classroom. Indeed, arguments about the contemporary canon often thinly disguise interventions on one side or another of the culture wars. The reading list can embody a wish to win the hearts and minds of readers to a favored cause. In the culture wars, books, including novels, apparently possess extraordinary persuasive and motivational power, but without passionate teachers (parents, librarians, and other book lovers) even classics remain inert.

I suggest that when we set the rare narratives of autodidacts who report conversions that came about through private reading into a broader context of all literary readers, the strongest testimony about the influence of books arises from circumstances during which teaching or active discussion accompanies reading. Even the remarkable working-class readers—Welsh miners, English weavers, and Scottish mechanics—who sought to educate themselves through books did so in social networks of mutual improvement.[2] This does not mean that reading circles result in unanimous responses to books: indeed, a group discussion may come closer to eliciting what Paul B. Armstrong calls the disjunctive tension between readers' experiences and the assertions of a fictional world (*Play and the Politics of Reading* xi). We respond to novels differently; novels do not subject us to uniform conclusions. Armstrong sees reading as an exercise in "nonconsensual reciprocity," which may help model peaceful, rational, democratic interactions among citizens. Larry P. Nucci argues that "effective educational use of . . . fictional characters depends on the engagement of students in reflective activities" such as writing, oral analysis, and especially discussion (*Education* 209). Fostering the development of moral selves in readers requires more than offering a reading list of novels and stories embodying specific character traits or virtues (including empathetic responsiveness!). What empathetic reading by itself may not accomplish, however, a teacher or guide may still achieve, if one considers the link between novel reading and active steps on behalf of real others desirable. Thus, while fiction reading alone may not form citizens committed to justice, democracy, and nuanced understandings of other cultures, pedagogical practices could respond to narrative empathy as an opportunity to transform "ideological and cultural conflicts into mutually beneficial and enlightening exchanges," as Armstrong puts his call for reformed language arts instruction (177). Conscious cultivation of narrative empathy by teachers and discussion leaders could at least point toward the potential for novel reading to help citizens respond to real others with greater openness and consciousness of their shared humanity.

Critics of empathy and, to a lesser extent, of empathetic reading quarrel with that very goal. For these critics, empathy is amoral (Posner, "Against" 19), a weak form of appeal to humanity in the face of organized hatred,[3] an obstacle to agitation for racial justice (Delgado, *Race War?* 4–36), a waste of sentiment and encouragement of withdrawal (Raymond Williams, *Culture and Society* 109), and even a pornographic indulgence of sensation acquired at the expense of suffering others (Wood, *Slavery* 36). To some feminist and postcolonial critics, empathy loses credence the moment it appears to depend on a notion of universal human emotions, a cost too great to bear even if basic human rights depend upon it.[4] Indeed, the suspicion of universalizing or essentializing concepts explains a great deal of the resistance to empirical disciplines (such as psychology) in the humanities and in some social sciences. "Empathy" becomes yet another example of the Western imagination's imposition of its own values on cultures and peoples that it scarcely knows, but presumes to "feel with," in a cultural imperialism of the emotions. Each of the sentences of this paragraph refers to rich debates, to which I cannot do justice in a short chapter, though I return below to the key areas of contestation: the relationship of empathy to altruism and community building; the hazards of empathy; the commonalities of human bodies; and the putative universality of the emotions. To further illustrate the point made in the preceding chapter, that contemporary fiction participates in the interrogation of empathy as a core value of novels, I approach these topics through the fiction of African American science fiction novelist Octavia Butler and Canadian Booker Prize winner Michael Ondaatje, who left his native Ceylon (now Sri Lanka) as a child.

Hyperempathy

In Octavia Butler's dystopic near-future California, fifteen-year-old Lauren Olamina lives a protected life within a walled community outside Los Angeles. Neighborhood walls keep marauders and drug-addicted pyromaniacs on the outside, where only the vestiges of civil society remain. *Parable of the Sower* (1993) relates in first-person diarylike entries the destruction of that safe haven and the journey of Olamina and a band of followers to a remote area where she founds a new faith, Earthseed. Butler's central character suffers from a brain disorder caused by her biological mother's drug abuse during pregnancy. She has the "organic delusional syndrome" hyperempathy (*Sower* 11), a condition that renders her helpless in shared sensation when she witnesses another's pain. Olamina's hyperempathy resembles real human empathy in a number of particulars: seeing (but not hearing about) another's wound sets it off; suffering animals as well as humans can evoke it (43); a fake injury can call it up as well as accurate perceptions of suffering (10). Butler exacerbates the gap between empathy's involuntary responsiveness and sympathy's more mature and deliberate channeling of feelings when she pushes Olamina's hyperempathy toward personal distress.[5] However, the sensations of hyperempathy are not only painful: like Hazlitt's sympathy, Olamina's hyperempathy intensifies the pleasure of sex (12), but that is just about the only good side effect of what Butler presents unstintingly as a disability and a closely guarded secret (162). If others knew of her empathy, the narrator explains, she would be vulnerable to incapacitation, exploitation, even enslavement.

Late in the novel, Olamina meets a family of fellow "sharers" and discovers that they have just escaped slavery, which after all has not been eliminated by the conclusion of the American Civil War. Their experiences, and Butler's expansion upon them in a concentration-camp episode in the sequel, *Parable of the Talents* (1998), demonstrate the hazards of hyperempathy.[6] Bosses pay more for "feelers," especially children with the syndrome, who can be effectively rendered docile without risk to the bodily health of the slave (*Sower* 278). Olamina is exceptional not only because she can hide her debility (it shows in the others sharers' cringing behavior), but also because she can push violent actions further than typical hyper-empaths. They cannot even engage in self-defense, but Olamina can shoot. We learn through Olamina's unusual experiences that "sharing" feelings of being shot and even dying does not destroy the hyperempath, though it knocks her out. Olamina can kill those who attack her (142, 215), but she consequently undergoes their agony. Her empathy has ironically made her a more effective fighter, for she cannot afford merely to injure her oppo-nent (256). She shoots (stabs, bludgeons) to kill. This ruthlessness on the part of Butler's protagonist makes her survival on the road plausible, but it would be missing a major part of Butler's defamiliarizing treatment of empathy to link it too easily with survival. Olamina survives in spite of her hyperempathetic feelings for suffering of others, some of whom she kills with her own hands.

Mitigating Olamina's violence (always in self-defense) is her persistent community building. Having perceived the risks of being in a group locked in behind walls, Olamina does not react by lighting out for the territory on her own. She judges people well through the fine-tuned skills of the habit-ual perspective taker, and she compensates for her lack of survival skills by recruiting companions. Cultivating trust in order to achieve improved safety through numbers, Olamina gathers a multiracial band of travelers around her. Deliberate acts of altruism often result in members joining the group.[7] Carrying out altruistic rescues exposes Olamina to hyperempathic agony, but the moral obligation to help victims and the pragmatic goal of making the whole group safer override the perils of empathy. The survivors become the core of the first Earthseed community, whose story Butler tells in the sequel, *Parable of the Talents*. Though Butler does not explicitly link Olamina's empathy to her success in reforging social bonds, the account of community arising in negative reaction to a state of anarchy is consistent with a Humean view of empathy, and Butler has asserted that the novel is "fundamentally about social power" (Potts, "We Keep Playing" 334).

While some critics of the novel have hastened to assure readers that But-ler makes Olamina's hyperempathy the source of her "deep sense of solidar-ity with others" (Miller, "Octavia Butler's Vision" 357), in fact, Butler con-sistently represents it as an obstacle to relationships, an alienating personal quality that is as likely to result in anger, hatred, distrust, resentment, and despair, as more positive emotions. The personal distress-suffering hyper-empath takes to heart the violence done to others, and she learns suspicion as a first strategy for survival. That the practical ethics of the road lead to the formation of a protective band emphasizes the dangers posed by others. There is no solidarity with predatory humans, whom Butler represents as ruthless individuals or members of barbaric gangs who can only imperil the weak, the careless, and the isolated. In a public lecture given at MIT, Butler explains that she intended to explore the negative possibilities of extreme empathy: "I remember talking to some people who thought this would be the perfect affliction to make us a better people because it's a kind of biological conscience, and you wouldn't be able to hurt people without feeling it. And I immediately began to think about ways in which that wouldn't be true and ways in which that would be disastrous" (Butler, "Devil-Girl"). Like Richard Posner, who argues that empathy may lead us into contact with the minds of "a torturer, a sadist, even a Hitler" ("Against" 19–20), Butler sees empathy as amoral and subject to abuse. Narrative empathy, as Posner observes, "may improve our skills in manipulating people to our own selfish ends" (20). By no means does it inevitably lead to better behavior, though the hyperempath Lauren Olamina admirably survives, which is the sort of selfish outcome that readers with a rooting interest in a self-narrating character tend to appreciate.

In juxtaposition to the perils of hyperempathy, Butler places two destructive alternatives, both addictions that play on human somatosensory vulnerabilities. By 2024, when the novel opens, television has become, for those who can afford it, a fully virtual experience. One enters other worlds in virtual reality gear through wall windows that a desperate government keeps going even as water supplies disappear and coastlines crumble. Olamina, like her creator Butler, is a voracious reader, but others cluster around the TVs until the signals fail. Television effectively immobilizes the middle class behind their walls, while the rich either seize power in the emerging fascist state or suffer the fates of affluent first adopters, dying of the drugs that only they can afford. An alternative to high-tech escapism is the street drug "pyro," a next-generation chemical that provides an ecstatic high, better than sex, when watching fires. The shaved and painted barbarians who terrorize the denizens of Butler's California spout a cheap Robin Hood rhetoric of class warfare, but theirs is no merry band in the greenwood. They literally torch the ground they stand on and dance in a frenzy of pleasure as their own fellow addicts die ablaze.

Butler's point, I believe, is that the very faculties of emotional contagion that make empathy possible can be hijacked all too readily by chemicals and sensory stimulation. Resistance is the extraordinary exception, like real-life altruism. Rare circumstances provide the crucible for the forging of a savior-leader such as Olamina. Most people fall victim to emotional weaknesses and don't even do a very canny job of surviving. It may help to be too poor for technology or drugs, but to her credit, Butler does not romanticize the poor as either abstainers or as victims. In one sense they have a survival advantage over those who have more to lose through inaction or addiction. Poverty provides a small protection, unless, like Olamina's ill-fated brother Keith, one gets swept into a temporarily lucrative life on the streets. Yet the desperate poor also endanger everyone else on the street. Butler depicts countless characters in states of grief, denial, numbness, and moral stupidity—competing for entrance to a town owned by a multinational corporation, for instance, in which inhabitants will shortly be ensnared in debt slavery. The few who will survive to found a new community Butler explicitly links to nineteenth-century fugitive slaves, fleeing north through hostile territory inhabited by racists, opportunists, and zealots.[8] This historical analogy certainly demands sympathy from the reader, but Butler estranges the reader from the usual associations of empathy with natural human bonds. Olamina and her community cannot afford to risk such an idealized view of the role of feelings.

Butler's comments in interviews illuminate her dissent from the mainstream notion of both empathy and the efficacy of fiction. Like students of human behavior during genocides, Butler sees empathy as a relatively weak form of appeal to common humanity.[9] She regards the desire for dominance, division, and hierarchal relationships as human beings' fatal weaknesses; further, "here on Earth, the worst behavior is rewarded" ("Persistence" 4). Butler worries about "the trivialization of empathy" (76) and reflects on the basis of her own experience that hurting other people exacts a price from empathic individuals and makes them hesitant to protect themselves.[10] This means that an empathic person is likely to be perceived as weak, as "some bleeding heart idiot" ("Persistence" 76). Butler rejects easy associations between empathy, understanding, and social good. In an early unpublished story, Butler reports, she depicted a group of telepaths constantly at one anothers' throats: "They were fighting because they understood each other. You know, we always feel that if we could just understand each other, we'd be fine. But the problem here was they couldn't conceal their disagreements and animosities and contempt, and they were killing each other" (Butler, "Devil Girl").

Despite her well-documented utopian imagination, Butler presents the obstacles to improvement in the human species vividly: sometimes hybridization with aliens is the only hope. About *Parable of the Sower*, Butler comments that it is a cautionary tale ("Devil Girl"), warning readers about an all-too-possible future. She remains skeptical about efficacy of fiction in improving human chances for flourishing amicably on earth. *Parable of the Sower* itself does not, as Madhu Dubey aptly observes, "invest any special redemptive power in the literary or fictional imagination as such," though it emphasizes the power of literacy ("Folk and Urban" 120). When interviewers Marilyn Mehaffy and AnaLouise Keating asked Butler whether she believed that "textual innovation and struggle" could be "politically, positively effective," Butler replied, "Can be, but there's no guarantee" ("Radio" 66). This is not to say that Butler has no ambitions to influence her readers; certainly the genre of dystopia in which she works depends upon extrapolations from present-day phenomena (walled communities, global warming, water shortages, debt slavery, and drug addiction) into their worst-case-scenario outcomes. She intends to warn readers, using the traditional vehicle of character identification to make us care about the fate of a black teenage girl who has ended up on the streets in a time of social upheaval. She just doesn't count on narrative empathy to achieve what real-life empathy fails to do, and she assesses the costs of overconfidence in the ethical, social, and political consequences of feeling with others. In this sense, she is in accord with Raymond Williams, whose argument against (literary) sympathetic engagement depends on the historical judgment that interventions on behalf of workers did not occur as a result of reading industrial fiction. Because she is a novelist and not a theorist, Butler keeps on writing fiction that offers an affective bridge between her imaginings and her diverse readership's desires. It will be an important aspect of the remaining argument to see how a novelist denies the cultural values attributed to empathy while establishing commonalities of brain and behavior that may cross borders and temporal lines. As I will suggest below, the consequence of this apparent paradox can be resolved by resituating empathy where it came from in the first place, in the realm of aesthetics.

"That False Empathy and Blame"

Michael Ondaatje's novel *Anil's Ghost* (2000) presents in shards and fragments aspects of a postcolonial problem: what (if anything) can a Western observer of a hybrid transnational identity discover when a human rights organization sends her into a place like Sri Lanka during its ongoing civil war? Can she employ her academically authorized empiricism in the task of truth seeking for the purposes of achieving justice, or is her very mission a product of a Western fantasy of drop-in intervention, as characters in the novel suggest? Do the feelings of the individuals involved matter at all? Michael Ondaatje complicates his task by refusing to create in Anil a heroic individual who might make an effectual response to crisis and in the process buoy the spirits of readers who also look on, through her fictional eyes. Structurally, Ondaatje's novel resists the empathetic invitation to character identification. Early reviewers decried its coolness and its apparently apolitical stance toward the Sri Lankan situation.[11] I argue that Ondaatje rebuffs readers who seek either an easy bridge character with whom to travel for a voyeuristic thrill, or a thinly fictionalized work of investigative journalism that can be harnessed for political use. These features participate in Ondaatje's skeptical interrogation of empathy and its uses.

Anil's Ghost, though a recent novel, has already been subjected to searching, intelligent critique by critics of Canadian and postcolonial literature, but none have zeroed in on the specific criticism that Ondaatje's novel makes of empathy and universal human emotions, especially fear, in their putative relations to justice.[12] Some background on a complex text will be helpful. Anil, the eponymous apparent protagonist, turns out to be one of a

handful of characters, professionals whose modes of truth seeking or repa-
ration Ondaatje holds up to scrutiny. They include: Anil Tissera, a forensic
pathologist, who investigates human rights abuses from skeletal remains;
Linus Corea, a kidnapped physician, who treats guerilla rebels in one of
the factions; the brothers Sarath and Gamini, one an archaelogist and the
other a physician; and Ananda, a drunken former gem miner who practices
the hereditary ritual profession of eye painting. All of the characters have
endured their own losses: Anil's parents die in an accident, and her best
friend suffers from early-onset Alzheimer's; Linus Corea has been violently
separated from his family; Sarath's wife has committed suicide, a death that
also grieves his brother, Gamini, who is emaciated from overwork and drug
abuse; and Ananda's wife is among the disappeared, like "Sailor," the anonymous skeletal remains of a political murder victim. Just as the novel provides grief to go around, it also parcels out culpability. No one's clothes are
without blood (*Anil's Ghost* 48), which (along with the destruction of evidence) makes the affixing of blame problematic (17).

Ondaatje's presentation of his characters' actions, memories, and motives
distances readers from easy pity or satisfaction on their behalf, and it also
engenders suspicion of the answers or truths that might be reached through
the investigations carried out within the novel. As Margaret Scanlan persuasively argues about this atypical novel of contemporary terrorism, it
"reproduces no political rhetoric, adjudicates no political claims, projects
no political solutions" ("Terrorism's Time" 302). In *Anil's Ghost*, Scanlan
observes, we find "no master narratives, no organic psychologies, no resolution and no moral" (302). Perhaps only fear, routed through the amygdala,
a brain structure with a Sri Lankan–sounding name (*Anil's Ghost* 135), can
effectively overcome cultural differences in order to permit characters to
respond humanely to one another. Even this proposition requires a collapse
in distance, so that the sharer comes close to the fearful one's circumstances.
But how can we come closer, and what tools do we take up in order to reach
one another, Ondaatje asks. Although he resists the easily recovered truth
of the romance of the archive, Ondaatje still represents the various crafts
of healing and recovery with a degree of hopefulness. The proving of Anil's
conclusions, however, Ondaatje displaces beyond the end of the story time,
which shifts the focus of the novel to the activities of those left on the
ground after Anil escapes Sri Lanka.

Anil's fascination with the "almond knot" (*Anil's Ghost* 135) of the
amygdala, sought out in the autopsies she performs, embeds her suspicion
of shared feeling in soft tissue, which she probes with a scalpel. Anil dis-
trusts "weepers" like her Sri Lankan ex-husband, who spends "all his spare
energy on empathy" (143). A global or transnational identity correlates with
an assumption of stylish cool, and Anil's career choice encourages distancing from her emotions. She enjoys the gallows humor of the autopsy room
and cuts off her relationship with her married lover Cullis with a knife. The

wobble into personal responsiveness Anil shows when she comes back to her country of origin and confronts the corpse of a political murder victim in a master-class with Sri Lankan medical students suggests that a return to home turf may restore Anil's emotions. Which emotions can be shared, though, in a country that has endured so much grief and routine horror that a crucifixion (of a truck driver onto a road using builders' nails) can seem relatively benign? (130). Indeed, as Sarath points out, Anil cannot help sharing the pervasive fear that everyone else on the island lives with daily—she whispers as if she can be overheard even when they have gone far from the capitol (53). This might seem a hopeful development, except that fear so often leads to paralysis, paranoia, disengagement, and broken trust. Anil herself falls victim to her own fear. She effectively betrays herself to the government because she cannot quell her suspicions of her collaborator Sarath. He responds altruistically, in an act of selfless rescue of both Anil and the skeletal remains that will provide evidence to pin one murder on the government that swiftly retaliates for his intervention by killing him. Prosocial action proves a dead end for this good world citizen.

Ondaatje's novel obliquely presents the concepts, empathy, altruism, and justice, but shatters the relationships among them. Ondaatje also arrays fragments of bone, rock, pencil erasers and clay in a celebration of material objects and artisans' skill that points toward putting back together. The novel ends on an up note, with Ananda painting the animating eyes on the reconstructed statue of a Buddha, but it qualifies aesthetic solutions to the larger-scale traumas that it depicts. The penultimate scene depicts a bomber's assassination of the Sri Lankan president, and one feels that the destruction and reconstruction could just as well be reversed. Though he cannot present them simultaneously, Ondaatje's juxtapositions enjoin the reader who wishes to emphasize the last words, on human contact with the artist as, "This sweet touch from the world" (*Anil's Ghost* 307), to admit the limited efficacy of an aesthetic response to carnage. Yet the crafting of a novel out of the materials of recent Sri Lankan history inevitably replaces the real irrevocable experiences of the silenced and disappeared with the creations of fictional representation. The necessary exercise of authorial empathy (which may accompany the most effective fictional world-making) produces a dilemma in a novel that disavows easy connections and solutions.

Guilty already of having escaped to the west, the author and his alter ego Anil meditate on the limits of an empirical truth quest. Like her maker Michael Ondaatje, Anil exits the country as a teenager. She returns in a professional capacity as a forensic investigator, sponsored by a human rights agency based in Geneva. Ondaatje's return journeys took place for less politically charged purposes than Anil's, but he concedes that the project of the novel still runs the risk of indulging in literary tourism, remarking in an interview with Maya Jaggi that "it's a real problem. I'm sure I'm as guilty as anyone. That's why I didn't want to make assured judgments about what should be done—which is often incendiary and facile. . . . I was very careful to try and avoid the easy solutions" (*Writing across Worlds* 253). The expatriate author indicts himself, as well as his character, when the archaeologist Sarath chides Anil: "You know, I'd believe your arguments more if you lived here. . . . You can't just slip in, make a discovery and leave'" (*Anil's Ghost* 44).

Anil has discovered a modern skeleton, a likely victim of a government-sponsored murder, among historical remains gathered from an archaeological site. The quest to put a name to the victim, to find his village, represents a larger project. One victim, one village—these stand in for hundreds of unidentified others (176), according to the logic of Anil's profession, which is necessarily synecdochic. If you are to examine only one bone, her teachers tell her, *"the bone of choice would be the femur"* (140, emphasis in original). The soft tissues that hold memories and emotions elude forensic investigation, so that inferences from the states of bones emphasize narratives of death. Anil is fortunate to have the entire skeleton, so she dates "Sailor" and locates him geographically by means of the subtle marks on his bones, made by larvae after his death, and by his posture at work while still living. Indeed, by the end of the novel, Anil and her Sri Lankan collaborator, the archaeologist Sarath, find witnesses to his abduction and learn "Sailor's" real name.

The discovery is anticlimactic, however. Sarath cautions Anil at the outset about the risks of such extrapolation, even when successful: "I want you to understand the archaeological surround of a fact. Or you'll be like one of those journalists who file reports about flies and scabs while staying at the Galle Face Hotel. That false empathy and blame" (*Anil's Ghost* 44). Ondaatje poses the question of whether narrative fiction, historically kin to journalism, can make itself more like archaeology, providing the dispassionate surround for the fact, rather than crafting a saleable tale for Western consumption. Is the novel as an art form too much devoted to the evocation of feeling and the invitation to character identification to provide such a rich and contextual understanding? Ondaatje's formal choices underscore his suspicion of illusory wholeness. The narration of *Anil's Ghost* Ondaatje breaks up and scatters in multiple centers of consciousness. Anil recedes from view in whole swaths of the book, though the goal of reassembling the picture, as in forensic bone gathering and art restoration work, still suggests a grid that may be of use in filling in. The order of events suggests that the methodology of recovering the past informs the process of repairing destruction, but Ananda makes the aesthetic decision, as far as the reconstructed Buddha goes, not to conceal the scars. Ondaatje sets process and objects in the foreground, with results and discoveries in the background. Individuals survive or don't make it, and their outcomes Ondaatje places in the complicated broader context that repels a sense of satisfaction or even connection. All of these estranging moves place obstacles in the way of empathy-seeking novel-readers, who report with puzzlement their experience of not liking Anil very much.[13]

I have already suggested that Ondaatje eschews the emotional effects of a character-centered psychological novel in *Anil's Ghost*. Ondaatje also throws out the usual moves of the character-driven research thriller, with which *Anil's Ghost* has something in common. As Margaret Scanlan observes, *Anil's Ghost* does not participate in the celebration of a recoverable truth that typifies romances of the archives ("Terrorism's Time" 310). Specifically, Ondaatje provides no strong closure to the conclusion of Anil's research quest. Anil receives no reward for her efforts, and Sarath pays a severe penalty for his role. The characters abjure pleasurable experiences, including aesthetic ones, in a novel that idealizes asceticism. The usual research tools (United Nations and Amnesty reports, atlases, encyclopedias, and newspapers) are revealed as patchy and unreliable. Instead, scientific expertise, local knowledge, and a knack for improvisation during times of scarcity receive Ondaatje's emphasis. Peculiarly, the creation of something approximating an archaeological surround for a fact in fiction requires jettisoning history and politics. The novel provides very little detail on the recent strife in Sri Lanka; though informed readers will recognize Ondaatje's fictionalized versions of some events, he leaves much deliberately vague. Ondaatje resists the generic pressure to provide a researcher hero or to reveal a heroic victim, a silenced life brought to voice by recovery. I have argued elsewhere that romances of the archive often place empathy at the center of a research quester's work, as a special form of recognition that permits the unlocking of mysteries.[14] Though the novel offers a brief portrait of an epigraphist (Palipana, Sarath's mentor) who makes up the evidence that ought to be there, Ondaatje does not endorse the maker's trance as a way through to truth. Similarly, Ananda's facial reconstruction of "Sailor," apparently following the Manchester protocol for rebuilding a face up from the skull, fails in accuracy because it becomes a portrait of the artist's dead wife, a work of mourning rather than of recovery. Though she experiences flashes of insight as she gains knowledge of her surroundings, Anil does not reach the truth about Sailor through feeling. Dispassionate recognition of the meaning of evidence replaces empathy, whose leaps to certainty Ondaatje places under skeptical scrutiny.

False empathy receives explicit condemnation in *Anil's Ghost*, as in critiques such as critical race theorist Richard Delgado's work. In *The Coming Race War*, Delgado creates characters that discover through dialogue how true empathy is in "shorter and shorter supply" (*Race War* 8). Whites in particular are prone to false empathy, a term Delgado relates to Gramsci's false consciousness: "False empathy, a sentimental, breast-beating kind, is common among white liberals, and is the mirror opposite of false consciousness, Gramsci's notion" (12). Whether one knows that he or she is faking or not, a white enjoying false empathy "pretends to understand and sympathize with a black" (13). From this grim assessment comes the inevitable disavowal of empathy itself, for "the most unsympathetic thing you can do is think you have empathized with those of a radically different background. You can easily end up hurting them" (13). As Thom Gunn's speaker in the poem "Save the word" counsels, "Think you can/ syphon yourself / into another human[?] . . ./ / Don't try it" (*Boss Cupid* 71). The task is too likely to end in self-delusion and, according to Delagdo, worse: empathy reproduces hierarchy and power relations (*Race War* 14, 15). Although Delgado and Ondaatje both hold out the possibility that true empathy exists, white or Western delusion discredits the claim of empathetic understanding before it can even be made. Since false empathy is worse than none at all, worse even than indifference (31), Delgado eschews empathy altogether: "We must realize," his character opines, "that persons of radically different background and race cannot be made vicariously to identify with us to any significant extent" (31). Instead, Delgado advocates, sympathetic whites should reject racial privilege, act in solidarity with minorities, and work to subvert the system from within.

Ondaatje's suspicion of empathy resembles Delgado's in many particulars, despite differences of historical situation. The Western observer—even the returned Sri Lankan who has been absent for the crucial years—must not presume to an understanding she, as an outsider, cannot possess. As Heike Härting aptly observes, the privilege of Anil's mobility "marks her as a cosmopolitan traveler in the postnational world" and her efforts after exiting Sri Lanka receive neither description nor guarantee ("Diasporic Cross-Currents" 46). While engaged in research, Anil's enjoyment of decent lodgings, professional respect, and a brief from an international agency discredit her insights as potentially engaging in false empathy (*Anil's Ghost* 41). Her Sri Lankan background does not go far to assuage doubts about her sincerity. She has been away too long and does not share the experience of the civil war. Because she has lost her ability to speak her native language (Sinhala), Anil cannot blend in with her countrymen, even those belonging to the same ethnic background. Her education sets her apart. The charge from Geneva may be interpreted (certainly by the Sri Lankan government and possibly also by the rebel groups) as an attempt at subversion, though Anil is officially an "invited" guest of the nation.

Nonetheless, Anil works in solidarity with that most silent of minorities, the dead, and that makes her position especially precarious, for they cannot defend her. In the end, Sarath helps her escape the country with the skeleton that will enable her to pin one crime on the government perpetrators. Perhaps he does it because Anil finally identifies herself, in a moment of life-risking public accusation, as a Sri Lankan herself: "I think you murdered hundreds of us" (*Anil's Ghost* 272). Sarath notes that "us" of belonging, after fifteen years away. Until this climactic scene, Anil, who bears a masculine name bartered from her brother, strenuously resists attempts to place her own identity: not the swimmer, not married, not Sri Lankan anymore. Yet professionally accustomed to placing the dead, Anil routinely turns "bodies into representatives of race and age and place" (55). Being fully alive embraces particularities of experience, memory, and emotion that elude the categories that contain the dead. (Hence Ondaatje depicts Leaf's descent into early-onset Alzheimer's disease as embedding the true meaning of death.) Defying fixed identity entails other distancing gestures, as in Anil's characteristic defense against the demand for a personal response to trauma: "there could never be any logic to the human violence without the distance of time. For now it could be reported, filed in Geneva, but no one could give meaning to it. . . . She saw that those who were slammed and stained by violence lost the power of language and logic" (55). Anil's expressed solidarity with the dead, about whom readers learn little, stems from her privilege to fly away from the scene and to regain her position in Europe or America. Judgments are to be left to history, conspicuously absent from the text. Anil's effort has the virtue of retaining language and logic employed on the dead's behalf, but it is disconnected from fellow feeling.

Eventually Anil gets past her fear of emotional responsiveness to arrive at what Martin Hoffman would call empathic injustice—by which the psychologist means an empathic recognition of injustice suffered by others (see 19 above). Anil finally lays blame on the government, allying herself with justice. Yet a pallid justice renders its verdicts from the safety of Geneva. On the ground in Ondaatje's Sri Lanka a starker reality rules, in which approaching justice endangers life, perhaps not the best choice in the circumstances. One victim who might be identified, one monument repaired: Ondaatje places these works of craft in stark juxtaposition to the healing arts of the novel's two doctors, who continue to strive for the wounded and sick. Ondaatje brings Anil into close proximity with the physicians on several occasions, as if to chart her cure from dispassion and her induction into professional caring through actions rather than through narration of psychological renovation. The conclusion of the novel, in which Ananda restores sight to the Buddha and receives the companionable gesture of a child, could not come about without Anil's swift medical intervention when Ananda attempts suicide. Gunesena, the man who drives Anil to the airport for her last-minute escape to the West, is the crucifixion victim whom she earlier rescues. If one cares about human rights, Ondaatje suggests, one could do worse than caring for living persons and human bodies.

Embodied human characters, for both Octavia Butler and Michael Ondaatje, present fearful dangers to one another. The extreme risk entailed in empathizing or identifying with others underscores the problems of empathic inaccuracy and the amorality of empathetic responsiveness to suffering. The victim with whom the empath resonates emotionally may be an assassin, an assailant, a person with blood on his hands. According to both writers, not until the archaeological surround of a fact can be established could one begin to know whether to trust an empathetic impulse. That process may require too much time—even the distance of historical regard—to be of any use in the immediate moment. In this sense it may be a consoling fact to know that empathy rarely leads directly to altruism.[15] For Butler, deliberate altruistic actions offer others the opportunity to overcome their distrust and join the utopian community; for Ondaatje, altruism costs lives, producing yet another corpse of a government-sponsored murder to replace the one that has been spirited away. Both Butler and Ondaatje suggest caution in matters of trust and put limits on the usefulness of universal human emotions. Using empathy to get at supposed commonalities or to reach certain judgments about complex events exposes the empathizer to risks of oversimplification, misunderstanding, and inadvertent harm.

Failed Empathy, False Empathy, and Universal Human Emotions

For a significant subset of empathy's critics, the implausibility of universal human emotions makes empathetic response a suspect end of literary representation. This differs from what we may call the *failed empathy* and *false empathy* critics' views. While *failed empathy* critics lament the inefficiency of shared feelings in provoking action that would lead to positive social or political change, *false empathy* critics emphasize the self-congratulatory delusions of those who incorrectly believe that they have caught the feelings of suffering others from a different culture, gender, race, or class. (Those who take the Hobbesian view that empathy is really only egoism and self-regard enhanced by means of a suffering other offer a variant of false empathy criticism.) Failed empathy critics focus on empathic inefficacy[16]; false empathy critics predict and deplore empathic inaccuracy.[17] A very small subset of false empathy critics construe empathy as antipathy under the guise of compassion; for these individuals, some of whom are Freudians, a sense of shared feeling does violence to the object of one's regard and hurts the object through aggressive identification or projection.

False empathy critics and failed empathy critics offer limited commentary on narrative empathy, by which readers experience sensations of empathetic identification with fictional representations. The worst a failed empathy critic could say would be a version of what Raymond Williams argues, that reading about fictional characters in pitiable situations actually leads to apathy. Catherine Gallagher explains the mechanisms at work (using the term *sympathy*), with an emphasis on the special contribution of fictional characters as "potential objects of universal identification":

Fiction, then, stimulates sympathy because, with very few exceptions, it is easier to identify with nobody's story and share nobody's
sentiments than to identify with anybody else's story and share anybody else's sentiments. But, paradoxically, we can always claim to be
expanding our capacity for sympathy by reading fiction, because, after
all, if we can sympathize with nobody, then we can sympathize with
anybody. Or so it would seem, but such sympathy remains on that
level of abstraction where anybody is "nobody in particular" (the very
definition of a novel character). Nobody was eligible to be the universally preferred anybody because nobody, unlike somebody, was never
anybody *else*. (*Nobody's Story* 172)

Thus the salutary effects of fiction reading fail, in inaction. The worst a false
empathy critic could say can be represented by cultural historian Marcus
Wood's condemnation of the liberal imagination, as offering onanistic indulgence of feeling at the expense of the enslaved (*Slavery* 36). There, consumption of the pitiable representation as pornography ostensibly makes
something happen, but the wrong thing (certainly not abolition, according
to Wood).

Both false empathy and failed empathy critics dislike the emotions that
empathizers enjoy, but, in a central irony, they confidently predict the
existence and effects of the feelings that they criticize. Their moralizing
depends upon the certainty that pride, disdain, or condescension related to
the empathizer's position in a social hierarchy truly undergirds any claim
of empathic resonance with another real or fictional being. While the same
critics who express false empathy or failed empathy views may also doubt
the existence of universal human emotions, their conclusions about the deleterious effects of empathy endorse a view of human nature (or at least of
white, Western, privileged human nature) as gravitating toward pleasurable
sensations of superiority over others. Some regard this as hardwired, especially in the male of the species.[18] Octavia Butler, for instance, believes that
a genetic tendency toward hierarchical behavior is the species' most negative and self-endangering trait (Mehaffey and Keating, "Radio Imagination"
54–55). Not all false empathy or failed empathy critics are biological deter-
minists, however, and they consistently emphasize the significance of recognizing and responding to cultural differences as a priority over any easy
assumption of understanding based on human universals.

For those whose main object of critique is the notion of universal human
emotion, the failure or falsity of empathy stems from the conviction that
humans do not share basic emotions, neither in the culturally diverse contemporary world, nor back in time, nor yet in prehistory on the savannah.
They would regard as risible reductionism a statement such as this, from
two psychologists: "Because humans share similar receptor mechanisms and
brains that are organized in roughly the same way, there is bound to be con-

siderable overlap between their experiences" (Gallup and Platek, "Cognitive Empathy" 36). This association of physiology with experience neglects the highly various cultural matrices in which humans develop social understandings. Schemes of universal emotions such as those described by Paul Ekman in his studies of facial expressions (including sadness, anger, surprise, fear, disgust, contempt, and enjoyment) run into semantic difficulties at the outset because even those who believe in their existence disagree about how many basic emotions exist and what to name them. However, contemporary psychologists consider the universal basis for emotional expression a cross-culture feature of psychological functioning in people and primates. Psychologists also recognize that cultures alter the display rules that govern emotional expressions, but they insist on the underlying basis for emotions. As putative human universals, however, a psychobiological view of the emotions also comes under attack as essentialism.[19]

Critiques of universality (or human universals) come in a variety of forms, shaped by the disciplines from which they emerge: history, anthropology, some feminist criticism, and most postcolonial theory. An excerpt from a handbook from the most recent of those fields, postcolonial studies, suggests the gist of the objection to human universals. Bill Ashcroft, Gareth Griffiths, and Helen Tiffin define "universalism/universality" as:

> The assumption that there are irreducible features of human life and experience that exist beyond the constitutive effects of local cultural conditions. Universalism offers a **hegemonic** view of existence by which the experiences, values and expectations of a dominant culture are held to be true for all humanity. For this reason, it is a crucial feature of imperial hegemony, because its assumption (or assertion) of a common humanity—its failure to acknowledge or value cultural difference—underlies the promulgation of imperial discourse for the "advancement" or "improvement" of the colonized, goals that thus mask the extensive and multifaceted exploitation of the colony. (*Key Concepts* 235, emphasis in original)

Deigning not to define human rights or capabilities (two empowering discourses that retain a commitment to some human universals[20]) allows the postcolonial theorists quoted here to eschew any generalizations about values, experiences, and expectations that might be shared by most human beings. Such generalizations, in the view of many postcolonial theorists, only serve the interests of those in power, recently the architects of the British and American empires. Unwitting participants in the exploitation of the colonized thus include those who efface their particular emotional experiences under the presumptuous belief in a common psychobiological inheritance.

Literary expressions of shared humanity are not exempt from this criticism, for, as Ashcroft, Griffiths, and Tiffin remark in another definition,

"Euro-centrism is masked in literary study by such concepts as literary universality" (*Key Concepts* 92). Not the only, but an influential source, for this idea can be found in the writings of the Nigerian novelist Chinua Achebe, whose essay "Colonialist Criticism" acerbically remarks,

> In the nature of things the work of a western writer is automatically informed by universality. It is only others who must strain to achieve it. So and so's work is universal; he has truly arrived! As though universality were some distant bend in the road which you may take if you travel out far enough in the direction of Europe or America, if you put adequate distance between you and your home. I should like to see the word *universal* banned altogether from discussions of African literature until such a time as people cease to use it as a synonym for the narrow, self-serving parochialism of Europe, until their horizon extends to include all the world. (*Morning Yet* 9)

Under the rule of the prohibitions articulated by postcolonial theory and its antecedent disciplines, then, empathy violates a sequence of taboos. First, empathy as understood by psychology depends upon generalizations about universal human traits (not that psychology describes all individuals as equally empathic). Second, a significant subvariant of this critique points out that psychology undertakes far too little cross-cultural comparison and generalizes too hastily from studies of college-aged Americans to human beings in general. Third, for those who regard emotion as culturally constructed, claims about human empathy (perhaps especially those based on studies of other primates) offend a fundamental notion of difference. If one disagrees that a shared neurophysiological makeup among human beings determines our possible range of feelings (and recognition of them in others), then empathy arising from the firing of mirror neurons gives short shrift to both cognition and culture.[21] Fourth, the directional quality of empathy offends because an empathizer feels with a subject who may or may not be empowered to speak for herself, to correct misconceptions about her feelings, and to refuse the pitying gaze. Finally, the threat that empathy justifies and precedes the imposition of "improving" programs that may or may not benefit the recipient or respond to a real need also makes it suspect.

These complaints about empathy raise several questions, some of which could be investigated through empirical studies. Does cross-cultural research reveal empathy to be an esteemed concept in a variety of world cultures?[22] Do people in a variety of cultures value empathy with one another (and do they have a word to label it, or exemplary case to illustrate it)? Do people in worldwide cultures empathize with, or express an emotional obligation toward, individuals that they would construe as outsiders? Do people generally welcome or disdain the notion of empathy as a source of helping and altruism? Most important for the subject of narrative empathy, do they connect novel reading (or narrative consumption) with the cultivation of the role-taking imagination? If so, is this association an artifact of post-Enlightenment liberal humanism, or is it too subject to vigorous reforming and hybridization, those celebrated qualities of postcolonial literature? In many parts of the postcolonial world, novel writing is a twentieth-century phenomenon. Does adoption of the novel as a form of narrative expression import recent Western expectations about empathy and character identification, or can the postcolonial novel accommodate narrative invocation of preexistent cultural understandings about empathy?

Examining texts from other cultures for signs of empathy or its close cognates (sympathy, compassion, fellow-feeling) reassures us that they cannot simply be newfangled notions that come in on the coattails of the novel. According to Patrick Colm Hogan, Sanskrit literary theorists (third century) describe *rasa*, or aesthetic feelings, as entailing empathic versions of emotions,[23] and Arabic Aristotelian theorists name *rahmah*, compassion or beneficence, as one of the "primary ethical emotions operating in literature."[24] Hogan rightly calls for attention to the literary theories and primary imaginative texts of non-Western traditions, and he finds in a variety of cultures significant evidence of literary universals, including empathy.[25] Contributions to this understanding come from many disciplinary approaches and interdisciplinary conversations. For instance, Richard J. Davidson and Anne Harrington gather the conversations of scientists and Buddhist monks in their collection, *Visions of Compassion: Western Scientists and Tibetan Buddhists Examine Human Nature* (2002). The Buddhist moral virtue *karuna* combines love and compassion in order to resist greed and hatred. More important, the practice of *karuna* models the movement toward sympathy and altruism, in Nancy Eisenberg's paraphrase, helping "a person to overcome indifference" and providing "an understanding of the suffering of others and a willingness to go out of one's way to help those in distress" ("Empathy-Related" 133).[26] All major world religions, it is sometimes claimed, have a version of the Golden Rule at the heart of their ethical codes. The Hebrew Bible enjoins the faithful to love their neighbors as themselves (Leviticus 19:18), and Jesus's gloss of Leviticus in the Sermon on the Mount insists that his followers go further, loving even their enemies (Matthew 5:44). The Golden Rule, to do unto others as you would have them do to you (Matthew 7:12; Luke 6:31), emphasizes the principle of reciprocity, as it comes down from the law and the prophets. The existence of versions of the Golden Rule (in Buddhist, Brahmin, Confucian, Sikh, and Hindu religious texts, as well as in ancient Greek philosophical writing, among others) suggests both the advantages of reciprocity and the relative weakness of compassion, especially when involving individuals marked as other.[27] In other words, the presence of Golden Rule variants may show a near universal worry that humans tend *not* to treat others as they would themselves.

Hogan's description of categorical empathy suggests that the ethics of group protection rules empathy through identity. Both identity and empathy are governed by "collective self-definition of an in-group, and opposition to an out-group" (*Mind and Its Stories* 141). This limits the extension of empathy to all human beings on the basis of perceived otherness. For instance, Paul Gilroy laments the obstacle of racial difference:

> Racial difference obstructs empathy and makes ethnocentrism inescapable. It becomes impossible even to imagine what it is like to be somebody else. . . . we are all sealed up inside our frozen cultural habits, and there seems to be no workable precedent for adopting a more generous and creative view of how human beings might communicate or act in concert across racial, ethnic, or civilizational divisions. (*Postcolonial Melancholia* 63)

The tendency of humans to exhibit ethnocentrism in their empathic responses has often been noted (sometimes approvingly, as in political philosophy that extrapolates from love of family to love of nation and ruler).[28] In some cases, as in Gilroy's complaint, noting the phenomenon precedes an ethical charge to go beyond the bounds of similarity. Indeed, good actions confined to taking care of members of the in-group may be regarded as a weaker or even deleterious form of prosocial action. Patrick Colm Hogan believes that only situational empathy, which involves personal memory and role taking, leads to the ethics of compassion (142). This austere position discounts the ethical effects of altruistic action undertaken on behalf of those sharing our categorical identity. The only community large enough to foster truly moral virtues in Hogan's scheme would be the whole world. One could argue, then, that the many parallels of the Golden Rule exist in order to compensate for a human tendency to tribalism, which makes of those outside the group enemies and strangers not obviously deserving mercy or compassion. A proposal derived from Hogan's theory, then, suggests that *empathy for group members emerging from categorical identity with a group does not, on its own, lead to an ethics of compassion.*

Religious instruction often urges believers to move beyond these limitations. Certainly, a selection of world religious texts urges believers to extend good treatment to all others, even to enemies and members of stigmatized groups. For this reason, the parable of the good Samaritan occupies an important place in a Christian understanding of the obligation to love one's neighbor, for it shames those who fail to help the beaten robbery victim as much as it honors the altruistic Samaritan (Luke 10: 25–37). A man learned in the law hears the parable from Jesus after seeking clarification—who is the neighbor that the law requires him to love? Jesus's reply extends the definition of neighbor beyond the neighborhood. If Hogan is correct, the commonness of categorical empathy (and the ubiquitous experience of feeling more intensely with our family members than with strangers) lends credence to the charges of failed empathy critics. Indeed, Jesus himself could be regarded as a failed empathy critic, though he sees a way through the impasse when he singles out for emulation the unusually "good" Samaritan, who acts on his compassionate feeling rather than hurrying by.

Clearly, many cultures value compassion, but their philosophers often observe the weakness of fellow-feeling in moving people to action on behalf of others. Religious teaching has sometimes (though by no means always) addressed this problem by attempting to get people to think of others in terms of similarities rather than differences, through attribution of universal traits. Belief in innate qualities, including virtues and vices, often accompanies attempts to define the nature of humanity. Though this does not always result in emphasis on positive qualities such as compassion, it can, and not only in the West. In the fourth century BCE, the Chinese philosopher Mencius places a concept close to empathy at the heart of his description of humanity. "No man," Mencius writes, "is devoid of a heart sensitive to the sufferings of others." The philosopher illustrates his observation with an example and an analysis of the authenticity of spontaneous empathetic responsiveness: "Suppose a man were, all of a sudden, to see a young child on the verge of falling into a well. He would certainly be moved to compassion, not because he wanted to get in the good graces of the parents, nor because he wished to win the praise of his fellow villagers or friends, nor yet because he disliked the cry of the child. From this it can be seen that whoever is devoid of the heart of compassion is not human" (Mencius 2.6, 82). Further, the "heart of compassion is the germ of benevolence," or *Jen* (sometimes translated as love), one of four fundamental virtues that embed the potential for good in human beings (83). Indeed, for Mencius, denying the existence of any one of these virtues in oneself is tantamount to robbing oneself of one's humanity.[29] The motivation to act upon one's empathic responses, in Mencius's philosophy, then becomes linked to the desire to remain inside the boundaries of the human group.

Our contemporary celebration of our diversity and our differences may make the call to recognize our similarities more difficult to heed, though advocates of virtue ethics and ethics of care hope not.[30] We should recall, however, what the Oliners found when they interviewed holocaust rescuers: those who had learned to see Jews as human beings like themselves were more likely to engage in rescuing than those who had been trained to focus on differences (*Altruistic Personality* 176). Ihab Hassan, an atypical theorist of postcoloniality and postmodernity, articulates some of the possible consequences of focusing on otherness to the exclusion of commonalities: "It can discourage mutual obligation, cripple empathy, defeat transcultural judgments, leaving only raw power to resolve human conflicts. It can lead to hostility, exclusiveness, less respect for others than solidarity with ourselves. . . . Still, the intractable question remains: *How and when, pragmati-*

cally, do we honor differences, ignore them, negotiate them?" ("Queries" 335, italics in original). Acknowledging near universals, for Hassan, represents a more hopeful direction: "many principles serve as working generalizations or soft universals. I do not mean only biological facts like death, hunger, or sexual reproduction. I also mean, empirically, some transcultural practices like languages, rituals, taboos, spirits, social organizations of marriage, hierarchy, and status. These, we know, vary immensely according to time, place and tribe. Yet as human practices, they pervade the earth. *Can postcolonial studies qualify, discriminate, contextualize the idea of universals, give it texture and nuance, instead of rejecting it outright?"* (336, italics in original). For Hassan, the goals of a cultivated role-taking empathy could follow upon recognition of commonalities to our common good: "is it not possible that by transcending both ourselves and our cultures we can project ourselves into other selves and other cultures . . .?" (341).

Azar Nafisi, writing of her years of teaching novels to women students in Iran, agrees that the activity of entering fictional worlds and experiencing imaginative transport matters. She regards the practice of what Hogan calls situational empathy through novel reading as an essential step in character formation as well as understanding. Nafisi recalls how she exhorted her students, "It is only through literature that one can put oneself in someone else's shoes and understand the other's different and contradictory sides and refrain from becoming too ruthless. Outside the sphere of literature only one aspect of individuals is revealed. But if you understand their different dimensions you cannot easily murder them . . ." (*Reading Lolita* 118). When an admirable individual such as Nafisi (who persisted in teaching in her home after the Iranian government made continued work at the university impossible) testifies to the ethical and political consequences of novel reading, the connection of empathy and the novel becomes harder to question. However, research on character education shows that reading alone results neither in reliable extraction of moral themes nor in traceable moral development.[31] The missing piece in Nafisi's account is her *own role* as a teacher who promoted the reflective connections between fiction and world that so influenced her students. Nafisi discounts the effect of her own charisma and gives all the credit to the books and her resilient students, which is certainly her prerogative. Looking in from the outside, we may be inclined to bestow our admiration on Nafisi as a teacher. Because she makes the cultivation of empathy through literature a central tenet of her teaching, Nafisi makes it more likely that her students will search for connections between literature and life. She writes, "A novel . . . is the sensual experience of another world. If you don't enter that world, hold your breath with the characters and become involved in their destiny, you won't be able to empathize, and empathy is at the heart of the novel" (111). Her students could not fail to learn this credo.

Since she writes about a context in which the act of novel reading stood in opposition to a regime that deprived citizens of basic freedoms, Nafisi's case for empathy through reading may seem more compelling than the common American and English versions that I have subjected to scrutiny in this study. This testimony from outside the Anglo-American academy (though Nafisi is now a professor at Johns Hopkins) suggests that we should not be quick to discount the symbolic importance of novel reading as a *sign* of one's empathy and one's commitments to humane principles. When announcing oneself as a reader of Nabokov and Fitzgerald runs the risk of censure by agents of a totalitarian state, then siding with imaginative transport looks more like courage than escapism. Nafisi's testimony also reminds us that before we discount the universal importance of empathy simply because it bears the label of a "universal," that we should attempt to put ourselves in the shoes of those who see value in the emotional transactions across time and culture that may be assisted by novel reading.

Nonetheless, the validity of claims about the relationship of empathy to altruism or good world citizenship should still be tested. These pervasive beliefs about the efficacy of fiction, advanced in many cases by novelists themselves, should be investigated in multiple historical contexts, with sensitivity to cultural differences. Striking similarities should also be collected and questioned. Nafisi's warning does not differ substantially from the English critic John Carey's comment, "The imaginative power reading uniquely demands is clearly linked, psychologically, with a capacity for individual judgement and with the ability to empathize with other people. Without reading, these faculties may atrophy" (*Pure Pleasure* xi). Nafisi and Carey stand in here for the thousands of similar utterances of teachers, librarians, and book-lovers all around the world who fear the consequences of an end to novel reading. This position deserves the respect of critical scrutiny.

The atrophy of faculties of judgment and empathy would certainly impoverish humans. The replacement of the novel with other forms of narrative may already be underway, and I am sure I am not alone in feeling that its total abandonment would be a loss. However, I strongly resist the notion that the decline of a novel-reading population among global citizens would inevitably result in stultified imaginations and civic lives ruled by antipathy or apathy. I also doubt that novels alone can cure what ails us: can novel reading really restore to vitality nearly extinguished civic virtues in a culture like my own, in which torture and routine violations of international law and human rights are carried out daily on our behalf? Can novel reading avert the course of genocide or rouse a torpid public to activism? Of course, no one goes so far. More modest expressions of hope invest fiction with the power to reverse the course of apathy and indifference to others. The evidence for such effects, I have argued, is not robust, and we will be bitterly disappointed if we expect novel reading to accomplish the work of forming world citizens for us. This is *our* responsibility as parents, teachers, writers, and, indeed, as novel readers. We should not fob it off on fiction and risk spoiling a great source of aesthetic pleasure, refreshing escape, and edification with a task it cannot accomplish.

In my judgment, readers themselves, especially those who discuss books and bring others into conversation about the implications of fiction, possess the power that they so often attribute to novels. We ought to take care not to confound the effect of teaching with the effects of reading, when it has been demonstrated that even a simple perspective-taking game can inspire altruism where reading alone does not. Readers, which is to say living people, bring empathy to the novel, and they alone have the capacity to convert their emotional fusion with the denizens of make-believe worlds into actions on behalf of real others. That they rarely decide to do so should not be taken as a sign of fiction's failings. I have argued throughout this study that the perception of fictionality releases novel-readers from the normal state of alert suspicion of others' motives that often acts as a barrier to empathy. This means that the contract of fictionality offers a no-strings-attached opportunity for emotional transactions of great intensity. A novel-reader may enjoy empathy freely without paying society back in altruism. Indeed, the appetite for such experiences of imaginative transport significantly diminishes when they become vehicles for arriving at improving ends. New ways of analyzing the lives of readers, especially longitudinal studies that might catch delayed or cumulative effects of novel reading, ought to be devised.

Further, the fiction that novel-readers actually choose and recommend to one another ought to command our attention, whether or not it passes critical tests of significance or literariness. If narrative empathy can be shown to spill over into prosocial action, then great care ought to be exerted to identify the full range of novels that make changes in the world. Even there we should proceed cautiously. A society that insists on receiving immediate ethical and political yields from the recreational reading of its citizens puts too great a burden on both empathy and the novel.

Appendix

A Collection Of Hypotheses About Narrative Empathy

While several of the hypotheses confute one another (as for instance in the directionality of empathy and character identification), I include both formulations to indicate possible directions for research. In its specificity, this collection of possibilities marks a significant advance over earlier broad assertions about narrative empathy that take the form of un-testable generalizations.

Proposals about Narrative Empathy

- Empathy for fictional characters may require only minimal elements of identity, situation, and feeling, not necessarily complex or realistic characterization;
- Character identification often invites empathy, even when the character and reader differ from each other in all sorts of practical and obvious ways;
- Spontaneous empathy for a fictional character's feelings opens the way for character identification;
- Empathetic responses to fictional characters and situations occur more readily for negative feeling states, whether or not a match in details of experience exists;
- Empathy with characters doesn't always occur as a result of reading an emotionally evocative fiction;
- The capacity of novels to invoke readers' empathy may change over time (and some novels may only activate the empathy of their first, immediate audience);
- Empathy for a fictional character need not correspond with what the author appears to set up or invite;

- Situational empathy, which responds primarily to aspects of plot and circumstance, involves less self-extension in imaginative role taking and more recognition of prior (or current) experience;
- Readers' empathy for situations depicted in fiction may be enhanced by chance relevance to particular historical, economic, cultural, or social circumstances;
- Generic differences are likely to play a role in inviting (or retarding) readers' empathic responses;
- (Miall and Kuiken) Unusual or striking representations in the literary text promote foregrounding and open the way to empathetic reading;
- (Bourg) Empathizers are better readers, because their role-taking abilities allow them to comprehend causal relations in stories;
- Readers' perception of a text's fictionality plays a role in subsequent empathetic response, by releasing readers from the obligations of self-protection through skepticism and suspicion;
- (Miall) Readers' empathy could producer verifiable results in the beliefs and actions of populations of actual readers;
- (Hoffman) Novel reading may participate in the socialization and moral internalization required for the transmutation of empathic guilt into prosocial action;
- Though a key ingredient of successful fictional world-making, authors' empathy does not always transmit to readers without interference;
- (Taylor) Novelists as a group may be more empathetic than the general population;
- Fiction writing may cultivate novelists' role-taking skills and make them more habitually empathetic;
- Authors' empathy can be devoted to socially undesirable ends;
- Empathic distress at feeling with a character whose actions are at odds with a reader's moral code may be a result of successfully exercised authorial empathy;
- Empathic inaccuracy may contribute to a reader's strong sense that the author's perspective is simply wrong;
- Both authors' empathy and readers' empathy have rhetorical uses, which become more readily to notice when they conflict in instances of empathic inaccuracy;
- Concord in authors' empathy and readers' empathy could be a motivating force to move beyond literary response to prosocial action;
- *Bounded strategic empathy* operates with an in-group, stemming from experiences of mutuality, and leading to feeling with familiar others;
- *Ambassadorial strategic empathy* addresses chosen others with the aim of cultivating their empathy for the in-group, often to a specific end;

- *Broadcast strategic empathy* calls upon every reader to feel with members of a group, by emphasizing common vulnerabilities and hopes (universalizing);
- (Hogan) Empathy for group members emerging from categorical identity with a group does not, on its own, lead to an ethics of compassion.

NOTES

Preface

1. To those who advance the empathy-altruism hypothesis, such as developmental psychologist Nancy Eisenberg, empathy means an "affective response that stems from the apprehension or comprehension of another's emotional state or condition, and which is identical or very similar to what the other person is feeling or would be expected to feel." Prosocial action is voluntary behavior intended to benefit another. A specialized form of prosocial behavior is altruism, "acts motivated by concern for others or by internalized values, goals, and self-rewards rather than by the expectation of concrete or social rewards or the avoidance of punishment" (Eisenberg, Fabes, and Spinrad, "Prosocial Development" [2006]) 647. Full discussions of empathy and related emotions (sympathy, personal distress), follow in chapter 1.

2. See C. Daniel Batson et al., "Benefits and Liabilities of Empathy-Induced Altruism" (2004), 360–70 for a discussion of the recent research on each of these results of empathy. For a warm, agent-based virtue ethics view of empathy and sympathy, see Michael Slote, *Morals from Motives* (2001), 47, 109–10.

3. See Christian Keysers et al., "Demystifying Social Cognition" (2004), 501 and Vittorio Gallese et al., "A Unifying View of the Basis of Social Cognition" (2004), 396.

4. For an overview of this research, see Vittorio Gallese, "'Being Like Me': Self-Other Identity, Mirror Neurons, and Empathy" (2005), 101–18.

5. See Marco Tettamanti, "Listening to Action-Related Sentences" (2005), 273. Though most neuroscientists working on mirror neurons agree that the effects are strongest in real-life, face-to-face interactions, the "shared manifold for intersubjectivity" still operates when subjects see videos, experience virtual reality through computer interfaces, and simply hear narration about others (Blakeslee, "Cells That Read Minds" (2006), F1, F4).

6. Christian Keysers, cited in Blakeslee, "Cells That Read Minds" F1, F4.

7. See for instance Daniel G. Linz et al., "Effects of Long-Term Exposure to Violent and Sexually Degrading Depictions of Women" (1988) and Brad J. Bushman and L. Rowell Huesmann, "Effects of Televised Violence on Aggression" (2001).

8. Some studies suggest that people with very empathetic dispositions respond more positively to members of out-groups than less empathetic people do, but for most people, perceived similarity encourages empathy. A classic study affirming sim-

ilarity's relationship to higher empathy scores is Dennis Krebs, "Empathy and Altruism" (1975). On out-groups, see E. P. Sheehan et al., "Reactions to AIDS and Other
Illnesses: Reported Interactions in the Workplace" (1989). On similarity, see the literature review in Mark H. Davis, *Empathy: A Social Psychological Approach* (1994),
15, 96–99, 105–6, 109, 116–18.

9. I treat Hume and Smith in detail in chapter 2. On evolutionary bases for empathy for those who are like us, see D. J. Kruger, "Evolution and Altruism: Combining
Psychological Mediators with Naturally Selected Tendencies," *Evolution and Human
Behavior* 24 (2003) and Martin Hoffman, *Empathy and Moral Development: Implications for Caring and Justice* (2000), 4, 13, 206.

10. See the account of empathy's potential to replace egocentrism with ethnocentrism in Nancy Sherman, "Empathy and Imagination" (1998).

11. For this catalog of helps and impediments to empathetic reading of first-person fiction, I draw upon the in-class essays of the students in English 232, The Novel,
composed on 20 February 2006, answering this question: "How does your recent
reading experience in this course square with the notion that first-person narration
is especially productive of empathetic reading? What differences in technique in the
variety of first-person narrative situations might alter readers' responses?"

12. For starting points in philosophy, see Susan L. Feagin's *Reading with Feeling:
The Aesthetics of Appreciation* (1996) and E. M. Dadlez's, *What's Hecuba to Him?
Fictional Events and Actual Emotions* (1997). Psychological critic Norman Holland
deserves attention, not only to his original *The Dynamics of Literary Response* (1968),
but also to his recent "Where Is a Text? A Neurological View" (2002). Two literary
cognitivists who attend (atypically) to the role of emotion in literary response are
David S. Miall, "Anticipation and Feeling in Literary Response: A Neuropsychological Perspective," *Poetics* 23 (1995), 275–98 and Keith Oatley, "A Taxonomy of the
Emotions of Literary Response and a Theory of Identification in Fictional Narrative"
(1994). Robyn Warhol's *Having a Good Cry: Effeminate Feelings and Pop-Culture
Forms* (2003) models the discussion of embodied emotional responses (other than
the individual critic's feelings) for narrative theory and literary criticism. Professional readers will have already discerned the profound influence of Wayne Booth on
this project. His *The Company We Keep: An Ethics of Fiction* (1988) shows the way.

13. For reception theory and reader-response criticism, see (respectively) Wolfgang Iser, *The Act of Reading* (1978) and Jane Tompkins's collection, *Reader-Response
Criticism: From Formalism to Post-Structuralism* (1980).

14. For some of the finest in this burgeoning area, see, variously, Charles Altieri,
The Particulars of Rapture: An Aesthetics of the Affects (2003); Isobel Armstrong, *The
Radical Aesthetic* (2000); Brian Massumi, *Parables for the Virtual: Movement, Affect,
Sensation* (2002); Sianne Ngai, *Ugly Feelings* (2005); and Rei Terada, *Feeling in The-
ory: Emotion after "The Death of the Subject"* (2001).

15. See Antonio R. Damasio, *Descartes' Error: Emotion, Reason, and the Human
Brain* (1994) and Joseph LeDoux, *The Emotional Brain: The Mysterious Underpinnings of Emotional Life* (1996).

16. See Tammy Bourg, "The Role of Emotion, Empathy, and Text Structure in
Children's and Adults' Narrative Text Comprehension" (1996).

17. See David S. Miall and Don Kuiken, "What Is Literariness?" (1999) and Miall,
"Beyond the Schema Given" (1989).

18. See Marjorie Taylor et al., "The Illusion of Independent Agency: Do Adult Fiction Writers Experience Their Characters as Having Minds of Their Own?" (2002/2003).

19. For the best study of the experience of immersion reading, see Victor Nell, *Lost in a Book: The Psychology of Reading for Pleasure* (1988).

20. See both Azar Nafisi's moving memoir, *Reading Lolita in Tehran* (2003) and Elizabeth Long's superb sociological study, *Book Clubs: Women and the Uses of Reading in Everyday Life* (2003).

21. David Miall reports that a 1992 pilot survey of adult readers in Canada yields an 8 percent rate of "regular readers of literary texts," but the definition of a "literary text" in the study he cites most likely rules out popular fiction readers. See "Empowering the Reader: Literary Response and Classroom Learning" (1996), 464. On the Canadian situation, see ABC Canada, http://www.abc-canada.org/literacy_facts/ (accessed 19 November 2004). These recent North American findings are matched by survey data for the United Kingdom. See the U.K. National Literacy Trust, http://www.literacytrust.org.uk (accessed 7 September 2004). The sources gathered at this site suggest that 40 percent of British adults do not read at all, with women reading more than men. See also Michail Skaliotis's "Key Figures on Cultural Participation in the European Union" (October 2002), available online at www.readingeurope.org/observatory.nsf/ (accessed 7 September 2004).

22. See Robert D. Putnam, *Bowling Alone: The Collapse and Revival of American Community* (2000). On rates of novel reading contrasted with other genres, see *Reading at Risk* (2004), 16–17.

23. Martha C. Nussbaum, *Cultivating Humanity: A Classical Defense of Reform in Liberal Education* (1997), 63. See also *Love's Knowledge: Essays on Philosophy and Literature* (1990) and *Poetic Justice: The Literary Imagination and Public Life* (1995).

24. See John Sanford, "Human Rights: A Novel Idea?" http://news-service.stanford.edu/news/2002/april17/hunt-417.html (accessed 10 September 2004), concerning Lynn Hunt's presidential lecture, "The Novel and the Origins of Human Rights: The Intersection of History, Psychology and Literature" (8 April 2004). See also Lynn Hunt, "The Paradoxical Origins of Human Rights" (2000).

25. Canonically, see Benedict Anderson, *Imagined Communities: Reflections on the Origin and Spread of Nationalism* (1983), 25–36.

26. Physiological measures have the advantage of being unaffected by the subjects' desire to present themselves favorably, as may occur in surveys, interviews, or self-reports. See Nancy Eisenberg et al., "Physiological Indices of Empathy" (1987). On deceleration of heart rate in response to negative experiences of others, see K. D. Craig, "Physiological Arousal as a Function of Imagined, Vicarious, and Direct Stress Experiences" (1968). On the measurement of palmar skin conductance and heart rate in response to images of people in pain, see R. S. Lazarus et al., "A Laboratory Study of Psychological Stress Produced by a Motion Picture Film" (1962). This study relies upon people's tendency to identify with "characters" in a nonfiction film (3). For a skin conductance study suggesting that empathetic arousal occurs when subjects believe a person is receiving a painful shock, see J. H. Geer and L. Jarmecky, "The Effect of Being Responsible for Reducing Another's Pain on Subject's Response and Arousal" (1973). On facial or gestural responses as indications of empathy, see the evaluation of Robert F. Marcus, "Somatic Indices of Empathy" (1987). See also

Martin Hoffman, "The Measurement of Empathy" (1982). On EMG and other physiological measurements of emotional responses, see J. T. Cacioppo and R. E. Petty, *Social Psychophysiology* (1983). On the fMRI imaging of empathy, see Tania Singer et al., "Empathy for Pain Involves the Affective but Not Sensory Components of Pain" (2004).

27. On the impact of photography on its viewers, see Susan Sontag's *Regarding the Pain of Others* (2003).

28. For the full grim tale, see Philip Gourevitch, *We Wish to Inform You That Tomorrow We Will Be Killed with Our Families: Stories from Rwanda* (1998).

29. Arguably, a book (though not a novel) has altered American public policy for responding to genocide. Samantha Powers's chilling *"A Problem from Hell": America and the Age of Genocide* (2002) has made American leaders more willing at least to condemn perpetrators of genocide.

30. This book does not attempt to relate the arguments about the paradox of fiction (its elicitation of emotional responses to nonexistent beings) that preoccupy contemporary aesthetics. For a superb resource on this problem, see the essays collected in Mette Hjort and Sue Laver, *Emotion and the Arts* (1997). For the record, I take what Jerrold Levinson calls an antijudgmentalist stance ("Emotion in Response" (1997) 24), since I do not see that emotional responses to fiction logically require belief in those objects' existence. Indeed, I argue that paratexts announcing a text as fictional enhance the work's opportunity to evoke emotion, by relieving readers of any sense of real-world obligation to act, while they engage in fictional world-making. In this I am in solid agreement with Keith Oatley and Mitra Gholamain, in "Emotions and Identification" (1997), on the constructed dream of fiction (264–65). As for the emotions themselves, I regard them as essentially the same as "real" emotions—sometimes less or more intense. Fiction enables us to experience our full emotional registers in risk-free, no-obligations mental simulations. The neuroscientists are getting quite close to an explanation of the neural shared manifold for intersubjectivity that makes this use of our brains as theaters for fictive projections possible. For a start on contemporary aesthetics featuring empathy, see Ellen Dissanayake, *Homo Aestheticus: Where Art Comes From and Why* (1992).

Chapter 1

1. See Davis, *Empathy: A Social Psychological Approach* (1994), 62–81 for a survey of this research.

2. See Carolyn Zahn-Waxler et al., "The Development of Empathy in Twins" (1992).

3. See R. Koestenbaum et al., "Individual Differences in Empathy among Preschoolers: Relation to Attachment History" (1989).

4. See Mark H. Davis et al., "The Heritability of Characteristics Associated with Dispositional Empathy" (1994).

5. See my treatment of the contextual and paratextual factors that govern readers' assumptions about the shifting boundary between fiction and nonfiction in Keen, *Narrative Form* (2003), 128–39. The literary historical evidence suggests that cultural assumptions about fictionality and factuality change over time. Thus, the

salient point is readers' *belief* that a work is fictional, activated as the work of cocreation begins. My contention here is congruent with the claims of Richard J. Gerrig and David N. Rapp, who argue that "readers must construct disbelief: literature will have an impact unless readers expend specific effort to forestall that consequence." See "Psychological Processes Underlying Literary Impact" (2004), 280. Gerrig and Rapp observe that "the probability that readers will construct disbelief is affected by the extent to which they are transported to narrative worlds. . . . the more vividly a work of literature carries its readers off, the more they will be affected by the journey" (280).

6. Daniel Batson and his group have shown that exposure to the testimony of a single member of a stigmatized group can improve attitudes toward those groups through induced empathy. See C. Daniel Batson et al., "Empathy and Attitudes: Can Feeling for a Member of a Stigmatized Group Improve Feelings Toward the Group?" (1997). Batson emphasizes the ease with which novels and films induce empathy and theorizes that the low-cost, low-risk situation may contribute to the effect: "Rather than the disruption of normal patterns of behavior required to create direct, equal-status, cooperative personal contact, we can be led to feel empathy for a stigmatized group member as we sit comfortably in our living room" (106).

7. Social psychologist Mark H. Davis's *Empathy* (1994) provides an excellent and accessible introduction to the subject. For a philosophical account of the role of empathy in the art of understanding (and the arts generally), see Karl F. Morrison, *"I Am You": The Hermeneutics of Empathy in Western Literature, Theology, and Art* (1988).

8. See Vittorio Gallese et al., "The Mirror Matching System: A Shared Manifold for Intersubjectivity" (2002), 35–36.

9. In chapter 2, I trace the fascinating literary careers of the related concepts, observing the convention of using the terminology actually employed by writers in the past.

10. See C. Daniel Batson, *The Altruism Question: Toward a Social-Psychological Answer* (1991), 56–57 and "Altruism and Prosocial Behavior" (1998), 282–316; see also Nancy Eisenberg, "Emotion, Regulation, and Moral Development" (2000), 671–72 and "The Development of Empathy-Related Responding" (2005), 73–117.

11. Students who read under compulsion in order to gain credit for a course may indeed experience personal distress and still soldier on in their reading. I regard this situation (and its results) as an extension of teaching, not to be attributed directly to the novel. Personal distress might contribute to a description of the obstacles to immersion (including disposition or emotional temperament) for reluctant readers.

12. For instance, the congruent theories of Batson and Eisenberg feature different uses of the terms *sympathy* and *empathy* and distinct positions on whether pure empathy precedes other-related sympathy or is defined by its orientation toward the other. See Eisenberg, "Emotion, Regulation, and Moral Development," 671–72. For an excellent recent summary of the different schools of thought about empathy, see Stephanie D. Preston and Frans B. M. de Waal, "Empathy: Its Ultimate and Proximate Bases" (2002).

13. Charles Darwin's treatment of sympathy clearly includes empathy, though he does not use the term. See *The Expression of the Emotions in Man and Animals* (1872). Paul Ekman, the leading authority on facial expressions as indicators of

universal human emotions, does not treat empathy as a core emotion, but as one of the nine starting points for emotional reactions (when we feel what others feel). See Ekman, *Emotions Revealed: Recognizing Faces and Feelings to Improve Communication and Emotional Life* (2003), 34, 37. Neuroscientist Jaak Panksepp argues that emotional systems in the brain involve central affective programs composed of neural anatomy, physiology, and chemicals. Panksepp considers empathy one of the higher sentiments (mixing lower reflexive affects and higher cognitive processes), emerging out of the recent evolutionary expansion of the forebrain. See "Emotions as Natural Kinds in the Brain," (2000), 142–43. For philosopher Martha C. Nussbaum, empathy comes into play as a part of compassion, which she treats as a human emotion. See Nussbaum, *Upheaveals of Thought: The Intelligence of Emotions* (2001), 327–35. For John Deigh and those working at the intersection of ethics and cognitive science, empathy is one of the moral emotions. See Deigh, "Empathy and Universalizability" (1995), 743–63. Social scientist Jon Elster, by way of contrast, does not treat empathy in his *Alchemies of the Mind: Rationality and the Emotions* (1999). This array of views reflects the current state of empathy studies: experts have not agreed whether it is primarily emotional, cognitive, or both: their judgments usually reflect their position on the rationality of the emotions or the emotionality of cognition.

14. See, for instance, the working definitions of different vicariously induced emotional states in Nancy Eisenberg and Richard A. Fabes, "Children's Disclosure of Vicariously Induced Emotions" (1995), 111. I follow Nancy Eisenberg in differentiating empathy, aversive personal distress, and sympathy. Empathic response includes the possibility of personal distress, but personal distress (unlike empathy) is less likely to lead to sympathy, if it proceeds beyond evanescent shared feeling.

15. Positive forms of empathy are drastically underemphasized in the literature. As recently as 2002, psychologists George Ainslie and John Monterosso call for more attention to the full range of emotions involved in empathy. See "Hyperbolic Discounting Lets Empathy Be a Motivated Process" (2002).

16. *Jouissance* is a nearly orgasmic pleasure to be experienced through reading, combining bodily pleasure with intellectual joy in finding meaning. See Roland Barthes, *The Pleasure of the Text* (1973, trans. 1975), in which Barthes distinguishes the relatively easy pleasure of the readerly text from the bliss that comes when the demanding writerly text helps readers break out of their subject positions. See also Julia Kristeva, *Revolution in Poetic Language* (1974, trans. 1984).

17. See, for instance, the treatment of happiness, joy, and love in Elaine Hatfield, John T. Cacioppo, and Richard L. Rapson, *Emotional Contagion* (1994). Theodor Lipps, an important early theorist of empathy, proposed motor mimicry as an automatic response to another's expression of emotion. See Lipps, "Das Wissen von Fremden Ichen" (1906).

18. See Carolyn Zahn-Waxler et al., "Empathy and Prosocial Patterns in Young MZ and DZ Twins: Development and Genetic and Environmental Influences" (2001). Zahn-Waxler reports genetic influences on prosocial acts and empathic concern, found across the time points studied.

19. Cultural differences implicate differences in the nature of emotional experience. Our understanding of what it means to be a person in our cultural context affects the way we experience, for instance, daily emotions of pleasantness

and unpleasantness, or whether we feel entitled as individuals to express a particular emotion. See Stephanie A. Shields, *Speaking from the Heart: Gender and the Social Meaning of Emotion* (2002) and Betja Mesquita and Mayumi Karasawa's cross-cultural comparison in "Different Emotional Lives" (2004). Some psychologists acknowledge cultural differences while emphasizing commonalities. See, for instance, Dylan Evans, *Emotions: A Very Short Introduction* (2001), 8.

20. Oral storytelling is not isolated to preliterate cultures. Children in literate cultures also absorb cultural values and narrative styles through collaborative storytelling. See the comments on rapport and empathy in Masahiko Minami and Alyssa McCabe, "Rice Balls and Bear Hunts: Japanese and North American Family Narrative Patterns" (1995), 443.

21. Other primates demonstrate empathy, with the apes in particular exhibiting consoling behavior and role-taking imagining. See Preston and de Waal, "Empathy: Its Ultimate and Proximate Bases," 7, 12–13. Other group-living mammals such as wolves and dolphins may also possess a version of empathy. See Marc Bekoff, "Empathy: Common Sense, Science Sense, Wolves, and Well-being" (2002).

22. Simon Baron-Cohen, *The Essential Difference: The Truth about the Male and Female Brains* (2003). Autism afflicts one in every 250 American children, most of them boys.

23. Dennis Krebs's work on empathy and altruism showed that high empathizers (who believed themselves to be similar to the performer in his experiment) did indeed behave most altruistically in a reward task. See "Empathy and Altruism" (1975), 1134–46.

24. For a recent survey of the evidence of modest gender differences in kindness, considerateness, and helping, see Nancy Eisenberg, Richard A. Fabes, and Tracy L. Spinrad "Prosocial Development" (2006), 646–718.

25. Among others, Rousseau, Hegel, Freud, Nancy Chodorow, and Carol Gilligan all argue in different ways that females possess innately caring natures. For a trenchant critique of the tendency to study male and female emotions by enumerating differences and similarities, see Shields, *Speaking from the Heart* (2002).

26. See Barbara A. Gault and John Sabini, "The Roles of Empathy, Anger, and Gender in Predicting Attitudes toward Punitive, Reparative, and Preventative Public Policies" (2000).

27. See for instance, Larry Cahill et al., "Sex-Related Hemispheric Lateralization of Amygdala Function in Emotionally Influenced Memory: An fMRI Investigation" (2004).

28. Developmental psychologist Carolyn Zahn-Waxler argues that "biological factors as well as socialization experiences undoubtedly contribute to heightened empathy in females seen even in the first years of life," but she also notes that "relatively few individuals are constitutionally incapable of caring in the early years of life and malleability is possible." See Zahn-Waxler, "Caregiving, Emotion, and Concern for Others" (2002), 48–49.

29. "When demand characteristics were high and participants had conscious control of their responses, gender differences were large; when demand characteristics were more subtle, gender differences were smaller. Finally, when demand characteristics were subtle and subjects were unlikely to exercise conscious control over their responding (e.g., physiological and somatic indices), no gender differences were

obtained." Randy Lennon and Nancy Eisenberg, "Gender/Age Differences in Empathy/Sympathy" (1987), 197, 203.

30. See Tiffany Graham and William Ickes, "When Women's Intuition Isn't Greater Than Men's" (1997).

31. See Ellen J. Ingmansan, "Empathy in a Bonobo" (2002). See also Stephanie D. Preston and Frans B. M. de Waal, "The Communication of Emotions and the Possibility of Empathy in Animals" (2002).

32. The sources of psychopaths' impaired empathy are still under investigation. Experiments conducted by R. J. R. Blair and his collaborators show that children with psychopathic tendencies are less sensitive to both fearful and sad facial expressions on others' faces, which may contribute to impaired empathy. Adult psychopaths and children with psychopathic tendencies show reduced responses to distress cues, as measured by skin conductance. See R. J. R. Blair et al., "A Selective Impairment in the Processing of Sad and Fearful Expressions in Children with Psychopathic Tendencies" (2001); R. J. R. Blair et al., "The Psychopathic Individual: A Lack of Responsiveness to Distress Cues?" (1997); Blair et al., "Responsiveness to Distress Cues in the Child with Psychopathic Tendencies" (1999).

33. See Diane Duane, *A Wizard Alone* (2002) and Mark Haddon, *The Curious Incident of the Dog in the Night-Time* (2003).

34. See for example R. L. Katz, *Empathy: Its Nature and Uses* (1963), 57–58.

35. See Lorna Wing, "Asperger's Syndrome: A Clinical Account" (1981). Asperger's syndrome is sometimes labeled high functioning autism. See Lisa Capps et al., "Understanding of Simple and Complex Emotions in Non-retarded Children with Autism" (1992). See also Tony Attwood, *Asperger's Syndrome: A Guide for Parents and Professionals* (1998), 11, 15–17 and Oliver Sacks's portrait of Temple Grandin, *An Anthropologist on Mars* (1995), 269.

36. See Brent E. Turvey, "Psychopathy and Sadism" (1999) and Vernon J. Geberth, "Antisocial Personality Disorder, Sexual Sadism, Malignant Narcissism, and Serial Murder" (1997).

37. For a full consideration of issues in the study of psychopaths, including their emotional dispositions, see David J. Cooke et al. *Psychopathy: Theory, Research and Implications for Society* (1998). For the philosophical significance of the behavior of psychopaths, see John Deigh, "Empathy and Universalizability."

38. For an overview of empathy in a therapeutic context, see Changming Duan and Clara E. Hill, "The Current State of Empathy Research" (1996). See also Edwin Kahn and Arnold W. Rachman, "Carl Rogers and Heinz Kohut: A Historical Perspective" (2000). Rogers's self-actualizing therapy depends upon empathy as a method for nonjudgmentally entering the private perceptual world of the other. See Carl Rogers, "Empathic: An Unappreciated Way of Being" (1975), 2–10. Hans Kohut's psychoanalytic emphasis on vicarious introspection also emphasized empathy as a basic human trait. See his "Introspection, Empathy, and Psychoanalysis" (1959).

39. See Haim Omer, "Narrative Empathy " (1997).

40. See Rita Charon, "Narrative Medicine: A Model for Empathy, Reflection, Profession, and Trust" (2001). See also the Web site for the Program in Narrative Medicine at Columbia University. It aims to "fortify medicine with ways of knowing about singular persons available through a study of humanities, especially literary studies and creative writing." The program articulates several goals, the most impor-

tant of which is developing "the individual patient-doctor relationship, which can be fortified with accuracy and empathy through narrative methods." http://www .narrativemedicine.org/about.html (accessed 5 October 2004).

41. See Scott Sundby, *A Life and Death Decision: A Jury Weighs the Death Penalty* (2005).

42. See Stephen R. Covey, *The 7 Habits of Highly Effective People: Powerful Lessons in Personal Change* (1990), 235–60.

43. While Daniel Batson and his collaborators have shown that empathy induced for a member of a stigmatized group does improve attitude toward that group (in "Empathy and Attitudes" [1997]) and that more positive attitudes toward a stigmatized group positively alter motivations to help that group (by voting to allocate funds that have already been gathered to the similarly afflicted), they also document defensive resistance to empathy and the negative effects of believing in a victim's responsibility for his condition. See "Empathy, Attitudes, and Action: Can Feeling for a Member of a Stigmatized Group Motivate One to Help the Group?" (2002). Other work by Batson and his colleagues in which empathy influences helping and impedes justice when rival claims for help are made is discussed below.

44. Two views from psychology support the notion that empathy can be taught. First, a behaviorist view: classical conditioning can inculcate a caring response to another's plight, as has been demonstrated with lab animals. See R. M. Church, "Emotional Reactions of Rats to the Pain of Others" (1959). Second, a developmental view: repeat occurrences or exposure can build a sense of familiarity that can overcome the bias against feeling for those who are dissimilar. See Carolyn Zahn-Waxler et al., "Development of Concern for Others" (1992).

45. I treat this question in chapter 3, "Readers' Empathy." See also S. Tötösy de Zepetnek and I. Sywenky, eds., *The Systematic and Empirical Approach to Literature and Culture as Theory and Application* (1997).

46. For an atypical acknowledgment of the impact of fictionality on psychological study of empathic emotional appraisal, see Becky Lynn Omdahl, *Cognitive Appraisal, Emotion, and Empathy* (1995), 170.

47. Evaluation of patients who show changes in behavior as a result of brain injuries, ailments, or surgery contributes to the understanding of empathy. See, for instance, Lynn M. Gratton and Paul J. Elsinger, "High Cognition and Social Behavior: Changes in Cognitive Flexibility and Empathy after Cerebral Lesions" (1989).

48. See note 26 to the preface (175–76) for references to physiological measures of empathy and emotional responsiveness.

49. The earliest empathy test is R. Dymond's "A Scale for the Measurement of Empathy Ability" (1949), 127–33; for another early empathy test, see W. A. Kerr and B. J. Speroff, *The Empathy Test* (1951). The Sherman-Stotland scale includes a factor (VI) measuring "fantasy empathy" for fictional characters in stories, plays, and films. See Ezra Stotland et al., *Empathy, Fantasy and Helping* (1978), 135–56. More recent tests of emotional intelligence include the Balanced Emotional Empathy Scale (BEES) and Davis's Interpersonal Reactivity Index (IRI). On BEES, see Albert Mehrabian, "Relations among Personality Scales of Aggression, Violence, and Empathy: Validational Evidence Bearing on the Risk of Violence Scale" (1997) and *Manual for the Balanced Emotional Empathy Scale (BEES)* (1996; available from Albert Mehrabian, 1130 Alta Mesa Road, Monterey, CA, USA 93940). For the IRI, which

has subscales in Empathic Concern, Perspective Taking, Fantasy (including narrative empathy), and Personal Distress, see Interpersonal Reactivity Index, M. H. Davis, "A Multidimensional Approach to Individual Differences in Empathy" (1980), 85 and "Measuring Individual Differences in Empathy: Evidence for a Multidimensional Approach" (1983). See also Davis, *Empathy* (1994), 55–58. Measuring empathy in children has contributed to developmental psychology. For scales in addition to those already cited, see H. J. Eysenck and S. B. G. Eysenck, "Impulsiveness-Venturesome-ness-Empathy Scale," *Manual of the Eysenck Personality Scales (EPS adult)* (1996). Hall and Rosenthal's Profile of Nonverbal Sensitivity (PONS) measures emotional identification that operates without language mediation. See Judith Hall and Robert Rosenthal et al., "Profile of Nonverbal Sensitivity" (1977) and Hall's recent reassessment, "The PONS Test and the Psychometric Approach to Measuring Interpersonal Sensitivity" (2001). Identifying emotions can be a component of perspective taking. More specialized empathy scales examine empathy toward those suffering from particular conditions. See, for instance, M. Wagner et al., "The AIDS Empathy Scale: Construction and Correlates" (2001) and S. Deitz et al., "Measurement of Empathy Toward Rape Victims and Rapists" (1982).

50. For a recent overview, see Nancy Eisenberg, "Empathy and Sympathy" (2000).

51. For a salutary caution on the interpretation of these fMRI studies, which feature such dazzling pictures and often receive quite credulous promotion in the press, see John T. Cacioppo et al., "Just Because You're Imaging the Brain Doesn't Mean You Can Stop Using Your Head: A Primer and Set of First Principles" (2003). New methods of brain imaging may alter or shore up the scientific understanding of empathy. For instance, Diffusion Tensor Imaging (DTI) reveals the directionality of brain activity by recording the activity in white matter connecting different parts of the brain.

52. Singer and her colleagues employed two empathy scales, Mehrabian's Balanced Emotional Empathy Scale and Davis's Empathic Concern Scale ("Empathy for Pain," 1159).

53. The amygdala, anterior temporal cortex, and orbital frontal cortex (as well as physiological synchrony of the autonomic nervous system) are probably involved in empathy, as the evidence of emotional impairment in brain-damaged or diseased patients suggests. See Leslie Brothers, "A Biological Perspective on Empathy" (1989), Robert Levenson and Anna Ruef, "Physiological Aspects of Emotional Knowledge and Papport" (1997), and Howard J. Rosen et al., "Emotion Comprehension in the Temporal Variant of Frontotemporal Dementia," *Brain* (2002).

54. See LeDoux, *The Emotional Brain* (1996), 168–78.

55. This account is consistent with the emotion theory of neuroscientist Edmund T. Rolls, who hypothesizes that human brain mechanisms provide two routes to action, one a quick, unconscious prompt for a behavioral response (which we share with other mammals) and the other a slower, language-mediated, rational planning faculty. According to Rolls, the two routes can produce conflicting results. See Rolls, "A Theory of Emotion, Its Functions, and Its Adaptive Value" (2002).

56. Mirror neurons fire not only when carrying out an action but also when observing another carrying out the same action. They provide a basis for understanding primates' mind reading, including human empathy. See Vittorio Gallese et al.,

"The Mirror Matching System: A Shared Manifold for Intersubjectivity" (2002) and M. Iacoboni et al., "Cortical Mechanisms of Human Imitation" (1999).

57. See, for instance, Leda Cosmides and John Tooby, "Cognitive Adaptations for Social Exchange" (1992).

58. D. J. Kruger, "Evolution and Altruism" (2003), 118–25. Cross-cultural research suggests that Westerners may differ from members of traditional societies in their emphasis on personal choice that mitigates the obligation to offer a caring response. See J. G. Miller and D. M. Bersoff, "Cultural Influences on the Moral Status of Reciprocity and the Discounting of Endogenous Motivation" (1994).

59. See Eisenberg, Fabes, and Spinrad, "Prosocial Development." 1.

60. See Martin L. Hoffman's table "Scheme for the development and transformation of empathic distress" (1987). See also his compressed version of his theory in the chapter "Toward a Comprehensive Empathy-Based Theory of Prosocial Moral Development" (2001), 61–86 and his earlier "Empathy, Its Limitations and Its Role in a Comprehensive Moral Theory" (1984).

61. See C. Daniel Batson, *The Altruism Question* (1991) and "Altruism and Prosocial Behavior" (1998); Eisenberg, Fabes, and Spinrad, "Prosocial Development." See also Nancy Eisenberg, "Emotion, Regulation, and Moral Development" (2000), 671–72.

62. For his evolutionary argument, see Martin L. Hoffman, "Is Altruism Part of Human Nature?" (1981). For a full-scale philosophical treatment of evolutionary altruism, see Elliot Sober and David Sloan Wilson, *Unto Others: The Evolution and Psychology of Unselfish Behavior* (1998). Mark Davis provides a concise summary of the sociobiological and psychological theories in *Empathy* (1994), 23–45.

63. By connecting caring and justice, Hoffman argues with John Rawls's influential *Theory of Justice* (1971). As Peter Singer notes, even in Rawls's more recent *The Law of Peoples* (1999), Rawls neglects "obligations towards individuals . . . currently destitute in other countries" (Singer, *One World* [2002], 176).

64. See Nancy Eisenberg, "Development of Empathy-Related Responding," 78–83.

65. Psychologists are not the only ones to offer critiques of empathy. Legal theorist Richard Posner considers empathy "amoral." See "Against Ethical Criticism" (1997), 19. Richard Delgado believes the cultivation of empathy should be rejected as poor strategy. See his *The Coming Race War? And Other Apocalyptic Tales of America after Affirmative Action and Welfare* (1996), 4–36. I discuss these and other criticisms of empathy in chapter 6, "Contesting Empathy."

66. See J. A. Piliavin et al., *Emergency Intervention* (1981).

67. See the summary of studies involving questionnaires administered to adults, in Nancy Eisenberg and Paul Miller, "Empathy, Sympathy, and Altruism" (1997).

68. See C. Daniel Batson, *The Altruism Question* (1991); C. Daniel Batson et al., "Empathic Joy and the Empathy-Altruism Hypothesis" (1991); "Empathy and the Collective Good: Caring for One of the Others in a Social Dilemma" (1995); "Immorality from Empathy-Induced Altruism: When Compassion and Justice Conflict" (1995); and "Influence of Self-Reported Distress and Empathy on Egoistic Versus Altruistic Motivation to Help" (1983). For a response to Batson's work, see Steven L. Neuberg et al., "Does Empathy Lead to Anything More Than Superficial Helping? Comment on Batson et al. (1997)" (1997).

69. See Samuel P. and Pearl M. Oliner, *The Altruistic Personality: Rescuers of Jews in Nazi Europe* (1988) and their edited collection, *Embracing the Other: Philosophical, Psychological, and Historical Perspectives on Altruism* (1992).

70. For the full questionnaire, see Appendix C of *The Altruistic Personality* (1988), 331–56.

71. See *The Altruistic Personality* (1988), 189–99, for accounts of several different empathic rescuers. For a positive view of the correlation of empathy and altruism, see John F. Dovidio et al., "Specificity of Empathy-Induced Helping: Evidence for Altruistic Motivation" (1990).

72. See Elizabeth Bowen, *The Collected Stories of Elizabeth Bowen* (1981), 671–85.

73. See Geoffrey H. Hartman, "Is an Aesthetic Ethos Possible? Night Thoughts after Auschwitz" (1994), 135–55, 137–38.

74. See Tom W. Smith, "Altruism in Contemporary America: A Report from the National Altruism Study" (2003).

75. See the variety of views in *Altruism*, edited by Ellen Frankel Paul, Fred D. Miller, and Jeffrey Paul (1993).

76. For instance, in *Unto Others* (1998), Sober and Wilson argue that social psychology has not explained away the role of egoism (seeking internal rewards) in altruism. They advance an evolutionary argument as an alternative.

77. See Patricia Greenspan, *Emotions and Reasons: An Inquiry into Emotional Justification* (1988).

78. For a historical survey, see Nico H. Frijda, "The Psychologists' Point of View" (2000), 70–71. Philosopher Patricia Greenspan offers a nuanced critique of psychological arguments in "Emotions, Rationality and Mind/Body" (2003).

79. See, for instance, Antonio Damasio et al., "Somatic Markers and the Guidance of Behavior: Theory and Preliminary Testing" (1991). Damasio's works for general readers have resulted in wide dissemination of his theories. See *Descartes' Error: Emotion, Reason, and the Human Brain* (1994), *The Feeling of What Happens: Body and Emotion in the Making of Consciousness* (1999), and *Looking for Spinoza: Joy, Sorrow and the Feeling Brain* (2003).

80. See Ronald deSousa, *The Rationality of the Emotions* (1987) and LeDoux, *The Emotional Brain*.

81. See Leda Cosmides and John Tooby, "Evolutionary Psychology and the Emotions" (2000).

82. My informant is neuroscientist Tyler S. Lorig.

83. See, for instance, Stephen K. Reed's introductory college text, *Cognition: Theory and Applications*, 6th ed. (2004). Emotional states receive fleeting mention on just three pages of this text.

84. See, for instance, Joseph P. Forgas, ed., *Handbook of Affect and Social Cognition* (2001).

85. Hoffman is less concerned with the matching of feelings as an end result of empathy, and more interested in the empathic process that may lead a person to feel, for instance, empathic anger on behalf of someone else's sadness. See *Empathy and Moral Development* (2000), 30.

86. See Janet Strayer and Marianne Schroeder, "Children's Helping Strategies: Influences of Emotion, Empathy, and Age" (1989), 86.

87. Novelist and critic Vernon Lee's (Violet Paget) 1895 lecture and 1897 essay "Beauty and Ugliness" contain early mentions of *Einfühlung*, integrated as empathy into her book-length aesthetic theory, *The Beautiful* (1913). The core elements of the modern concept of empathy can legitimately be traced to Lee, who was also a novelist. As with several key dates in psychology, rival claimants to earliest usage appear. Late nineteenth-century German aesthetics makes a claim. Theodor Lipps's *Einfühlung* (1897, in book form *Äesthetik* [1903]), was translated in 1909 by experimental psychologist E. B. Titchener as *empathy*. Lee drew on Lipps' work for *The Beautiful*. Freud also had Lipps's books in his library and adopted the term *Einfühlung*. See Lauren Wispé, "History of the Concept of Empathy" (1987). For speculations on the role of aesthetics in human evolution, see Leda Cosmides and John Tooby, "Does Beauty Build Adapted Minds? Toward an Evolutionary Theory of Aesthetics, Fiction and the Arts" (2001).

88. Philosopher Lawrence Blum believes that insofar as emotions of sympathy and empathy promote perspective taking, they may result in better prosocial responses than rationality alone. See Blum, *Friendship, Altruism and Morality* (1980), 122–39.

89. Alexander McCall Smith, *Morality for Beautiful Girls* (2001).

90. Received from "USMAM BELLO" usmanbello20004@telstra.com on 24 February 2004.

91. On the 419 advance fee fraud, see the London Metropolitan Police Web site, http://www.met.police.uk/fraudalert/419.htm (accessed 16 September 2004).

92. Personal collection of the author. Letter from Noor Nazziwa to Suzanne Keen, no date (received in February 2004).

93. Washington and Lee University students' responses were gathered by Suzanne Keen in a postcolonial literature course in 2003. Students were asked of each document, "What does it make you feel?" and "What would you do?" Everyone quoted in the subsequent discussion gave me permission to reproduce his or her words.

94. http://www.soschildrensvillages.org.uk/ (accessed 7 October 2004). Alternatively, contact the SOS Children's Village Association in Botswana at P.O. Box 30396, Gaborone, Botswana, tel. +267-395 32 20; fax +267-395 32 20. Ordinarily, the notion of intervention on behalf of a fictional character is considered "absurd," as Susan L. Feagin has it ("Imagining Emotions and Appreciating Fiction" [1997], 54).

95. David S. Miall argues that literary reading characteristically "provides a forum within which the concerns of the self are mediated" and results in strong differences among readers (as opposed to nonliterary reading, in which a consensus about meaning tends to emerge). I note that only two students made the move of self-application. See David S. Miall, "Anticipation and Feeling in Literary Response: A Neuropsychological Perspective" (1995), 294.

96. For a useful interrogation of the uses to which moral philosophy puts the novel, see Peter Johnson, *Moral Philosophers and the Novel: A Study of Winch, Nussbaum and Rorty* (2004).

97. See Ellen J. Esrock, *The Reader's Eye: Visual Imaging as Reader Response* (1994).

98. See Davis, *Empathy* (1994) and Stotland, ed., *Empathy, Fantasy, and Helping* (1978).

Chapter 2

1. For a collection of responses from the early days of the form, see *Novel and Romance 1700–1800: A Documentary Record*, edited by Ioan Williams (1970).

2. Stowe's novel was not the only American narrative of the nineteenth century to make an impact on reform movements. Richard Henry Dana's autobiographical *Two Years before the Mast: A Personal Narrative of Life at Sea* (1840) brought the abuse of sailors to public attention and may have influenced congressional debate over the following decade. Some celebrated cases of fiction related to reform, such as Herman Melville's *White Jacket* (1850), which also condemned flogging, accompany rather than directly influence legislation. T. S. Arthur's temperance novel *Ten Nights in a Bar-Room and What I Saw There* (1854) rivaled even *Uncle Tom's Cabin* for popularity in its time and may have assisted in the spread of temperance sentiment.

3. In 1909, the experimental psychologist E. B. Titchener translated as "empathy" aesthetician Theodor Lipps's term *Einfühlung* (which meant the process of "feeling one's way into" an art object or another person). See *Experimental Psychology of the Thought Processes* (1909), 181–85. Notably, Titchener's 1915 elaboration of the concept in *Beginner's Psychology* exemplifies empathy through a description of a reading experience: "We have a natural tendency to feel ourselves into what we perceive or imagine. As we read about the forest, we may, as it were, become the explorer; we feel for ourselves the gloom, the silence, the humidity, the oppression, the sense of lurking danger; everything is strange, but it is to us that strange experience has come" (198). For *Einfühlung*, see Theodor Lipps, *Ästhetik* (1903, 1906).

4. On film, see Alex Neill, "Empathy and (Film) Fiction" (1996). A negative view of empathetic effects in film occurs in film theory employing the Lacanian psychoanalytic term *suture* to describe impositions of identifications on film viewers. See Jean-Pierre Oudart, "Suture (elements of the logic of the signifier)" (1969). See Kaja Silverman's assessment of suture (1983), excerpted in *Narrative, Apparatus, Ideology: A Film Theory Reader* (1986). For a critique of suture theory, see Noel Carroll, *Mystifying Movies: Fads and Fallacies in Contemporary Film Theory* (1988), 196–97.

5. Edmund Burke, for example, writes of sympathy's paradoxical role in aesthetic response: "It is by this principle that poetry, painting, and other affecting arts, transfuse their passions from one breast to another, and are often capable of grafting a delight on wretchedness, misery, and death itself." See *A Philosophical Enquiry into the Origin of Our Ideas of the Sublime and Beautiful* (1757), 41.

6. See Aristotle's *Rhetoric*, Book 3, 2. *On Rhetoric: A Theory of Civic Discourse* (1991), 38, 152–53. Aristotle treats emotions as an aspect of the art of persuasion, mentioning the arousal of the audience's emotion (by inviting role taking) and the refutation of the audience's sympathy for an opponent's view. Elements of empathy appear in his brief accounts of pity and pathos.

7. For instance, Henry Home, Lord Kames's treatment of the topics "Grandeur and Sublimity" (in the chapter so named) includes aspects of motor mimicry, as when a tall object inspires stretching in the beholder, or when a broad prospect of land or sea causes a feeling of expansiveness that Kames links to an enlargement of mind. See Henry Home, Lord Kames, *Elements of Criticism* (1762), 150–78.

8. For a contemporary psychological update of Hume's insight, see Leslie Brothers, *Friday's Footprint: How Society Shapes the Human Mind* (2001), in which social

neuroscientist Brothers argues that the human brain has evolved a specialized capacity for exchanging signals with other brains. In common with primate brains, our brains have evolved to be social, as their sensitive attunement to facial expressions and physical gestures (the basis for emotional contagion) and their way of assigning mental life to animate and inanimate others demonstrate.

9. See also Adela Pinch's subtle reading of Hume's sympathy, *Strange Fits of Passion* (1996), 24–44.

10. They do differ: Hume accentuates the automatic nature of sympathy; in Smith, the harmonious connection between feeling spectator and the object of his gaze receives emphasis.

11. See Ann Jessie Van Sant, *Eighteenth-century Sensibility and the Novel: The Senses in Social Context* (1993) and the discussion of sympathy in Catherine Gallagher, *Nobody's Story: The Vanishing Acts of Women Writers in the Marketplace 1670–1820* (1994), 162–75.

12. Of course, this phenomenon was not confined to the British Isles, as the responses to Goethe's *Sorrows of Young Werther* (1774) and Rousseau's *La Nouvelle Héloïse* (1761) demonstrate. For a cultural reading of the latter case, see Robert Darnton, *The Great Cat Massacre and Other Episodes of French Cultural History* (1984), 215–56.

13. Henry Home, Lord Kames, "Emotions Caused by Fiction," *Elements of Criticism* (1762), 66–77.

14. For one of the few recent treatments of sensibility to entertain a version of the positive, activist view represented here by Kames, see Markman Ellis, *The Politics of Sensibility: Race, Gender, and Commerce in the Sentimental Novel* (1996).

15. Henry Mackenzie, paper from *The Lounger* 20 (18 June 1785), reprinted in *The Works of Henry Mackenzie* (1996), 176–87.

16. For an important version of this critique, see Raymond Williams's criticism of the structure of feeling of industrial fiction, in *Culture and Society, 1780–1950* (rpt. 1983), 88–109.

17. See William Godwin, *An Enquiry Concerning Political Justice* (1798 edition), vol. 2. 499–500. For suspicion of sympathy as instigating contagious panic, see Shaftesbury, *Characteristics of Men, Manners, Opinions, Times, etc.* (1711), 10. A magistrate's sympathy, in contrast, can absorb and calm the people's panic.

18. See Audrey Jaffe, *Scenes of Sympathy: Identity and Representation in Victorian Fiction* (2000). For Jaffe, modern sympathy is inseparable from representations. She usefully comments on the dynamics of projection, displacement, and imagined exchange that characterize sympathy: "Thus the distinction between sympathy for fictional characters and sympathy for actual people dissolves into . . . the difference between the pleasurable sympathetic feelings fiction invites and the potential threat of an encounter with an actual person. Pleasure, here, coincides with an absence of reciprocity: a fictional character cannot look back" (7). Contrast this view with Catherine Gallagher, *Nobody's Story*, which emphasizes the difference between fictional characters ("nobodies") and real people (171).

19. For a classic statement of this legacy, see Walter Jackson Bate, "The Sympathetic Imagination in Eighteenth-Century Criticism" (1945), 144, 159.

20. On the sentimental novel as political, see Markman Ellis's excellent *The Politics of Sensibility* (1996).

21. For a view emphasizing the disconcerting effects of sympathy, especially loss of self, indulgence in voyeurism, and the dangers of mistaking the feelings of others, see David Marshall, *The Surprising Effects of Sympathy* (1988).

22. When in the early twentieth century the concepts of *Einfühlung* and empathy became semantically separate from sympathy, the Romantic poets (and Shakespeare) seemed obvious places to turn to detect representational empathy at work. Richard Harter Fogle describes poetic empathy as the "presence of motor, kinesthetic, or organic imagery, so powerful in effect as to evoke kindred impulses in the reader" ("Empathetic Imagery" 149). For Fogle, poetic empathy begins with physiological response and culminates in a psychological effect, the sensory fusion of body and spirit: "If this fusion is perfect the total effect is not merely of physical and emotional self-projection, but of imaginative projection balanced and tempered by an objective self-possession born of intense contemplation" (*Imagery* 151). The best examples of empathic poetic imagery Fogle locates in the work of Keats. Projecting himself into the inanimate realm, while preserving the sense of embodied perception results, Keats exercises empathy as the "best and most complete means of contemplation" (151). Fogle sees poetic empathy as exercised by Keats and Keats's attuned reader as "a kind of sensuous imagination, which bases perception firmly upon our muscular, nervous, and organic processes" (151). Fogle's views of the physical and affective functions of romantic imagery took issue with the then-dominant school of thought known as the New Criticism and perhaps for this reason they were never widely accepted. A very different attitude toward empathy and sympathy prevailed in the modern period, and the New Critics derived many of their attitudes toward affect from the modern rather than the Romantic writers. Taking the long view afforded by twenty-first-century interests in the embodied mind and metaphor, Fogle can perhaps now be appreciated as a perceptive student of metaphor and empathy. On metaphor as a product of embodied minds, see canonically George Lakoff and Mark Johnson, *Metaphors We Live By* (1980); George Lakoff, *Women, Fire, and Dangerous Things: What Categories Reveal about the Mind* (1987); and George Lakoff and Mark Turner, *More Than Cool Reason: A Field Guide to Poetic Metaphor* (1989).

23. For an exhaustive treatment of this topic, see Thomas J. McCarthy, *Relationships of Sympathy: The Writer and the Reader in British Romanticism* (1997), which trawls through the poetry, prose, and the voluminous correspondence of writers of the period.

24. For a brilliant and exhaustive account of the topicality of Victorian fiction, see Richard D. Altick's *The Presence of the Present: Topics of the Day in the Victorian Novel* (1991).

25. See both the account and extensive bibliography of the periodical literature in Richard Stang's useful *The Theory of the Novel in England, 1850–1870* (1959), 67–72, 228–41.

26. For details of these events, see Peter Ackroyd's *Dickens* (1990), 255–57.

27. Sensation fiction records changing attitudes about domestic violence as the marriage laws undergo reform. See Marlene Tromp, *The Private Rod: Marital Violence, Sensation, and the Law in Victorian Britain* (2000).

28. For an extended treatment of the narrative strategies employed by Victorian novelists as they tackled ostensibly forbidden or impossible topics, see Suzanne

Keen, *Victorian Renovations of the Novel: Narrative Annexes and the Boundaries of Representation* (1998).

29. See, for instance, Wilkie Collins's depiction of the moral agriculturalist Captain Wragge in *No Name* (1862). This con man cultivates sympathy in order to harvest cash.

30. Dickens's great favorite type for satirizing, the moral hypocrite, invariably attempts to cultivate sympathy, though he doesn't deserve it.

31. For a lucid account of the philosophical differences between German aesthetics and British associationism, as they effect the development of the notion of empathy, see Charles Edward Gauss, "Empathy" (1973–74), vol. 2, 86–9.

32. For the original essays, see Vernon Lee and C. Anstruther-Thomson, "Beauty and Ugliness," *Contemporary Review* 72 (October 1897): 544–69 and (November 1897): 669–88. Lee subjects this material to revision in her later book, *The Beautiful* (1913).

33. See Suzanne Clark's account of the reversal of values in modernism, stressing disruption and experiment over sentiment, in *Sentimental Modernism: Women Writers and the Revolution of the Word* (1991).

34. Brecht's statements about the V-effekt appear in many different interviews and essays. See, for instance, "Alienation Effects in Chinese Acting" (1964), 91–99.

35. Brecht's word for empathy was of course the German *Einfühlung*. V-effekt is sometimes rendered A-effect in translation. As I discuss in the next chapter, defamiliarization and estrangement have not been demonstrated to cause alienation. Indeed, some theorists of reading response suggest that defamiliarization, or foregrounding, can slow the reader's pace and invite empathetic identification. See, for instance, David S. Miall and Donald Kuiken, "The Form of Reading: Empirical Studies of Literariness" (1998).

36. See, for instance, Ezra Pound's brief manifesto, "A Few Don'ts by an *Imagiste*" (1913), 5.

37. For an account of how empathy fell out of favor as a consequence of the shift from romantic theories of the imagination to modern theories of form, see Ellen Dissanayake, *Homo Aestheticus* (1992), 142–47.

38. Exceptions among modernists: some of Hemingway's stories and virtually all of Ivy Compton-Burnett's novels focus on an externalized view of characters, relying on the readers' ability to infer psychological states from plain reports of dialogue. Wyndham Lewis notoriously created abstract characters whose traits would work against readers' efforts to recuperate believable fictional worlds and confute what he regarded as a noxious tradition of English individualism.

39. See Percy Lubbock, *The Craft of Fiction* (1926) for an early and influential elaboration of the implications of James's narrative technique. Henry James's brother, the psychologist William James, contributed the term *stream of consciousness* to his discipline in his *Principles of Psychology* (1890, 1892). See Dorrit Cohn's account in *Transparent Minds: Narrative Modes for Presenting Consciousness in Fiction* (1978), 87.

40. For a good historical treatment of this trend, see Nicola Humble, *The Feminine Middlebrow Novel, 1920s to 1950s* (2001), 7–56.

41. For demographics and details about selections, see Elizabeth Long, *Book Clubs* (2003).

42. For my treatment of the changing reputation of one of those subgenres and the relationship of the gender of a subgenre's readership to its status, see Suzanne Keen, "The Historical Turn" (2006).

43. My account is indebted to Janice A. Radway, *A Feeling for Books* (1997). See also Joan Shelley Rubin, *The Making of Middle/brow Culture* (1992).

44. Martha Nussbaum, "Exactly and Responsibly: A Defense of Ethical Criticism" (1998), 350. Not all empathy results in compassion, she concedes in this essay. For Nussbaum, empathy is "thinner" than compassion (351).

45. For a summary of critical responses to Oprah Winfrey's Book Club, see Kathleen Rooney, *Reading with Oprah: The Book Club That Changed America* (2005).

Chapter 3

1. See Alan Richardson's overview of the role of affect in "Studies in Literature and Cognition: A Field Map" (2004), 8–11.

2. For a fictional version, see the discussion in A. S. Byatt, *Babel Tower* (1996), 307–18.

3. Acknowledging that features other than literary character can be involved in empathy distinguishes my approach from that of Ed S. Tan, whose *Emotion and the Structure of Narrative Film: Film as an Emotion Machine* (1996) argues that emotions determined by fictional events are nonempathetic: "An empathetic emotion is characterized by the valence of the events in relation to the concerns of the protagonist" (171). My research suggests that while readers feel narrative empathy primarily with characters, other features of narrative also evoke empathetic responses.

4. Kathryn Miele, "empathetic readings of Victorian novels," VICTORIA-L (Tuesday, 16 November 2004). This response is one of sixty archived responses to a query on the topic that I posted on 12 November 2004 to the 1500-plus subscribers on the VICTORIA-L listserv. See the archives at https://listserv.indiana.edu/archives/victoria.html for the full public discussion. The pages that follow also contain excerpts from private e-mail responses to my query, during the same period of 12 November–3 December 2004.

5. Sheldon Goldfarb, "empathetic reading experiences of c19 novels," VICTORIA-L (Monday, 15 Movember 2004).

6. British objects relations theory is informative on the developmental role animals (real and imaginary) play in a child's growth. See, for instance, D. W. Winnicott's treatment of transitional objects in *Playing and Reality* (1971). Psychoanalytic critic Norman Holland regards literary works themselves as transitional objects, but his adoption of the term erases the developmental context vital to Winnicott. See Holland, *Five Readers Reading* (1975), 286–88. On anthropomorphism as an interpretive signal to the reader, see Hans Robert Jauss's brief account of animal tales in "The Identity of the Poetic Text in the Changing Horizon of Understanding" (1985), 146–74.

7. David Miall, private correspondence (12 May 2005).

8. Beth Sutton-Ramspeck, "empathetic reading experiences of c19 novels," VICTORIA-L (Monday, 15 November 2004).

9. Margot K. Louis, "empathetic reading experiences of c19 novels," VICTORIA-L (Sunday, 14 November 2004).

10. Pat Menon, "empathetic reading experiences of c19 novels," VICTORIA-L (Sunday, 14 November 2004).

11. Michael Hargreave Mawson, "empathetic reading experiences of c19 novels," VICTORIA-L (Monday, 15 November 2004).

12. Ralf Schneider idealistically suggests that the term *character identification,* with its Freudian baggage, ought to be avoided and replaced with the term *empathy.* Ralf Schneider, "Emotion and Narrative" (2005), 136–37.

13. To gather this particular set of responses, I administered a six-question survey eliciting hand-written prose responses in the tenth week of the course World Fiction in English (10 March 2004). The subsequently quoted replies were elicited by the question: "Have you experienced empathy (feeling *with* a character, as opposed to pity, in which your feeling is different from the character's) at any point while doing the course reading? If so, which book(s) and character(s)?

14. Meredith Walker, survey (10 March 2004).

15. Amanda Lueders, survey (10 March 2004).

16. Paige Halter, survey (10 March 2004).

17. Megan Brooks, survey (10 March 2004).

18. Anonymous respondent, survey (10 March 2004).

19. For every generalization there is an exception. Richard Fulton writes of such positive empathy: "looking through my old collection of books from my childhood, I was flooded with memories of certain characters that I not only empathized with, but pretended to be: Joe Hardy, Tom Quest, Red Randall, Chip Hilton, Dave Dawson of the Air Force, and, more to the point of this discussion, Jim Hawkins and Rob Roy (and maybe Ivanhoe, just a little bit)." Richard Fulton, "empathy for literary characters," VICTORIA-L (Friday, 19 November 2004).

20. Lindsay Pace, survey (10 March 2004).

21. Ellen Moody, "empathetic reading experience of c19 novels," VICTORIA-L (Tuesday, 16 November 2004).

22. Robert Lapides, "Rethinking empathy," VICTORIA-L (Sunday, 21 November 2004).

23. Robert Lapides, "empathetic reading experiences of c19 novels," VICTORIA-L (Sunday, 14 November 2004). The subsequent quotations in this section come from private correspondents, answering the same query in November 2004, whose anonymity I have agreed to preserve and whose permission to quote I have secured.

24. Maria, "empathetic reading experiences of c19 novels," VICTORIA-L (Friday, 19 November 2004).

25. Jean Rhys's *The Wide Sargasso Sea* (1966) initiates this tradition for the Anglophone postcolonial novel. It remains a frequently used strategy in feminist fiction and contemporary historical fiction, as well as in the popular generation of sequels to classic texts. Peter Carey's *Jack Maggs* (1997), which reimagines Dickens's returned convict Magwitch, is a recent excellent example.

26. Mary Lenard, "empathy for literary characters," VICTORIA-L (Thursday, 18 November 2004). For her scholarly elaboration of this position, see Mary Lenard's *Preaching Pity: Dickens, Gaskell, and Sentimentalism in Victorian Culture* (1999) and

"'Mr. Popular Sentiment': Dickens and the Gender Politics of Sentimentalism and Social Reform Literature" (1998).

27. Sara L. Maurer, "empathetic reading experiences of c19 novels," VICTORIA-L (Monday, 15 November 2004).

28. Ellen Moody, "empathetic reading experiences of c19 novels," VICTORIA-L (Friday, 19 November 2004).

29. Kerryn Goldsworthy, "empathy for literary characters," VICTORIA-L (Saturday, 20 November 2004).

30. Private correspondence (14 November 2004).

31. Kathleen O'Neill Sims, "empathy (and sympathy) for literary characters," VICTORIA-L (Saturday, 20 November 2004).

32. Michel Faber, "empathy (and sympathy) for literary characters," VICTORIA-L (Friday, 19 November 2004).

33. Els Andringa, "The Interface between Fiction and Life: Patterns of Identification in Reading Autobiographies" (2004).

34. Sheldon Goldfarb, "empathetic reading experiences of c19 novels," VICTORIA-L (Monday, 15 November 2004).

35. Deborah D. Morse, "empathy, again," VICTORIA-L (Monday, 15 November 2004).

36. For an excellent recent work historicizing emotions relevant to the history of empathy, see Julie Ellison, *Cato's Tears and the Making of Anglo-American Emotion* (1999).

37. Cross-cultural studies of this kind are uncommon. See W. F. Brewer and K. Ohtsuka, "Story Structure, Characterization, Just World Organization, and Reader Affect in American and Hungarian Short Stories" (1988).

38. See Peter J. Rabinowitz, *Before Reading: Narrative Conventions and the Politics of Interpretation* (1987). Rabinowitz offers a nuanced account of the different kinds of narrative audiences to which an individual reader may belong.

39. Both Michael Steig and David Bleich emphasize the meaning making of readers over authoritative, professional critical interpretation. That feature of reader-response criticism provoked concern in the 1970s and 1980s, as literary theorists worried about what would happen to interpretation. Today, interpretation is more threatened by aliteracy than by empowered meaning-making readers.

40. Margot K. Louis, "empathetic reading experiences of c19 novels," VICTORIA-L (Sunday, 14 November 2004).

41. See Bonnie Brennan, "Bridging the Backlash: A Cultural Material Reading of *The Bridges of Madison County*" (1996). Most of the critical commentary concerns the film, dignified by association with Clint Eastwood and Meryl Streep.

42. Diana Ostrander, "empathetic reading experience of c19 novels," VICTORIA-L (Monday, 15 November, 2004).

43. June Siegel, "empathetic reading experiences of c19 novels," VICTORIA-L (Monday, 15 November 2004).

44. Michel Faber, "empathy (and sympathy) for literary characters," VICTORIA-L (Saturday, 20 November 2004).

45. See Don Kuiken et al., "Forms of Self-Implication in Literary Reading" (2004). Though empathy is important for the theories of Kuiken and Miall, they concede

here, "the effects of empathy, identification, and their associated narrative feelings have not been systematically examined in empirical studies" (175 n).

46. Victor Nell studied larger numbers of readers; Norman Holland drew conclusions from study of just five readers. David S. Miall and Don Kuiken break stories into segments.

47. By no means all reader-response criticism involves experiments with actual readers. The methods of introspection and philosophical speculation about reading often feature an abstract single "reader," bearing closest resemblance to the author. See, for instance, Stanley Fish's early intervention in this area, "Literature in the Reader: Affective Stylistics" (1970).

48. See, for example, C. D. Brisbin's unpublished dissertation, "An Experimental Application of the Galvanic Skin Response to the Measurement of Effects of Literature on Attitudes of Fifth Grade Students towards Blacks" (1971).

49. Understandably, medical research is the dominant application of neuroimaging. The subfields of psycholinguistics, cognition, and developmental psychology and the related field of education feature a great deal of work on reading.

50. See the recent article by W. D. Gaillard et al., "fMRI Identifies Regional Specialization of Neural Networks for Reading in Young Children" (2003). This group ascertains that the neural networks processing reading are strongly lateralized (in most subjects, in the left brain, associated with language) and are similar in early readers and in adults.

51. I treat Patrick Colm Hogan's cognitive theory of aesthetic empathy in chapter 6. His interesting theories draw on wide reading of world literature, including Arab and Indian aesthetic treatises, and support a general argument about literary universals. He does not conduct empirical research on reading. Similarly, philosopher Susan L. Feagin's *Reading with Feeling: The Aesthetics of Appreciation* (1996) theorizes a role for emotion in reading but does not study actual readers empirically. Several literary critics treat empathy as a thematic element of fiction. These include J. Brooks Bouson, whose book, *The Empathic Reader: A Study of the Narcissistic Character and the Drama of the Self* (1989), draws reader-response theory into dialogue with psychoanalytic theory of Heinz Kohut. As a result, the study focuses on narcissistic characters and contributes little to the understanding of readers' empathy. An influence on the concerns of the present study, Judith Kegan Gardiner's *Rhys, Stead, Lessing, and the Politics of Empathy* (1989) traces thematics of empathy in three postcolonial women writers. Gardiner gestures toward the impact of empathic representations or intentions on readers.

52. Despite its subtitle, János László's *Cognition and Representation in Literature: The Psychology of Literary Narratives* (1999) proves an exception to the general trend. László treats the notion of distinctive literariness with more skepticism than his colleagues in the field.

53. Few go as far as David S. Miall in openly advocating moving "beyond interpretation," as in his lecture "Beyond Interpretation: The Cognitive Significance of Reading" (2004).

54. Perhaps the possibility of observing beneficial results from reading mass-market junk fiction deters professionals from designing experiments that might suggest the redundancy of postsecondary literary education. Miall, however, is an exact-

ing critic of literary education as it is carried out in the United States and Canada. He sees it as interfering with or even destroying the pleasure of reading. See his "Empowering the Reader: Literary Response and Classroom Learning" (1996).

55. See, for instance, David S. Miall, "On the Necessity of Empirical Studies of Literary Reading" (2000); David S. Miall and Don Kuiken, "What Is Literariness? Three Components of Literary Reading" (1999); and David S. Miall, "Beyond the Schema Given: Affective Comprehension of Literary Narratives" (1989).

56. See Tammy Bourg, "The Role of Emotion, Empathy, and Text Structure in Children's and Adults' Narrative Text Comprehension" (1996). See also Tammy Bourg et al., "The Effects of an Empathy-Building Strategy on 6th-graders' Causal Inferencing in Narrative Text Comprehension" (1993), 117–33.

57. See Norma D. Feshbach and Seymour Feshbach, "Affective Processes and Academic Achievement" (1987).

58. Paul Ekman, *Emotions Revealed* (2003), 35. For David S. Miall's speculative treatment of the neurophysiology of literary response, see "Anticipation and Feeling in Literary Response" (1995).

59. For experimental support of this claim, see Rolf A. Zwaan, "The Immersed Experiencer: Toward an Embodied Theory of Language Comprehension" (2004).

60. A common view coming out of the Artificial Intelligence area of cognitive science holds that literature enables humans to run simulations that may provoke revisions of our models of self. See Keith Oatley, *Best Laid Schemes: The Psychology of Emotions* (1992), 225–61. For experimental results substantiating aspects of Oatley's theories, see G. C. Chupchik, Keith Oatley, and L. Vorderer, "Emotional Effects of Reading Excerpts from Short Stories by James Joyce" (1998).

61. David S. Miall and Don Kuiken, "Aspects of Literary Response: A New Questionnaire" (1995). Subsequently cited as LRQ.

62. On this topic, see Jonathan Rose's magisterial *The Intellectual Life of the British Working Classes* (2001). Rose details the reading habits, attitudes, and preferences of ordinary British readers.

63. Jèmeljan Hakemulder, *The Moral Laboratory: Experiments Examining the Effects of Reading Literature on Social Perception and Moral Self-Concept* (2000). See also Jèmeljan Hakemulder, "Foregrounding and Its Effect on Readers' Perception" (2004), 193–96. Here Hakemulder efficiently surveys the assumptions and existing research, conceding that few studies showing positive effects for reading literature establish the particularity of those effects to literature or a positive correlation to literariness.

64. Hakemulder's own research after *The Moral Laboratory* contributes to the literature on foregrounding, but his focus is on the relationship between textual features and literary reading experiences. See his "Foregrounding and Its Effect on Readers' Perception" (2004).

65. The four studies examined by Hakemulder include three dissertations, two of which focus on preschool children, a drawback he de-emphasizes.

66. See C. Daniel Batson et al. "Empathy, Attitudes, and Action" (2002), 1658–61. While Batson regards fiction reading as the equivalent of the high empathy condition (in which subjects are instructed to engage in perspective taking), he finds that empathic feelings are lower among those who believe the experiment's interviewee Jared, a heroin addict and dealer, is a fictional character (1661).

67. For a fantasy empathy measure that could be used to study such questions, see Mark H. Davis, *Empathy* (1994), 55–58 and "Measuring Individual Differences in Empathy: Evidence for a Multidimensional Approach" (1983), 113–26.

68. Very little empirical research has been attempted to verify the theoretical speculations about aspects of characterization that operate in readers' character identification. Marisa Bortolussi and Peter Dixon's pioneering study *Psychonarratology* (2003) report their findings that character actions contribute to readers' assessments of character traits, while self-evaluations provided by the narrator (description) do not. However, the test stories employed first-person narrators, so narrators' evaluations of characters in third-person fiction cannot be included in this preliminary conclusion. See *Psychonarratology*, 160–65.

69. For John Dewey, "esthetic emotion is native emotion transformed through the objective material to which it has committed its development and consummation." See *Art as Experience* (1985), 85. E. M. Dadlez surveys the controversy about the status of aesthetic emotions in *What's Hecuba to Him? Fictional Events and Actual Emotions* (1997), a lively area of debate. In addition to the works of Martha Nussbaum, most recently *Upheavals of Thought: The Intelligence of Emotions* (2001), see the following: Charles Altieri, *The Particulars of Rapture: An Aesthetics of the Affects* (2003); Susan L. Feagin, *Reading with Feeling* (1996); Patrick Colm Hogan, "From Mind to Matter: Art, Empathy, and the Brain," in his *Cognitive Science, Literature, and the Arts* (2003), 166–90; Peter Lamarque and Stein Haugum Olsen, *Truth, Fiction, and Literature: A Philosophical Perspective* (1994); Alex Neill, "Fiction and the Emotions" (1993); Keith Oatley, *Best Laid Schemes* (1992); Robert C. Solomon, ed., *Thinking about Feeling: Contemporary Philosophers on Emotions* (2004); Rei Terada, *Feeling in Theory: Emotion after "The Death of the Subject"* (2001); Kendall Walton, *Mimesis as Make-Believe: On the Foundations of the Representational Arts* (1990); and L. S. Vygotsky, *The Psychology of Art* (1925). The recent revival of Silvan Tomkins has enlivened the literary study of negative affects such as shame and disgust: see *Shame and Its Sisters: A Silvan Tomkins Reader* (1995).

70. For a summary of major ideas about and theorists of narrative situation, see Keen, *Narrative Form* (2003), 30–50. Ralf Schneider represents narrative situation as a factor in eliciting readers' empathy and lack of representation of inner life as a likely inhibitor of it, in "Toward a Cognitive Theory of Literary Character: The Dynamics of Mental-Model Construction" (2001).

71. See Robyn R. Warhol on affective responses to serial fiction in *Having a Good Cry* (2003), 71–72. See also Hakemulder, *The Moral Laboratory* ([2000], 93, 143), drawing on N. D. Feshbach's observations of the effects of repetitive role taking in "Studies of Empathic Behavior in Children" (1978).

72. Martha Nussbaum's empathy-inducing novels are invariably long, though not always the longest works by the authors she mentions. Writing about the reading habits of the character David Copperfield in Dickens's novel of that name (1849–50), Nussbaum comments, "he remains with [books] for hours in an intense, intimate, and loving relationship. As he imagines, dreams, and desires in their company, he becomes a certain sort of person." Nussbaum believes that novels, as *David Copperfield* highlights, have the effect of making readers perceive "the social world around them with a new freshness and sympathy." For Nussbaum, the length of the immersion (in what Victor Nell describes as ludic reading) is a vital component of

the process, permitting intensity, dreaming, and desiring that develops the reader's loving heart. See Martha C. Nussbaum, *Love's Knowledge: Essays on Philosophy and Literature* (1990), 230–31.

73. Canonically, see Fredric Jameson, *The Political Unconscious: Narrative as a Socially Symbolic Act* (1981). See also Rolf Zwaan, "Effect of Genre Expectations on Text Comprehension" (1994), which compares readers' behavior when processing texts labeled as "news stories" or "narratives." In *Psychonarratology* (2003), Bortolussi and Dixon caution that research in discourse processing has focused on broad generic distinctions rather than on narrative fiction's subgenres (253–54). However, a body of work on emotional responses to fictional subgenres in television exists in the field of mass communications, as in the essays collected in Jennings Bryant and Dolf Zillmann's *Responding to the Screen: Reception and Reaction Processes* (1991). Literary genre critics have been reluctant to adopt findings from mass communications research, perhaps because audiovisual (iconic) representations are assumed to be more emotionally stimulating than the verbal representations of prose narrative fiction. This assumption, however, has not been investigated systematically.

74. Feminist criticism often celebrates the power of women's writing's vividly represented spaces and places, in tandem with identity themes, to work out boundary-crossing potentials for connection, communication, and change. See, for instance, Susan Stanford Friedman's *Mappings: Feminism and the Cultural Geographies of Encounter* (1998).

75. See Monika Fludernik's account of Ansgar Nünning's remarks on empathy-inducing functions of metanarration in "Metanarrative and Metafictional Commentary: From Metadiscursivity to Metanarration and Metafiction" (2003), 39.

76. On slower pace as potentially fostering empathy, see Dolf Zillmann, "Empathy: Affect from Bearing Witness to the Emotions of Others" (1991), 160–61. Zillmann hypothesizes that the fast pace of television news stories and dramas may impede empathetic response. David S. Miall's previously mentioned work on foregrounding and empathy in literary texts correlates a slower reading pace with enhanced empathy.

77. See, for instance, Willie van Peer's judgment that the notion of perspective influencing empathy is due for a shake-up in his "Justice in Perspective" (2001).

78. Character identification is thus an example of what Marisa Bortolussi and Peter Dixon identify as readers' mental constructions, as opposed to textual features (*Psychonarratology* 28). They systematically measure how particular readers process specific textual features in narratives, but the experimental results bridging disciplines of discourse processing and narrative theory are still quite scanty, and the accuracy of Bortolussi and Dixon's narratology has been questioned. See Nilli Diengott, "Some Problems with the Concept of the Narrator in Bortolussi and Dixon's *Psychonarratology*" (2004).

79. See Peter Dixon, et al., "Literary Processing and Interpretation: Towards Empirical Foundations" (1993).

80. See Dolf Zillman, "Mechanisms of Emotional Involvement with Drama" (1994). Writing about identification with dramatic characters rather than narrative personae, Zillman argues that the audience members' disposition precipitates empathic and counterempathic reactions and suggests that audiences must be made

to care about characters one way or another. He believes that enactment of good or evil deeds by protagonists and antagonists, in circumstances that prompt moral appraisal of their actions, promotes strong emotional reactions.

81. See Keith Oatley, "A Taxonomy of the Emotions of Literary Response and a Theory of Identification in Fictional Narrative" (1994).

82. In this respect, Miall and Kuiken are in accord with earlier work that demonstrates a relationship between a subject's prior similar experiences and empathy felt for another in the same situation. See Ezra Stotland, *Empathy, Fantasy and Helping* (1978), 52.

83. See Miall and Kuiken, "What Is Literariness?" (1999) and Miall, "Beyond the Schema Given" (1989).

84. See Don Kuiken et al., "Locating Self-Modifying Feelings within Literary Reading" (2004).

85. Max Louwerse and Don Kuiken, "The Effects of Personal Involvement in Narrative Discourse" (2004), 170. This research confirms some of what Wolfgang Iser proposes about active reading as gap filling, in *The Act of Reading: A Theory of Aesthetic Response* (1978), 168–69.

86. For good critiques of this assumption from different disciplinary bases, see Elly A. Konijn and Johan F. Hoorn, "Reality-based Genre Preferences Do Not Direct Personal Involvement" (2004) and Richard Walsh, "Why We Wept for Little Nell: Character and Emotional Involvement" (1997).

87. See Edith Klemenz-Belgardt, "American Research of Response to Literature" (1981), 368 and P. E. Jose and W. F. Brewer, "Development of Story Liking: Character Identification, Suspense, and Outcome Resolution" (1984). In *The Moral Laboratory*, Hakemulder reports on recent studies confirming the importance of personal relevance for intensity of reader response (71).

88. M. Wünsch (1981), cited in Hakemulder (*Moral Laboratory* 73).

89. G. C. Chupchik and János László, "The Landscape of Time in Literary Reception: Character Experience and Narrative Action" (1994).

90. Research into the empathy evoked by various genres of television advertisements suggests that discontinuous, nonlinear "vignette" ads discourage empathy, whereas classical, character-centered dramatic form in ads evokes viewers' empathy. See Barbara B. Stern, "Classical and Vignette Television Advertising Dramas: Structural Models, Formal Analysis, and Consumer Effects" (1994).

91. For a good application of cognitive theory on levels of embedding to readers' capacity to comprehend embedded accounts of characters' mental states, see Lisa Zunshine, "Theory of Mind and Experimental Representations of Fictional Consciousness" (2003).

92. For a subtle treatment of the variety of techniques by which sympathy for characters may be cultivated, see Wayne C. Booth, *The Rhetoric of Fiction*, 2nd. ed. (1983), 129–33, 243–66, 274–82, and 379–91. Ultimately Booth prefers the use of an "inside view" for invoking sympathy, but he describes the full range of strategies that authors from the classical period to the modernists actually employ. For an excellent recent look at how cognitive science can revise narratological views of representation of consciousness, see Alan Palmer, *Fictional Minds* (2004).

93. See David S. Miall, "Affect and Narrative: A Model of Responses to Stories" (1988).

94. For the best description of how readers imaginatively construct characters, see Steven Cohan, "Figures Beyond the Text: A Theory of Readable Character in the Novel" (1983).

95. See Richard J. Gerrig, "The Construction of Literary Character: A View from Cognitive Psychology" (1990). See also his account of participatory responses to fiction in his book *Experiencing Narrative Worlds: On the Psychological Activities of Reading* (1993).

96. See Patrick Colm Hogan, "The Epilogue of Suffering: Heroism, Empathy, Ethics" (2001). Though this article suggests a preference for the cognitive role taking Hogan associates with situational empathy, his later, very brief treatment of readers' empathy in *Cognitive Science, Literature, and the Arts* improves on his theory by describing how emotion triggers invoke quick-and-dirty responses, as well as imaginative role taking, neither of which need be denigrated as egocentric (186–87). Work confirming the role of lived experience in spontaneous situational empathy with characters on film has been carried out by Barry Sapolsky and Dolf Zillmann, "Experience and Empathy: Affective Reactions to Witnessing Childbirth" (1978). Women who had given birth who responded to a medical film of actual childbirth showed more intense physiological reactions; otherwise, gender and related experiences had a negligible effect on empathy. Note that the film was not fictional.

97. See Hans Robert Jauss, *Aesthetic Experience and Literary Hermeneutics* (1982), 152–88, especially his summary figure, "Interaction Patterns of Identification with the Hero," 159. See also Patrick Colm Hogan on emotions and prototypes in narrative, in *The Mind and Its Stories: Narrative Universals and Human Emotion* (2003).

98. This insight has received preliminary confirmation from studies of the effect of point of view and voice-over in film. See Els Andringa, Q et al., "Point of View and Viewer Empathy in Film" (2001), 154–55.

99. See the definitions of narrated monologue, psycho-narration, and quoted monologue in Dorrit Cohn, *Transparent Minds* (1978), 14. Parallel terminology exists for the representation of consciousness in first-person narration.

100. See Sylvia Adamson, "The Rise and Fall of Empathetic Narrative: A Historical Perspective on Perspective" (2001).

101. See Wayne Booth's discussing of traditional literature's use of "telling" in *The Rhetoric of Fiction*, 3–16 and Dorrit Cohn on psycho-narration in *Transparent Minds*, 46–57.

102. For a subtle exploration of the intersection between cognitive science and narratology on this point, see Alan Palmer, *Fictional Minds* (2004), 49, 170–204.

103. Three good starting points for recent work on the representation of consciousness include: Monika Fludernik's magisterial *The Fictions of Language and the Languages of Fiction* (1993); the essays of Lisa Zunshine, "Theory of Mind" (2003) and "Richardson's Clarissa and a Theory of Mind" (2004); and the phenomenological theory of George Butte, *I Know That You Know That I Know* (2004).

104. See F. K. Stanzel, *Narrative Situation in the Novel* (1971) and *A Theory of Narrative* (1984).

105. See Willie van Peer and H. Pander Maat, "Perspectivation and Sympathy: Effects of Narrative Point of View" (1996). They designed experiments using five versions of stories, rewritten to allow them to test the relationship between positive internal focalization and readers' allocation of sympathy (145).

106. For a thorough investigation of the issues raised here, see Monika Fludernik, *Towards a "Natural" Narratology* (1996).

107. See Keen, *Narrative Form*, 45–47, 171.

108. Bertolussi and Dixon have done the best work on this subject, though they phrase the question differently (*Psychonarratology* 166–99). They are interested in the degree to which readers fuse narrators and characters as a result of perceptual access to a particular character's perspective, and thus develop a rooting interest in that character and making assumptions about the narrator's and author's gender.

Chapter 4

1. See Don Kuiken et al., "Forms of Self-Implication in Literary Reading" for a fascinating exploration, replete with testimony from individual readers, of how reading deepens self-understanding.

2. E. M. Forster used the term *word-masses* for members of the species *homo fictus* (*Aspects* 44, 55–6). Roland Barthes emphasizes the textual nature of characters by calling them "paper beings" in his essay "Introduction to the Structural Analysis of Narratives" ([1977], 111); Catherine Gallagher labels them "Nobodies" in *Nobody's Story* (1995), xiii. On the other side of the argument, stressing the humanlike quality of character, see W. J. Harvey, *Character and the Novel* (1965) and Martin Price, *Forms of Life: Character and Moral Imagination in the Novel* (1983). See Baruch Hochman's *Character in Literature* (1985) for a treatment of both critical positions and a flexible taxonomy that takes into account both mimetic and more stylized, nonnaturalistic kinds of character.

3. For a full treatment of this paradigm, see James Phelan, *Reading People, Reading Plots: Character, Progression, and the Interpretation of Narrative* (1989).

4. See, for instance, Frank Palmer, *Literature and Moral Understanding* (1992). He opines, "good literary works provide the opportunity for knowledge by acquaintance, and . . . the educative power of literature is linked with its artistic merit" (220).

5. The ubiquity of this belief has had an effect on experimental design, which tends to emphasize quality literature over mass-market fiction. Some work in discourse processing directly investigates traits of literariness. For both subjects, see chapter 3, 85–87

6. For a bracing reconsideration of what female readers seek in the fiction they choose, see Holly Virginia Blackford, *Out of This World: Why Literature Matters to Girls* (2004). Blackford argues that for the thirty-three racially, socioeconomically, and geographically diverse girls she studied, a good story that "looks *nothing* like the life they know" was consistently preferred (6).

7. The number of books produced and the number of books sold tell different stories. Although it is a growing segment of the market, with some titles breaking sales barriers, fiction still accounts for a little over 10 percent of the books produced annually in the U.S. See *U.S. Book Production (All Hardback and Paperback)*, compiled by Andrew Grabois (accessed 28 January 2004). Fiction accounts for 26 percent of books sold in the United Kingdom, according to statistics for 1999–2000. See Simon Howitt, ed., *Bookselling: 2000 Market Report* (2000), 12.

8. See the compilation of data in Appendix 10 of Clive Bloom's *Bestsellers: Popular Fiction Since 1900* (2002), 252–53.

9. Biweekly data on the fifteen most frequently borrowed library books in the United States has been provided since 2004 by *Library Journal* at http://www.libraryjournal.com/. Mysteries and thrillers dominate the lists, with works of general fiction (mainly fiction aimed at women) appearing occasionally. Focusing on best sellers and most-requested library books obviously does not tell the whole story about adults' reading preferences; but given that the average American now spends only 109 hours per year reading (a figure that has steadily diminished even as television watching increases: 1661 hours on average per person per year), best-seller statistics do suggest what most readers spend most of their time on. U.S. Census Bureau, *Statistical Abstract of the United States* (2003), No. 1125. Media Usage and Consumer Spending: 1998 to 2006, *Information and Communications*, 720.

10. Yann Martel's *The Life of Pi* (2001) sold 903,268 copies in 2003 after winning the 2002 Booker Prize. Not all Booker winners enjoy such longevity in sales, but *The Life of Pi* has been taken up as a book club selection and as a teaching text in colleges, universities, and some secondary schools. See McEvoy and Maryles, "Paperback Bestsellers" (2004), 585.

11. *The Secret Life of Bees*, endorsed on *Good Morning America*, sold 1,852,721 copies in paperback in 2003 ("Paperback Bestsellers" 585). *The Lovely Bones*, a Book of the Month Club selection, sold 2,815,900 copies in hardcover in 2002 and 2003 combined. See Daisy Maryles and Laurele Riippa, "Bestsellers of 2003: Hardcover Bestsellers; The Stakes Rise for Chart Toppers" (2004), 576.

12. Cecilia Konchar Farr persuasively argues that Winfrey cleverly oscillated between easier and more challenging works in order to draw readers in and teach them how to approach more demanding fiction. See *Reading Oprah: How Oprah's Book Club Changed the Way America Reads* (2005).

13. For a full account, see Kathleen Rooney, *Reading with Oprah: The Book Club That Changed America* (2005).

14. Els Andringa's research into the reading preferences of Dutch students confirms this notion. She found two times the amount of words indicating character identification among the female readers in her sample. See "The Interface between Fiction and Life" (2004), 226.

15. For recent research on the empathy-altruism thesis, see C. Daniel Batson et al. "Empathy, Attitudes, and Action" (2002). Batson believes that empathy felt for a fictional character can improve attitudes and stimulate concern for members of a stigmatized group (1666). However, in the resource-allocation task by which Batson measures subjects' willingness to act to help members of the group represented by drug addict Jared, allocations by those in the group believing Jared is fictional lagged behind the allocations made by high-empathy perspective takers who believed he was real. The differences in this component of the experiment did not reach the threshold of statistical significance (1662).

16. Two aspects of the analogy deserve attention: that emotional reaction to fiction, like human empathy, takes us out of ourselves, and that we recognize through role taking (practiced through reading) that others are different from us but still "real humans." This emphasis defends the spontaneous sharing of empathy's "feel-

ing with" against charges of egoism and bolsters the case for the effects of reading without explaining how readers actually transpose the experience of empathy for fictional characters from a fictive context to empathy for real people in the actual world. Philosopher Frank Palmer writes, "to be moved in the way that great art can move us is to be put in touch with something that in a way dwarfs our own little concerns, which is a step nearer to being sensitive to the 'reality' of other people. . . . But to appreciate the 'reality' of another person involves not just an act of identification with him, but a sense of his 'otherness.'" Note how Palmer slides from responsiveness to art to understanding of real people (*Literature and Moral Understanding* (1992), 240).

17. Lindsay Pace, survey (10 March 2004).

18. Meredith Walker, survey (10 March 2004).

19. Courtney Fitzgerald, survey (10 March 2004).

20. Paige Halter, survey (10 March 2004).

21. See Krystina A. Finlay and Walter G. Stephan, "Improving Intergroup Relations: The Effects of Empathy on Racial Attitudes" (2000). Of the students in this experiment who read, some received realistic "scenarios" that were presented to them as nonfictional first-person accounts of African Americans, and some read the same accounts framed as American students' reports about their experiences studying abroad in Hong Kong. Neither manipulation changed rates of reactive empathy associated with helping.

22. Psychologist C. Daniel Batson and his collaborators argue that empathy may indeed spur prosocial action, but they also show that empathy can hinder justice. See "Immorality from Empathy-Induced Altruism: When Compassion and Justice Conflict" (1995), 1042–54.

23. Hakemulder believes that the novel excerpts' ironic tone may have cued literature students to the intention of the study ("Foregrounding" [2004], 206). It is also possible that the use of short extracts, while essential for fine-grained analysis of discourse processing, interferes with the study of the effects of reading long works that ordinarily invite hours and hours of involved reading. Since the grandest claims for fictions' beneficial role in society inevitably refer to long novels, it would make sense to devise ways of studying them as they are actually read.

24. Research on television-viewing habits shows that empathy with characters of comedies and dramas increases the likelihood of watching reruns. See P. H. Tannenbaum, "Entertainment as Vicarious Emotional Experience" (1980).

25. See Skaliotis (2002), cited in Wim Knulst and Andries van den Broek, "The Readership of Books in Times of De-Reading" (2003), 233. Exceptionally, Knulst and van den Broek examine the relative popularity of different genres of reading, using data on Dutch readers. As I have already shown, most of the theorizing and empirical research on effects of reading has focused on literary fiction and has set aside the effects of a diet of subliterary kinds of mass-market fiction.

26. This has not always been the case. In the past, middlebrow reading marked individuals as aspirant middle-class professionals. See Janice Radway, *A Feeling for Books* (1997), 221–60.

27. For the most up-to-date statistics, see *Book Retailing—US* (2004). In the U.K., the percentage of books bought by women is slightly lower than in the U.S. but

still accounts for 65 percent or more of consumer book purchases. See *Bookselling* (2004), tables 18, 19, 20. For summary European data, see *Publishing Market Watch. Sectoral Report 2: Book Publishing* (2004), 9.

28. Online excerpted transcript, "*A Fine Balance Discussion*," Oprah's Book Club (accessed 15 February 2002). Currently accessible at http://www.oprah.com/obc/pastbooks/rohinton_mistry/obc_20020124_discussion.jhtml.

29. Seventy-three percent of Oprah's books were written by women. She selected books by ten men between 1996 and 2002. Her new book club reverses this trend, with Steinbeck, Paton, Garcia Marquez, and Tolstoy outnumbering McCullers and Pearl S. Buck.

30. Winfrey recently included Alan Paton's *Cry the Beloved Country* in her new club's selections.

31. See the discussion of the vogue for "Commonwealth" authors in Elizabeth Long, *Book Clubs* (2003).

32. Salil, SASIALIST listserv discussion group (accessed 2 April 1998).

33. Chandra, SASIALIST listserv discussion group (accessed 3 April 1998).

34. This is neither a callow nor an abnormal response. See Kuiken et al., "Forms of Self-Implication," in which the authors argue that the "search for concepts that potentially subsume narrative particulars will sometimes involve self-relevant concepts, especially those that represent personal strivings" (177).

35. Rooney sees this pattern of response as debasing and oversimplifying the literary texts, but she also admires Winfrey for establishing "practical protocols" for reading that have contributed to the enlargement of the audience for fiction (*Oprah* xii).

36. On Winfrey's emphasis on empathetic reading practices, juxtaposed to "more reflective" habits, see Farr, *Reading Oprah*, 61. Farr embraces the social function of the novel as a genre and admires Winfrey's way of integrating fiction into readers' "talking life," a phrase borrowed from Toni Morrison (*Reading Oprah* 45–51, 60).

37. Though it would be interesting to study changes in attitude toward bullying or rule breaking, in groups of *Harry Potter* readers.

38. See B. Latane and J. M. Darley, *The Unresponsive Bystander—Why Doesn't He Help?* (1970). This famous research was spurred by the 1964 murder of Kitty Genovese, in which dozens of people within earshot of the victim's cries failed to intervene. See Darley's recent summary of three decades' worth of work in this field, in "Bystander Phenomena" (2000), 493–95.

39. These numbers add up to 118 percent because I tallied emotion, understanding, and moralizing separately. Eighteen percent of responses mentioned both emotional intensity and improved understanding.

Chapter 5

1. What novelists hope to do in writing fiction has not, of course, remained consistent over the centuries, nor do writers of a single tradition or generation agree in their aims. Though subjected to criticism for decades since they put it forth in 1946 in the *Sewanee Review*, Wimsatt and Beardsley's "intentional fallacy" (which sought to move the literary critic's role toward evaluation and away from subjec-

tive response) has never been completely dislodged. While I concur that scrutiny of texts must be literary critics' first task, that much of an author's intentions cannot be recovered, and also that authors often do more in texts than they can explain or understand, my perspective as a narrative theorist leads me to believe that writers craft narratives using tools in order to accomplish ends that they can, and often do, articulate.

2. Though once again I draw upon my experience as a teacher of fiction in making this generalization, see for documented cases the Amazon.com's readers' reviews of *The Handmaid's Tale*.

3. See "Envisioning the Past," in Keen, *Romances of the Archive in Contemporary British Fiction* (2001), for the romance of the archive's cultivation of the sympathetic historical imagination (181–207).

4. Smiley defines empathy cognitively, as "perceiving with" or "seeing through" a character (*13 Ways* [2005], 76, 118), but despite her disavowal of the affective component of empathy, she argues that "the novel has made a world in which people are fairly adept at both feeling and thinking, and at thinking about feeling" (176).

5. "High fantasizers," or individuals who score high on a Fantasy-Empathy scale, tend to assume that people in general are more altruistic than low scorers assume. See Ezra Stotland et al., *Empathy, Fantasy and Helping* (1978), 88–9, 107. If novelists are likely to score as high fantasizers, then they may also be prone to believe in the power of empathy because they positively estimate the altruism of others.

6. See, for example, Caro Clarke, ed., "Writing Advice," http://www.caroclarke.com/ (accessed 10 February 2005).

7. Anti-Defamation League press release, "Q and A on the Turner Diaries" (16 May 1996) http://www.adl.org/PresRele/Militi_71/2737_71.asp (accessed 22 February 2005).

8. Nancy Eisenberg argues that "it is more often cognitively-based processes like perspective taking, and, to a lesser degree, empathy, that can be devoted to socially undesirable ends." These readers might share the perspective or feel with Pierce's protagonist. However, according to Eisenberg, "one would seldom expect sympathy to be related to undesirable ends." Personal correspondence with the author.

9. F. R. Conway, Amazon.com review of *The Turner Diaries* (posted 6 March 2002).

10. The twenty-eight-item Bernstein and Putnam's Dissociative Experiences Scale (DES) asks subjects to rate the percentage of time they spend having fantasies and daydreams (absorption) and the frequency of their gaps in episodic memory (amnesia) and experiences of derealization and depersonalization.

11. Leslie Marmon Silko, interviewed on *In Search of the Novel*, http://www.learner.org/channel/workshops/isonovel/Pages/subpage7.html (accessed 14 February 2005).

12. Arthur Golden, interviewed on *In Search of the Novel*, http://www.learner.org/channel/workshops/isonovel/Pages/subpage7.html (accessed 14 February 2005).

13. J. K. Rowling, interviewed on *In Search of the Novel*, http://www.learner.org/channel/workshops/isonovel/Pages/subpage7.html (accessed 15 February 2005).

14. The first edition of this novel (Spiral, 1983) is so scarce that I provide instead page number references to the most widely disseminated version, the 1986 Penguin paperback.

15. See, for instance, Mary Ann Hughes, "Transgressing Boundaries" (1994). Hughes argues that Hulme "chooses to upset our idea of corporeal boundaries in her ambivalent attitude to violence with *The Bone People*. While the assaults upon Simon are deplored and regretted, they are also glorified as the transgression of the boundary between internal and external, spiritual and material, one human and another" ("Transgressing" 57).

16. Stead faults the prize more than the winner. See C. K. Stead, "Keri Hulme's *The Bone People* and the Pegasus Award for Maori Literature" (1985). See also Margery Fee's rejoinder, "Why C. K. Stead Didn't Like Keri Hulme's *the bone people*: Who Can Write as Other?" (1989).

17. Ato Quayson notices the novel's discursive nervousness but attributes that to Hulme's unresolved feelings about disabilities. Though Quayson describes the scene of beating, he misses Kerewin's clear judgment of Joe, or perhaps he forgets it, because it is not the negative judgment his argument would predict. This critical aversion from the novel's statements bespeaks the exquisite difficulty of facing the implications of Hulme's representation. See Ato Quayson, "Looking Awry: Tropes of Disability in Post-colonial Writing" (1999).

18. See, for instance, Philip Armstrong's nuanced article, "Good Eating: Ethics and Biculturalism in Reading *"The Bone People"* (2001) and Gay Wilentz, "Instruments of Change: Healing Cultural Dis-ease in Keri Hulme's *the bone people*" (1995).

19. On empathic accuracy, see the research reported in William Ickes, ed., *Empathic Accuracy* (1997).

20. See Suzette A. Spencer, "Shall We Gather at the River? Ritual, Benign Forms of Injury, and the Wounds of Displaced Women in Opal Palmer Adisa's *It Begins with Tears*" (2001).

21. Opal Palmer Adisa, interviewed by Suzette A. Spencer (quoted in Spencer's "Shall We Gather at the River?" 108). See also Opal Palmer Adisa, "A Writer/Healer: Literature, a Blueprint for Healing" (2001).

22. The most neutral term currently in favor, Female Genital Cutting (FGC), describes a range of practices from reduction of the clitoris to the removal of parts of the labia (infibulation). Amnesty International sticks with Female Genital Mutilation (FGM) in order to emphasize its decision to treat these practices as torture and as human rights violations. Terms used by those who wish to indicate respect for cultural practices include female circumcision and excision. Nwapa's term "bath" emphasizes FGC's role in a purification ritual.

23. Nwapa does not specify which form of circumcision is performed, but it seems likely from the geographical and cultural locations, as well as from the later narration of childbirth, that Efuru has undergone excision of her clitoris rather than the more radical infibulation. See U. Megafu, "Female Ritual Circumcision in Africa: An Investigation of the Presumed Benefits among Ibos of Nigeria" (1983).

24. A later novelist, Buchi Emecheta, takes up Nwapa's phrase, "the joys of motherhood," and gives it a darkly ironic reworking in her novel of that name.

25. See the summary, "Female Genital Cutting," at http://www.4woman.gov/faq/fgc.htm#11 (accessed 8 March 2005). The U.K., several European nations, and indeed some African countries have similar laws. Whether they can be enforced is another matter.

26. For an exploration of insider and outsider views of the practice, see Ellen Gruenbaum, *The Female Circumcision Controversy: An Anthropological Perspective* (2001).

27. See Isabelle R. Gunning, "Uneasy Alliances and Solid Sisterhood: A Response to Professor Obiora's Bridges and Barricades" (1997). Gunning reports that "it is not an accident that it is [Walker's] work that has been frequently identified as having elevated the surgeries in the popular consciousness of Western feminists; African activists whose concern and activity preceded Walker's were not heard" (452–53). See also Elisabeth Bekers, "Daughters of Africa W/Riting Change: Female Genital Excision in Two African Short-Stories and in Alice Walker's *Possessing the Secret of Joy*" (1999), in which Bekers argues that Walker creates "the impression that African women are not able to fight their battles completely by themselves" (267).

28. Micere Githae Mugo, "Elitist Ant-Circumcision Discourse as Mutilating and Anti-Feminist" (1997). Mugo criticizes Walker for her depiction of Africa as "condescending and touristic," arguing that Walker's "philosophical outlook is informed by colonial and missionary conceptions of Africa" and that Walker's denunciation of female genital cutting silences and vilifies the victims of the practice (464).

29. On the external messiah syndrome exemplified by Alice Walker, see L. Amede Obiora, "The Issue of Female Circumcision: Bridges and Barricades, Rethinking Polemics and Intransigence in the Campaign against Female Circumcision" (1997).

Chapter 6

1. See, for instance, the teaching anthology edited by Peter and Renata Singer, *The Moral of the Story: An Anthology of Ethics Through Literature* (2005).

2. See Jonathan Rose, *The Intellectual Life of the British Working Classes* (2001), 76. Solitary reading and private study were distrusted, Rose discovers, as "selfish and unneighborly" (86).

3. See Philip Gourevitch, who not only writes of the hard-hearted responses to the pleas of Rwandan victims, but also offers an explanation: "Genocide, after all, is an exercise in community building." *We Wish to Inform You That Tomorrow We Will Be Killed with Our Families* (1998), 95. See also Batson, "Empathy-Induced Altruism" (2004) on the limitations of empathy in dealing with large-scale problems of long duration (372–73).

4. Indeed, human rights are not exempted from criticism. Some regard "the whole idea of 'universal' human rights" as a "gigantic fraud, where Western imperialist or excolonial powers try to pass off their own, very specific and localized idea of what 'rights' should be as universal, trampling roughly over everyone elses's beliefs and traditions." See Stephen Howe, *Empire: A Very Short Introduction* (2002), 3. For a good starting point on this debate, see Mary Williams's collection, *Human Rights: Opposing Viewpoints* (1998).

5. See 3–4 above for the distinction between personal distress, a nonmoral emotional reaction that is not likely to lead to prosocial behavior, and empathy (or sympathy). See Nancy Eisenberg, "Emotion, Regulation, and Moral Development" (2000) for a review of the current research on the role of emotion in morality.

6. On this point, see also Patricia Melzer, "'All that you touch you change'" (2002), 45.

7. See also Peter G. Stillman, "Dystopian Critiques, Utopian Possibilities, and Human Purposes in Octavia Butler's *Parables*" (2003), 23.

8. On *Parable of the Sower* as slave narrative, see Raffaela Baccolini, "Gender and Genre in the Feminist Critical Dystopias of Katharine Burdekin, Margaret Atwood, and Octavia Butler" (2000); on race, see Jerry Phillips, "The Intuition of the Future: Utopia and Catastrophe in Octavia Butler's *Parable of the Sower*" (2002).

9. See Samuel and Pearl Oliner, *The Altruistic Personality* (1988), 188 and Gourevitch's account of failed appeals from genocide victims in *We Wish to Inform You* (1998), 42–43, 135, 141–42. Butler would probably concur with Richard Delgado's character Roderigo's assessment that empathy for racial minorities is on the decline (*Coming Race War?* 8). She depicts mixed race and minority characters as especially vulnerable to persecution, robbery, rape, and murder.

10. For extrapolation of these views, see Charles Rowell's interview with Butler, "An Interview with Octavia E. Butler" (1997), 47–66.

11. See, for examples, Tom Le Clair, "The Sri Lankan Patients" (2000), 31 and the unsigned review "Brrr!" (2000), 14.

12. Among the finest articles are those by Teresa Derrickson, on the narratives of justice that global human rights discourse produces and Ondaatje's oblique intervention in the debate about globalization; and Antoinette Burton, on the evidence of bones in the archives of twentieth-century violence. See Teresa Derrickson, "Will the 'Un-Truth' Set You Free? A Critical Look at Global Human Rights Discourse in Michael Ondaatje's *Anil's Ghost*" (2004) and Antoinette Burton, "Archive of Bones: *Anil's Ghost* and the Ends of History" (2004).

13. Novel readers in this case include my college-aged students and a group of mature readers with whom I discussed *Anil's Ghost* at the Rockbridge Regional Library, Lexington, Virginia, in 2001. See also the reviews posted by readers at Amazon.com.

14. For a list of the qualities that define the subgenre of archival research quests, see Keen, *Romances of the Archive* (2001), 35. For the role of empathy in realistic narratives of archival research, see 183–207.

15. Surveying the recent studies, Nancy Eisenberg concludes that a "real, albeit sometimes modest" relation between situational sympathetic concern and prosocial responses exists in children. The leap between the original empathetic response and sympathy does not invariably occur if, for instance, personal distress provokes an aversive emotional state rather than an other-oriented emotion. See Eisenberg, "Emotion, Regulation, and Moral Development," 671–73.

16. In social psychology, this problem is investigated under the term *moral disengagement*, by which people take restraints and self-judgments offline. Deficient empathy explains inhumanity more widespread than can be explained by the existence of sociopaths. See Albert Bandura, "Moral Disengagement in the Perpetuation of Inhumanities" (1999) and "Reflexive Empathy: On Predicting More Than Has Ever Been Observed" (2002).

17. These critics assume that empathy will be inaccurate and that misunderstanding and harm will result from the misunderstanding. Psychologists who work on empathic accuracy agree that incorrect empathetic assessments can have bad

results in human relations and communication, but they emphasize the relative rarity of failures of empathy. For my discussion of what I term *empathic inaccuracy*, see 136–41 above.

18. The reverse statement of this gender determinism praises females for their empathy while noticing the dominating habits of males.

19. See, for instance, Lila Abu-Lughod and Catherine A. Lutz, "Introduction: Emotion, Discourse, and the Politics of Everyday Life" (1990). For a survey of recent cross-cultural work on the emotions, see David Matsumoto, "Culture and Emotion" (2001).

20. See, for instance, the text of the United Nations' *Universal Declaration of Human Rights* (1948) at the UN's Web site, http://www.un.org/Overview/rights .html (accessed 5 May 2005); on human capabilities, see Amartya Sen, *Inequality Reexamined* (1992).

21. Developmental psychologists, as we have earlier seen, regard empathy as a faculty that develops in individuals over time, from simple emotional contagion to mature sympathy. Some thus criticize as mechanistic the overemphasis on neuroanatomical explanations of empathy. See, for example, Phillipe Rochat, "Various Kinds of Empathy as Revealed by the Developing Child, Not the Monkey's Brain" (2002).

22. One recent study of advertising shows that "other-focused" appeals lead to more favorable attitudes in members of individualist cultures, while "ego-focused" appeals garner better responses from members of collectivist cultures (based on a comparison of the responses of American and Chinese students). See Jennifer L. Aaker and Patti Williams, "Empathy Versus Pride: The Influence of Emotional Appeals across Cultures" (1998).

23. See Patrick Colm Hogan, *The Mind and Its Stories* (2003), 46, 66, 74–75, 81.

24. See Patrick Colm Hogan, "Stories and Morals: Emotion, Cognitive Exempla, and the Arabic Aristotelians" (2004), 43.

25. Absolute universals need not recur in all works, but in all traditions; statistical universals occur across traditions with greater frequency than chance alone predicts (Hogan, *Mind and Its Stories* 19).

26. On *mahakaruna*, or great compassion, see Hammalawa Saddhatissa, *Buddhist Ethics* (1997) 27–29, 136–37.

27. For an array of views and subtle interrogations of compassion, see Laren Berlant, ed., *Compassion: The Culture and Politics of an Emotion* (2004).

28. Often, in recent years, disapprovingly. A typical strong case against what Hogan calls categorical identity and empathy appears in Audrey Jaffe, *Scenes of Sympathy* (2000), 22.

29. See I. A. Richards's gloss in *Mencius on the Mind: Experiments in Multiple Definition* (1932), 20.

30. On the imperatives of warm, agent-based virtue ethics regarding the treatments of others, including sentient nonhumans such as dolphins and chimpanzees, see Slote, *Morals from Motives* (2001), 37. Slote writes, "If we assume that human beings have a basic capacity for empathy and sympathy with others (an assumption the moral sentimentalists tended to make . . .), then making someone vividly aware of the effects of certain kinds of actions (or attitudes) on people's welfare can change the way that person *feels* about those actions (or attitudes) and make a difference, for

good, to her act-effecting motives." On caring, see in addition to Slote, Nel Noddings, *Caring: A Feminine Approach to Ethics and Moral Education* (1984).

31. On the limitations of reading alone, see Darcia Narvaez, "Does Reading Moral Stories Build Moral Character" (2002). Narvaez finds that children do not predictably understand the themes of moral stories as intended by the author (or by the adult presenting them).

WORKS CITED

Aaker, Jennifer L., and Patti Williams. "Empathy Versus Pride: The Influence of Emotional Appeals across Cultures." *Journal of Consumer Research* 25, 3 (December 1998): 241–61.

Abu-Lughod, Lila, and Catherine A. Lutz. "Introduction: Emotion, Discourse, and the Politics of Everyday Life." *Language and the Politics of Emotion.* Ed. Catherine A. Lutz and Lila Abu-Lughod. Cambridge: Cambridge University Press, 1990. 1–23.

Achebe, Chinua. *Morning Yet on Creation Day.* London: Heinemann, 1975.

Ackroyd, Peter. *Dickens.* London: Sinclair Stevenson, 1990.

Adamson, Sylvia. "The Rise and Fall of Empathetic Narrative: A Historical Perspective on Perspective." *New Perspectives on Narrative Perspective.* Ed. Willie van Peer and Seymour Chatman. Albany: SUNY Press, 2001. 83–99.

Adisa, Opal Palmer. *It Begins with Tears.* London: Heinemann, 1997.

———. "She Scrape She Knee." *Caribbean Women Writers: Essays from the First International Conference.* Ed. Selwyn R. Cudjoe. Wellesley, MA: Calaloux, 1990. 145–50.

———. "A Writer/Healer: Literature, a Blueprint for Healing." *Healing Cultures: Art and Religion as Curative Practices in the Caribbean and Its Diaspora.* Ed. Margarite Fernández Olmos and Lizabeth Paravisini-Gebert. London: Palgrave, 2001. 179–93.

Aiken, Anna Laetitia. "An Enquiry into Those Kinds of Distress Which Excite Agreeable Sensations." 1773. Rpt. *Novel and Romance 1700–1800: A Documentary Record.* Ed. Ioan Williams. New York: Barnes and Noble 1970. 289.

Ainslie, George, and John Monterosso. "Hyperbolic Discounting Lets Empathy Be a Motivated Process." *Behavioral and Brain Sciences* 25, 1 (February 2002): 20–21.

Ainsworth, William Harrison. *Jack Sheppard.* London, 1839.

Altick, Richard D. *The Presence of the Present: Topics of the Day in the Victorian Novel.* Columbus: Ohio State University Press, 1991.

Altieri, Charles. *The Particulars of Rapture: An Aesthetics of the Affects.* Ithaca and London: Cornell University Press, 2003.

Anand, Mulk Raj. *Untouchable.* 1935. London and New York: Penguin, 1986.

Anderson, Benedict. *Imagined Communities: Reflections on the Origin and Spread of Nationalism.* London: Verso, 1983.

Andringa, Els. "The Interface between Fiction and Life: Patterns of Identification in Reading Autobiographies." *Poetics Today* 25, 2 (Summer 2004): 205–40.

Andringa, Els, et al. "Point of View and Viewer Empathy in Film." *New Perspectives on Narrative Perspective*. Ed. Willie van Peer and Seymour Chatman. Albany: SUNY Press, 2001. 133–57.

Anti-Defamation League. "Q and A on the Turner Diaries." (16 May 1996) http://www.adl.org/PresRele/Militi_71/2737_71.asp. Accessed 22 February 2005.

Aristotle. *Rhetoric*. Trans. George A. Kennedy. Oxford and New York: Oxford University Press, 1991.

Armstrong, Isobel. *The Radical Aesthetic*. Oxford: Blackwell, 2000.

Armstrong, Paul B. *Play and the Politics of Reading: The Social Uses of Modernist Form*. Ithaca and London: Cornell University Press, 2005.

Armstrong, Philip. "Good Eating: Ethics and Biculturalism in Reading 'The Bone People.'" *Ariel* 32, 2 (April 2001): 7–27.

Ashcroft, Bill, Gareth Griffiths, and Helen Tiffin. *Key Concepts in Post-Colonial Studies*. London and New York: Routledge, 1998.

Attwood, Tony. *Asperger's Syndrome: A Guide for Parents and Professionals*. London and New York: Jessica Kingsley, 1998.

Atwood, Margaret. *The Handmaid's Tale*. Toronto: McClelland and Stewart, 1985.

Baccollini, Raffaela. "Gender and Genre in the Feminist Critical Dystopias of Katharine Burdekin, Margaret Atwood, and Octavia Butler." *Future Females, the Next Generation: New Voices and Velocities in Feminist Science Fiction Criticism*. Ed. Marleen S. Barr. Lanham, MD: Rowman and Littlefield, 2000. 13–34.

Bandura, Albert. "Moral Disengagement in the Perpetuation of Inhumanities." *Personality and Social Psychology Review* 3 (1999): 193–209.

———. "Reflexive Empathy: On Predicting More Than Has Ever Been Observed." *Behavioral and Brain Sciences* 25, 1 (February 2002): 24–25.

Baron-Cohen, Simon. *The Essential Difference: The Truth about the Male and Female Brains*. New York: Basic Books, 2003.

Barthes, Roland. "Introduction to the Structural Analysis of Narratives." Trans. Stephen Heath. *Image-Music-Text*. New York: Hill and Wang, 1977. 79–124.

———. *The Pleasure of the Text*. 1973. Trans. Richard Miller. New York: Hill and Wang, 1975.

Bate, Walter Jackson. "The Sympathetic Imagination in Eighteenth-Century Criticism." *Journal of English Literary History* 12 (1945): 144–64.

The Altruism Question: Toward a Social-Psychological Answer. Hillsdale, NJ: Erlbaum, 1991.

Batson, C. Daniel. "Altruism and Prosocial Behavior." *The Handbook of Social Psychology*. Ed. D. T. Gilbert, S. T. Fiske, and G. Lindzey. v. 2. New York: McGraw-Hill, 1998. 282–316.

———. *The Altruism Question: Toward a Social-Psychological Answer*. Hillsdale, NJ: Erlbaum, 1991.

Batson, C. Daniel, et al. "Benefits and Liabilities of Empathy-Induced Altruism." *The Social Psychology of Good and Evil*. Ed. Arthur G. Miller. New York and London: Guilford Press, 2004. 359–85.

———. "Empathic Joy and the Empathy-Altruism Hypothesis" *Journal of Personality and Social Psychology* 61, 3 (September 1991): 413–26.

————."Empathy and Attitudes: Can Feeling for a Member of a Stigmatized Group Improve Feelings toward the Group?" *Journal of Personality and Social Psychology* 72 (1997): 105–18.

————. "Empathy, Attitudes, and Action: Can Feeling for a Member of a Stigmatized Group Motivate One to Help the Group?" *Personality and Social Psychology Bulletin* 28, 12 (December 2002): 1656–66.

————."Empathy and the Collective Good: Caring for One of the Others in a Social Dilemma." *Journal of Personality and Social Psychology* 68, 4 (April 1995): 619–31.

————."Immorality from Empathy-Induced Altruism: When Compassion and Justice Conflict." *Journal of Personality and Social Psychology* 68, 6 (June 1995): 1042–54.

————."Influence of Self-Reported Distress and Empathy on Egoistic Versus Altruistic Motivation to Help." *Journal of Personality and Social Psychology* 45 (1983): 706–18.

Bekers, Elisabeth. "Daughters of Africa W/Riting Change: Female Genital Excision in Two African Short-Stories and in Alice Walker's *Possessing the Secret of Joy*." *Thamyris* 6, 2 (Autumn 1999): 255–71.

Bekoff, Marc. "Empathy: Common Sense, Science Sense, Wolves, and Well-being." *Behavioral and Brain Sciences* 25, 1 (February 2002): 26–27.

Bennett, William J., ed. *The Children's Book of Virtues*. New York and London: Simon and Schuster, 1995.

Berlant, Lauren, ed. *Compassion: The Culture and Politics of an Emotion*. New York and London: Routledge, 2004.

Blackford, Holly Virginia. *Out of This World: Why Literature Matters to Girls*. New York: Teachers College Press, 2004.

Blair, R. J. R., et al. "The Psychopathic Individual: A Lack of Responsiveness to Distress Cues?" *Psychophysiology* 34 (1997): 192–98.

————. "Responsiveness to Distress Cues in the Child with Psychopathic Tendencies." *Personality and Individual Differences* 27 (1999): 135–45.

————. "A Selective Impairment in the Processing of Sad and Fearful Expressions in Children with Psychopathic Tendencies." *Journal of Abnormal Child Psychology* 29 (December 2001): 491–98.

Blakeslee, Sandra. "Cells That Read Minds." *The New York Times* (10 January 2006): F1, F4.

Bleich, David. *Subjective Criticism*. Baltimore: Johns Hopkins University Press, 1978.

Bloom, Allan. *The Closing of the American Mind*. New York: Simon and Schuster, 1987.

Bloom, Clive. *Bestsellers: Popular Fiction Since 1900*. London: Palgrave, 2002.

Bloom, Harold. *How to Read and Why*. New York: Scribner, 2000.

Blum, Lawrence A. *Friendship, Altruism and Morality*. London and Boston: Routledge and Kegan Paul, 1980.

Book Retailing—US. London and Chicago: University of Chicago Press: Mintel International Group, 2004.

Bookselling. Chesham: Keynote, 2004.

Booth, Wayne C. *The Company We Keep: An Ethics of Fiction*. Berkeley: University of California Press, 1988.

————. *The Rhetoric of Fiction*, 2nd ed. Chicago: University of Chicago Press, 1983.

Bortolussi, Marisa, and Peter Dixon. *Psychonarratology: Foundations for the Empirical Study of Literary Response*. Cambridge and New York: Cambridge University Press, 2003.

Bourg, Tammy. "The Role of Emotion, Empathy, and Text Structure in Children's and Adults' Narrative Text Comprehension." *Empirical Approaches to Literature and Aesthetics*. Ed. Roger J. Kreuz and Mary Sue MacNealy. Norwood, NJ: Ablex, 1996. 241–60.

Bourg, Tammy, et al. "The Effects of an Empathy-Building Strategy on 6th-graders' Causal Inferencing in Narrative Text Comprehension." *Poetics* 22 (1993): 117–33.

Bouson, J. Brooks. *The Empathic Reader: A Study of the Narcissistic Character and the Drama of the Self*. Amherst: University of Massachusetts Press, 1989.

Bowen, Elizabeth. *The Collected Stories of Elizabeth Bowen*. New York: Ecco Press, 1981.

Brecht, Bertolt. "Alienation Effects in Chinese Acting." *Brecht on Theatre: The Development of an Aesthetic*. Ed. John Willett. New York: Hill and Wang, 1964. 91–99.

————. "Conversation with Bert Brecht." *Brecht on Theatre: The Development of an Aesthetic*. Ed. John Willett. New York: Hill and Wang, 1964. 14–17.

————. "Short Description of a New Technique of Acting." *Brecht on Theatre: The Development of an Aesthetic*. Ed. John Willett. New York: Hill and Wang, 1964. 141–47.

————. "A Short Organum for the Theatre." *Brecht on Theatre: The Development of an Aesthetic*. Ed. John Willett. New York: Hill and Wang, 1964. 179–205.

Brennan, Bonnie. "Bridging the Backlash: A Cultural Material Reading of *The Bridges of Madison County*." *Studies in Popular Culture* 19, 1 (1996): 59–78.

Brewer, W. F., and K. Ohtsuka. "Story Structure, Characterization, Just World Organization, and Reader Affect in American and Hungarian Short Stories." *Poetics* 17 (1988): 395–415.

Brisbin, C. D. "An Experimental Application of the Galvanic Skin Response to the Measurement of Effects of Literature on Attitudes of Fifth Grade Students towards Blacks." Dissertation. Wayne State University Press, 1971.

Brontë, Charlotte. *Jane Eyre*. London, 1847.

Brothers, Leslie. "A Biological Perspective on Empathy." *American Journal of Psychiatry* 146, 1 (1989): 10–19.

————. *Friday's Footprint: How Society Shapes the Human Mind*. Oxford and New York: Oxford University Press, 2001.

"Brrrr!" Review of Michael Ondaatje's *Anil's Ghost*. *The Economist* (17 June 2000), 14.

Bryant, Jennings, and Dolf Zillmann. *Responding to the Screen: Reception and Reaction Processes*. Hillsdale, NJ: Erlbaum, 1991.

Burke, Edmund. *A Philosophical Enquiry into the Origin of our Ideas of the Sublime and Beautiful*. 1757. Ed. Adam Phillips. Oxford and New York: Oxford University Press, 1990.

Burnett, Frances Hodgson. *The Secret Garden*. London: Heinemann, 1911.

Burton, Antoinette. "Archive of Bones: *Anil's Ghost* and the Ends of History." *The Journal of Commonwealth Literature* 39, 1 (March 2004): 39–56.

Bushman, Brad J., and L. Rowell Huesmann. "Effects of Televised Violence on Aggression." *Handbook of Children and the Media*. Ed. Dorothy G. Singer and Jerome L. Singer. Thousand Oaks, CA: Sage, 2001. 223–54.

Butler, Octavia E. "'Devil Girl from Mars': Why I Write Science Fiction." *MIT Communications Forum*. http://web.mit.edu/comm-forum/papers/butler.html. Accessed 18 April 2005.

———. "Octavia E. Butler: Persistence." *Locus* (June 2000): 4, 75–78.

———. *Parable of the Sower*. New York and London: Four Walls Eight Windows, 1993.

———. *Parable of the Talents*. New York and Toronto: Seven Stories, 1998.

Butler, Octavia E., and Charles Rowell. "An Interview with Octavia E. Butler." *Callaloo* 20, 1 (1997): 47–66.

Butte, George. *I Know That You Know That I Know: Narrating Subjects from* Moll Flanders *to* Marnie. Columbus: Ohio State University Press, 2004.

Byatt, A. S. *Babel Tower*. London: Chatto and Windus, 1996.

Cacioppo, John T., and R. E. Petty. Social Psychophysiology. New York and London: Guilford Press 1983.

Cacioppo, John T., et al. "Just Because You're Imaging the Brain Doesn't Mean You Can Stop Using Your Head: A Primer and Set of First Principles." *Journal of Personality and Social Psychology* 85, 4 (October 2003): 650–61.

Cahill, Larry, and Melina Uncapher, et al. "Sex-Related Hemispheric Lateralization of Amygdala Function in Emotionally Influenced Memory: An fMRI Investigation." *Learning and Memory* 11, 3 (May–June 2004): 261–66.

Calvino, Italo. *Cosmicomics*. 1965. Trans. William Weaver. New York: Harcourt, 1968.

Card, Orson Scott. *Ender's Game*. New York: Tor, 1985.

Carey, Peter. *Jack Maggs*. London: Faber, 1997.

Capps, Lisa, et al. "Understanding of Simple and Complex Emotions in Non-retarded Children with Autism." *Journal of Child Psychology and Psychiatry* 33, 7 (1992): 1169–82.

Carey, John. *Pure Pleasure: A Guide to the 20th Century's Most Enjoyable Books*. London: Faber, 2000.

Carroll, Noel. *Mystifying Movies: Fads and Fallacies in Contemporary Film Theory*. New York: Columbia University Press, 1988. 196–97.

Charon, Rita. "Narrative Medicine: A Model for Empathy, Reflection, Profession, and Trust." *JAMA* 286 (2001): 1897–1902.

Chupchik, G. C. and János Lázló. "The Landscape of Time in Literary Reception: Character Experience and Narrative Action." *Cognition and Emotion* 8 (1994): 297–312.

Chupchik, G. C., Keith Oatley, et al. "Emotional Effects of Reading Excerpts from Short Stories by James Joyce." *Poetics* 25 (1998): 363–78.

Church, R. M. "Emotional Reactions of Rats to the Pain of Others." *Journal of Comparative and Physiological Psychology* 52 (1959): 132–34.

Clark, Suzanne. *Sentimental Modernism: Women Writers and the Revolution of the Word*. Bloomington: Indiana University Press, 1991.

Clarke, Caro. "Writing Advice." http://www.caroclarke.com/. Accessed 10 February 2005.

Cohan, Steven. "Figures beyond the Text: A Theory of Readable Character in the Novel." *Novel: A Forum on Fiction* 17, 1 (1983): 5–27.

Cohn, Dorrit. *Transparent Minds: Narrative Modes for Presenting Consciousness in Fiction*. Princeton: Princeton University Press, 1978.

Coleridge, Samuel Taylor. *Biographia Literaria*. Vol. 7, *Collected Works of Samuel Taylor Coleridge*. Ed. James Engell and Walter Jackson Bate. Routledge and Princeton: Princeton University Press, 1983.

————. *Lectures 1795 on Politics and Religion*. Vol. 1, *Collected Works of Samuel Taylor Coleridge*. Ed. Lewis Patton and Peter Mann. London: Routledge; Princeton: Princeton University Press, 1971.

————. *The Watchman*. Vol. 2,. *Collected Works of Samuel Taylor Coleridge*. Ed. Lewis Patton. London: Routledge; Princeton: Princeton University Press, 1970.

Collins, Wilkie. *No Name*. 1862. Ed. Virginia Blain. Oxford and New York: Oxford University Press, 1998.

Conrad, Joseph. *A Personal Record and the Shadow Line: A Confession*. Malay Edition. New York: Doubleday, 1928.

Cooke, David J., et al. *Psychopathy: Theory, Research and Implications for Society*. Dordrecht and Boston: Kluwer Academic, 1998.

Cosmides, Leda, and John Tooby. "Cognitive Adaptations for Social Exchange." *The Adapted Mind*. Ed. J. Barkow, Leda Cosmides, and John Tooby. Oxford and New York: Oxford University Press, 1992. 163–228.

————. "Does Beauty Build Adapted Minds? Toward an Evolutionary Theory of Aesthetics, Fiction and the Arts." *SubStance* 30, 1–2 (2001): 6–27.

————. "Evolutionary Psychology and the Emotions." *Handbook of Emotions*. 2nd ed. Ed. Michael Lewis and Jeanette M. Haviland-Jones. New York and London: Guilford Press, 2000. 91–115.

Covey, Stephen R. *The 7 Habits of Highly Effective People: Powerful Lessons in Personal Change*. New York: Free Press, 1990.

Craig, K. D. "Physiological Arousal as a Function of Imagined, Vicarious, and Direct Stress Experiences." *Journal of Abnormal Psychology* 73 (1968): 513–20.

Cunningham, Michael. *The Hours*. New York: Farrar, Straus and Giroux, 1998.

Dadlez, E. M. *What's Hecuba to Him? Fictional Events and Actual Emotions*. University Park: Pennsylvania State University Press, 1997.

Damasio, Antonio R. *Descartes' Error: Emotion, Reason, and the Human Brain*. New York: Putnam, 1994.

————. *The Feeling of What Happens: Body and Emotion in the Making of Consciousness*. San Diego and London: Harcourt, 1999.

————. *Looking for Spinoza: Joy, Sorrow and the Feeling Brain*. Orlando and London: Harcourt, 2003.

Damasio, Antonio R., et al. "Somatic Markers and the Guidance of Behavior: Theory and Preliminary Testing." *Frontal Lobe Function and Dysfunction*. Ed. H. S. Levin, H. M. Eisenberg, and A. L. Benton. Oxford and New York: Oxford University Press, 1991. 217–29.

Dangarembga, Tsitsi. *Nervous Conditions*. 1988. Rpt. Seattle: Seal Press, 1989.

Darley, J. M. "Bystander Phenomena." *Encyclopedia of Psychology*. Vol. 1 Ed. Alan Kazden. Washington, DC: American Psychological Association, 2000. 493–495.

Darnton, Robert. *The Great Cat Massacre and Other Episodes of French Cultural History*. New York: Basic Books, 1984. 215–56.

Darwin, Charles. *The Expression of the Emotions in Man and Animals*. 1872. Ed. Paul Ekman. Oxford and New York: Oxford University Press, 1998.

Davies, Stevie. *Impassioned Clay*. London: Women's Press, 1999.

Davis, Mark H. *Empathy: A Social Psychological Approach*. Boulder: Westview, 1994.

———. "Measuring Individual Differences in Empathy: Evidence for a Multidimensional Approach." *Journal of Personality and Social Psychology* 44 (1983): 113–26.

———. "A Multidimensional Approach to Individual Differences in Empathy." *JSAS Catalog of Selected Documents in Psychology*, 10 (1980): 85.

Davis, Mark H., et al. "The Heritability of Characteristics Associated with Dispositional Empathy." *Journal of Personality* 62 (September 1994): 369–91.

Deigh, John. "Empathy and Universalizability." *Ethics* 105, 4 (July 1995): 743–63.

Deitz, S., et al. "Measurement of Empathy toward Rape Victims and Rapists." *Journal of Personality and Social Psychology* 43 (1982): 372–84.

Defoe, Daniel. *Robinson Crusoe*. London: 1719.

Delgado, Richard. *The Coming Race War? And Other Apocalyptic Tales of America after Affirmative Action and Welfare*. New York: New York University Press, 1996.

DeLillo, Don. *Libra*. New York: Viking, 1988.

Derrickson, Teresa. "Will the 'Un-Truth' Set You Free? A Critical Look at Global Human Rights Discourse in Michael Ondaatje's *Anil's Ghost*." *Literature Interpretation Theory* 15 (2004): 131–52.

Desai, Anita. *Fire on the Mountain*. London: Heinemann, 1977.

de Sousa, Ronald. *The Rationality of the Emotions*. Cambridge: MIT Press, 1987.

Dewey, John. *Art as Experience. The Later Works*. Vol. 10. Ed. Jo Ann Boydston. Carbondale: Southern Illinois University Press, 1985.

Dick, Philip K. *Do Androids Dream of Electric Sheep?* New York: Doubleday, 1968.

Dickens, Charles. *Dombey and Son*. London: 1848.

———. *Nicholas Nickelby*. London: 1839.

———. *Oliver Twist*. London: 1837–38.

Diengott, Nilli. "Some Problems with the Concept of the Narrator in Bortolussi and Dixon's *Psychonarratology*." *Narrative* (October 2004): 306–16.

Disraeli, Benjamin. *Coningsby*. London: 1844.

———. *Sybil*. London: 1845.

Dissanayake, Ellen. *Homo Aestheticus: Where Art Comes From and Why*. New York: Free Press, 1992.

Dixon, Peter, et al. "Literary Processing and Interpretation: Towards Empirical Foundations." *Poetics* 22 (1993): 5–33.

Donnelly, Daria. "Studies Abroad." *Commonweal* (23 April 2004): 22–24.

Dovidio, John F., et al, "Specificity of Empathy-Induced Helping: Evidence for Altruistic Motivation." *Journal of Personality and Social Psychology* 59, 2 (August 1990): 249–60.

Duan, Changming, and Clara E. Hill. "The Current State of Empathy Research." *Journal of Counseling Psychology* 43, 3 (July 1996): 261–74.

Duane, Diane. *A Wizard Alone*. New York: Harcourt, 2002.

Dubey, Madhu. "Folk and Urban Communities in African-American Women's Fiction: Octavia Butler's *Parable of the Sower.*" *Studies in American Fiction* 27, 1 (Spring 1999): 103–28.

Dubus, Andre. *House of Sand and Fog.* New York: Norton, 1999.

Dymond, R. "A Scale for the Measurement of Empathy Ability." *Journal of Consulting Psychology* 13 (1949): 127–33.

Edmundson, Mark. "The Risk of Reading: Why Books Are Meant to Be Dangerous." *New York Times Magazine* (1 August 2004): 11–12.

———. *Why Read?* New York and London: Bloomsbury, 2004.

Eisenberg, Nancy. "The Development of Empathy-Related Responding." *Moral Motivation through the Life Span.* Ed. Gustavo Carlo and Carolyn Pope Edwards. Lincoln and London: University of Nebraska Press, 2005. 73–117.

———. "Emotion, Regulation, and Moral Development." *Annual Review of Psychology* 51 (2000): 665–97.

———. "Empathy and Sympathy." *Handbook of Emotions.* 2nd ed. Ed. Michael Lewis and Jeannette M. Haviland-Jones. New York and London: Guilford Press, 2000. 677–91.

———. "Empathy-Related Emotional Responses, Altruism, and Their Socialization." *Visions of Compassion: Western Scientists and Tibetan Buddhists Examine Human Nature.* Ed. Richard J. Davidson and Anne Harrington. Oxford and New York: Oxford University Press, 2002. 131–64.

Eisenberg, Nancy, and Richard A. Fabes. "Children's Disclosure of Vicariously Induced Emotions." *Disclosure Processes in Children and Adolescents.* Ed. Ken J. Rotenberg. Cambridge: Cambridge University Press, 1995. 111–34.

Eisenberg, Nancy and Paul Miller. "Empathy, Sympathy, and Altruism." *Empathy and Its Development.* Ed. Nancy Eisenberg and Janet Strayer. Cambridge: Cambridge University Press, 1997. 299–302.

Eisenberg, Nancy and Janet Strayer. eds. *Empathy and Its Development.* Cambridge: Cambridge University Press, 1987.

Eisenberg, Nancy, Richard A. Fabes, and Tracy L. Spinrad. "Prosocial Development." *Handbook of Child Psychology,* 6th ed., Ed. William Damon. Vol. 3, *Social, Emotional, and Personality Development.* Ed. Nancy Eisenberg. Hoboken, NJ: Wiley, 2006.

Eisenberg, Nancy, et al. "Physiological Indices of Empathy." *Empathy and Its Development.* Ed. Nancy Eisenberg and Janet Strayer. Cambridge: Cambridge University Press, 1987. 380–85.

Ekman, Paul. *Emotions Revealed: Recognizing Faces and Feelings to Improve Communication and Emotional Life.* New York: Henry Holt, 2003.

Eliot, George. *Adam Bede.* London: 1859.

———. *The George Eliot Letters.* 9 vols. Ed. Gordon S. Haight. New Haven and London: Yale University Press, 1954–78.

———. *Middlemarch.* London: 1871–72.

———. "The Natural History of German Life," *Essays of George Eliot.* Ed. Thomas Pinney. New York: Columbia University Press; London: Routledge and Kegan Paul, 1963. 266–99.

Eliot, T. S. "The Metaphysical Poets." *Selected Essays, 1917–32.* New York: Harcourt, 1932. 241–50.

Ellis, Markman. *The Politics of Sensibility: Race, Gender, and Commerce in the Sentimental Novel*. Cambridge: Cambridge University Press, 1996.

Ellison, Julie. *Cato's Tears and the Making of Anglo-American Emotion*. Chicago: University of Chicago Press, 1999.

Elster, Jon. *Alchemies of the Mind: Rationality and the Emotions*. Cambridge: Cambridge University Press, 1999.

Esrock, Ellen J. *The Reader's Eye: Visual Imaging as Reader Response*. Baltimore: Johns Hopkins University Press, 1994.

Evans, Dylan. *Emotions: A Very Short Introduction*. Oxford and New York: Oxford University Press, 2001.

Eysenck, H. J., and S. B. G. Eysenck. "Impulsiveness-Venturesomeness-Empathy Scale." *Manual of the Eysenck Personality Scales (EPS adult)*. Rev. ed. Hodder and Stoughton, 1996.

Farr, Cecilia Konchar. *Reading Oprah: How Oprah's Book Club Changed the Way America Reads*. Albany: SUNY Press, 2005.

Feagin, Susan L. "Imagining Emotions and Appreciating Fiction." *Emotion and the Arts*. Ed. Mette Hjort and Sue Laver. New York and Oxford: Oxford University Press, 1997. 50–62.

———. *Reading with Feeling: The Aesthetics of Appreciation*. Ithaca and London: Cornell University Press, 1996.

Fee, Margery. "Why C. K. Stead Didn't Like Keri Hulme's *the bone people*: Who Can Write as Other?" *Australian and New Zealand Studies in Canada* 1 (1989): 11–32.

"Female Genital Cutting." Department of Health and Human Services' National Women's Health Information Center. http://www.4woman.gov/faq/fgc.htm#11. Accessed 8 March 2005.

Feshbach, Norma D. "Studies of Empathic Behavior in Children." *Progress in Experimental Personality Research*. Vol. 8. Ed. Brendan A. Maher. New York: Academic Press, 1978. 1–47.

Feshbach, Norma D., and Seymour Feshbach. "Affective Processes and Academic Achievement." *Child Development* 58, 5 (1987): 1335–47.

Finlay, Krystina A., and Walter G. Stephan. "Improving Intergroup Relations: The Effects of Empathy on Racial Attitudes." *Journal of Applied Social Psychology* 30, 8 (2000): 1720–37.

Fish, Stanley. "Literature in the Reader: Affective Stylistics." *New Literary History* 2, 1 (1970), 123–62.

Fludernik, Monika. *The Fictions of Language and the Languages of Fiction*. London and New York: Routledge, 1993.

———. "Metanarrative and Metafictional Commentary: From Metadiscursivity to Metanarration and Metafiction." *Poetica* 35 (2003): 1–39.

———. *Towards a "Natural" Narratology*. London and New York: Routledge, 1996.

Fogle, Richard Harter. "Empathetic Imagery." *The Imagery of Keats and Shelley: A Comparative Study*. North Carolina, 1949. 139–83.

Forgas, Joseph P., ed. *Handbook of Affect and Social Cognition*. Mahwah, NJ: Erlbaum, 2001.

Forster, E. M. *Aspects of the Novel*. New York: Harcourt, 1927.

Fox, Stephen D. "Keri Hulme's *The Bone People*: The Problem of Beneficial Child Abuse." *Journal of Evolutionary Psychology* (March 2003): 40–55.

Franzen, Jonathan. *The Corrections*. New York: Farrar, Straus and Giroux, 2001.

Freud, Sigmund. "Creative Writers and Day-Dreaming." 1907. *Standard Edition of the Complete Psychological Works of Sigmund Freud*. Vol. 9. Ed. James Strachey. London: Hogarth Press and Institute of Psycho-Analysis, 1959. 141–54.

Friedman, Susan Stanford. *Mappings: Feminism and the Cultural Geographies of Encounter*. Princeton: Princeton University Press, 1998.

Frijda, Nico H. "The Psychologists' Point of View." *Handbook of Emotions*. 2nd ed. Ed. Michael Lewis and Jeanette M. Haviland-Jones. New York and London: Guilford Press, 2000. 59–74.

Gaillard, W. D., et al. "fMRI Identifies Regional Specialization of Neural Networks for Reading in Young Children." *Neurology* 60, 1 (2003): 94–100.

Gallagher, Catherine. *Nobody's Story: The Vanishing Acts of Women Writers in the Marketplace, 1670–1820*. Berkeley: University of California Press, 1995.

Gallese, Vittorio. " 'Being Like Me': Self-Other Identity, Mirror Neurons, and Empathy." *Perspectives on Imitation: From Neuroscience to Social science, vol. 1. Mechanisms of Imitation and Imitation in Animals*. Ed. Susan Hurley and Nick Chater. Cambridge: MIT Press, 2005. 101–18.

———. "The Roots of Empathy: The Shared Manifold Hypothesis and the Neural Basis of Intersubjectivity." *Psychopathology* 36, 4 (July–August 2003): 171–80.

———. "A Unifying View of the Basis of Social Cognition." *Trends in Cognitive Science* 8, 9 (September 2004): 396–403.

Gallese, Vittorio, et al. "The Mirror Matching System: A Shared Manifold for Intersubjectivity." *Behavioral and Brain Sciences* 25, 1 (February 2002): 35–36.

Gallup, Gordon G., Jr., and Steven M. Platek. "Cognitive Empathy Presupposed Self-awareness: Evidence from Phylogeny, Ontogeny, Neuropsychology, and Mental Illness." *Behavioral and Brain Sciences* 25, 1 (February 2002): 36.

Gardiner, Judith Kegan. *Rhys, Stead, Lessing, and the Politics of Empathy*. Bloomington: Indiana University Press, 1989.

Gaskell, Elizabeth. *Mary Barton*. London: 1848.

———. *Ruth*. London: 1853.

———. *Sylvia's Lovers*. London: 1863.

Gault, Barbara A., and John Sabini. "The Roles of Empathy, Anger, and Gender in Predicting Attitudes toward Punitive, Reparative, and Preventative Public Policies." *Cognition and Emotion* 14, 4 (2000): 495–520.

Gauss, Charles Edward. "Empathy." *Dictionary of the History of Ideas: Studies of Selected Pivotal Ideas*, 2 vols. Ed. Philip P. Wiener. New York: Scribner, 1973–74. v. 2, 86–9.

Geberth, Vernon J., and Ronald N. Turco. "Antisocial Personality Disorder, Sexual Sadism, Malignant Narcissism, and Serial Murder." *Journal of Forensic Science* 42, 1 (1997): 49–60.

Geer, J. H., and L. Jarmecky. "The Effect of Being Responsible for Reducing Another's Pain on Subject's Response and Arousal." *Journal of Personality and Social Psychology* (1973): 232–37.

Gerrig, Richard J. "The Construction of Literary Character: A View from Cognitive Psychology." *Style* 24, 3 (Fall 1990): 380–92.

————. *Experiencing Narrative Worlds: On the Psychological Activities of Reading.* New Haven and London: Yale University Press, 1993.

Gerrig, Richard J., and David N. Rapp. "Psychological Processes Underlying Literary Impact." *Poetics Today* 25, 2 (Summer 2004): 265–81.

Gilroy, Paul. *Postcolonial Melancholia.* New York: Columbia University Press, 2005.

Godwin, William. *An Enquiry Concerning Political Justice and Its Influence on Morals and Happiness.* 1798 edition. 2 vols. Ed. F. E. L. Priestley. Toronto: University of Toronto Press, 1946.

Golden, Arthur. *Memoirs of a Geisha.* Westminster, MD: Knopf, 1997.

————. "Workshop 7—WHO AM I IN THIS STORY?" *In Search of the Novel.* http://www.learner.org/channel/workshops/isonovel/Pages/subpage7.html. Accessed 14 February 2005.

Goleman, Daniel. *Emotional Intelligence.* New York: Bantam, 1995.

Gordimer, Nadine. *The Conservationist.* London: Jonathan Cape, 1974.

Gourevitch, Philip. *We Wish to Inform You That Tomorrow We Will Be Killed with our Families: Stories from Rwanda.* New York: Farrar, Straus and Giroux, 1998.

Grabois, Andrew. *U.S. Book Production (All Hardback and Paperback).* BookWire. http://www.bookwire.com/bookwire/decadebookproduction.html. Accessed 28 January 2004.

Graham, Tiffany, and William Ickes. "When Women's Intuition Isn't Greater Than Men's," *Empathic Accuracy.* Ed. William Ickes. New York and London: Guilford Press, 1997. 117–43.

Gratton, Lynn M., and Paul J. Elsinger. "High Cognition and Social Behavior: Changes in Cognitive Flexibility and Empathy after Cerebral Lesions." *Neuropsychology* 3, 3 (1989): 175–85.

Greene, Sandra E. "Flora Nwapa's *Efuru.*" *African Novels in the Classroom.* Ed. Margaret Jeran Hay. Lynne Rienner, 2000. 215–28.

Greenspan, Patricia. "Emotions, Rationality and Mind/Body." *Philosophy* 52, supp. (2003): 113–25.

————. *Emotions and Reasons: An Inquiry into Emotional Justification.* London and New York: Routledge, 1988.

Gruenbaum, Ellen. *The Female Circumcision Controversy: An Anthropological Perspective.* Philadelphia: University of Pennsylvania Press, 2001.

Gunn, Thom. "Save the Word." *Boss Cupid.* New York: Farrar, Straus and Giroux, 2000. 71.

Gunning, Isabelle R. "Uneasy Alliances and Solid Sisterhood: A Response to Professor Obiora's Bridges and Barricades." Colloquium: Bridging Society, Culture, and Law. *Case Western Reserve Law Review* 47 (Winter 1997): 445–60.

Gupta, Sunetra. *Memories of Rain.* New York: Grove Press, 1992.

Haddon, Mark. *The Curious Incident of the Dog in the Night-Time.* New York: Doubleday, 2003.

Haight, Gordon S. *George Eliot: A Biography.* Oxford and New York: Oxford University Press, 1968.

Hakemulder, Jèmeljan. "Foregrounding and Its Effect on Readers' Perception." *Discourse Processes* 38, 2 (2004): 193–218.

———. *The Moral Laboratory: Experiments Examining the Effects of Reading Literature on Social Perception and Moral Self-Concept*. Utrecht Publications in General and Comparative Literature 34. Amsterdam: John Benjamins, 2000.

Hall, Judith. "The PONS Test and the Psychometric Approach to Measuring Interpersonal Sensitivity." *Interpersonal Sensitivity: Theory and Measurement*. Ed. Judith Hall and Frank Bernieri. Mahwah, NJ: Erlbaum, 2001. 143–60.

Hall, Judith, et al. "Profile of Nonverbal Sensitivity." *Advances in Psychological Assessment*. Vol. 4. Ed. P. McReynolds. San Francisco: Jossey-Bass, 1977. 179–211.

Hardwick, Elizabeth. "Reading." *Reading in the 1980s*. Ed. Stephen Graubard. New York: Bowker, 1983. 13–18.

Härting, Heike. "Diasporic Cross-Currents in Michael Ondaatje's *Anil's Ghost* and Anita Rau Badami's The Hero's Walk." *Studies in Canadian Literature* 28, 1 (2003): 43–70.

Hartman, Geoffrey H. "Is an Aesthetic Ethos Possible? Night Thoughts after Auschwitz." *Cardozo Studies in Law and Literature* 6 (1994).

Harvey, W. J. *Character and the Novel*. Ithaca and London: Cornell University Press, 1965.

Hassan, Ihab. "Queries for Postcolonial Studies." *Philosophy and Literature* 22, 2 (1998): 328–42.

Hatfield, Elaine, John T. Cacioppo, and Richard L. Rapson. *Emotional Contagion*. Studies in Emotion and Social Interaction. Cambridge: Cambridge University Press, 1994.

Hazlitt, William. "A Essay on the Principles of Human Action, Being an Argument in Favour of the Natural Disinterestedness of the Human Mind." 1805. *The Selected Writings of William Hazlitt*. Vol. 1. Ed. Duncan Wu. London: Pickering & Chatto, 1998. 1–82.

Highsmith, Patricia. *The Talented Mr. Ripley*. New York: Coward McCann, 1955.

Hjort, Mette, and Sue Laver eds. *Emotion and the Arts*. New York and Oxford: Oxford University Press, 1997.

Hochman, Baruch. *Character in Literature*. Ithaca and London: Cornell University Press, 1985.

Hoffman, Martin. "Empathy, Its Limitations and Its Role in a Comprehensive Moral Theory." *Morality, Moral Behavior and Moral Development*. Ed. William Kurtines and Jacob Gewirtz. New York: John Wiley, 1984.

———. *Empathy and Moral Development: Implications for Caring and Justice*. Cambridge: Cambridge University Press, 2000.

———. "Is Altruism Part of Human Nature?" *Journal of Personality and Social Psychology* 40 (1981): 121–37.

———. "The Measurement of Empathy." *Measuring Emotions in Infants and Children*. Ed. C. E. Izard. Cambridge: Cambridge University Press, 1982. 279–96.

———. "Scheme for the Development and Transformation of Empathic Distress." *Empathy and Its Development*. Ed. Nancy Eisenberg and Janet Strayer. Cambridge: Cambridge University Press, 1987. 50.

———. "Toward a Comprehensive Empathy-Based Theory of Prosocial Moral Development." *Constructive and Destructive Behavior: Implications for Family, School, and Society*. Ed. Arthur C. Bohart and Deborah J. Stipek. Washington, DC: American Psychological Association, 2001. 61–86.

Hogan, Patrick Colm. *Cognitive Science, Literature, and the Arts: A Guide for Humanists*. London and New York: Routledge, 2003.

———. "The Epilogue of Suffering: Heroism, Empathy, Ethics." *SubStance* 30, 1–2 (2001): 119–43.

———. *The Mind and Its Stories: Narrative Universals and Human Emotion*. Cambridge: Cambridge University Press, 2003.

———. "Stories and Morals: Emotion, Cognitive Exempla, and the Arabic Aristotelians." *The Work of Fiction: Cognition, Culture, and Complexity*. Ed. Alan Richardson and Ellen Spolsky. Aldershot, Hampshire, and Burlington, VT: Ashgate, 2004. 31–50,

Holland, Norman. *The Dynamics of Literary Response*. Oxford and New York: Oxford University Press, 1968.

———. *Five Readers Reading*. New Haven and London: Yale University Press, 1975.

———. "Where Is a Text? A Neurological View." *New Literary History* 33, 1 (2002): 21–38.

Home, Henry. Lord Kames. *Elements of Criticism*. 1762. 2 vols. Ed. Peter Jones. Indianapolis: Liberty Fund, 2005.

Howe, Stephen. *Empire: A Very Short Introduction*. Oxford and New York: Oxford University Press, 2002.

Howitt, Simon, ed. *Bookselling: 2000 Market Report*. Hampton, Middlesex: Key Note, 2000.

Hughes, Mary Ann. "Transgressing Boundaries." SPAN 39 (October 1994): 56–68.

Hugo, Victor. *Les Miserables*. Paris: 1862.

Hulme, Keri. *the bone people*. 1983. Rpt. Harmondsworth: Penguin, 1986.

Hulme, Keri, and Antonella Sarti. "Keri Hulme, March 1995." Interview. *Spiritcarvers: Interviews with Eighteen Writers from New Zealand*. Amsterdam: Rodopi, 1998. 57–69.

Hulme, Keri, and Gerry Turcotte. "Reconsidering *the bone people*." *Australian and New Zealand Studies in Canada* 12 (December 1994): 135–54.

Humble, Nicola. *The Feminine Middlebrow Novel, 1920s to 1950s*. Oxford and New York: Oxford University Press, 2001.

Hume, David. 1739. *A Treatise of Human Nature*. Ed. L. A. Selby-Bigge. Oxford: Clarendon Press, 1978.

Hunt, Lynn. Lecture. "The Novel and the Origins of Human Rights: The Intersection of History, Psychology and Literature." Presidential Lecture in the Humanities and Arts at Stanford University (8 April 2004).

———. "The Paradoxical Origins of Human Rights." *Human Rights and Revolutions*. Ed. Jeffrey N. Wasserstrom, Lynn Hunt, and Marilyn B. Young. Lanham, MD: Rowman and Littlefield, 2000. 3–17.

Iacoboni, M., et al. "Cortical Mechanisms of Human Imitation." *Science* 286 (1999): 2526–28.

Ickes, William, ed. *Empathic Accuracy*. New York and London: Guilford Press, 1997.

Ingmansan, Ellen J. "Empathy in a Bonobo." *Pretending and Imagination in Animals and Children*. Ed. Robert W. Mitchell. Cambridge: Cambridge University Press, 2002. 280–84.

Iser, Wolfgang. *The Act of Reading: A Theory of Aesthetic Response*. Baltimore: Johns Hopkins University Press, 1978.

Israel, Nico. "Globalization and Contemporary Literature." *Literature Compass* 1 (2004) 20C 104, 4. http://www.literature-compass.com. Accessed 10 March 2005.

Jaffe, Audrey. *Scenes of Sympathy: Identity and Representation in Victorian Fiction.* Ithaca and London: Cornell University Press, 2000.

James, William. *Principles of Psychology.* 1890, 1892. *The Works of William James.* 3 vols. Cambridge, MA: Harvard University Press, 1981.

Jameson, Fredric. *The Political Unconscious: Narrative as a Socially Symbolic Act.* Ithaca and London: Cornell University Press, 1981.

Jauss, Hans Robert. *Aesthetic Experience and Literary Hermeneutics.* Trans. Michael Shaw. Minneapolis: University of Minnesota Press, 1982.

———. "The Identity of the Poetic Text in the Changing Horizon of Understanding." *The Identity of the Literary Text.* Ed. Mario J. Valdis and Owen Miller. Toronto: University of Toronto Press, 1985. 146–74.

Johnson, Peter. *Moral Philosophers and the Novel: A Study of Winch, Nussbaum and Rorty.* London: Palgrave, 2004.

Johnson, Samuel, "To Sympathise." *A Dictionary of the English Language.* 1755. Facsimile. New York: Times, 1979.

Jose, P. E., and W. F. Brewer. "Development of Story Liking: Character Identification, Suspense, and Outcome Resolution." *Developmental Psychology* 20 (1984): 911–24.

Joyce, James. *Ulysses.* 1922. Ed. Hans Walter Gabler. New York: Garland Press, 1984.

Kahn, Edwin, and Arnold W. Rachman. "Carl Rogers and Heinz Kohut: A Historical Perspective." *Psychoanalytic Psychology* 17, 2 (Spring 2000): 294–312.

Katz, R. L. *Empathy: Its Nature and Uses.* New York: Free Press, 1963.

Keen, Suzanne. "The Historical Turn in British Fiction." *A Concise Companion to Contemporary British Fiction* Ed. James English. Oxford: Blackwell, 2006. 167–87.

———. *Narrative Form.* London: Palgrave, 2003.

———. *Romances of the Archive in Contemporary British Fiction.* Toronto: University of Toronto Press, 2001.

———.*Victorian Renovations of the Novel: Narrative Annexes and the Boundaries of Representation.* Cambridge: Cambridge University Press, 1998.

Kehoe, John W., and Charles Ungerleider. "The Effects of Role Exchange Questioning on Empathic Perceptiveness." *The Alberta Journal of Educational Research* 25, 1 (1979): 48–52.

Kerr, W. A., and B. J. Speroff. *The Empathy Test.* Chicago: Psychometric Affiliates, 1951.

Keysers, Christian. "Demystifying Social Cognition: a Hebbian Perspective." *Trends in Cognitive Science* 8, 11 (November 2004): 501–7.

Kidd, Sue Monk. "A Common Heart: A Bestselling Novelist Argues for Empathy Through Fiction." *Washington Post* Book World (Sunday, 4 December 2005): 9.

———. *The Secret Life of Bees.* New York: Viking, 2002.

Kingsley, Charles. *Westward Ho!* London: 1855.

Klemenz-Belgardt, Edith. "American Research of Response to Literature." *Poetics* 10 (1981): 357–80.

Knulst, Wim, and Andries van den Broek. "The Readership of Books in Times of De-Reading." *Poetics* 31 (2003): 213–33.

Koestenbaum, R., et al. "Individual Differences in Empathy among Preschoolers: Relation to Attachment History." *New Directions for Child Development* 44 (1989): 51–64.

Kohut, Hans. "Introspection, Empathy, and Psychoanalysis." *Journal of the American Psychoanalytic Association* 7 (1959): 459–83.

Konijn, Elly A., and Johan F. Hoorn. "Reality-based Genre Preferences Do Not Direct Personal Involvement." *Discourse Processes* 38, 2 (2004): 219–46.

Krebs, Dennis. "Empathy and Altruism." *Journal of Personality and Social Psychology* 32, 6 (1975): 1134–46.

Kristeva, Julia. *Revolution in Poetic Language*. 1974. Trans. Margaret Waller. New York: Columbia University Press, 1984.

Kruger, D. J. "Evolution and Altruism: Combining Psychological Mediators with Naturally Selected Tendencies." *Evolution and Human Behavior* 24 (2003): 118–25.

Kuiken, Don, et al. "Locating Self-Modifying Feelings within Literary Reading." *Discourse Processes* 38, 2 (2004): 267–86.

Kuiken, Don, et al. "Forms of Self-Implication in Literary Reading." *Poetics Today* 25, 2 (Summer 2004):171–203.

Lahiri, Jhumpa. *Interpreter of Maladies*. New York: Houghton Mifflin, 1997.

Lakoff, George. *Women, Fire, and Dangerous Things: What Categories Reveal about the Mind*. Chicago: University of Chicago Press, 1987.

Lakoff, George, and Mark Johnson. *Metaphors We Live By*. Chicago: University of Chicago Press, 1980.

Lakoff, George and Mark Turner. *More Than Cool Reason: A Field Guide to Poetic Metaphor*. Chicago: University of Chicago Press, 1989.

Lamarque, Peter, and Stein Haugum Olsen. *Truth, Fiction, and Literature: A Philosophical Perspective*. Oxford: Clarendon Press, 1994.

Lang, Andrew. "Introduction." *The Pleasures of Literature and the Solace of Books*. Ed. Joseph Shaler. Wilbur B. Ketcham, no date. 9–10.

Latane, B., and J. M. Darley. *The Unresponsive Bystander—Why Doesn't He Help?* New York: Appleton-Century-Crofts, 1970.

László, János. *Cognition and Representation in Literature: The Psychology of Literary Narratives*. Budapest: Akadémiai Kiadó, 1999.

Lazarus, R. S., et al. "A Laboratory Study of Psychological Stress Produced by a Motion Picture Film." *Psychological Monographs* 76 (1962): 1–35.

Leavis, F. R. *The Great Tradition: George Eliot, Henry James, Joseph Conrad*. London: Chatto and Windus, 1948.

Le Clair, Tom. "The Sri Lankan Patients." *The Nation* (19 June 2000): 31.

LeDoux, Joseph. *The Emotional Brain: The Mysterious Underpinnings of Emotional Life*. New York and London: Simon and Schuster, 1996.

Lee, Harper. *To Kill a Mockingbird*. Philadelphia: Lippincott, 1960.

Lee, Vernon. [Violet Paget]. *The Beautiful. An Introduction to Psychological Aesthetics*. Cambridge: Cambridge University Press, 1913.

Lee, Vernon, and C. Anstruther-Thomson. "Beauty and Ugliness." *Contemporary Review* 72 (October 1897): 544–69; (November 1897): 669–88.

Lenard, Mary. "'Mr. Popular Sentiment': Dickens and the Gender Politics of Sentimentalism and Social Reform Literature." *Dickens Studies Annual* 27 (1998): 45–68.

———. *Preaching Pity: Dickens, Gaskell, and Sentimentalism in Victorian Culture.* New York: Peter Lang, 1999.

Lennon, Randy, and Nancy Eisenberg. "Gender/Age Differences in Empathy/Sympathy." *Empathy and Its Development.* Ed. Nancy Eisenberg and Janet Strayer. Cambridge: Cambridge University Press, 1987. 195–217.

Levenson, Robert, and Anna Ruef. "Physiological Aspects of Emotional Knowledge and Rapport." *Empathic Accuracy.* Ed. William Ickes. New York and London: Guilford Press, 1997. 44–72.

Levinson, Jerrold. "Emotion in Response to Art: A Survey of the Terrain." *Emotion and the Arts.* Ed. Mette Hjort and Sue Laver. New York and Oxford: Oxford University Press, 1997. 20–34.

Linz, Daniel G., et al. "Effects of Long-Term Exposure to Violent and Sexually Degrading Depictions of Women." *Journal of Personality and Social Psychology* 55, 5 (November 1988): 758–68.

Lipps, Theodor. *Äesthetik: Psycholgie des Schönen und der Kunst,* 2 vols. Hamburg and Leipzig: Voss, 1903, 1906.

———. "Das Wissen von Fremden Ichen." *Psychologische Untersuchungen* 1 (1906): 694–722.

———. *Zur Einfühlung.* Leipzig: Engleman, 1913.

Lodge, David. *Consciousness and the Novel: Connected Essays.* Cambridge, MA: Harvard University Press, 2002.

Long, Elizabeth. *Book Clubs: Women and the Uses of Reading in Everyday Life.* Chicago: University of Chicago Press, 2003.

Louwerse, Max, and Don Kuiken. "The Effects of Personal Involvement in Narrative Discourse." *Discourse Processes* 38, 2 (2004): 169–72.

Lowry, Lois. *The Giver.* Boston: Houghton Mifflin, 1993.

Lubbock, Percy. *The Craft of Fiction.* 1926. Rpt. New York: Viking, 1957.

Mackenzie, Henry. *The Man of Feeling.* 1771.

———. *The Works of Henry Mackenzie.* Vol. 5. 1808. Facsimile. London: Routledge/ Thoemmes, 1996.

Marcus, Robert F. "Somatic Indices of Empathy." *Empathy and Its Development.* Ed. Nancy Eisenberg and Janet Strayer. Cambridge: Cambridge University Press, 1987. 374–79.

Marlyn, John. *Under the Ribs of Death.* Toronto: McClelland and Stewart, 1957.

Marshall, David. *The Surprising Effects of Sympathy: Marivaux, Diderot, Rousseau, and Mary Shelley.* Chicago: University of Chicago Press, 1988.

Maryles, Daisy, and Laurele Riippa. "Bestsellers of 2003: Hardcover Bestsellers; The Stakes Rise for Chart Toppers." *The Bowker Annual: Library and Book Trade Annual, 2004.* 49th ed. Ed. Dave Bogart. New York: Information Today, 2004. 576.

Massumi, Brian. *Parables for the Virtual: Movement, Affect, Sensation.* Durham: Duke University Press, 2002.

Matsumoto, David. "Culture and Emotion." *The Handbook of Culture and Psychology.* Ed. David Matsumoto. Oxford and New York: Oxford University Press, 2001. 171–94.

McCarthy, Thomas J. *Relationships of Sympathy: The Writer and the Reader in British Romanticism.* Aldershot: Scolar Press; Brookfield, VT: Ashgate Press, 1997.

McEvoy, Dermot, and Daisy Maryles. "Paperback Bestsellers: Numbers Up; Fiction Dominates." *The Bowker Annual: Library and Book Trade Annual, 2004.* 49th ed. Ed. Dave Bogart. New York: Information Today, 2004. 584–85.

McLemee, Scott. "Literary Reading Is Declining." *The Chronicle of Higher Education* (9 July 2004): A1, A16.

Megafu, U. "Female Ritual Circumcision in Africa: An Investigation of the Presumed Benefits Among Ibos of Nigeria." *East African Medical Journal* (November 1983): 793–800.

Mehaffy, Marilyn, and AnaLouise Keating. "'Radio Imagination': Octavia Butler on the Poetics of Narrative Embodiment." *MELUS* 26, 1 (Spring 2001): 45–76.

Mehrabian, Albert. *Manual for the Balanced Emotional Empathy Scale (BEES),* 1996.

———. "Relations among Personality Scales of Aggression, Violence, and Empathy: Validational Evidence Bearing on the Risk of Violence Scale." *Aggressive Behavior* 23 (1997): 433–45.

Melzer, Patricia. "'All that you touch you change': Utopian Desire and the Concept of Change in Octavia Butler's *Parable of the Sower* and Parable of the Talents." *Femspec* 3, 2 (2002): 31–52.

Mencius. Trans. D. C. Lau. Harmondsworth: Penguin, 1970.

Mesquita, Betja, and Mayumi Karasawa. "Different Emotional Lives." *Cognition and Emotion* 16, 1 (2004): 127–41.

Miall, David S. "Affect and Narrative: A Model of Responses to Stories." *Poetics* 17 (1988): 259–72.

———. "Anticipation and Feeling in Literary Response: A Neuropsychological Perspective." *Poetics* 23 (1995): 275–98.

———. "Beyond Interpretation: The Cognitive Significance of Reading." Lecture delivered at the conference Cognition and Literary Interpretation in Practice. (29 August 2004) University of Helsinki, Helsinki, Finland.

———. "Beyond the Schema Given: Affective Comprehension of Literary Narratives." *Cognition and Emotion* 3, 1 (1989): 55–78.

———. "Empowering the Reader: Literary Response and Classroom Learning." *Empirical Approaches to Literature and Asethetics.* Ed. Roger J. Kreuz and Mary Sue MacNealy. Norwood, NJ: Ablex, 1996. 463–78.

———. "On the Necessity of Empirical Studies of Literary Reading." *Frame* 14, 2–3 (2000): 43–59.

Miall, David S., and Donald Kuiken. "Aspects of Literary Response: A New Questionnaire," *Research in the Teaching of English* 29, 1 (February 1995): 37–58.

———. "The Form of Reading: Empirical Studies of Literariness." *Poetics* 25 (1998): 327–31.

———. "What Is Literariness? Three Components of Literary Reading." *Discourse Processes* 28, 2 (1999): 121–38.

Miller, J. G., and D. M. Bersoff. "Cultural Influences on the Moral Status of Reciprocity and the Discounting of Endogenous Motivation." *Personality and Social Psychology Bulletin* 20 (1994): 592–602.

Miller, Jim. "Octavia Butler's Vision." *Science-Fiction Studies* 25 (1998): 336–60.

Minami, Masahiko, and Alyssa McCabe. "Rice Balls and Bear Hunts: Japanese and North American Family Narrative Patterns." *Journal of Child Language* 22 (1995): 423–45.

Mistry, Rohinton. *A Fine Balance*. Toronto: McClelland and Stewart, 1995.

———. Interview. "Rohinton Mistry with Robert Mclay (1996)." *Writing across Worlds: Contemporary Writers Talk*. Ed. Susheila Nasta. London and New York: Routledge, 2004. 198–206.

Morrison, Karl F. *"I Am You": The Hermeneutics of Empathy in Western Literature, Theology, and Art*. Princeton: Princeton University Press, 1988.

Morrison, Toni. *Beloved*. New York: Knopf, 1987.

———. *Song of Solomon*. New York: Knopf, 1977.

Mott, Frank Luther. *Rewards of Reading*. New York: Henry Holt, 1926.

Mugo, Micere Githae. "Elitist Ant-Circumcision Discourse as Mutilating and Anti-Feminist." Colloquium: Bridging Society, Culture, and Law. *Case Western Reserve Law Review* 47 (Winter 1997): 461–80.

Mukherjee, Bharati. *Jasmine*. New York: Grove Press, 1989.

———. *The Holder of the World*. London: Chatto, 1993.

Nafisi, Azar. *Reading Lolita in Tehran*. New York: Random, 2003.

Narvaes, D. "Does Reading Moral Stories Build Moral Character?" *Educational Psychology Review* 14, 2 (2001): 155–71.

Nehring, Cristina. "Books Make You a Boring Person." *The New York Times Book Review* (27 June 2004): 23.

Neill, Alex. "Empathy and (Film) Fiction." *Post-Theory: Reconstructing Film Studies*. Ed. David Bordwell and Noël Carroll. Madison: University of Wisconsin Press, 1996. 175–94.

———. "Fiction and the Emotions." *American Philosophical Quarterly* (1993): 1–13.

Nell, Victor. *Lost in a Book: The Psychology of Reading for Pleasure*. New Haven and London: Yale University Press, 1988.

Neuberg, Steven L., et al. "Does Empathy Lead to Anything More Than Superficial Helping? Comment on Batson et al. (1997)." *Journal of Personality and Social Psychology* 73, 3 (September 1997): 510–16.

Ngai, Sianne. *Ugly Feelings*. Cambridge, MA: Harvard University Press, 2005.

Noddings, Nel. *Caring: A Feminine Approach to Ethics and Moral Education*. Berkeley: University of California Press, 1984.

Nucci, Larry P. *Education in the Moral Domain*. Cambridge: Cambridge University Press, 2001.

Nussbaum, Martha C. *Cultivating Humanity: A Classical Defense of Reform in Liberal Education*. Cambridge, MA: Harvard University Press, 1997.

———. "Exactly and Responsibly: A Defense of Ethical Criticism." *Philosophy and Literature* 22, 2 (1998): 343–65.

———. *Love's Knowledge: Essays on Philosophy and Literature*. Oxford and New York: Oxford University Press, 1990.

———. *Poetic Justice: The Literary Imagination and Public Life*. Boston: Beacon Press, 1995.

———. *Upheavals of Thought: The Intelligence of Emotions*. Cambridge: Cambridge University Press, 2001.

Nwapa, Flora. *Efuru*. London: Heinemann, 1966.

Nwapa, Flora, and Marie Umeh. "The Poetics of Economic Independence." *Research in African Literature* 26, 2 (Summer 1995): 22–30.

Oatley, Keith. *Best Laid Schemes: The Psychology of Emotions*. Cambridge: Cambridge University Press, 1992.

———. "A Taxonomy of the Emotions of Literary Response and a Theory of Identification in Fictional Narrative." *Poetics* 23 (1994): 53–74.

Oatley, Keith, and Mitra Gholamain. "Emotions and Identification: Connections Between Readers and Fiction." *Emotion and the Arts*. Ed. Mette Hjort and Sue Laver. New York and Oxford: Oxford University Press, 1997. 263–81.

Obiora, L. Amede. "The Issue of Female Circumcision: Bridges and Barricades, Rethinking Polemics and Intransigence in the Campaign against Female Circumcision." Colloquium: Bridging Society, Culture, and Law. *Case Western Reserve Law Review* 47 (Winter 1997): 324–28.

Oliner, Samuel P., and Pearl M. Oliner. *The Altruistic Personality: Rescuers of Jews in Nazi Europe*. New York: Free Press, 1988.

Oliner, Samuel P., and Pearl M. Oliner, eds. *Embracing the Other: Philosophical, Psychological, and Historical Perspectives on Altruism*. New York: NYU Press, 1992.

Omdahl, Becky Lynn. *Cognitive Appraisal, Emotion, and Empathy*. Mahwah, NJ: Erlbaum, 1995.

Omer, Haim. "Narrative Empathy. " *Psychotherapy* 34, 1 (Spring 1997): 19–27.

Ondaatje, Michael. *Anil's Ghost*. Toronto: McClelland & Stewart, 2000.

Ondaatje, Michael, and Maya Jaggi. *Writing across Worlds: Contemporary Writers Talk*. Ed. Susheila Nasta. London and New York: Routledge, 2004. 250–65.

Oudart, Jean Pierre. "Suture (elements of the logic of the signifier)." 1969. Trans. Kari Hamet. *Screen* 18, 4 (1977–78): 35–47.

Palmer, Alan. *Fictional Minds*. Lincoln: University of Nebraska Press, 2004.

Palmer, Frank. *Literature and Moral Understanding*. Oxford: Clarendon Press, 1992.

Panksepp, Jaak. "Emotions as Natural Kinds in the Brain." *Handbook of Emotions*. 2nd ed. Ed. Michael Lewis and Jeannette M. Haviland-Jones. New York and London: Guilford Press, 2000. 137–56.

Paton, Alan. *Cry, the Beloved Country*. London: Jonathan Cape, 1948.

Paul, Ellen Frankel, Fred D. Miller, and Jeffrey Paul, eds. *Altruism*. Cambridge: Cambridge University Press, 1993.

Phelan, James. *Reading People, Reading Plots: Character, Progression, and the Interpretation of Narrative*. Chicago: University of Chicago Press, 1989.

Phillips, Jerry. "The Intuition of the Future: Utopia and Catastrophe in Octavia Butler's *Parable of the Sower*." *Novel* 35, 2–3 (Spring 2002): 299–311.

Piliavin, J. A., et al. *Emergency Intervention*. New York: Academic Press, 1981.

Pinch, Adela. *Strange Fits of Passion: Epistemologies of Emotion, Hume to Austen*. Stanford: Stanford University Press, 1996.

Pinker, Steven. Interview. "The Seed Salon: Steven Pinker and Rebecca Goldsmith." *Seed* 10 (2004): 44–49, 97–99.

Pinsent, Pat. *Children's Literature and the Politics of Equality*. New York: Teachers College Press, 1997.

Pirandello, Luigi. *Six Characters in Search of an Author.* New York: Dutton, 1922.

Plaatje, Sol T. *Mhudi*. 1930. Rpt. London: Heinemann, 1978.

Pope, Alexander. *An Essay on Man*. 1733–34. Ed. Maynard Mack. *The Twickenham Edition of the Poems of Alexander Pope*. Vol. 3, part 1. New Haven and London: Yale University Press, 1950. 163–64.

Posner, Richard. "Against Ethical Criticism." *Philosophy and Literature* 21, 1 (1997): 1–27.

Potts, Stephen W. "'We Are Playing the Same Record': A Conversation with Octavia E. Butler." *Science-Fiction Studies* 23 (1996): 331–38

Pound, Ezra. "A Few Don'ts by an *Imagiste*." *Poetry* 1 (Feb. 1913): 5.

Powers, Samantha. *"A Problem from Hell": America and the Age of Genocide*. New York: Basic Books, 2002.

Preston, Stephanie D., and Frans B. M. de Waal. "The Communication of Emotions and the Possibility of Empathy in Animals." *Altruism and Altruistic Love: Science, Philosophy, and Religion in Dialogue*. Ed. Stephen G. Post and Lynn G. Underwood. Oxford and New York: Oxford University Press, 2002. 284–308.

———. "Empathy: Its Ultimate and Proximate Bases." *Behavioral and Brain Sciences* 25, 1 (February 2002): 1–20, 49–71.

Price, Leah. *The Anthology and the Rise of the Novel: From Richardson to George Eliot*. Cambridge: Cambridge University Press, 2000.

Price, Martin. *Forms of Life: Character and Moral Imagination in the Novel*. New Haven and London: Yale University Press, 1983.

Publishing Market Watch. Sectoral Report 2: Book Publishing. n.p.: European Commission, 2004.

Putnam, Robert D. *Bowling Alone: The Collapse and Revival of American Community*. New York and London: Simon and Schuster, 2000.

Quayson, Ato. "Looking Awry: Tropes of Disability in Post-colonial Writing." *An Introduction to Contemporary Fiction*. Ed. Rod Mengham. Cambridge: Polity Press, 1999. 53–68.

Rabinowitz, Peter J. *Before Reading: Narrative Conventions and the Politics of Interpretation*. Ithaca and London: Cornell University Press, 1987.

Radway, Janice. *A Feeling for Books: The Book-of-the-Month Club, Literary Taste, and Middle-class Desire*. Chapel Hill: University of North Carolina Press, 1997.

Rawls, John. *The Law of Peoples*. Cambridge, MA: Harvard University Press, 1999.

———. *Theory of Justice*. Cambridge, MA: Harvard University Press, 1971.

Reading at Risk: A Survey of Literary Reading in America. Research Division Report #46. Washington, DC: The National Endowment for the Arts, June 2004.

Reed, Stephen K. *Cognition: Theory and Applications*. 6th ed. Belmont, CA: Wadsworth, 2004.

Richards, I. A. *Mencius on the Mind: Experiments in Multiple Definition*. London and New York: Routledge and Kegan Paul, 1932.

Richardson, Alan. "Studies in Literature and Cognition: A Field Map." *The Work of Fiction: Cognition, Culture, and Complexity*. Ed. Alan Richardson and Ellen Spolsky. Aldershot, Hampshire and Burlington, VT: Ashgate, 2004. 1–30.

Richardson, Samuel. *Pamela*. London: 1740.

Rochat, Phillipe. "Various Kinds of Empathy as Revealed by the Developing Child, Not the Monkey's Brain." *Behavioral and Brain Sciences* 25, 1 (February 2002): 45–46.

Rogers, Carl. "Empathic: an Unappreciated Way of Being." *The Counseling Psychologist* 2 (1975): 2–10.

Rolls, Edmund T. "A Theory of Emotion, Its Functions, and Its Adaptive Value." *Emotions in Humans and Artifacts*. Ed. Robert Trappl, Paolo Petta, and Sabine Payr. Cambridge: MIT Press, 2002. 11–34.

Rooney, Kathleen. *Reading with Oprah: The Book Club That Changed America*. Fayetteville: Univeristy of Arkansas Press, 2005.

Rose, Jonathan. *The Intellectual Life of the British Working Classes*. New Haven and London: Yale University Press, 2001.

Rosen, Howard J., et al. "Emotion Comprehension in the Temporal Variant of Frontotemporal Dementia." *Brain* 125, 10 (October 2002): 2286–95.

Rosenblatt, Louise M. *Literature as Exploration*. New York and London: Appleton-Century, 1938.

Rowling, J. K. "Workshop 7—WHO AM I IN THIS STORY?" *In Search of the Novel*. http://www.learner.org/channel/workshops/isonovel/Pages/subpage7.html. Accessed 15 February 2005.

Roy, Arundhati. *The God of Small Things*. New Delhi: India Ink, 1997.

Rubin, Joan Shelley. *The Making of Middle/brow Culture*. Chapel Hill: University of North Carolina Press, 1992.

Rushdie, Salman. *The Satanic Verses*. London: Viking, 1988.

Sacks, Oliver. *An Anthropologist on Mars*. New York: Knopf, 1995.

Saddhatissa, Hammalawa. *Buddhist Ethics*. Boston: Wisdom Press, 1997.

Said, Edward W. *Culture and Imperialism*. New York: Knopf, 1993.

Sapolsky, Barry, and Dolf Zillmann. "Experience and Empathy: Affective Reactions to Witnessing Childbirth." *Journal of Social Psychology* 105, 1 (1978): 133–44.

Scanlan, Margaret. "*Anil's Ghost* and Terrorism's Time." *Studies in the Novel* 36, 3 (Fall 2004): 302–17.

Schneider, Ralf. "Emotion and Narrative." *Routledge Encyclopedia of Narrative Theory*. Ed. David Herman, Manfred Jahn, and Marie-Laure Ryan. London and New York: Routledge, 2005. 136–37.

———. "Toward a Cognitive Theory of Literary Character: the Dynamics of Mental-Model Construction." *Style* 35, 4 (2001): 607–42.

Scholes, Robert. *Protocols of Reading*. New Haven and London: Yale University Press, 1989.

Schulman, Sarah. *Empathy*. New York: Dutton, 1992.

Sebold, Alice. *The Lovely Bones*. Boston: Little Brown, 2002.

Sedgewick, Eve Kosofsky, and Adam Frank. *Shame and Its Sisters: A Silvan Tomkins Reader*. Durham and London: Duke University Press, 1995.

Sen, Amartya. *Inequality Reexamined*. Cambridge, MA: Harvard University Press, 1992.

Seth, Vikram. *A Suitable Boy*. London: Sixth Chamber Press, 1993.

Shaftesbury, Third Earl of, Anthony Ashley Cooper. *Characteristics of Men, Manners, Opinions, Times, etc.* 1711. Ed. Lawrence E. Klein. Cambridge: Cambridge University Press, 1999.

Shattuck, Roger. *Forbidden Knowledge: From Prometheus to Pornography*. New York: St. Martin's Press, 1996.

Sheehan, E. P., et al. "Reactions to AIDS and Other Illnesses: Reported Interactions in the Workplace." *The Journal of Psychology* 123 (1989): 525–36.

Shelley, Percy Bysshe. *A Defence of Poetry.* 1821. *Shelley's Poetry and Prose.* Ed. Donald H. Reiman. New York: Norton, 1977. 480–508.

———. "A Treatise on Morals." 1840. *Shelley's Prose.* Ed. David Lee Clark. Albuquerque: University of New Mexico Press, 1954.

Sherman, Nancy. "Empathy and Imagination." *Philosophy of Emotions. (Midwest Studies in Philosophy, XXII).* Ed. Peter French and Howard K. Wettstein. Notre Dame: University of Notre Dame Press, 1998. 82–119.

Shields, Stephanie A. *Speaking from the Heart: Gender and the Social Meaning of Emotion.* Cambridge: Cambridge University Press, 2002.

Showalter, Elaine. *Teaching Literature.* Oxford: Blackwell, 2003.

Shute, Nevil. *The Pied Piper.* New York: William Morrow, 1942.

Silko, Leslie Marmon. "Workshop 7—WHO AM I IN THIS STORY?" *In Search of the Novel.* http://www.learner.org/channel/workshops/isonovel/Pages/subpage7 .html. Accessed 14 February 2005.

Silverman, Kaja. "Suture [Excerpts]." 1983. *Narrative, Apparatus, Ideology: A Film Theory Reader.* Ed. Philip Rosen. New York: Columbia University Press, 1986. 219–35.

Singer, Peter. *One World.* New Haven and London: Yale University Press, 2002.

Singer, Peter, and Renata Singer. *The Moral of the Story: An Anthology of Ethics Through Literature.* Oxford: Blackwell, 2005.

Singer, Tania, et al. "Empathy for Pain Involves the Affective but Not Sensory Components of Pain." *Science* 303 (20 February 2004): 1157–62.

Slote, Michael. *Morals from Motives.* Oxford and New York: Oxford University Press, 2001.

Smiley, Jane. *13 Ways of Looking at the Novel.* New York: Knopf, 2005.

Smith, Adam. *The Theory of Moral Sentiments.* 1759. Ed. D. D. Raphael and A. L. Macfie. Vol. 1. *Glasgow Edition of the Works and Correspondence of Adam Smith.* Oxford and New York: Oxford University Press, 1976.

Smith, Alexander McCall. *Morality for Beautiful Girls.* New York: Polygon, 2001.

Smith, Tom W. "Altruism in Contemporary America: A Report from the National Altruism Study." *GSS Topical Report No. 34.* NORC, 2003.

Sober, Elliot, and David Sloan Wilson. *Unto Others: The Evolution and Psychology of Unselfish Behavior.* Cambridge, MA: Harvard University Press, 1998.

Solomon, Robert C. Ed. *Thinking about Feeling: Contemporary Philosophers on Emotions.* Oxford and New York: Oxford University Press, 2004.

Sontag, Susan. *Regarding the Pain of Others.* New York: Farrar, Straus and Giroux, 2003.

Spencer, Herbert. *Principles of Psychology.* London: Longmans, 1855.

Spencer, Suzette A. "Shall We Gather at the River? Ritual, Benign Forms of Injury, and the Wounds of Displaced Women in Opal Palmer Adisa's *It Begins with Tears.*" *MaComère* 4 (2001): 108–18.

Spryi, Joanna. *Heidi.* 1885. Trans. Boston: 1885.

Stang, Richard. *The Theory of the Novel in England, 1850–1870.* New York: Columbia University Press; London: Routledge and Kegan Paul, 1959.

Stanzel, F. K. *Narrative Situation in the Novel.* Trans. James P. Pusack. Bloomington: Indiana University Press, 1971.

————. *A Theory of Narrative*. 1979. Trans. Charlotte Goedsche. Cambridge: Cambridge University Press, 1984.

Stead, C. K. "Keri Hulme's *The Bone People* and the Pegasus Award for Maori Literature." *Ariel* 16, 4 (October 1985): 101–8.

Steiber, Ellen. *Empathy, X files #5*. Novelization based on the teleplay by Charles Grant Craig. New York: HarperCollins, 1997.

Steig, Michael. *Stories of Reading: Subjectivity and Literary Understanding*. Baltimore: Johns Hopkins University Press, 1989.

Steinbeck, John. *East of Eden*. New York: Viking, 1952.

————. *The Grapes of Wrath*. New York: Viking, 1939.

Stern, Barbara. "Classical and Vignette Television Advertising Dramas: Structural Models, Formal Analysis, and Consumer Effects." *The Journal of Consumer Research* 20, 4 (1994): 601–15.

Stern, Daniel N. *The Interpersonal World of the Infant: A View from Psychoanalysis and Developmental Psychology*. New York: Basic Books, 1985.

Stillman, Peter G. "Dystopian Critiques, Utopian Possibilities, and Human Purposes in Octavia Butler's *Parables*." *Utopian Studies* 14, 1 (2003): 15–35.

Stockwell, Peter. *Cognitive Poetics: An Introduction*. London and New York: Routledge, 2002.

Stotland, Ezra, et al. *Empathy, Fantasy and Helping*. Beverly Hills, CA: Sage, 1978.

Stowe, Harriet Beecher. *Uncle Tom's Cabin*. Boston, 1852.

Strayer, Janet, and Marianne Schroeder. "Children's Helping Strategies: Influences of Emotion, Empathy, and Age." *New Directions for Child Development* 44 (Summer 1989): 85–105.

Sundby, Scott. *A Life and Death Decision: A Jury Weighs the Death Penalty*. London: Palgrave, 2005.

Tademy, Lalita. *Cane River*. Boston: Warner Books, 2001.

Tan, Amy. *The Kitchen God's Wife*. New York: Putnam, 1991.

Tan, Ed. S. *Emotion and the Structure of Narrative Film: Film as an Emotion Machine*. Hillsdale, NJ: Erlbaum, 1996.

Tannenbaum, P. H. "Entertainment as Vicarious Emotional Experience." *The Entertainment Functions of Television*. Ed. P. H. Tannenbaum. Hillsdale, NJ: Erlbaum, 1980. 107–31.

Taylor, John Tinnon. *Early Opposition to the English Novel: The Popular Reaction from 1760 to 1830*. New York: King's Crown Press, 1943.

Taylor, Marjorie. *Imaginary Companions and the Children Who Create Them*. Oxford and New York: Oxford University Press, 1999.

Taylor, Marjorie, et al. "The Illusion of Independent Agency: Do Adult Fiction Writers Experience Their Characters as Having Minds of Their Own?" *Imagination, Cognition and Personality* 22, 4 (2002/2003): 361–80.

Terada, Rei. *Feeling in Theory: Emotion after "The Death of the Subject."* Cambridge, MA: Harvard University Press, 2001.

Tettamanti, Marco, et al. "Listening to Action-related Sentences Activates Fronto-parietal Motor Circuits." *Journal of Cognitive Neuroscience* 17, 2 (February 2005): 273–81.

Titchener, E. B. *Beginner's Psychology*. London: Macmillan, 1915.

————. *Experimental Psychology of the Thought Processes*. London: Macmillan, 1909.

Todd, Janet. *Sensibility: An Introduction*. London and New York: Methuen, 1986.

Tolstoi, Leo. *Anna Karenina*. 1878. Trans. London: Dent, 1912.

Tompkins, Jane, ed. *Reader-Response Criticism: From Formalism to Post-Structuralism*. Baltimore: Johns Hopkins University Press, 1980.

Treece, Henry. *The Horned Helmet*. London: Brockhampton, 1963.

Tromp, Marlene. *The Private Rod: Marital Violence, Sensation, and the Law in Victorian Britain*. Charlottesville: University Press of Virginia, 2000.

Turvey, Brent E. "Psychopathy and Sadism." *Criminal Profiling: An Introduction to Behavioral Evidence Analysis*. New York: Academic Press, 1999. 193–207.

United Nations, *Universal Declaration of Human Rights*. General Assembly resolution 217 A (III) (10 December 1948). http://www.un.org/Overview/rights.html. Accessed 5 May 2005.

U. S. Census Bureau, *Statistical Abstract of the United States* (2003). No. 1125. Media Usage and Consumer Spending: 1998 to 2006, *Information and Communications*.

van Peer, Willie. "Justice in Perspective." *New Perspectives on Narrative Perspective*. Ed. Willie van Peer and Seymour Chatman. Albany: SUNY Press, 2001. 325–38.

van Peer, Willie, and H. Pander Maat. "Perspectivation and Sympathy: Effects of Narrative Point of View." *Empirical Approaches to Literature and Aesthetics*. Ed. Roger J. Kreuz and Mary Sue MacNealy. Norwood, NJ: Ablex, 1996. 143–54.

Van Sant, Ann Jessie. *Eighteenth-century Sensibility and the Novel: The Senses in Social Context*. Cambridge: Cambridge University Press, 1993.

VICTORIA-L archives. https://listserv.Bloomington: Indiana UP,.edu/archives/victoria.html 12 November–3 December 2004.

Vygotsky, L. S. *The Psychology of Art*. 1925. Trans. Scripta Technica. Cambridge, MA: MIT Press, 1971.

Wagner, M., et al. "The AIDS Empathy Scale: Construction and Correlates." *New Directions in the Psychology of Human Sexuality: Research and Theory*. Ed. W. E. Snell, Jr. Cape Girardeau, MO: Snell, 2001.

Walker, Alice. *Possessing the Secret of Joy*. New York: Harcourt, 1992.

Waller, Robert James. *The Bridges of Madison County*. New York: Time Warner, 1992.

Walsh, Richard. "Why We Wept for Little Nell: Character and Emotional Involvement." *Narrative* 5, 3 (October 1997): 306–21.

Walton, Kendall. *Mimesis as Make-Believe: On the Foundations of the Representational Arts*. Cambridge, MA: Harvard University Press, 1990.

Warhol, Robyn. *Having a Good Cry: Effeminate Feelings and Pop-Culture Forms*. Columbus: Ohio State University Press, 2003.

Weber, Bruce. "Poet Brokers Truce in Culture Wars." *Washington Post* (7 September 2004): B1, B5.

Weldon, Fay. *The Bulgari Connection*. London: Flamingo, 2001.

Wilentz, Gay. "Instruments of Change: Healing Cultural Dis-ease in Keri Hulme's *the bone people*." *Literature and Medicine* 14, 1 (1995): 127–45.

Williams, Ioan, ed. *Novel and Romance 1700–1800: A Documentary Record*. New York: Barnes and Noble, 1970.

Williams, Mark. "Keri Hulme and Negative Capability." *Leaving the Highway: Six Contemporary New Zealand Novelists.* Auckland: Auckland University Press, 1990. 84–109.

Williams, Mary. Ed. *Human Rights: Opposing Viewpoints.* San Diego: Greenhaven Press, 1998.

Williams, Preston N. "A Personal Perspective on the Elimination of Female Circumcision." Colloquium: Bridging Society, Culture, and Law. *Case Western Reserve Law Review* 47 (Winter 1997): 491–500.

Williams, Raymond. *Culture and Society, 1780–1950.* 1958. Rpt. with a new introduction. New York: Columbia University Press, 1983.

———. *Keywords: A Vocabulary of Culture and Society.* Rev. Ed. Oxford and New York: Oxford University Press, 1983.

Wimsatt, W. K., and Monroe Beardsley. "The Affective Fallacy." *The Verbal Icon: Studies in the Meaning of Poetry.* Lexington: University of Kentucky Press, 1954. 21–39.

Wing, Lorna. "Asperger's Syndrome: A Clinical Account." *Psychological Medicine* 11 (1981): 115–30.

Winnicott, D. W. *Playing and Reality.* London: Tavistock, 1971.

Wispé, Lauren. "History of the Concept of Empathy." *Empathy and Its Development.* Ed. Nancy Eisenberg and Janet Strayer. Cambridge: Cambridge University Press, 1987. 17–37.

Wood, Marcus. *Slavery, Empathy and Pornography.* Oxford and New York: Oxford University Press, 2002.

Woolf, Virginia. "Middlebrow." *The Death of the Moth and Other Essays.* London: Hogarth Press, 1942. 176–86.

———. "Modern Fiction." 1919. Rpt. *The Common Reader.* New York: Harcourt, 1925. 207–18.

———. *Mrs. Dalloway.* London: Hogarth Press, 1925.

Zahn-Waxler, Carolyn. "Caregiving, Emotion, and Concern for Others." *Behavioral and Brain Sciences* 25, 1 (February 2002): 48–49.

Zahn-Waxler, Carolyn, et al. "Development of Concern for Others." *Developmental Psychology* 28 (1992): 126–36.

———. "The Development of Empathy in Twins." *Developmental Psychology* 28 (1992): 1038–47.

———. "Empathy and Prosocial Patterns in Young MZ and DZ Twins: Development and Genetic and Environmental Influences." *Infancy to Early Childhood: Genetic and Environmental Influences on Developmental Change.* Ed. Robert M. Emde and John K. Hewitt. Oxford and New York: Oxford University Press, 2001. 141–62.

Zepetnek, S. Tötösy de, and I. Sywenky, eds. *The Systematic and Empirical Approach to Literature and Culture as Theory and Application.* Edmonton: University of Alberta Press, 1997.

Zillmann, Dolf. "Empathy: Affect from Bearing Witness to the Emotions of Others." *Responding to the Screen: Reception and Reaction Processes.* Ed. Dolf Zillmann and Jennings Bryant. Hillsdale, NJ: Erlbaum, 1991. 135–67.

———. "Mechanisms of Emotional Involvement with Drama." *Poetics* 23 (1994): 33–51.

Zunshine, Lisa. "Richardson's *Clarissa* and a Theory of Mind." *The Work of Fiction: Cognition, Culture, and Complexity*. Ed. Alan Richardson and Ellen Spolsky. Aldershot, Hampshire, and Burlington, VT: Ashgate, 2004. 127–46.

———. "Theory of Mind and Experimental Representations of Fictional Consciousness." *Narrative* 11, 3 (October 2003): 270–91.

Zwaan, Rolf A. "Effect of Genre Expectations on Text Comprehension." *Journal of Experimental Psychology: Learning, Memory and Cognition* 20 (1994): 920–33.

———. "The Immersed Experiencer: Toward an Embodied Theory of Language Comprehension." *The Psychology of Learning and Motivation* 44 (2004): 35–62.

INDEX